ECUMENICAL
PILGRIMS

ECUMENICAL
PILGRIMS

Profiles of Pioneers
in Christian Reconciliation

Edited by
Ion Bria *&* **Dagmar Heller**

WCC Publications, Geneva

Cover design: Edwin Hassink

ISBN 2-8254-1145-0

© 1995 WCC Publications, World Council of Churches,
150 route de Ferney, 1211 Geneva 2, Switzerland

Printed in Switzerland

Preface

Reflections on the theme of the seventh assembly of the World Council of Churches (Canberra 1991) — "Come, Holy Spirit — Renew the Whole Creation" — have revealed new insights into the nature of the ecumenical movement and the vocation of the WCC. While the WCC is a fellowship whose members are churches as institutions and communities, this historical community is the work of the Holy Spirit, the Spirit of *koinonia*, who called several generations of people to commit themselves existentially to an ecumenical pilgrimage, on the way to the unity and renewal of Christianity in their time. Without the devotion and commitment of this "cloud of witnesses", the historical realization of the movement would not have been possible.

To illustrate this, we present here a collection of fifty short profiles of women and men who have lived during this century and, by making that ecumenical pilgrimage, have brought a major impetus to the movement for the unity of the church. In the process of preparing this collection we identified numerous personalities — Orthodox, Protestant, Roman Catholic — who were attached in one way or another to the goals of the World Council of Churches and who pioneered or inspired various schools, streams, institutions out of a deep spiritual commitment and vocation and not primarily because of their position in one or another ecumenical or church organization. Certainly, many ecumenical pilgrims of the same excellence and celebrity as those portrayed in these pages have gone unmentioned, due to limitations of space. Our choice was determined in some cases by the intent not to repeat what has already been said about people in other places. And in some cases we were limited by the availability of contributors.

A rich diversity of gifts, vocations, spiritual sensibilities and practical commitments is represented within this communion of pilgrims. There are charismatic and visionary leaders, models of devotion and piety, creators of Christian poetry and literature, theologians and biblical scholars. But all of them represent true ecumenical witnesses due to their considerable experience and profound knowledge of the ecumenical questions and problems which have confronted the churches during this century.

The purposes of this book are modest, but important:
— to keep alive in the "ecumenical memory" personalities who particularly inspired, by their work, writings and example, the search for unity and renewal;
— to recover in the practice of ecumenism the energy of spiritual life, which is not an escape, but a call to commitment to move people to enter into the process of reconciliating humanity;

— to offer resources to the younger generation for their own spiritual rootage and development;

— to illustrate the diversity of spiritualities among the churches, which need to be recognized and made known as our common ecumenical heritage.

The Worship and Spirituality team of the WCC's Programme Unit on Unity and Renewal, which has been responsible for the preparation of the book, is especially grateful to two former general secretaries of the WCC, Emilio Castro, who wholeheartedly encouraged its publication, and Philip Potter, who offered his wisdom and his vast acquaintance with ecumenical history in the construction of the book. We would also like to express our deep gratitude to all who contributed the portraits of pilgrims and to colleagues who helped us in compiling, translating and editing the articles, especially to Irene Bouman, Rosemary Green, Caroline McComish, Valerie Medri, Renate Sbeghen, Isa Schmidtkunz and Audrey Smith.

In a time when ecumenism is so often reduced to the static acceptance of the contradictions among the various traditions, *Ecumenical Pilgrims* is an invitation to all Christians to cross confessional and historical lines to live together "with all humility and gentleness, with patience, bearing with one another in love, making every effort to maintain the unity of the Spirit in the bond of peace. There is one body and one Spirit..." (Eph. 4:2-4).

Ion Bria and Dagmar Heller

Athenagoras I
1886–1972

I prayed at his grave, and listened to Nikos Nissiotis tell of his greatness

GEORGES TSETSIS

WCC

There is no doubt that one of the outstanding ecumenical figures of the twentieth century was Athenagoras I, Ecumenical Patriarch from 1949 until his death in 1972.

He was born in the village of Vassilikon in the province of Ioannina, then part of the Ottoman Empire, the son of a medical doctor named Matthaios Spyrou and of Helen, née Mokoros. The name given him at baptism was Aristocles.

After attending primary and secondary schools in his native province, he entered the Theological School of Halki, in 1903, at 17. One of his professors was Germanos Strinopoulos, an ecumenical pioneer who became internationally known as Metropolitan Germanos of Thyateira. When Aristocles Spyrou was ordained deacon in March 1910, he received the monastic name of Athenagoras, in honour of both his spiritual father Athenagoras Eleftheriou, the grand chancellor of the Patriarchate, and the 2nd-century Christian philosopher and apologist Athenagoras, for whom he had a great admiration.

Following graduation Athenagoras served in the diocese of Pelagonia from 1910 until he was called to become archdeacon of Athens Cathedral in 1916. In 1922, at the very early age of 36, he was elected metropolitan of Corfu, where he carried out an extraordinary pastoral activity while developing significant ecumenical contacts. He became involved in the work of the YMCA, attended the World Youth Assembly in 1926 and represented the Church of Greece at the Lambeth Conference of Anglican bishops in 1930.

When W.A. Visser 't Hooft visited Corfu in connection with a project of the Youth Commission of the Life and Work Movement, he was greatly impressed by Metropolitan Athenagoras, recalling later that he "was already deeply concerned about Christian unity":

> I noted especially his questions: "Is unity not the desire of Christ? And is not Christ strong enough to realize it even if we go on sleeping? Does not the whole peace of the world depend finally on this condition of unity among the followers of Christ?" It was fortunate

N.B.

that the first Eastern Orthodox church leader whom I came to know personally was a man of such spiritual calibre and of such deep conviction about the common destiny of all Christians. He made me believe that it was not an illusion that East and West could meet again.[1]

On 12 August 1930, with the consent of the Church of Greece, the Holy Synod of the Ecumenical Patriarchate elected Athenagoras Archbishop of North and South America. An enthusiastic crowd attended his enthronement on 26 February 1931. The 1920s had been a turbulent period for Greek-American Orthodoxy, and the new archbishop promised no easy solutions. Instead, his enthronement message was a simple message about the cross:

> I accepted the mission to come and preach to you Christ crucified. This is my only desire; this is the main objective of my ministry. I believe that only through the cross will men come in peace with one another. Why have the nations, our beloved Orthodox Church and Greek-Americans been deprived of peace? I think the reason is that we are running in every direction in search of peace except in the direction that leads to the cross... The mistakes of the past should become lessons for us in the future... To be creative and productive we must have faith, we need to pray, study and prepare ourselves for continuous struggles... It is not enough to have ideals and traditions; it is absolutely necessary also to have Christian will for their realization... To strengthen my faith and my will I turn to the only source, Jesus Christ and his cross. I do not know if I will be able to meet your expectations and fulfill my duties and obligations, but I can assure you of one thing, that I will love you, that I love you now and I loved you even before I came to you. For this love, I am willing to carry the cross.[2]

For 17 years Archbishop Athenagoras remained in the USA, re-organizing this vast and important archdiocese and building it up on solid ground. Then, on 1 November 1948, the Holy Synod of the Constantinopolitan Church elected him Ecumenical Patriarch to succeed Maximos V, who had resigned for health reasons. Enthroned on 26 January 1949, Patriarch Athenagoras worked assiduously throughout his 24-year pontificate to strengthen pan-Orthodox unity and thus give meaning to the concept of Orthodox conciliarity. Besides convening several pan-Orthodox conferences, he was also instrumental in re-establishing links with Western Christendom and in establishing the ground for meaningful ecumenical cooperation.

Athenagoras was convinced that the unity of the church and the unity of humankind are two closely linked ideas. He deeply believed that the 20th century ought to be a century of love and fraternity, that there was no place for intra-Christian disputes and quarrels. He often remarked that Christian leaders ought to give up their defensiveness, come out of the trenches of the past and become fighters on the outposts of *oikoumene*, promoting love, Christian edification and unity.

One such stronghold of the Christian *oikoumene*, he believed, was the World Council of Churches, in which Orthodox and Protestants could cooperate as equal partners in a common effort to witness together to the world, to help each other and to create conditions that would later lead them towards their unity. His own election as Ecumenical Patriarch had come only a few months after the founding assembly of the WCC in Amsterdam, and his church was already a member of the WCC.

The World Council itself was a realization of the proposal made by the Ecumenical Patriarchate in an encyclical of 1920, which called on the churches to form a "League (*Koinonia*) of Churches" along the lines of the newly established "League of Nations". The importance of this encyclical for the ecumenical movement and for the evolution of the WCC has often been recognized. Visser 't Hooft described it as an initiative "without precedent in church history".[3]

At the first synodical meeting following his enthronement Patriarch Athenagoras declared: "I bring nothing new, but I will follow the centuries'-old tradition and programme of the church." On inter-church matters he appeared as someone determined to continue the ecumenical *diakonia* of the Ecumenical Patriarchate along the lines set out by his predecessors, particularly Joachim III, whose encyclicals of 1902 and 1904 had pleaded not only for pan-Orthodox unity but also for closeness and cooperation in the wider Christian family.

Athenagoras believed that the problems faced by today's society could be solved only if a united Christendom would acquire again the fullness of spiritual strength which characterized the undivided church. Thus he often repeated that the Orthodox Church was present in the ecumenical movement precisely in order to reveal to the non-Orthodox the treasures of its faith and the richness of its tradition, since the objective of both is the transfiguration of the whole world in Jesus Christ.

He developed these convictions in a 1952 encyclical issued on the occasion of the third Faith and Order Conference in Lund:

> In an epoch in which peoples and nations of the world are working intensely for some kind of rapprochement, in order to confront the great problems which face humanity today, and when the need for some manifestation of the unity of the Christian world, in opposition to the anti-Christian tendencies in the world, has acquired particular importance, the task of rapprochement and cooperation between all the Christian confessions and organizations is a sacred obligation and a holy duty, derived from their own identity and mission. The constitution of the World Council of Churches stipulates that the Council's function is to facilitate common action by the churches, to promote cooperation in the study of the Christian spirit, to promote the growth of the ecumenical consciousness in the members of all the churches, to encourage the dissemination of the holy gospel, to preserve and uplift within the wider Christian context the spiritual values of man. It becomes, therefore, obvious that the primary purpose of the Council is of a practical nature, while its God-pleasing task constitutes an attempt and a manifestation of a noble desire of the Christian world, wishing the churches of Christ to face together the great problems of humanity.
>
> Therefore because of the above aim of the World Council of Churches, but also because, in participating in this pan-Christian movement, the Orthodox Church has primarily sought to make known and to impart to the non-Orthodox the treasures of her faith, worship and order, her religious and ascetic experience, and at the same time get acquainted with new methods and conceptions of church life and activity... (which the Orthodox Church could not possess and foster, because of the particular conditions under which she lived), we consider that the future participation and cooperation of the Orthodox Church with the World Council of Churches is, in many ways, imperative.[4]

Evidence of Patriarch Athenagoras' determination to promote the Orthodox presence in the Council was his decision in 1955 to create a Permanent Delegation of the Ecumenical Patriarchate to the WCC. This patriarchal "embassy" to the WCC has not only been a link between the Phanar and Geneva, but also (particularly in its early days, when a great many Orthodox churches were not yet members of the WCC) provided the WCC with resource materials with regard to Orthodox ecclesiastical order, theology and tradition.

During the final decade of his pontificate, Patriarch Athenagoras manifested a genuine interest in the Roman Catholic Church, believing that repairing the painful historic split between Christianity East and West ought in the first instance to be the responsibility of its two protagonists, Rome and Constantinople. The spectacular but deeply meaningful encounters between Athenagoras and Pope Paul VI in Jerusalem (1964), Constantinople (1965) and Rome (1967) may have led some to conclude that the patriarch's ecumenical interests were changing direction. This impression was contradicted by Athenagoras himself when he visited the WCC in November 1967, immediately after his meeting with Paul VI in the Vatican. Addressing a distinguished ecumenical and international audience at the Ecumenical Centre, Athenagoras could not have been clearer about the stand of his church vis-à-vis the Council:

> We come not as strangers to strangers, but as members of the same family, to this our common home, in witness of our church's profound awareness that it is one of the founding churches of this Council and — along with the other sister Orthodox churches — a deeply engaged and active member of it in the inter-Christian dialogue of love and unity. But, at the same time, we come to bear witness to the fact that our Ecumenical Patriarchate is conscious of how much it has owed in the past, owes now and will also owe in the future to the World Council of Churches — and most rightly so, for this Council is destined to act in all things against the sin of division within the Christian church, and to serve the holy purpose of Christian unity, by bringing closer together the various denominations.[5]

Recalling the commitment of the Ecumenical Patriarchate, since the time of the 1920 encyclical, to "the true ecumenical ideal and true ecumenical dialogue", he went on to explain its new "initiatives in Christian reconciliation":

> A new era in relations between the Roman Catholic Church and the Orthodox church has opened up into one of sincere collaboration with His Holiness Pope Paul VI. For this reason [the Ecumenical Patriarchate also] cultivates and promotes bilateral relations with member churches of the World Council of Churches, such as the Anglican, Old Catholic and Post-Chalcedonian Churches, and the Lutheran Church. The Ecumenical Patriarchate, in working in these directions, is firmly convinced that it is promoting the work of the World Council of Churches.[6]

During his long pontificate Patriarch Athenagoras persuasively spread the ecumenical idea of the Church of Constantinople. At the same time, he was tireless in his efforts to make the *"koinonia* of churches" fully representative of the Christian world rather than resting content with what had been achieved, which would, he warned, lead to ecumenical stagnation. "We have the opportunity to give to this movement a new dynamism leading towards our renewal, which is a fundamental presupposition for the encounter of the churches in the path towards their unity." And he wanted the Orthodox to be pioneers in this effort.

He passed away on 7 July 1972, after a life of working and praying for the universal church, which he believed would emerge, regenerated in the waters of the Apostolic Tradition, from its present chaotic situation, allowing world Christendom to be united in Christ, in the common eucharistic cup.

NOTES

[1] W.A. Visser 't Hooft, *The Genesis and Formation of the World Council of Churches*, Geneva, WCC, 1982, p.1.
[2] *Atlantis*, New York, 28 February 1931.
[3] Visser 't Hooft, *op. cit.*, p.1.
[4] See *Orthodoxia*, 27, 1952, pp.96-99. See also in C. Patelos, ed., *The Orthodox Church and the Ecumenical Movement*, WCC, Geneva, 1978, pp.44-45.
[5] Address by His All Holiness Athenagoras I, Ecumenical Patriarch of Constantinople, in *The Ecumenical Review*, vol. XX, no. 1, 1968, p.86.
[6] *Ibid.*, p.87.

BIBLIOGRAPHY

Works on Athenagoras I

C. Bonis, "Athenagoras Was Predestined to be Leader of Christianity", in *The Orthodox Observer*, special issue, June 1966.
S. Castanos de Medicis, *Athenagoras Ier, l'apport de l'Orthodoxie à l'œcuménisme*, Lausanne, L'Age d'Homme, 1968.
O. Clément, *Dialogues avec le Patriarche Athenagoras*, Paris, Fayard, 1969.
V. Gheorgiu, *La vie du Patriarche Athenagoras*, Paris, Plon, 1969.
V. Istavridis, "The Ecumenical Patriarch Athenagoras I", in *Kleronomia*, 4, 1972, pp.453-63 (in Greek).
V. Istravridis, *The Ecumenical Patriarchs, 1860-Today*, ed. Society of Macedonian Studies, Thessaloniki, 1977 (in Greek).
P. Mojzes, "Athenagoras I: The Charismatic Orthodox Ecumenist", in *Journal of Ecumenical Studies*, 7, 1970, pp.94-97.
B. Ohse, *Der Patriarch Athenagoras I*, Göttingen-Regensburg, Vandenhoeck & Ruprecht, 1968.
G. Papaioannou, *The Odyssey of Hellenism in America*, Thessaloniki, Patriarchal Institute for Patristic Studies, 1985.
D. Tsakonas, *A Man Sent by God: The Life of Patriarch Athenagoras of Constantinople*, Brookline, MA, Holy Cross Orthodox Press, 1977.

Christian Goncalves Kwami Baëta
1908–1994

I met him first at the Accra meeting of the F+O Commission (1974)

JOHN S. POBEE

A distinguished African church leader and ecumenist, theologian and theological educator, Christian Baëta also played a significant role in the national political life of the Gold Coast and later Ghana. The breadth of his contributions is reflected in the honours bestowed on him. The British colonial government conferred on him the Order of the British Empire (OBE); the national government of Ghana awarded him its Grand Medal; and he received honorary doctorates from Tokyo Union Theological Seminary (Japan), Hope College (USA), Humboldt University (Berlin) and Debrecen, Hungary.

Born on 23 May 1908 in a Christian clergy home in Keta, in the Trans-Volta Region of what was then the Gold Coast, Baëta was educated at the Evangelisches Missionsseminar in Basel, Switzerland, and at King's College, University of London, where he took a Ph.D. His thesis on prophetism in Ghana was one of the pioneer published studies on the African Instituted Churches (AICs) which are a significant feature of the religious and Christian scene of Africa. In January 1936 he was ordained. From 1945 to 1949 Baëta served as synod clerk (chief executive) of the Evangelical Presbyterian Church in the Gold Coast, a product of the missionary endeavours of the North German Evangelical Missionary Society in Bremen. The years of the second world war had been difficult for missions with German connections. Although based in the eastern Gold Coast, the EP Church extended into what is today Togo — a German colony taken over by the French after the war. But these political changes had no impact on the local affection for the Germans, and for a long time there was a pro-German political movement called the Togo-Bund. Thus Baëta's service came at a delicate period of the struggle of the EP Church to develop its own identity, against the background of suspicions that it was a political fifth column in the British colony. Moreover, by the principle of comity, this church was very much a tribal church; indeed, it was once called the Ewe Presbyterian Church. The Ewes stretched from eastern Ghana into Togo; and part of Baëta's task was handling the delicate relationship between the parts of the church in the two colonies.

Baëta moved from being synod clerk to serving (among other things) as the Presbyterian chaplain of the University of Ghana, a position he kept until his retirement. But his church life went beyond his denomination and home base, notably through his role in the International Missionary Council. He attended the IMC's world mission conference in Tambaram, India, in 1938; and in 1958 he became vice-chair of the IMC, in which capacity he oversaw its long and difficult integration into the WCC. A joint committee of WCC and IMC had been set up already in 1954 to study the full integration of the two. There were hesitations about what it would do to the genius of the IMC constituency to become part of a large bureaucracy. Moreover, the IMC was a forum of very disparate groups, including theological conservatives whose sole commitment was to mission and who had no interest in organizational unity. Baëta's superintending of these negotiations to a successful conclusion in 1961 attests to his wisdom and tact and the general respect he commanded.

The story of ecumenism in Ghana is inextricably intertwined with Baëta's life. He was a longtime member of the board of the Christian Council of the Gold Coast/ Ghana; and when that council had to confront the challenge of nationalism versus faith and the increasing dictatorship of the first nationalist government, Baëta was the mature leader it needed. Championing the cause of the church in facing the difficulties raised by the administration of Kwame Nkrumah, that prince of African nationalism and self-styled "Marxian socialist", Baëta was happy to involve himself in the fray because he believed church-state relations and the connection between religion and politics were cutting edges of mission.

During and after the second world war the British colonial administration had to come to terms with African nationalism. Accordingly, in 1942 it amended the 1925 constitution of the Gold Coast. The former constitution had taken seriously the chiefs as the natural leaders and, therefore, as representatives of the people. This made for a kind of indirect rule, though in practice the authority of the rulers was undermined. [1] In 1942 the Joint Provincial Council of Chiefs elected two non-chiefs to serve alongside them on the Legislative Council of the Gold Coast: Joseph Boakye Danquah, the revered doyen of Ghanaian politics, a lawyer from Kibi in the eastern region, and Baëta, who represented the entire Trans-Volta region. The minutes of the chiefs' December 1946 meeting commented:

> The Joint Provincial Council in allocating two of its seats to these gentlemen has been able not only to create a remarkable landmark in the political history of the country but also to disperse the allegations that the chiefs were selfish as they were unwilling to cooperate with that section of the country known as the "intelligentsia".

In many churches today there is debate and uneasiness about clergy going into politics. As far back as 1946 that question was on the agenda of the church in the Gold Coast. The decision then was that Baëta could do so. Whether or not that was a deeply considered position is not clear, and it should be noted that Baëta did not go into *partisan* politics. Perhaps the fact that his appointment did not ruffle the feathers of the people of God was largely an expression of confidence in him as a man, but his accepting the position attests to his conviction that a modern secular state could be constituted on the principles discovered in traditional social and political institutions.

In fact it was nothing new for the church in the Gold Coast to be at the cutting edge of national political life. Already in the 19th century the Methodist periodical *The Christian Reporter* had demanded the inclusion of African representatives in the

Legislative Council; and African clergy like S.R.B. Solomon, alias Attoh-Ahuma (Methodist) and C.K. Dovlo (EP Church) were in the forefront of national political life.

In 1948 Baëta also served on the Coussey Committee, which examined constitutional reforms for the Gold Coast. Its proposals were an important landmark on the road to self-government, which became a reality in 1957 under Kwame Nkrumah.

Nkrumah remained in power until 1966, but the promise and hope invested in his government both at home and abroad went sour somewhere down the line. His virulent anti-Western rhetoric, alleged Marxist inclinations, especially towards China and the USSR, dictatorship and corruption at home left much room for fence-mending on all fronts. The military government that succeeded Nkrumah, therefore, sent delegates to major capitals of the world to discuss the economic and political plight of Ghana and to seek understanding and support. Baëta, by then a respected elder statesman, was on the delegation that went to Bonn and Paris. Again, when the first military government was preparing the nation for a return to civilian rule, Baëta was a member of the Constituent Assembly which drafted the new constitution for the Second Republic.

Baëta thus made an impressive contribution to national political life, though he remained first and foremost a churchman. He had thought through his vocation. He understood that involvement in crafting a peaceful and just nation was a religious and spiritual commitment. His self-understanding of his ministry may be summed up in the words of Trevor Huddleston: "if the church refuses to accept responsibility in the political sphere as well as in the strictly theological sphere, then she is guilty of betraying the very foundation of her faith: the Incarnation".[2]

Baëta was also an academic. From 1949 to 1961 he served on the staff of the University College of the Gold Coast/Ghana as a senior lecturer in divinity. His areas of concentration were Old Testament, Hebrew and comparative religions. From 1961 until his retirement in 1972 he was the first occupant of the professorial chair of the reorganized Department for the Study of Religions, which was meant to introduce students to the scientific understanding of religions, taking seriously not only the traditional disciplines of theology but also African traditional religions and other world faiths, especially Islam.

Within this orientation, the department carried out a pioneering study of African Instituted Churches in Ghana. Although the so-called historic churches wanted virtually nothing to do with the AICs at that time, Baëta understood well that it was in those churches that many Christians felt at home while the historic churches seemed to be in North Atlantic captivity. Moreover, the ecumenical vision would be incomplete until the AICs were also engaged in the dialogue to manifest the one body of Christ.

For Baëta, the role of the department was not just to bring together religious systems but, more important, to engage persons with different faith commitments in dialogue with one another for mutual challenge, critique and affirmation. He understood that religion is ultimately about what it is to be human, despite the plurality of humanity. Theology from the ecumenical perspective meant seeking the human face of God in contemporary society. And in that quest, Baëta sought to bring the African jewel to adorn the crown of Christ alongside the inherited jewels.

Baëta's concentration on research into African Instituted Churches has a deeper significance. The missionaries of the historic churches had, by and large, had a very negative attitude to African cultures. And yet culture is the realm of meaning and value, not just of ephemeral behavioural patterns. Not to engage AICs is to miss the opportunity to engage Africans — body, mind and soul — for Christ. David Brown Vincent (1860-1917), who in his pursuit of Ethiopianism changed his name to Mojola Agbebi, said: "to render Christianity indigenous to Africa it must be watered by native hands, turned by native hatchets and tended with native earth".[3] Baëta's research was an attempt to reflect on what Africans had done for themselves and to put it at the disposal of the churches. It reached to the heart of mission ideology and method. Gospel and culture was for him one of the cutting edges of mission and ecumenism. His 1972 farewell lecture on retiring from the university was on the relationship of Christians with persons of other living faiths. He was also one of the prime movers of the timely conference of the Christian Council of Ghana on Christianity and African culture in Accra in 1955. On that occasion his contribution was on "The Challenge of African Cultures to the Church and the Message of the Church to African Culture".

Baëta was not only a theologian but also an educationist. From 1929 to 1930 and again from 1936 to 1940 he taught at Akropong Training College, which was established by the Basel Mission to train teachers and catechists for the Presbyterian Church. In his long service at the University of Ghana he served in several important positions where he had opportunity to interact with and form people. He was the second Master (and the first African) of Legon Hall, the premier hall of residence of the University (1961-69); Dean of the Faculty of Arts (1967-69); and Pro-Vice-Chancellor (1966-68).

In the history of efforts to foster ecumenical formation through exchanges of teachers as well as students, Baëta was one of the persons from the South who went to the North, rather than vice versa. He was a visiting professor at Union Theological Seminary in New York (1958-59); and at Selly Oak Colleges, Birmingham, England (1969-75), as well as doing several shorter stints elsewhere in Europe and America. But he also encouraged students from other parts of the world to come and study at the University of Ghana.

I have noted that Baëta probed the issue of gospel and culture because he realized that theology, mission and ecumenism are about engaging people for God. In that context he saw language as crucial. He himself took Greek and Hebrew seriously and tried to inspire students with that dream. He also spoke and worked comfortably in English, German and French. But above all, he was at home in Ewe, his mother tongue, and Twi, a major Ghanaian language. He was part of a team which translated the Bible into Ewe. Baëta used to say that "language is the soul of a people". But he saw not only the need to recognize different languages and to give all languages a face, but also the need for the different languages to struggle together to speak a common language. That was his ecumenical hope.

NOTES

[1] K.A. Busia, *Africa in Search of Democracy*, London, Routledge & Kegan Paul, 1967, p.49.
[2] Trevor Huddleston, *Naught for Your Comfort*, London, Collins, 1956, p.171.
[3] D.B. Vincent, *Africa and the Gospel*, (1889), cited in E.A.A. Ayandela, *The Missionary Impact of Modern Nigeria 1842-1914*, London, Longmans, Green & Co., 1966, p.200.

BIBLIOGRAPHY

Works by Christian Baëta:

Ed., *Christianity in Tropical Africa*, London, Oxford UP, 1968.
"My Pilgrimages in Mission", in *International Bulletin*, vol. 12, no. 4, October 1988, pp.165-68.
Prophetism in Ghana, London, SCM, 1963.
The Relationships of Christians with Men of Other Living Faiths, Accra, Ghana Universities Press, 1971.

Works on Christian Baëta:

J.S. Pobee, ed., *Religion in a Pluralist Society: Essays in Honour of Prof. C.G. Baëta*, Leiden, E.J. Brill, 1976.
Walter Ringwald, "Christian Baëta. Führender Christ seiner afrikanischen Kirche", in *Ökumenische Profile, Brückenbauer der Einen Kirche*, Band II, Günter Gloede, Hg., Stuttgart, Evangelischer Missionsverlag, 1963.
Theo Sundermeier, "Auf dem Weg zu einer afrikanischen Kirche, Christian G. Baëta, Ghana", in *Theologen der Dritten Welt*, Munich, Verlag H.C. Beck, 1982.

Sante Uberto Barbieri
1902–1991

LUIS E. ODELL

Many years ago, speaking to a group of young people about pastors I had known, I mentioned a person whose experience of life and high culture, combined with a passion for preaching the gospel, had impelled him — like the Apostle Paul and, centuries later, John Wesley — to consider the world as his parish. I was referring to Bishop Sante Uberto Barbieri, one of the heroes of the Christian faith in Latin America and in the *oikoumene* in general. Now that he has entered his rest, according to the promise made in the letter to the Hebrews, let us remember his remarkable and gifted personality, his devotion to the cause of the kingdom, his uprightness and his humanness.

Born in 1902 into an Italian home, Sante Uberto Barbieri spent the first nine years of his life in Switzerland and Germany. His family then moved to Brazil. Attending school there, he soon evidenced his great intelligence and his passion for reading and writing. At the age of 20, he was writing regularly for the only newspaper in Passo Fundo in southern Brazil where he then lived.

Although neither he nor his parents considered themselves religious, he wrote an article defending the city's Methodist church against unfair criticism. This incident, and a subsequent encounter with the local pastor, as well as the sadness he experienced upon the death of his father, aroused in him a need to know more about the Christian faith. In 1923 both he and his mother accepted Christ as their Lord and Saviour and became full members of the Methodist church.

Some months later, the depth of Barbieri's conversion moved him to answer the call to enter the Christian ministry. No one could have imagined then that this young man would, in a few years' time, become one of the most outstanding Christian leaders in Latin America.

After several years of experience in different pastorates, he undertook four years of intensive study in the United States at Southern Methodist and Emory Universities, earning the Bachelor of Arts, Master of Arts and Bachelor of Divinity degrees. For the next twenty-five years he taught theology in Brazil and Argentina. In 1949 he was elected bishop, with responsibility for supervising the Methodist Church in Argentina, Bolivia and Uruguay, a post he held until his retirement in 1970. During this period he was awarded several academic honours. In 1969 the government of Bolivia made him a Knight of the Order of the Condor of the Andes.

We customarily associate the concept of a pastoral vocation with responsibility for the spiritual leadership of a Christian congregation. Barbieri held this position in several churches in both Brazil and Argentina. One of the most memorable features in his church services was the vibrant way in which he brought the Word of God to life as he read the Bible from the pulpit. His profound, vigorous sermons, stressing the evangelistic responsibility of the Christian, were both inspiring and compelling. His book on this topic, *Colaboradores de Dios* ("Co-workers with God"), has been of immense help to lay people.

God called Bishop Barbieri to widen the scope of the ministry entrusted to him, and he spent many years of his life visiting and supervising the work in the three countries in his charge. The many pastors, missionaries and Christian workers under his care found in him the older brother, always understanding, always generous, always ready to help them in their difficulties, encouraging them to renew their enthusiasm and to continue working for the extension of the kingdom of God. During his ministry at large, many new congregations came into being and many chapels, schools and clinics were built or enlarged. His preaching reached many other churches in Latin America, as well as in Portuguese-speaking countries of Africa, where he was regularly invited to preach and to give courses in the theological seminaries.

Over a period of many years Bishop Barbieri made a valuable contribution to the cause of Christian unity worldwide. At the second assembly of the World Council of Churches in 1954 he was elected one of the six presidents for the period 1954-1961. At the next assembly (New Delhi, 1961), he was elected a member of the Central and Executive Committees. From 1958 until 1970 he served as vice-chairman of the World Council of Christian Education (which was then integrated into the WCC). Barbieri also participated in various continental church meetings and consultations, and presided over the First Latin American Protestant Conference in Buenos Aires in 1949. His many activities in this field aroused interest in the ecumenical movement in Latin America and encouraged the churches of this continent to find their way to a stronger mutual relationship with the WCC.

Barbieri became bishop emeritus of the Methodist Church in 1970, but continued an active life of writing, preaching and lecturing. He left to be with his Lord on 13 February 1991.

* * *

As we said earlier, Barbieri showed a talent for creative writing already in his youth. His acceptance of Christ as his Lord, far from limiting this calling, merely emphasized it. Some forty books on biblical and theological issues and on the church's mission, as well as poems, devotional writings and meditations in Spanish, English, Portuguese and Italian, offer proof of his gift. In 1943 he was involved in setting up a major journal entitled *El Predicador Evangélico* ("The Protestant

Preacher"), and he chaired its editorial committee for many years. His last book, *Coloquios Intimos* ("Intimate Dialogues"), consists of 365 short poems based on the gospel of Mark.

Barbieri's literary work, unequalled in the Latin American Protestant world, reminds us that the printed word can be one of the best instruments for educating the Christian in discipleship and proclaiming the good news of the kingdom of God. It is appropriate to conclude this brief portrait of him with three excerpts from his many writings.

World citizenship

Do we have, as Christians, a true conception of what it means to belong to God's kingdom? Sometimes it seems that we do not. We are subjected to the same temptation as the church of Jerusalem: that of confining ourselves within certain boundaries; of thinking that we can reach our salvation alone, without the help of other people; that we do not have other obligations except those which our own traditions and blood prescribe; that the social, political and religious structures of our country are the best in the world. When we come to belong to God's kingdom, through our conversion and allegiance to Jesus, we no longer have frontiers. God's kingdom does not recognize geographical, social or any other kind of boundaries which may make a difference in the rights and duties between one human being and another.

We have to recognize, though, with grief and contrition, that much of the trouble and confusion in the world, its warlike, competitive and unbalanced conditions, we owe to the much-divided church, which for long engaged in internal strife, in fruitless polemics of doctrinal or ecclesiastical matters, alienated from the world and its grave problems. Fortunately, the Holy Spirit is making the church aware of the reality of its situation, exhorting it to assemble in unity, to seek to be the instrument for the salvation of the world. All of humanity cannot be united if the Christian church is divided or interested only in saving itself. In this state of disunion and isolation it will neither be saved nor save the world. It has to hear again, on its knees, our Lord's prayer:

"As thou didst send me into the world, so I have sent them into the world. And for their sake I consecrate myself, that they also may be consecrated in truth. I do not pray for these only, but also for those who believe in me through their work, that they may all be one, even as thou, Father, art in me, and I in thee, that they also may be in us, so that the world may believe that thou hast sent me (John 17:18-21)."

To pray on one's knees, yes; and then get up, conscious that it is, and to answer affirmatively this prayer of its Master, and carry out the mission with which it was entrusted, marching as an obedient servant of a Lord who "came not to be served but to serve, and to give his life as a ransom for many" (Mark 10:45). Only then can we hope to see humankind united as one family and at home in any place on the earth.

Jesus is calling us today to be part of a world citizenship. He calls us urgently, before it is too late and because this is the only hope of salvation for humanity. We have, therefore, to make efforts towards integrating the whole human race, in the common vocation of Christ, which is the vocation of life. The responsibility of the Christian church is tremendous. We have to summon the young people and give them a place so that they may feel challenged by this kingdom of Jesus, so that they may dedicate themselves to struggle against all oppressive force, be it military or civil, against all intolerance, lack of cooperation, exploitation of man by man, hate, poverty, discrimination.

When I found myself, during my life, a pilgrim in the world — a pilgrim even before being born, in my mother's womb — I felt my national orphanhood; and when people called me a foreigner, I felt it even more deeply. I found, though, in Jesus, my world brother; and I found in his kingdom my citizenship, which nobody can take from me. Today I no longer feel a stranger anywhere, in the midst of any people, because the whole earth is God's earth, and all people have their origin in God, because Christ gave me a dimension of life which does not know geographical limits, and gave me a humanistic vision with which to see every man and woman as my companion towards eternity. I give thanks to God for his infinite grace.

* * *

N.B.

What troubles me

It is not my salvation or damnation
that disturbs my spirit;
I want to know if I have lived in vain
or if my life has served for something,
specially for someone.

I want to know if what is left behind me
is straw, ashes, stubble,
or deeds that will last eternally
because of the love and grace of my hands and spirit
among sorrowful souls and aching hearts.

I want to know if I have sown thistles and thorns
or hopes and blessings
along the path of my pilgrimage through this world.

I want to know if the song that has come from my lips
carried anyone to the Mountain of Enchantment
to hear the silence of the starry sky
and the harmony of imperishable things.

I want to know if my countenance and my glance
have inspired a holy enthusiasm,
an ardent zeal, a noble aspiration
in someone who was struggling in the valley of this life.

I do not need to know if for me there is
heaven or hell,
joy or torment.
I want to know, indeed, that this body
which I touch and this soul which I feel
aflame with unrest
have served, by God's grace,
if only for one day
or for just one hour,
to carpet the path of others
with some few petals of fraternal grace
and let fall some drops of heavenly balm
which will soften the bitter wounds
of their daily life.

Sent by Christ

Jesus does not say that we should wait for people to come to us: we should go to find them as Jesus "went about doing good and healing all that were oppressed by the devil" (Acts 10:38). We may ask: how will we find Christ and where should we start and end? There is no fixed boundary; wherever a human need is detected: physical, moral, spiritual, there the disciple of Christ should be found. That human need is the voice of Christ, calling at the door of our conscience: "I stand at the door and knock" (Rev. 3:20). And if we open, he will say: "'Truly, I say to you, as you did it to one of the least of these my brethren, you did it to me'" (Matt. 25:40).

And who are these "least of my brethren"? The hungry, the thirsty, the homeless, the lost, the ragged, the prisoner, the sick, the forgotten, those lost in vices and sin, the violent, the envious, the tyrant. All of them in some way are lost people, void of love, subject to pain or passion, all of them under God's grace. We all are "God's fellow workers" (1 Cor. 3:9), sent by Christ...

For the true disciple of Christ the mandate is: "Take up (your) cross and follow me" (Mark 8:34). This cross is the call for an integral testimony, through proclamation and action. The task is every day more complex and, therefore, more urgent and necessary, requiring more daring and fidelity.

Evidently, we have to first meet the human needs of persons who are closest to us, without waiting for the day when social structures will be changed, because we do not know for sure when this will come about. In whatever social condition we may find ourselves, our most urgent duty is to assist the fellow being closest to us who is lost or suffering...

BIBLIOGRAPHY

Works by Sante Uberto Barbieri:

Colaboradores de Dios, Buenos Aires, La Aurora, 1945.
Coloquios Intimos, Buenos Aires, Methopress, 1978.

Karl Barth
1886–1968

ADRIAAN GEENSE

Without a doubt the best way to introduce Karl Barth among the long procession of ecumenical pilgrims would be to tell the story of his life, 82 years of intense living, stopping at every junction to recall the events of the outside world in which this life was lived and to listen to the voice of the theologian speaking a message to the situation and at the same time transcending it. So strong is the unity of "life and work" in Karl Barth's theological existence that the life of this theologian who never developed any theology of ministry is itself a ministry, lived on behalf of the church universal — a ministry which, though widely received during his lifetime, has still to be fully accepted by that church universal.

This was the method chosen by Eberhard Busch, Barth's last assistant, in a fascinating biography of his master crammed into 550 pages. In this sketch we must content ourselves with only highlights, but understanding these as the space and time in which Barth responded to the challenges with which his life was confronted by God and the history of our time — or, as he himself used to say, by the Bible and the newspaper.

Karl Barth was born in Basel, Switzerland, on 10 May 1886. He died there on 8 December 1968. Except for a trip to the United States in his old age, he never left Europe. Apart from Switzerland, Germany was the country that left the strongest mark on Barth's theology. At the beginning of the century he studied theology under W. Herrmann in Marburg and A. von Harnack in Berlin. From 1921 to 1935 he was a professor at the universities of Göttingen, Münster and Bonn. Finally, he involved himself deeply in the political history of Germany: the aftermath of the first world war, the rise of Nazism, the second world war and the period of reconstruction that followed. It was with sharp criticism and a deep love that Barth accompanied the political and intellectual history of Germany, a country where more than anywhere else philosophy, theology and literature reflected the spiritual and political story of the transition from the 19th to the 20th centuries.

Another challenge which shaped Barth's theological existence was the ten-year period from 1912 to 1921, following his studies, when he was a pastor in the small Swiss town of Safenwil. It was here that this son of the traditional bourgeois milieu of Basel was confronted by the class struggle between workers and employers and all the social questions it posed. Above all, he took seriously his own position as a pastor, not in any clerical sense but rather as the challenge to preach the gospel, the Word of God week by week.

What was the Word of God in this local situation, lived out in a period of tremendous change in Europe and in the world? This was the time of the first world war, with all the atrocities committed by cultured and indeed Christian peoples; the rise of the Russian Revolution; the church's impotence as it sought to articulate its message. With fresh and full expectation, Barth the young theologian turned again to the Bible, a Bible which, through the critical liberal theology of his teachers, had lost its authority for the life of the church. Is it possible to listen to the Bible in such a way that the Bible criticizes us — especially those of us who claim to live by it?

Barth turned in particular to Paul's letter to the Romans, a summary of the gospel by Christ's greatest interpreter. The result was a completely new and penetrating interpretation offered to the theological world by the young Barth. The reworked second edition (1922) aroused wide interest in the theological debates within church and university. Without ever having to defend a doctoral thesis in the classic academic sense, Barth was called to the chair of Reformed theology at the University of Göttingen. He found himself faced with the need to translate the prophetic voice of his first book into a disciplined systematic theology. After ten years of gestation, from 1932 onwards, this was to result in the monumental *Church Dogmatics*: thirteen large volumes still unfinished at his death in 1968.

In 1935, when Barth was suspended from his chair in Bonn by the Nazi government which had come to power in 1934, his hometown University of Basel offered him the chair of dogmatics. There Barth worked till his death, theologically active long after retirement and surrounded by growing numbers of students and scholars from all over the world.

* * *

What is the deepest motive behind Barth's theology, his lasting contribution, the reason he should be placed among the ecumenical pilgrims? The deepest motive behind the work of this theological giant is at the same time the simplest: taking seriously the assumption of the reality of the theme of theology, its "object", God — an object that in reality is the subject of theology that speaks for God himself and makes him known by his own virtue. The simplest message of theology is "let God be God".

God is the totally Other. If we take that confession seriously, theology becomes a critical science, that is, a discipline which must make a critical distinction between the God revealed in Scripture and the gods we project in our religion(s) and philosophy, who far too often play the dominant role in the identification of our causes and interests (national, class, economic, denominational) with the cause of God ("nostrification", to use Barth's term). The equation of "for God's sake" with "for our sake", the belief that God is on our side in all the conflicts that mark human history, reinforces such conflicts instead of healing them.

Thus Barth looks at religion (including the Christian religion) with what would later come to be called the "hermeneutics of suspicion". At the same time, the critical distance that God takes to all our religious endeavours opens a space of dialogue in which reconciliation becomes possible, and this is liberating. The basis of all human liberation is the liberty of God, his identity, his majesty, his glory, none of which depends on what human beings think of him. But God's freedom should not be understood as arbitrary detachment. Rather, it is the source of the free grace in which God himself turns to the human being. This is the dominant message in the second stage of Barth's theology: the critical "No" that God in his judgment addresses to humanity is precisely the reverse of his deep unconditional love for humanity, his grace.

Increasingly, Barth's *Church Dogmatics* began to develop this central truth of the Christian faith in spelling out the name of Jesus Christ — the servant Lord — in ever new ways. In him God's love for humankind becomes visible, and here theology must learn to spell out the deepest mystery of God's love. Theology cannot speak about God in a general way; if this concept of God is not filled from the very beginning by the name of Jesus Christ, it is an abstraction.

Theology, especially when it enters into dialogue with other religions, might be tempted to look for such a general concept of God, apart from Jesus Christ, simply for the sake of finding a common base with others. Barth's approach is the contrary: Christian theology does not achieve the universality it seeks by doing away with the specific nature of biblical revelation, the concreteness of the name of the God of Israel and of Jesus Christ, but, on the contrary, by starting from this foundation. God is always Immanuel, God-with-us, Jesus Christ, and this is the basis for understanding God's love for all humankind, irrespective of its religious or non-religious character. This insight in no way privileges Christians above others as the happy possessors of the true religion. Rather, it looks away from Christians and non-Christians alike to the one who stands as a prophet over against all of them in a sovereign way.

One of the greatest misunderstandings of Barth's theology is the characterization of it as "Christomonism", a view that would limit its ecumenical potential. Barth's aim was to offer a synthetic ecumenical theology which is comprehensive simply by its very particularity and its biblical concreteness. It is in this thorough concentration on the specific nature of theology that the scientific value of systematic theology is also to be found. The openness, the ecumenical nature of Christian theology cannot be gained by forgetting or relativizing its theme, but rather by reinforcing it: the continuous reflection of the mystery of God's love in Jesus Christ. This concentration means two things: on the one hand no greater mystery is conceivable between heaven and earth than this love of God; at the same time, our concepts can never adequately capture the breadth of this mystery, so that theology is constantly invited to move beyond its own local, denominational and historical boundaries and limitations and to enter into any new situation which the church may encounter on its pilgrimage through space and history.

* * *

Apart from a fundamental and critical contribution to the first assembly of the World Council of Churches (Amsterdam 1948) on the theme "Man's Disorder and God's Design" and active cooperation in the preparation of the theological working document on Christian hope for the second assembly (Evanston 1954), Barth was not directly or continuously involved in the "business" of ecumenism. Indirectly, however, his contribution has been fundamental to ecumenical theology. Here let us set out four points at which Barth's theology still — or perhaps again — awaits reception by the ecumenical movement.

1. The scope of ecumenical theological reflection is to find and to formulate a concept of the unity of the church which might become operative for all the churches involved. Barth's theology reminds us again and again that the source of unity, the reason for coming together, is simply the common knowledge of and common witness to the love of God in Christ. The churches are invited to look away from themselves and from the historical conditions and obligations which prevent their unity towards him in whom they are all reconciled.

2. In dealing with what separates the churches, much theological energy has been invested in baptism, eucharist and ministry, three areas in which our being open or closed to others and to the recognition of their ecclesiastical existence is manifested. Surprisingly, perhaps, these questions play scarcely any role in Barth's voluminous theology. In the final period of his theological writings he avoided using the concept of "sacrament" for anything belonging to the actions of the church: if the concept is to be used at all, it should apply to Jesus Christ alone as the presence of God among us.

Barth questions the baptismal practice of all the historic churches which seek to establish their continuity by the rite of infant baptism. On the other hand, he stresses the New Testament concept of confession as inherent to baptism, which confers on the Christian the responsibility to become a witness. He had planned to write a reflection on the eucharist to crown the volume on the ethics of reconciliation, just as baptism had been understood as its foundation. Based on the original meaning of the word "eucharist" it would be the thanksgiving and expression of the Christian's gratitude for the newness of life received in Christ. Although he himself never finished his work on the ethics of reconciliation, the major book written by his son Markus, *The Meal of the Lord: Communion with Israel, with Christ and among the Participants*, can be seen as an elaboration of his father's ideas in this area. Finally, Barth's reflections on congregational order and the ministry of the congregation can relativize our discussions on the structure of ministry, which tend to suffer from an ecclesiocentrism and an exclusive claim on the Holy Spirit for the tradition in which we stand.

3. Dialogue with people of living faiths as a programmatic concern of the World Council of Churches still awaits thorough theological formulation, despite a continuing process of reflection on the "theological significance of other religions". While Barth himself never actively took part in such dialogue and never visited a non-European country where these are burning questions, the fact that he dealt with the phenomenon of religions as such within his doctrine of revelation is not without importance for such dialogue.

Ecumenical reflections on "my neighbour's faith and mine" are accustomed to identify the biblical concept of faith with the general concept of religion. We try to see whether God has revealed himself in other religions, we compare the authenticity of the religious commitment of others with our own and we do our best to arrive at a positive evaluation of other religions as the basis for dialogue. In so doing, we normally neglect the whole biblical aspect of God's judgment on our religious activities — "There is no one who understands, no one who seeks God" (Rom. 3:11) — in an attempt to be polite to others and to avoid Christian arrogance. In this context, Barth's characterization of religion as unbelief is usually misinterpreted as an arrogant Christian judgment about others, whereas in reality it is meant to be applied first and foremost to Christians. Would it not be much more liberating for dialogue to reflect together on God's judgment of our religion rather than to look for elements of truth in the religion of others as a basis for our understanding?

4. Barth died in 1968, the year in which the World Council of Churches held its fourth assembly in Uppsala. Here, for the first time, the needs and the theologies of the southern hemisphere came to the attention of the WCC in a major way. The inspiration of this assembly was one of the driving forces behind discussions of "contextual theology", and a few years later the Ecumenical Association of Third-World Theologians was formed. European theology, and especially European academic theology, which had laid claim to scientific universalism, was suddenly revealed as very contextual. The contextual nature of Barth's own theology, which, as we have seen took shape in Germany and Switzerland, was obvious. But his strong and fundamental criticism of academic European theology and his rejection of any identification of God's interests with our own interests (even when these are understood as the cultural values of the European tradition) open the way to dialogue with theologians from the South regarding this specific type of European theology, which could bring the biblical message of grace and new Christian responsibility in their situation. Some liberation theologians have discovered this potential; for others it has still to come to fruition.

* * *

A fitting conclusion to this portrait comes in the words of a moving and challenging Pentecostal prayer from Karl Barth:

> Dear heavenly Father, we pray that you may give us all your Holy Spirit and again give it to us, that it may revive, enlighten, encourage us, and make us capable of making the small and yet so big step: away from the consolations by which we try to comfort ourselves to the hope in you alone. Turn us away from ourselves to you. Do not permit us to hide away from you. Show us how wonderful you are and how wonderful it is to trust and to obey you.
>
> This we pray for all people: that peoples and their governments submit themselves to your word and so become ready for justice and peace on earth. We pray that your Word may be made known in good counsel and right action to all who are poor and ill, to all prisoners, to all who are in distress or oppressed, to all who do not believe, and that it may be heard and understood as an answer to their cries, and taken to heart. We pray that all Christianity, all churches and denominations, may learn your Word in a new way and may serve you in a new faithfulness, that the truth of your Word becomes clear already here and now and that it will remain a guideline in all human confusion, until it finally enlightens all and everything.
>
> Praise to you who in Jesus Christ, your Son, has freed us to confess this and to hold this: that our hope is in you.
>
> Amen!

BIBLIOGRAPHY

Books by Barth and about Barth already number several thousand titles in many languages. It is impossible to make a good and fair selection, as there are many excellent introductions among them. A must in the above-mentioned sense of describing the unity of Barth's life and work remains the biography of Eberhard Busch, *Karl Barth: His Life from Letters and Autobiographical Texts*, London, SCM, 1976.

A general introduction to Barth's early theology:

T.F. Torrance, *Karl Barth: An Introduction to His Early Theology 1910-1931*, London, SCM, 1962.

"Appetizers" for the whole of his theology are:

Donald Kim, ed., *How Karl Barth Changed My Mind*, Grand Rapids, MI, Eerdmans.
K.H. Miskotte, *Über Karl Barths Kirchliche Dogmatik, Kleine Präludien und Phantasien*, Th. Existenz heute 89, Munich, 1961.
Thomas C. Oden, *The Promise of Barth, the Ethics of Freedom*, Philadelphia, Lippincott, 1969.

More difficult but important are the following studies by a Roman Catholic author and a Dutch Reformed systematician:

Hans Urs von Balthasar, *Karl Barth. Darstellung und Deutung seiner Theologie*, Cologne, Hegner, 1951.
G.C. Berkouwer, *The Triumph of Grace in the Theology of Karl Barth*, Grand Rapids, MI, 1956.

A more recent book in French:

Pierre Gisel, ed., *Karl Barth. Genèse et réception de sa théologie*, Geneva, 1987.

Augustin Cardinal Bea
1881–1968

STJEPAN SCHMIDT

A leading figure of the Second Vatican Council, Augustin Bea was born on 28 May 1881 at Riedböhringen, Baden, Germany. He studied theology in Freiburg, classical philology in Innsbruck and Oriental sciences in Berlin. He was a professor of Old Testament biblical exegesis in Germany (1917-21) and in Rome (1924-59). From 1930 to 1949 he was rector of the Pontifical Biblical Institute. In 1959 he was created cardinal by Pope John XXIII and from 1960 to 1968 was the first president of the Secretariat for Promoting Christian Unity.

For Bea, the basis of ecumenical commitment is the doctrine of the sacrament of baptism and its consequences. According to his successor as president of the Secretariat for Promoting Christian Unity, Johannes Cardinal Willebrands, Bea "worked out and expounded this point of doctrine

to the general church public perhaps better than anybody".[1] His starting point was St Paul's teaching that "by one Spirit we were all baptized into one body, whether we be Jew or Greek, slaves or free" (1 Cor. 12:13). In baptism, Paul writes to the Galatians (3:27ff.), we "have put on Christ", we are "all one in Christ Jesus".[2] Given this basis, Bea affirms that other Christians are,

> in virtue of baptism, subjects and members of the church... Because fundamentally, even if not fully, they belong to the church, they also have the benefit of the influence of God's grace... The Holy Spirit, then, works in a special and powerful way in them too, although... not in such a full manner as in the members visibly united with the Catholic Church.[3]

From this follows "the great duty of every baptized person to show concern over everybody else who has been baptized in Christ, and hence over their union. This duty springs from baptism itself."[4] Thus Bea proposed that, thanks to the impetus of the Second Vatican Council, there would be "a general mobilization of all ranks of the Catholic Church in favour of ecumenism".[5] Although 80 years of age, he made himself an "ambassador of unity" to enable Christian people at all levels to become more aware of the cause of unity. For the clergy he proposed the image of "the priest as minister of unity". He also explained "what Christian unity requires of the laity". To intellectuals Bea spoke of "how university research and teaching can further Christian unity".

The inspiration for Bea's ecumenical method came from the Pauline concept of truth in charity as expressed in the letter to the Ephesians: "Speaking the truth in love, we must grow up in every way into him who is the head, into Christ" (Eph. 4:15). His commentary on these words of the apostle was: "Truth and charity are inseparable in this task. Truth without charity becomes intolerant and repelling; charity without truth is blind and does not endure."[6] Applying this principle to the exposition of the church's doctrine, Bea makes clear that we must put forward the truth, "the whole, undivided, undiluted catholic truth, as made known by Scripture and Tradition and laid down by the teaching authority of the church".[7] This attitude, he adds, is motivated by a "spirit of zealous love: love of truth, of unity, of the souls of the faithful and also of those of the wanderers".[8]

These words may seem hard. In response, Bea points to the appropriate way of bearing witness to the truth, a way which is inspired by charity and thus by the

> humility and the high esteem and respect we should bear towards our separated brethren... "Charity feels no envy, charity is never perverse or proud" (1 Cor. 13:4)... We shall not try to make them surrender by force of argument but by force of truth. We shall not seek to be triumphant ourselves, but look only and always for the triumph of Christ and his truth... Much less should we argue with such insistence as to give the impression that at all costs we want to force others to give up their faith and to accept ours. Such methods do not take into consideration the difference between the evidence for a truth and the objective certainty of it and the difficulty a man has in understanding and realizing it. We must respect the secrets of the human heart and the freedom of man.[9]

Since Bea dealt all his life with Holy Scripture, it is not surprising that he was convinced of the fundamental ecumenical importance of the Bible:

> All who take part in the ecumenical movement or who come into contact with it will need knowledge of Sacred Scripture. This knowledge should be wide, exact and based upon a sound, methodical analysis. It should not be confined to exegesis in the narrow sense but should include true biblical theology, which is a synthesis of detailed exegetical work. Publications dealing with problems of unity should be grounded in a real scholarly knowledge of the Bible.[10]

More than once Bea emphasized the importance of collaboration in ecumenical work "in fields where questions of faith are not directly concerned, especially in matters of social cooperation, of defending Christian principles in public, social and cultural life, in charitable undertakings and especially in international relations".[11] A key example was the search for world peace: "What could it mean for humanity if the whole Christian world, nearly one thousand million men, a third of the human race, were to act in complete unanimity on the momentous questions of nuclear arms, disarmament and peace!"[12]

* * *

The Vatican II document *Nostra Aetate*, which deals with the Catholic Church's relationships with non-Christian religions and, more particularly, with the Jewish people, of which Cardinal Bea was the principal supporter, encountered a great deal of opposition at the Council. After the document had been approved and promulgated, Bea confessed, "If I had been able to foresee all the difficulties we would have encountered, I do not know whether I would have had the courage to undertake this task."[13]

For Bea, the enumeration in *Nostra Aetate* of the essential points which determine the Catholic Church's relations with the Jewish people are basic points of the doctrine of the faith, in other words, purely and exclusively religious relationships. Indeed, herein lay the great pitfall to be avoided in all the Council discussions. Bea never ceased to affirm: "Since we are here treating a merely religious question, there is obviously no danger that the Council will get entangled in those difficult questions regarding the relations between the Arab nations and the State of Israel, or regarding the so-called Zionism."[14]

Restricted thus to religious relations, the document had as its primary aim

> to recall in a solemn way those things which the church of Christ, by hidden design of divine providence, received through the hands of the chosen people of Israel. It received first of all, in the words of St Paul in his Epistle to the Romans, "the oracles of God" (Rom. 3:2), that is, the Word of God in the Old Testament. Besides, to use the words of the same St Paul, to the Israelites "belong the sonship, the glory, the covenants, the giving of the Law, the worship, and the promises"; to them belong the patriarchs, and "of their race, according to the flesh, is Christ, who is over all things, God-blessed forever" (cf. Rom. 9:4-5).[15]

More concretely, Bea explains:

> In other words, not only was the whole preparation of the work of the Redeemer and his church done in the Old Testament, but also the execution of his work, the foundation of the church and its propagation in the world were either in the chosen people of Israel or through members of this people whom God chose as instruments.[16]

Bea has a brief and simple response to those who object that the leaders of the Jews, with the people in agreement, condemned Jesus to be crucified, clamouring "His blood be on us and on our children" (Matt. 27:25), and that Christ himself spoke severely about Jews and their punishment:

> It is true that Christ spoke severely, but only with the intention that the people might be converted and might "recognize the time of its visitation" (cf. Luke 19:42-48). But even as he is dying on the cross he prays: "Father, forgive them, for they know not what they do" (Luke 23:24).[17]

The apostles did not act in a different way:

> St Peter, in preaching to the Jewish people on the crucifixion of the Lord, said, "I know that you acted through ignorance, as did also your rulers..." (Acts 3:17). Thus he excuses even the rulers themselves. Likewise St Paul (Acts 13:27).[18]

Bea concludes that the church must conform to the example of ardent charity given by the Lord and the apostles. "If Christ, the Lord, and the apostles, who personally experienced the grievous effects of the crucifixion, maintained an ardent charity towards their very persecutors, how much more must we be motivated by the same charity?"[19]

In Bea's address to the Council he observed further that the collaborators who shouted, "His blood be on us and on our children" (Matt. 27:25), in fact formed a very small part of the chosen people, noting that the leaders of the Jews were unwilling to kill Jesus "during the feast, lest there be tumult among the people" (Matt. 26:5). From this he concludes:

> If therefore not even all the Jews in Palestine or in Jerusalem could be accused, how much less the Jews dispersed throughout the Roman Empire? And how much less again those who today, after nineteen centuries, live scattered throughout the whole world? [20]

When Vatican II addressed the painful two thousand-year-old problem of relationships with the Jewish people, it also looked at the wider area of relations with the great variety of non-Christian religions. Just as relationships with the Jewish people were marked by painful division, so, too, were those with these other creeds.

Presenting the draft of *Nostra Aetate* to the Council, Bea noted that it

> does not propose to offer a complete account of religions nor of the divergences that exist among themselves and from the Catholic religion. Rather, the Council... intends to point out the bond between men and religions as the foundation of dialogue and cooperation. Thus the stress is placed on those things which unite men and lead to mutual fellowship. [21]

What is this bond which is the foundation of dialogue and cooperation? Bea, in summarizing the introduction to the conciliar document, writes:

> In speaking of the unity of the whole human family, our document points to our unity in God as the indestructible foundation on which it rests: all men come from God, our Creator; we journey back to him as our final goal; and on this journey we are the objects of his providence and his gracious guidance. God wishes to bring all men to salvation in union with himself and he guides them to this happy final state. [22]

Many years before this conciliar document was enlarged to include relations with non-Christian religions in general, Bea had written a book entitled *Unity in Freedom: Reflections on the Human Family*. [23] In it he dealt with the vast gamut of divisions which afflict the human family and sought to indicate the means and the path by which one human family, freely united in truth, justice and love can come into being.

To anyone who would point to the painful and winding path of humanity across history as evidence that such a vision is an illusion, Bea would have replied: "Certainly the path of humanity, seen merely through human eyes, is as tortuous as could be, full of failures and grave misadventures. It is nonetheless certain that it is guided, in a manner secret and unseen yet real and effective, towards the realization of God's plan with and for mankind." [24]

NOTES

[1] Quoted by S. Schmidt, *Augustin Bea: The Cardinal of Unity*, New York, New City Press, 1992, p.402.
[2] Augustin Cardinal Bea, *The Unity of Christians*, London, Geoffrey Chapman, 1963, p.30.
[3] *Ibid.*, pp.32f.
[4] Quoted by Schmidt, *op. cit.*, p.406.
[5] Bea, *op. cit.*, p.36.
[6] *Ibid.*, p.115.
[7] *Ibid.*, p.108.
[8] *Ibid.*, p.24.
[9] *Ibid.*, pp.78f.
[10] *Ibid.*, p.101.
[11] *Ibid.*, pp.89f.
[12] *Ibid.*, p.90.

[13] Schmidt, *op. cit.*, p.500.
[14] Bea, *The Church and the Jewish People*, London, Geoffrey Chapman, 1966, p.59.
[15] *Ibid.*, p.155.
[16] *Ibid.*
[17] *Ibid.*, pp.155f.
[18] *Ibid.*, p.157.
[19] *Ibid.*
[20] *Ibid.*, p.158.
[21] *Ibid.*, p.169.
[22] *Ibid.*, p.31.
[23] New York, Harper & Row, 1964.
[24] Bea, "Paths to Ecumenism", in *What I have Learned: A Collection of 20 Autobiographical Essays by Great Contemporaries*, New York, Simon & Schuster, n.d., p.22.

BIBLIOGRAPHY

Works by Cardinal Bea:

The Unity of Christians, London, Geoffrey Chapman, 1963.
The Church and the Jewish People, London, Geoffrey Chapman, 1966.
Unity in Freedom. Reflections on the Human Family, New York, Harper & Row, 1964.
"Paths to Ecumenism" in, *What I have Learned: A Collection of 20 Autobiographical Essays by Great Contemporaries*, New York, Simon & Schuster, no date, pp.13-23.

Works on Cardinal Bea:

S. Schmidt SJ, *Augustin Bea, the Cardinal of Unity*, New York, New City Press, 1992.

Dom Lambert Beauduin
1874–1960

EMMANUEL LANNE

If ever a servant of Christian unity merited the title "ecumenical pilgrim", it was Dom Lambert Beauduin. Throughout his long life he was a "man of God and of the church" (to echo the sober inscription on his grave: *Vir Dei et Ecclesiae*). As a priest of the diocese of Liège (Belgium), he entered the monastic life at 33, influenced above all by the high quality of the liturgical celebrations he had seen in the Benedictine abbeys. His aim was to restore to diocesan parishes a sense of common prayer rooted in the beauty of the texts, the chants and the liturgy. Thus it was that, as a monk of the Keizersberg (Mont-César) Abbey in Leuven (Louvain), he came to launch the "liturgical movement" in Belgium in 1909.

But it would be incorrect to see Dom Lambert Beauduin as an aesthete. At the heart of the liturgical movement for him was the unity of Christian people in the celebration of the eucharist, unity in Christ, unity with the Father, the unity of all those — brothers and sisters — who are baptized. The slim volume he published in launching the liturgical movement bore the inscription *Ut unum sint!* — "That they all may be one; as thou, Father, art in me, and I in thee" (John 17:21) — and already then his spiritual vision was the unity of the members of the body of Christ made visible in the eucharistic celebration of the local church.

Dom Lambert was a friend of Cardinal Mercier, archbishop of Mechelen (Malines) and primate of Belgium, who from 1921 until his death in 1926 oversaw the Malines Conversations between Roman Catholics and Anglicans. Despite the fact that these "conversations" were not official, they were the first of their kind between a leading Catholic prelate and the leaders of the Anglican communion, and both Rome and Canterbury were kept informed of them.

In 1920 Dom Lambert was sent to Rome as professor of theology at St Anselm College. Teaching ecclesiology was a real eye-opener for him; and the issue of unity among visibly divided Christians became his overriding concern. In the same period, the flood of Russian emigrés fleeing the Bolshevik Revolution deepened his awareness of the Orthodox Church and the richness of its liturgical and spiritual tradition. Also, 1920 was the year of the meetings in Geneva out of which grew the Life and Work movement and the 1925 Stockholm conference, as well as the Faith and Order conference in Lausanne in 1927. Dom Lambert's disciples and friends kept him informed of these first steps in the newly born ecumenical movement.

All these factors lay behind his dream of a monastery devoted to the search for unity among Christians, and in 1925 he seized the opportunity to found it. With a group of followers he established himself at Amay-sur-Meuse, close to Liège, and a few months later set up the review *Irénikon*, the first issue of which appeared in April 1926. Henceforth the monastery in Amay and its journal were to be the focus of a completely new opening up within the Catholic Church to other Christians and to their churches, aimed at bringing together spirits and hearts as the fundamental first step in the search for the unity of all the followers of Christ.

Among the friends who helped to guide Dom Lambert's ecumenical thinking and action was a remarkable personality, Fr Fernand Portal. As early as 1894, Portal, who had links with Lord Halifax, had begun attempts to bring Catholics and Anglicans closer together. These ran aground in 1896 when Rome rejected the validity of Anglican ordination. In 1920, however, Portal relaunched the initiative, and it was he and Halifax who convinced Mercier to begin the Malines Conversations. In the course of the last Conversations in which Mercier was to take part, in 1925, the cardinal asked Dom Lambert to prepare an unsigned memorandum, for which Mercier took responsibility, entitled "The Anglican Church United but not Absorbed". The memorandum represented a very daring statement for a Catholic of the time, and when it became known after Mercier's death that Dom Beauduin was the real author, he found himself at the centre of polemical argument.

A special characteristic of the foundation in Amay-sur-Meuse (which moved to Chevetogne in the province of Namur in 1939), which it retains to this day, is the double celebration of the liturgical offices according to the Byzantine and the Roman rites. The community is divided into two groups, each of which celebrates in its own place of worship by one of these two rites. During the eucharist and on feast days the monks come together for common prayer in one of the two churches. Dom Lambert was very much attached to this practice, which not only brought the monks to pray within the context of the two principal Christian traditions, but also led them to learn, love and teach the liturgical and spiritual tradition of Orthodoxy. So for more than six decades, the monks of Amay and now Chevetogne, praying in spiritual union with Orthodox and Catholic monks everywhere, have offered a modest witness to the hope of unity in their daily life.

In 1926 Dom Lambert wrote to one of the monks in his new monastery: "Let us first bring about among ourselves this perfect unity which we would see among all Christians." Later he took up the same idea more specifically:

> The monastery of the Union... has of necessity become a place of welcome... a hearth which vibrates with the ecumenical spirit and togetherness, where everything, human beings and things, harmonize and repeat the same echo. In tune with those who live there, everything seeks to make Chevetogne into a welcoming post-house on the road to union, the Emmaus where, together, with a burning heart, we can listen to the words of the Master.

From the outset Dom Lambert, who had been indirectly brought into the Malines Conversations by writing the memorandum for Cardinal Mercier, wanted Amay to be especially open to Anglican guests. Indeed, until the end of his life he had an undisguised admiration for the liturgical services of the Church of England, though he welcomed all Christians of the Reformation at the monastery, considering them as brothers who honoured, first and foremost, the Word of God. He also wanted the monks to have a true veneration for the Bible, and he required them to spend much of their time in personal prayer and in long and attentive study of the Bible. Dom Lambert believed that in order to experience community and liturgical celebrations authentically, monks — and indeed all Christians — must be impregnated in their deepest being by the Scripture. While this may seem quite obvious to post-Vatican II Catholics, it was not quite so evident in those days.

No portrait of Dom Lambert Beauduin would be complete without mentioning the difficulties he encountered. Not only did the memorandum he wrote for the Malines Conversations arouse a veritable storm among the Catholic leadership in England, but authorities in Rome were the source of other difficulties. Nor was the use of the Byzantine rite in his new foundation without ambiguity. Some hoped that it would help draw the Orthodox into the Catholic Church, whereas Dom Lambert was totally against any form of proselytism, no matter how hidden. At a time when well-meaning but misguided persons were seeking to draw Russian emigrés into the Catholic Church by offering them material assistance and by demonstrating to them the power of the Roman Catholic Church, this attitude on the part of the founder of Amay upset many people even in the highest echelons of the Catholic Church. In a short note in the second issue of *Irénikon* in May 1926, he laid to rest any doubts on this score: "In what spirit do we wish to work? Neither that of proselytism, nor that of charity, nor that of an imperialist conception." A short passage from this note gives eloquent expression to the courage and the prophetic spirit of the man who wrote it:

The unionist action [the term used for ecumenical activity in those days] arouses among many legal and diplomatic associations: patient negotiations between various ecclesiastical hierarchies and, at the end of these negotiations, the integration of what are at present divided societies into a society which is juridically one. It is as though they are haunted by a dream of unification, by nostalgia for the universal empire. They think only of one thing: achieving the external obedience of wills through dictatorial power. This aspiration towards the union of the churches is the fruit of a centralizing spirit which only wishes to widen the cradle if it means engulfing a whole new flow of consciousness by discipline. This imperialist concept, so abhorrent to our separated brethren, must never be that of the true apostles of union. There is only one doctrine in terms of which we can reflect on the concept of the union of all the churches — at least if we wish to reflect on it in all its depth and in all its richness: that is the doctrine of the church as the mystical body of Christ. [1]

That such words created a shock is quite understandable. Not only did they do away with any idea of proselytism and self-interested charity, they also undermined the very basis of any so-called "apostolic" action — a false vision of the ecclesial reality — in the name of a vision which focused on faith, the sacraments and love. A few years later Dom Lambert set out the method of unity he himself advocated, which he called "psychological". It meant "bringing about this spiritual encounter of minds and hearts through fervent personal work: coming to know, to understand, to esteem and to love our separated brethren, to pray with them for the concord of the holy churches". He went on: "It means carrying out work of a psychological nature, in all charity and humility, a work which will help dispel prejudices and open up illuminating inroads of confidence and love." [2]

As for concrete results in the short term, Dom Lambert expected no more than this growth in love and mutual confidence. From the outset, he rejected the prospect of possible "successes" as a temptation. Down through the years, with all the trials and tribulations to which he was subjected, he inculcated in his disciples the gratuitousness of this action. A memorandum in 1940 reiterated his conviction: "Let us have no illusions: our generation, and — alas — in all probability a great many others after it, will not see reconciliation... Such resignation is important; it will give us a mentality which is disinterested and without any ulterior motives; it is what we could call the purity of intent or, in the scientific world, intellectual objectivity." The same memorandum anticipated perspectives that would see the light of day only very much later in the ecumenical movement: "The basic and characteristic attitude of the monks of Amay (Chevetogne): an ecumenical attitude. Indeed, it is impregnated with a doctrine in which everything is universal, catholic, ecumenical: universalism through the unity rediscovered in the risen Christ; universalism through humanity rediscovered in the new humanity."

Not surprisingly, such a standpoint attracted some fierce enemies in the 1920s and 1930s. When Pope Pius XI published the encyclical *Mortalium Animos* in 1928, which condemned the budding ecumenical movement, Dom Lambert was given to understand that it was aimed at him. He defended himself in *Irénikon*, but at the end of that same year he resigned as prior of his monastery in the hope of saving his life's work. From 1930 to 1932 proceedings against him were instituted in Rome and when they ended, he was punished by being relegated to the En-Calcat Abbey in the south of France for two years. There his presence won the hearts of all the monks, and soon he could count them all as friends. Although he was given permission to live close to Paris, he was forbidden to return to his monastery in Amay; and only in 1951 was he authorized to go to Chevetogne, where he spent his final days.

The infectious joy he retained during his exile in En-Calcat shines through a letter he wrote to a friend:

> For some months now I have felt the austere but profound joy of suffering for an ideal... I greatly enjoy the silence and the contemplation of this solitude and I do my best to re-experience and meditate for myself on what I preached to others. I am like a wine merchant whose shop has been closed temporarily by the police for the illegal sale of alcohol (*Ebrietatem Spiritus*: cf. Acts 2:15) and who, in the meantime, makes an inventory of his storeroom and finds unsuspected reserves which he uses to his own good ends.

* * *

Dom Lambert's ecumenical vision was incarnated in a "style" which attracted disciples, admirers and a very diverse group of friends. He won over and drew in those whose spirit was not broad enough to grasp at once the "vision" of unity. This innate style largely contributed to the success of the liturgical movement which he launched in Belgium before the first world war and thereafter placed entirely at the service of the quest for the union of the churches. We could almost describe it by using St Paul's words to the Corinthians, "love believes all things, hopes all things", even when a lack of confidence in him offered such apparent contradictions.

From the outset no daily task was too humble for him. And when he returned to Chevetogne in his later years, he wanted to share in all the little obligations of fraternal life. Without any ostentation, with laughing eyes, he set the example. The most striking aspect of his style was his unbelievable gift for making people feel welcome. No matter who turned to him, for whatever reason, that person was received with a smiling face and with the most surprising consideration. And no matter what the point of the visit, the tenor of the conversion often moved on spontaneously to the vast realities of the Christian faith, revealing the interior vision which was always present within Dom Lambert. Sometimes he would crack a joke. Less perceptive people took it at face value and either burst out laughing or were offended, when in fact it was a sign of modesty and of respect for the other person.

Above I used the words of 1 Corinthians 13 to describe this style. Even more appropriate for linking this style to the "vision" of John 17 "that they should be one" are the verses in Philippians 2 in which St Paul introduces the hymn to Christ humiliated on the cross and exalted in glory: "If then our common life in Christ yields anything to stir the heart, any loving consolation, any sharing of the Spirit, any warmth of affection or compassion, fill up my cup of happiness by thinking and feeling alike, with the same love for one another, the same turn of mind and a common care for unity."

In Dom Lambert Beauduin, vision and style were intertwined. The union of the churches and the ecumenical task is first of all a search for unanimity of spirit. The face of each and every Christian brother and sister reveals the visage of Christ in which the glory of the Father is resplendent. That was the message of this ecumenical pilgrim. Six decades later it is no less valid.

NOTES

[1] *Irénikon*, 1926, p.119.
[2] *Ibid.*, 1930, pp.393ff.

George Allen Kennedy Bell
1883–1958

ANS J. VAN DER BENT

Shortly after the Universal Christian Conference on Life and Work in Stockholm in 1925,
Archbishop Nathan Söderblom of Sweden wrote to
Archbishop of Canterbury Randall Thomas Davidson: "This Bell never rings for nothing." Indeed,
the man to whom Söderblom was referring, George
A.K. Bell, then dean of Canterbury cathedral,
never stopped ringing throughout his life, and the
echoes of that life reverberate even today. He was
truly a world churchman, one of the most creative
personalities of the ecumenical movement, the advocate of an international Christian ethos based on
forgiveness and reconciliation, a resolute opponent
of Britain's policy of bombing Germany during the
second world war, the trusted advisor to the Confessing Church in Germany and a prominent figure
in the reconstruction of relationships with German
churches during and after the war.

The eldest of seven children, George Bell was born in Norwich, England, on
4 February 1883. Educated at Westminster School and Christ Church, Oxford, he
spent two years at Wells Theological College before being ordained in 1907. From
then until his death he held five appointments: curate in Leeds (1907-10), student and
tutor at Christ Church (1910-14), chaplain to the Archbishop of Canterbury (1914-24),
dean of Canterbury (1924-29) and Bishop of Chichester (1929-58). He earned a
doctorate of divinity from Oxford in 1924, and later received honorary doctorates in
Britain and abroad.

He became dean of Canterbury under the socialist prime minister Ramsey Mac-
donald and cared deeply and practically about social and industrial questions. His
personality and temperament were well-suited to the demands of the unusual position of
a Lambeth chaplain. Davidson, of whom Bell wrote a lucid biography in 1935, trusted
Bell and delegated many responsibilities to him. His academic training had produced
a disciplined mind which knew how to tackle and master an unfamiliar subject.

Bell attended four Lambeth Conferences from 1920 to 1958, serving as episcopal
secretary at the 1930 conference. He was secretary to the Anglican panel in conversa-

tion with the Free Churches after Lambeth 1920, joint chairman of the first round of negotiations between the Church of England and the Methodist Church and a keen advocate of the South India scheme. From 1932 to 1934 he chaired the Universal Council for Life and Work and was the movement's leading spokesman. Few did more to facilitate the launching of the World Council of Churches. He was the first moderator of the WCC Central Committee and was elected Honorary President of the World Council in 1954. He gave his last sermon at the 1958 WCC Central Committee meeting. He died quietly at his home in Canterbury on 3 October 1958. That same year the Federal Republic of Germany announced that he would be awarded its Order of Merit, but he died before receiving it.

Bell was no ordinary ecclesiastical bureaucrat. In his early years he was much interested in poetry, and his poem "Delphi" won him the Newdigate Prize. As dean of Canterbury he fostered the arts and the use of drama in worship, including John Masefield's *Coming of Christ* and T.S. Eliot's *Murder in the Cathedral*. In Chichester he appointed a diocesan director of religious drama, the first appointment of its kind in Britain, and he was later active in organizing the first International Conference on Religious Drama at Lincoln College, Oxford, in 1955, which led to consultations on religion and drama in the ecumenical movement.

Disliking the telephone, Bell sat up late into the night writing long letters to colleagues and friends. His massive correspondence throws valuable light on his theological views, and numerous incidents in his life show his readiness for action and his originality in making crucial decisions. But although he planned to write his memoirs, no autobiography exists.

Already in 1915, he explained his understanding of church and kingdom:

> The war and its terrible results, mourning and sorrow, loss and suffering, disaster and death, are the wages of sin. And when we speak of sin we do not mean the sins of a political system — in the narrow sense in which that word "political" is used; nor are we primarily concerned with the political causes which brought the war on. We are concerned with the moral and religious causes which lie behind all these... But while it is our first duty to denounce these sins from which the war springs, and to call men to repentance, we have a higher and better task than this. Behind our call to repentance lies a great hope. We bid men repent because we would point them to the kingdom of God... It is for us as members of his church to press forward and strain eagerly towards it, that we may be worthy of it when in all its completeness it comes.

And this is what he said in his farewell address at Chichester:

> It has been my aim to encourage a growing consciousness of what the church means, and what membership involves. I have stood for common order in Christ's church... In the questions of international justice and world peace I am an ardent, though I hope neither an unreal nor too impatient, champion. Certainly my championship dates from even before the first world war; and in different sections of this immense field I have worked and prayed and spoken right through my time in Chichester, going sometimes, it has to be acknowledged, against the stream. I have spoken on these themes not only in convocations and church assemblies, but also in the House of Lords. I have risen in my place in Parliament in the belief that bishops, as spiritual peers, have a duty to make responsible contributions from time to time on public questions, not as party politicians, but as Christian men specially concerned with moral issues and the well-being of the nation as a whole.

Bell's generally empirical approach to ecumenical questions did not mean that he was unaware of doctrinal problems under discussion in the Faith and Order movement.

But he rarely contributed to the theoretical debates on the unity of the church and indeed dismissed the first world conference on Faith and Order (Lausanne 1927) as a "waste of time of self-satisfied theologians". He was far more concerned with practical steps towards unity, such as practising intercommunion first and then discussing the theology behind it. Yet his own ecumenical involvements did not mean that he abandoned his confessional position; he remained a devoted and uncomplicated Anglican.

W.A. Visser 't Hooft once remarked about Bell: "Theology for the sake of theology, unity for the sake of unity, organization for the sake of organization, he could not accept. Theology was to help confused modern man to understand the gospel, unity was to make the Christian church a better servant of humanity, organizations existed to serve the cause of Christ."

From the 1930s onwards, George Bell symbolized for many people the reality of the *Una Sancta* — the universal Christian fellowship unbroken by war and other human evil. As few others he lived his life in an extremely wide context. But it was not only that he felt that he belonged to the whole church of Christ; it was equally true that countless men and women in other churches felt that he belonged to them. In 1953 Bell said to the members of the WCC Central Committee: "The World Council of Churches stands before the nations, and before the United Nations, as a worldwide fellowship appealing for an end of hatred and suspicion and war, declaring that the world of nations is one single family and that all are responsible for their neighbour's welfare."

During the Cold War, said Visser 't Hooft, there were few church leaders who spoke as clearly as Bell about the violation of human rights in communist countries. "But he could never forget that communists were human beings. I have been with him in some meetings with communist leaders. He spoke firmly and took his stand on Christian principles, but he did not speak to them as enemies, rather as men who must be able to understand the truth of God. Thus all that he said, whether in denouncing evil or in advocating mutual understanding, was said for, never against, men. 'The church and humanity' meant for him the church *for* humanity, for all, persecuted and persecutors, the weak and the strong."

It was no surprise that Bell was elected to be the first moderator of the World Council of Churches Central Committee in 1948. In a young movement without a solid tradition, personal leadership was necessarily predominant, and no one could represent better than Bell what the World Council was going to be in the future. The confidence he inspired and his example of completely disinterested consecration to a transcendent cause, as well as the informality of his chairmanship, created a spirit of partnership which moved the Central and Executive Committees in the right direction. At the end of his term he reported to the Evanston assembly in 1954:

> I have been intimately concerned with the ecumenical movement for 35 years. The individual members and officers, the councils and committees, in the earlier phases, rendered an unforgettable service to the cause of Christian unity. Without these pioneers there would be no World Council today, but... I do not hesitate to say that the partnership of members of many churches on the outgoing Central Committee has involved an even more precious spiritual experience and carries a deeper significance for Christendom. We must expect difficulties of various kinds. Yet what has engraved itself so clearly on my mind in the past six years has been the steady growth of mutual trust, and deep understanding, as well as a greater sense of urgency. In subjects which ordinarily afford ample ground for

controversy, whether political or theological, complete freedom, frankness and charity have prevailed. There has been no thought, even in the most difficult matters, of one bloc lining up against another bloc; but always the sense of being an instrument of a World Council of Churches, not a Council of the West or the East, or the North or the South, and of a common desire to know the mind of Christ and to follow its leading to the best of our ability in all our relationships.

George Bell's friendship with Dietrich Bonhoeffer began in 1933 when the young German pastor came to work with the German congregation in London. From the outset Bell showed an immense trust in Bonhoeffer, who considered Bell as a spiritual father who, like Karl Barth, had real authority over him. Through Bonhoeffer, Martin Niemöller, Alphons Koechlin and Visser 't Hooft, Bell was well aware of the real nature of the German situation. But it was through Bonhoeffer's personal struggle that he came to comprehend the justification of resistance in a situation in which God's law is violated. On the day before his execution Bonhoeffer sent his last message to Bell through a British fellow-prisoner: "Tell him that for me this is the end but also the beginning — with him I believe in the principle of our universal Christian brotherhood which rises above all national interests, and that our victory is certain."

After the war Bell was among the foreign church leaders at the meeting of repentance and reconciliation in Stuttgart where leaders of the Evangelical Church in Germany drafted a declaration of guilt. While in Germany he also gave an address in the windowless Marienkirche in the Russian sector of Berlin. With European reconstruction in mind, he said there must be repentance by all for the sins which all had committed. He believed that the churches of the entire world must work together to their utmost to relieve Germany in its bitter distress and all suffering countries in proportion to their needs. This fundamental view would be of great importance to the whole ecumenical movement. In awarding him an honorary doctorate in 1949, the Protestant Theological Faculty of the University of Münster spoke of his extraordinary work in promoting the fellowship of Christians in Britain and Germany and throughout the world:

> His unreserved and undaunted stand for truth, justice and reconciliation has brought anew to consciousness for many weary and tortured hearts, not least in Germany, the comforting presence of Jesus Christ in his church, and he has thereby shown himself a true bishop in apostolic fashion.

Martin Niemöller called Bell "a man of the ecumenical movement... because he was a Christian who was led and driven by the love of Jesus Christ himself. He could not see somebody suffering without suffering himself. He could not see people left alone without becoming their brother. He will remain in the memory of the church for a long time to come, and his blessing for the church will not cease."

The crowning event in Bell's life was when he preached his final sermon in the cathedral in Odense, Denmark, on the occasion of the tenth anniversary of the World Council of Churches. His text was Luke 17:10: "So you also, when you have done all that you were ordered to do, say, 'we are worthless slaves; we have done only what we ought to have done'." That same text had been chosen by Bonhoeffer for his first sermon as a young student for the ministry. Archbishop Söderblom used it constantly, and the text is engraved on his tomb in Uppsala cathedral.

BIBLIOGRAPHY

Works by George Bell:

Christian Unity: The Anglican Position, London, Hodder & Stoughton, 1948.
Christianity and World Order, Harmondsworth, Penguin, 1940.
Documents on Christian Unity, 4 vols, London, Oxford UP, 1967.
The Kingship of Christ: The Story of the WCC, Harmondsworth, Penguin, 1945.

Works on George Bell:

Ronald C.D. Jasper, *George Bell — Bishop of Chichester*, London, Oxford UP, 1967.

Kathleen Bliss
1908–1989

JANET CRAWFORD

It was said of Kathleen Bliss after her death in 1989 that "she might well have been Archbishop of Canterbury had ordination been open to women, for she was a pastor and administrator as well as a thinker". In many ways she was a person well ahead of her time, not only in the professional appointments she held but also in her thinking. Certainly she made an outstanding contribution to the growth and effectiveness of the World Council of Churches in its early years, when very few women were involved. William Temple, T.S. Eliot, George Bell and Dietrich Bonhoeffer were among her friends and colleagues. Who was this remarkable woman?

Internationally, Kathleen Bliss first became known at the WCC's Amsterdam assembly in 1948, where she was an alternate delegate of the Church of England. With Jacques Ellul, John Foster Dulles and Josef Hromádka she addressed an assembly plenary session on the theme of the disorder of modern society. She "pleaded with the church no longer to evade the task of understanding modern scientific-technical society... nor to condemn it wholesale" but to face its problems in their depth, for "this is the only society there is now throughout the world". In her opinion, the problems of society lay neither in science nor in technology, but "in the unsolved problem of power and the control of power". The church might become a new order of life within society, offering a home and a faith to "the suffering souls of modern men" but the church itself was divided, "suffering from a division far more disastrous than denominationalism: the division between clergy and laity, church and world". Bliss urged that if clergy were to understand modern society, they needed the help of the laity — a theme that was to echo constantly throughout her work. If the need for renewal were felt deeply enough, the divided church might become the people of God in the world, "a people ready to die to the sins of our present society, and quietly but courageously work in market-place and council-chamber for its deep transformation".

At Amsterdam Bliss also chaired the committee of alternate delegates on the laity and wrote the preliminary draft of the assembly message because, according to

N.B.

Visser 't Hooft, "we had come to the conclusion that the best person to write that was Kathleen Bliss". "We intend to stay together", the widely-quoted sentence from the message, came from her pen.

Her earlier life had prepared her for international and ecumenical leadership. At Girton College, Cambridge (where she was then the only woman studying theology), she was a leader in the Student Christian Movement. After graduating with honours in history and theology, she married Rupert Bliss (then a layman, later a minister in the Congregational Church) and with him sailed to missionary service with the London Missionary Society in South India. There they served in educational work, returning to England with their children when the second world war broke out.

Upon her return to England Bliss became assistant to J.H. Oldham, an outstanding lay Christian and ecumenical leader and the editor of the fortnightly *Christian Newsletter*, the main organ of English Christian thinking about the war and post-war reconstruction. Oldham was both friend and mentor to Bliss; and it was through him that she first became involved with the WCC when in 1946 she deputized for him at a meeting in Geneva of the Provisional Committee. In 1945 Bliss replaced Oldham as editor, continuing till 1949 in that position, which kept her in touch with many of the most formative people and ideas of the time. Her work was recognized in 1949 with an honorary doctorate from the University of Aberdeen.

Although Bliss left the *Christian Newsletter* when she gave birth to another child, motherhood did not prevent her from accepting an invitation to write a book based on the responses to a survey on the role of women in the churches worldwide, conducted by the WCC prior to the Amsterdam Assembly. After all, she said, "writing the book was the sort of job I could do while I rocked the cradle with one hand". The result was *The Service and Status of Women in the Churches*, described by Visser 't Hooft as a "highly illuminating survey... which may claim to represent the first worldwide study on this subject which has ever been made". Bliss gave her own personal interpretation to the material gathered in the survey, adding two chapters in which she sketched the history of interaction between church and society as it affected the role of women in both. This careful study, charitable and compassionate in tone, solidly rooted in concrete historical examples, has been credited with preparing the way for the rise of Christian feminism years later. In it, Bliss pleads eloquently for women's rights, above all for women's right to *serve* the church.

N.B.

> It is not in order to prove something to others, but as a matter of her own integrity that a woman who feels that she has God-given powers must prove them by exercising them. Society, the community outside the institutional church (which is just as much the world for which Christ died as the church is), lies open before her, and if she fulfils her calling by using her gifts there and obeys God in so doing, she *is* serving the church. More than that, she is serving the church in a way it particularly needs and a way that women particularly have it in their power to serve.

While writing this book, Bliss was also greatly involved with the newly formed WCC Commission on the Life and Work of Women in the Church, first as its chairperson and then, from mid-1951 to early 1953, as part-time secretary. She helped to influence the commission to focus on the issue of women-in-relationship with men in the church, rather than on women working in separate groups. Her own attitude was clear:

> Women have never found their place in the church by imposing their will and their views: whether they find fulfilment or frustration depends on the relationship of the sexes — not

only the relation of an individual man and an individual woman in marriage but the total relationship, governed by what men think of women, how they behave towards them and what women think of themselves. The question of the place of women in the churches is not a "women's question". It might more truly be called a "men's question". Fundamentally it is a question of *relationship*.

According to Bliss,

this relationship between men and women on which fundamentally the status and the function of women in the churches depend is never entirely fixed. There is always a tension between what comes to a church from the gospel and from the church's own past history and tradition and what comes from outside, from society, where the economic, social and educational position of women is always changing. It is not a case of a fixed unchangeable Christian principle and church tradition being in tension with changing social attitudes.

The overriding question was always, "Are the gifts and willingness of women being used to the best advantage by the churches?" Bliss hoped through her work to suggest ways in which the service of women could be enlarged, the life of the church enriched and its message strengthened.

Bliss herself was one of the most prominent lay people involved in the WCC. She was named to the select group of theologians called together before the second assembly (Evanston 1954) to produce the main report on the theme "Christ — the Hope of the World". In Evanston she was elected to the Central Committee and by it to the Executive Committee, the first woman to serve in this position. From 1954 to 1968 she was at the heart of the central workings of the WCC, and greatly respected as a wise and trusted guide. She chaired the board of the Ecumenical Institute in Bossey and was a member of the editorial board of *The Ecumenical Review*. At the third assembly (New Delhi 1961) she became the chairperson of the Division of Ecumenical Action and a little later moderator of the commission responsible for the integration of the WCC and the World Council of Christian Education. She was one of the chief authors of a study paper, "Education and Nature of Man", prepared for the fourth assembly (Uppsala 1968).

During the same period she was active in the British Council of Churches, as well as serving from 1957 to 1966 as general secretary of the Board of Education of the Church of England — the first woman general secretary of a general synod board. When she left that position, she became one of the first women to head a university religious studies department — at the University of Sussex (1967-72).

After her retirement in 1972 Bliss and her family developed an interest in agricultural and environmental concerns which, like her concern for education, had begun in India. She withdrew somewhat from church affairs, impatient with the slow rate of change and disappointed by the failure of hopes for Anglican-Methodist reunion. Her last major project, a biography of Oldham, remained unfinished.

Kathleen Bliss died on 13 September 1989, after a long battle with cancer. Despite her illness, she had lost none of her intellectual vigour at 81. She died peacefully, surrounded by her family, praying the service of Compline, which had been her daily habit. As they came to the canticle *Nunc Dimittis* — "Lord, now lettest thy servant depart in peace..." — she smiled and stopped breathing.

Bliss described herself as "an Anglican inclining towards the Catholic wing", though very averse to extremes. Her parents were Baptists and she was brought up in the evangelical tradition, choosing later in life to join the Church of England. She wrote of her own spiritual journey:

> I was, in late childhood and adolescence, converted rather more times than is good for either the spiritual or mental health of anybody. But that these conversions never lasted shows that I am one of the failures of this kind of education... Even my baptism at 16, though I was impressed by the solemnity of it, both the preparation and the event, did not bring the lasting feeling of secure salvation that I had been led to expect.
>
> My school studies brought persistent nagging doubts. I found my religious vocation therefore in service and only years later did I find what, perhaps, I had been seeking all the time — the release from reliance on assessment of my own feelings which came when I could accept the bread and wine as the body and the blood of Christ, objectively there, given facts.

Bliss wrote of conversion in more general terms in her book *The Future of Religion*, published in 1969 in response to the "Death of God" debate.

> There are those who say "our image of God must go": the old man in the sky must be burnt like Guy Fawkes and we must set out to find a new way of thinking of God. I do not see it quite that way. I have had experience of waiting on the platform for a train: it comes in, but from the opposite direction: I get in and it moves off. Nothing corrects the overmastering impression that I am headed away from my destination. Thinking back to the place I was in and the journey to the station only confirms my worst forebodings of lost connections and broken engagements. I try to read, I look out of the window. Suddenly without being able to say why or how I feel I am travelling the opposite way: the train, the rails, the scenery have all done a volte-face. I can in my mind now repeat my journey to the station mirrorwise.
>
> I believe this happens in relation to the experience of God. What one thinks one ought to believe contradicts or does not connect with a lot of what one experiences and most values in life: you do what is the practical right next thing (get on the train in spite of the nagging "ought I not to have faith and go the other way?"), and lived experience asserts itself as reality and reorganizes past experience into continuity with it.
>
> This may well be a form of conversion experience in the modern world: that from searching the heavens to find God and attempting to be very spiritually-minded one slowly or suddenly becomes aware that what one needed but could not express was discernible by clues or flashes of insight or unexpected awareness as one's life was opened up to receive whatever would come largely unsought through events, sights, sounds, encounters, delight and afflictions.

Bliss was a *lay* Christian, and not just because in her lifetime the Church of England did not ordain women. With J.H. Oldham, Suzanne de Diétrich, Hendrik Kraemer and others she saw the role of the laity as a crucial matter of ecumenical concern if the church was to be present and relevant in the modern secularized world. In 1963 she published *We the People: A Book about Laity*, in which she emphasized the missionary vocation of every lay Christian to be the church in the world. All Christians, whatever their ultimate status and responsibilities, are first of all lay Christians, and the majority of Christians live their whole lives as lay people. She insisted that "both the ordained and the lay ministry are ministries in and to the world, within the wholeness of the people of God". The calling of the church is to be the people of God in the world to share in the sufferings of Christ in and for the world. "Christ asks us to share his sufferings in a world in which he is continuously at work. The promise to be with us comes from one who is always in front of us and beckons us on."

Her belief in the crucial importance of lay ministry influenced Bliss's attitude to the ordination of women, which she saw as secondary to the question of the possibilities open to lay women in the churches.

> The ministry of women directly affects only a very tiny minority of women in the church, whether one looks at the number who are actually ordained or at those who might want to be if the situation in their church were different. It is no slight upon the service of these women to their own churches to say that the most important part about the discussion of the ministry of women has been its indirect influence. The raising of the question, "should women be ministers?", has compelled those charged with answering it to re-examine the nature of the ministry, and without exception all churches which have seriously discussed the question of women in the ministry have also had to look to the broader aspect of the place of all women in the church.

Bliss spent most of her professional life working for the church and the ecumenical movement, but her concern was for the world. As she wrote:

> Unity means far more than uniting denominations or changing their relationships to one another. A united church concentrating only on its own life within ecclesiastical frontiers, however widely drawn, is not a *whole* church in any proper meaning of the word "whole"... What makes the word "ecumenical" so valuable today is that it holds together two things that must not be separated. It refers at once to the *whole* church and to the *whole* world...

Bliss was not an obviously pious person, and her keen intellect led her to be impatient with muddled thinking and critical of many aspects of the church. She was, however, a woman of faith who used her intellectual and spiritual gifts to serve the church and the ecumenical movement. In so doing she gave an outstanding example of lay leadership — all the more important at a time when leadership was predominantly a male clerical preserve. A long-time male colleague wrote after her death:

> A characteristic memory is of the act of worship with which the retiring Central Committee closed the short meeting in which they had run through the preparations for the Uppsala assembly, starting the next day. With a hundred thousand details to be cared for, the time was not appropriate for a long and meditative address, but few present had expected Kathleen to content herself with no more than three sentences! Yet they were three sentences which trenchantly pulled together the threads of vision and commitment in the work of that Central Committee over seven years, and when one of the younger men present dared to ask her afterwards how she had managed to be so brief, she replied, "Ah, but it took me more than two hours last night to think it out."

Bliss was also a person of hope, looking always to the future which God was making possible. Shortly before she died, she told the Archbishop of Canterbury, "God has opened so many doors to the church. We need more courage to go through them."

BIBLIOGRAPHY

Works by Kathleen Bliss:

The Future of Religion, Harmondsworth, Penguin, 1969.
The Service and Status of Women in the Churches, London, SCM, 1952.
We the People: A Book about Laity, London, SCM, 1963.

Dietrich Bonhoeffer
1906–1945

MARTIN CONWAY

Born into a wide and influential family network of intellectuals and public servants, Dietrich Bonhoeffer made his mark as an outstanding theology student in Berlin and quickly embarked on an academic career. Study opportunities in Rome, Barcelona and New York opened his mind and heart to other cultures, while the fiery conviction of Karl Barth's Christ-centred theology drew him into passionate opposition to anything self-serving and narrowly nationalistic in his own milieu, which flowered into a lifelong commitment to the Confessing Church called into being around Martin Niemöller soon after Hitler's accession to power.

At a conference in Cambridge in September 1931 Bonhoeffer was named one of three part-time youth secretaries for the World Alliance for Promoting Friendship through the Churches and for the Ecumenical Council for Life and Work, two key bodies in the nascent ecumenical movement of the 1930s. Between 1933 and 1935 he spent a crucial 18 months as pastor of one of the German congregations in London. There he devoted most of his energies to the early struggles of the Confessing Church and became a trusted friend of Bishop George Bell of Chichester, for whose prophetic leadership against Hitler's Nazi government of Germany Bonhoeffer provided much of the material and inspiration.

Returning to Germany, he took charge of an unofficial, later illegal, theological seminary of the Confessing Church at Finkenwalde in Pomerania. Its distinctive ethos, not least its innovations in spirituality and community living, are reflected in his books *The Cost of Discipleship* and *Living Together*. When this activity was totally proscribed, friends from the US invited him in June 1939 across the Atlantic, intending to preserve him from the likely storms of war. Within days he knew he had made the wrong decision, and he returned to Germany in a deliberate act of willing to share with his own people whatever was to come.

Family members then invited him into the demanding double life of a secret agent in the counter-espionage service, where a plot against Hitler was being prepared. This enabled him to visit W.A. Visser 't Hooft in Geneva, as well as church leaders in occupied Norway; and in May 1942 he met Bell in Stockholm in order to appeal for support for the plotters from the British and other Allied governments.

Bonhoeffer was arrested in April 1943 on suspicion of evading military service. The remaining two years of life he spent in prison, outwitting his interrogators, impressing his guards and fellow-prisoners with a deeply human and Christian style of living and writing the letters, poems and fragments of his *Ethics* which remain his finest memorial. In the confusion of the last weeks of war he was removed from Berlin to an extermination camp at Flossenbürg, near the Czech border, where he was hanged on 9 April 1945, minutes after entrusting to a British prisoner a message to Bell:

> Tell him that for me this is the end but also the beginning. With him I believe in the principle of our universal Christian brotherhood which rises above all national interests, and that our victory is certain — tell him too that I have never forgotten his words at our last meeting.

It was from listening to Bell's address at a broadcast memorial service in St Martin-in-the-Fields, London, on 27 July 1945 that Bonhoeffer's parents learned the details of his death.

Bonhoeffer was deeply respected, admired and loved in his lifetime by those who knew him. His lasting inspiration came through the devoted work of one of his students, Eberhard Bethge, husband of Bonhoeffer's niece, who discovered, deciphered, published and interpreted Bonhoeffer's writings in a long series of books from 1946 onwards. These have inspired, shaped and fortified countless other Christian witnesses in the former German Democratic Republic, South Africa, Korea and wherever else Christians have struggled for an integrity of life and obedience in face of the distinctive demands of the late 20th century.

Dietrich Bonhoeffer's life and work witness to a marvellously rounded and whole human being. Gifted with a powerful intellect, he was also a keen sportsman; strongly and passionately committed to the cause he espoused, he was also known for his ready humour and his ability to give time to relaxation and to friends and family. His friends remember him at least as much for the inspiration he was as for all that he said or wrote or did.

Those who can rely only on the records of his writing and speaking are nevertheless struck again and again by his insistence on bringing together features that so easily fall apart. His constant study of the Bible provides both fresh insight into what the stories meant then and what they point readers to for today. His unswerving insistence on the priority of what God has done in Jesus leads no less insistently into pointers to what God requires of his people in the here and now, not only in "religious" terms but also in regard to the human situations, often social or political, which face Christians as part of the total human community. His travel reports from Rome and the USA show at least as much interest in the overall culture and the social and historical particularities of those places as in the specific features of their churches or Christianity.

Thus Dietrich Bonhoeffer stands out as an ecumenical pilgrim in his witness to the God-given and God-encouraged wholeness of human living and human obedience.

Second, Bonhoeffer was one of the earliest and most convincing witnesses to the recovery of a sense of the church in the ecumenical movement between the two world wars. The key thesis in his promotion for his doctorate (at the age of 21!) was "The church is Christ 'existing in community'". In all his subsequent writing, as in his tireless struggles for the health and integrity of the Confessing Church, what rings out is this sense of the church as Christ's own body, Christ's own hands and voice, and so not subjected to any conventional worldly expectations or patterns of humanity.

This can be illustrated in at least two very different fields. On the one hand, Bonhoeffer's early travels and the encouragement of his teachers soon won him for the movement for the unity of Christ's church, for a vision of the church as nothing less than the entire flock of Christ's followers beyond all the barriers of time and space, language, race or culture, denominational or theological allegiance. Not that he was indifferent to these human factors. At times he could richly enjoy them, as is evident in his account of black churches in the USA. At other times he was fierce in his attack on heresy or betrayal: a long polemic over how international Christian bodies were handling the split between the "official" church and the Confessing Church in Germany led to his disengagement from and considerable disillusionment with the structures of ecumenical movement in the late 1930s. But he never faltered in believing in the church, the companionship of disciples, as Christ's sign and instrument in and for the world.

On another front, Bonhoeffer's practical guidance for his students at Finkenwalde, compiled in *Life Together*, is again and again eloquent, not to say startling, for the way in which it plunges familiar questions into the depths of Jesus' own — and continuing — spirituality. Those difficult psalms, for instance:

> A psalm we cannot utter as a prayer, that makes us falter and horrifies us, is a hint to us that here Someone else is praying, not we; that the One who is here protesting his innocence, who is invoking God's judgment, who has come to such infinite depths of suffering, is none other than Jesus Christ himself. He it is who is praying here, and not only here but in the whole Psalter. [1]

Or consider his commendation — astonishing for a "mainline" Protestant — of personal confession of sins to a brother:

> Christ became our Brother in order to help us. Through him our brother has become Christ for us in the power and authority of the commission Christ has given to him. He hears the confession of our sins in Christ's stead and he forgives our sins in Christ's name. He keeps the secret of our confession as God keeps it. When I go to my brother to confess, I am going to God. [2]

This is of course a deeply costly discipline. There is no triviality about belonging to Christ, but no lack of humour and humanity either. All that is good in human friendship and human loyalty is summoned to incarnate the grace of Christ's calling to all humanity to service in his body, the one, holy catholic and apostolic church.

Third, Bonhoeffer as a man and a thinker was always keenly aware of the concrete demands of faith and of obedience. His writing is often apparently quite "general" (*The Cost of Discipleship* is a sustained exhortation with hardly a post-biblical name in it and never a date or contemporary story to fix it in time and place); yet it breathes the immediacy, indeed the urgency, of being constantly and most practically directed towards the actual questions, needs and dilemmas of his increasingly demanding, even dangerous context.

From 1933 onwards Bonhoeffer was well aware of the precarious situation in which the Confessing Church was having to live and witness, personally committed to solidarity with it (think of his decision to abandon the safety of the USA in June 1939) and in the end well able to rise to the spiritual demands of the long months in prison while remaining a man of the universal church, witnessing to the Lordship of Christ in and over all humanity. In this way he foreshadowed the growing dilemma of the late 20th century, how to hold together the particularity of the very different cultures, situations and thus spiritualities of a complex world in a single, universal form of church that avoids both anarchy and dictatorship.

Fourth, mention must be made of Bonhoeffer's signal witness to God's commandment of peace. This may sound somewhat rhetorical in the case of a man who, while tempted in early years to a heroic pacifism, repeatedly thereafter denied that idealistic approach and in the end died because of his involvement in a murder plot. But in 1934, as a young man of 28, he was called to preach the sermon at a conference in Fanö of the Universal Christian Council of Life and Work. Announcing the threat of war to be expected from fascism and setting a marker for the later tensions and struggles of the 1930s, his words still ring out with their call for each succeeding age:

> Who will call us to peace so that the world will hear, will have to hear, so that all peoples may rejoice...? Only the one great ecumenical council of the holy church of Christ over all the world can speak out so that the world, though it gnash its teeth, will have to hear, so that the peoples will rejoice because the church of Christ, in the name of Christ, has taken the weapons from the hands of their sons, forbidden war, proclaimed the peace of Christ against the raging world.[3]

Ten years later, Bonhoeffer's understanding of the obedience of the Christian had grown immeasurably, not denying the hope and faith of that vivid sermon but deepening it with a sense of the suffering that had to be borne by men and women in discipleship of the Christ who had already borne it on the cross. In turn, that meant not just accepting suffering, but sharing in the guilt for Christ's sake, in order that humanity could share in the forgiveness and the new life of Christ's resurrection. A long section of his *Ethics*, entitled "The Structure of Responsible Life", offers an interpretation of what God expects from human behaviour which is remarkable both for its freedom from set rules or maxims and for its radical dependence on God and what God has done in Christ.

> Responsible action does not lay claim to knowledge of its own ultimate righteousness. When the deed is performed with a responsible weighing up of all the personal and objective circumstances and in the awareness that God has become man and that it is God who has become man, then this deed is delivered up solely to God at the moment of its performance. Ultimate ignorance of one's own good and evil, and with it a complete reliance upon grace, is an essential property of responsible historical action. The man who acts ideologically sees himself justified in his idea; the responsible man commits his action into the hands of God and lives by God's grace and favour.

That may stand both as the moving testimony of a Christian who has found his obedience in plotting the murder of his nation's leader, and as a profound call to a God-centred responsibility in all the ensuing ideological struggles and ideologically shaped tensions in any and every part of our world.

Bonhoeffer's personal involvement in the conferences and discussions of the ecumenical movement was short-lived, but the weight, import and indeed authority of his witness in these and other areas deservedly has been and remains immense.

* * *

To conclude the portrait of this ecumenical pilgrim, two excerpts from Bonhoeffer's writings. The first, from the Fanö sermon cited above, is a striking illustration of how his theological approach to the catholicity of Christ's church becomes immediately a vital appeal for the overcoming of the hatreds and nationalisms that scar our common humanity:

> What God has said is that there shall be peace among men — that we shall obey him without further question, that is what he means. He who questions the commandment of God before obeying has already denied him.
>
> There shall be peace because of the church of Christ, for the sake of which the world exists. And this church of Christ lives at one and the same time in all peoples, yet beyond all boundaries, whether national, social, political or racial. And the brothers who make up this church are bound together, through the commandment of the one Lord Christ, whose word they hear, more inseparably than men are bound by all the ties of common history, of blood, of class, and of language. All these ties, which are part of our world, are valid ties, not indifferent; but in the presence of Christ they are not ultimate bonds. For the members of the ecumenical church, in so far as they hold to Christ, his word, his commandment of peace, is more holy, more inviolable than the most revered words and work of the natural world. For they know that whoso is not able to hate father and mother for his sake is not worthy of him, and lies if he calls himself after Christ's name. These brothers in Christ obey his word; they do not doubt or question, but keep his commandment of peace. They are not ashamed, in defiance of the world, even to speak of eternal peace. They cannot take up arms against Christ himself — yet this is what they do if they take up arms against one another! Even in anguish and distress of conscience there is for them no escape from the commandment of Christ that there shall be peace.

The second is one of the poems that Bonhoeffer wrote while in prison. Perhaps his "masterpiece", it was written "in a few hours" on the evening of the day when he received the news that the 20 July 1944 plot against Hitler had failed. Death did not come for nearly nine months, but Bonhoeffer is clearly already facing that prospect with an unconquerable faith and hope.

Stations on the Road to Freedom

Discipline
If you set out to seek freedom, then learn above all things
to govern your soul and your senses, for fear that your passions
and longing may lead you away from the path you should follow.
Chaste be your mind and your body, and both in subjection,
obediently, steadfastly seeking the aim set before them;
only through discipline may a man learn to be free.

Action
Daring to do what is right, not what fancy may tell you,
valiantly grasping occasions, not cravenly doubting —
freedom comes only through deeds, not through thoughts taking wing.
Faint not nor fear, but go out to the storm and the action,
trusting in God whose commandment you faithfully follow;
freedom, exultant, will welcome your spirit with joy.

Suffering
A change has come indeed. Your hands, so strong and active,
are bound; in helplessness now you see your action
is ended; you sigh in relief, your cause committing
to stronger hands; so now you may rest contented.

Only for one blissful moment could you draw near to touch freedom;
then, that it might be perfected in glory, you gave it to God.

Death
Come now, thou greatest of feasts on the journey to freedom eternal;
death, cast aside all the burdensome chains, and demolish
the walls of our temporal body, the walls of our souls that are blinded,
so that at last we may see that which here remains hidden.
Freedom, how long we have sought thee in discipline, action, and suffering;
dying, we now may behold thee revealed in the Lord.

NOTES

[1] *Life Together*, London, SCM, 1954, p.31.
[2] *Ibid.*, p.87.
[3] *No Rusty Swords: Letters, Lectures and Notes 1928-1936*, London, Collins, 1965, p.286.

BIBLIOGRAPHY

Any full listing would be too long to be of use. The few suggestions here will get the reader started; several
   contain longer lists.

Works by Dietrich Bonhoeffer:

Letters and Papers from Prison (the original German title provided by Bethge was *Widerstand und
   Ergebung* — "Resistance and Submission"), enlarged ed. London, SCM, 1971. The indispensable
   window onto the prayers, thinking, conversations and interrogations of an unforgettable Christian.
Ethics, ed. E. Bethge, London, SCM, 1955. The very substantial, if often also tantalizing, fragments of a
   major work that Bonhoeffer was working on since his return to Germany in 1939.
The Cost of Discipleship, first ed. in German 1937, abridged ed. in English 1948, complete ed. in English
   with a foreword by Bishop George Bell and a memoir by G. Leibholz, London, SCM, 1959. Written
   for his students, and out of shared Bible study with them, this is a profound study of the theology and
   spirituality that sustained the adult Bonhoeffer.
Life Together, published in English 1954 by SCM, London, and Harper & Brothers, New York. A short
   manual for the community life, spirit and worship of Christians, modelled largely on the experience at
   Finkenwalde, bringing together careful theology and a radical attention to actual practice.

Biographies:

Eberhard Bethge, *Dietrich Bonhoeffer — Theologian, Christian, Contemporary*, first German ed., 1967; in
   English: London, Collins, and New York, Harper & Row, 1970. The definitive account and
   interpretation, admirably detailed and precise.
Mary Bosanquet, *Bonhoeffer: True Patriot*, London, Mowbrays, 1983. Possibly the most readable of the
   shorter biographies and interpretations drawn essentially from Bethge's monumental work.

Interpretations:

Keith Clements, *A Patriotism for Today — Dialogue with Dietrich Bonhoeffer*, first published 1984, 2nd ed.
   London, Collins, 1986. An inspiring example of Bonhoeffer's witness enabling and deepening the
   witness of other Christians — in this case the British struggling with economic decline and the
   nationalism aroused by the Falklands war. The same author has more recently published a set of essays
   all in one way or another taking Bonhoeffer's witness further into later explorations: *What Freedom?
   The Persistent Challenge of Dietrich Bonhoeffer*, Bristol Baptist College, 1990.
Eberhard Bethge, ed., *Bonhoeffer: Exile and Martyr*, with an essay by John de Gruchy, London, Collins,
   1975. Lectures written for visits to South America and South Africa, in which Bethge pulls together the
   significance of Bonhoeffer's life and witness for other situations of crisis and danger. The South
   African editor has since published his own *Dietrich Bonhoeffer: Witness to Jesus Christ*, London,
   Collins, 1988, with a selection of Bonhoeffer's writings.

Antoinette Butte
1898–1986

ELIZABETH PONTOPPIDAN

Antoinette Butte was born in Lunéville on 12 July 1898. Her father was a Catholic from Lorraine, her mother a Protestant from Alsace.

> I think my entire religious life has been guided by what I received from my upbringing. I come from a confessionally mixed family going back to the 19th century... marriage in both churches, contributions to both parishes, the boys belonging to their father's confession, the girls to their mother's; it worked very well, for the good of everyone... until it was forbidden. [1]

Baptized in a Lutheran church and confirmed in the Reformed Church, she showed her theological lucidity at an early age: "I very quickly realized what Catholicism added to the Christian faith and what Protestantism left out... I was strongly aware of Catholic paganism and Calvinist omissions." [2] As a teenager she listened in fascination to the discussions between her father and the parish priest of Parney as they analyzed and compared the two confessions.

Her father was killed in 1914 at the very beginning of the first world war. As a young woman she went to work at the hospital in Saumur, caring for the seriously wounded. The human tragedies she experienced there touched her deeply. The following year her family moved to Paris, and in 1916 she began her studies in law, developing an interest in free thinking and philosophical works. She also came into contact with the World Student Christian Federation and the *Mission populaire*, where in 1918 she underwent a conversion that led her to a deep faith. She wrote of being able "to feed and form myself at other sources" within the fantastic diversity of French Protestantism, including the Salvation Army, the Quakers, the Oxford groups and the revivals in the Drôme.

In the years that followed she and some friends — Protestant, Catholic and atheist — founded the Unionist Girl Guide Movement, which became the French Girl Guide Federation in 1921, with Butte as its first national commissioner. She also led a Christian students' group and was a good friend of Suzanne de Diétrich. Later she was also close to Madeleine Barot and Marc Boegner, with whom she shared the same ecumenical vision.

Having begun to train for the bar in Nancy, she fell seriously ill and had to abandon her many activities. For two years she could do nothing. This was when she discovered the life of prayer, of listening to God, of life with direction. She joined the *Tiers Ordre des Veilleurs* ("Third Order of Watchmen"), recently founded by Wilfred Monod. After her recovery, she set aside three days of retreat every month in a Salvation Army home.

In 1929 she left the bar, her scouting and her students behind and opened a place of spiritual retreat at Saint-Germain-en-Laye, in a house lent by the Reformed Church. So began her life in faith: silence, meditation on the Beatitudes, discipline in prayer, a life of poverty and dependence on God and on others for Christ's sake. She discovered the richness of the prayers of the Christians during the first centuries and in 1936 wrote her first book. [3]

In 1938, the *Association des Pasteurs de France* offered Antoinette Butte the château at Pomeyrol, near Tarascon (Provence), as a place of spiritual retreat. There she passed the war years with a few other women, leading a life of extreme poverty in very precarious conditions. The vigil of prayer continued uninterrupted. When the Catholic villagers heard the bell ringing four times a day to announce the offices, they said, "They are praying sisters, like our Sisters of the Visitation in Tarascon." After a few years they also talked about "our Pomeyrol sisters".

Throughout the years of war and occupation, Pomeyrol was a crossroads for Jews and others persecuted by the Vichy government, as well as a place where French Protestants met for reflection. In September 1941, W.A. Visser 't Hooft, general secretary of what was then the World Council of Churches in process of formation, came to Pomeyrol to present a report on the position of the European churches in regard to National Socialism. There the "Theses of Pomeyrol" were drafted, reworked and signed by leading Protestant personalities. In the name of the church they protested solemnly against "any legislation which rejects the Jews from the communities in which men live" and insisted that "resistance against every totalitarian and idolatrous influence is a spiritual necessity". [4]

After the war many Protestants came to Pomeyrol on retreats. With the other members of her team Butte set up home in the park of the château, using huts left by the occupying forces. The château itself was turned into a secular children's home called *Le rayon de soleil* ("Sunbeam"). In the winter Butte answered the request of the Protestant parishes in Alsace to organize spiritual retreats. In November 1951 the first four members founded the Community of Pomeyrol. Two years later, Pomeyrol, with Grandchamp and Taizé, affirmed their common calling to the service of Jesus Christ and the unity of their witness in the churches of the Reformation, acknowledging a deep level of communion in the diversity of the different forms practised by each community.

Sr Antoinette defended a thesis on *L'offrande: Office sacerdotal de l'Eglise* ("The Offering: A Priestly Office of the Church") at the Protestant Faculty of Theology in Montpellier. In 1963 she set out on a pilgrimage of several months with the Benedictines in the Holy Land, where she came into contact with a wide variety of Christians, Jews and Muslims. Ten years later the first edition of the *Chant des Bien-Aimés* ("Song of the Beloved") was published. In it Sr Antoinette tells of the wonders of God that she had witnessed since her youth. At 77, she passed the responsibility of the community over to Sr Elisabeth.

In 1981 Sr Antoinette had the great joy of opening a second community in the Cevennes, a region which has historically a majority of Protestants, a few kilometres from a community of Cistercian (Trappist) sisters in Cabanoule, with whom a friendship soon grew up.

On 30 April 1986 the Lord called his servant Antoinette Butte to himself.

* * *

The mystery of life in Christ sustained and inspired Antoinette Butte's whole life and made her an "ecumenical pilgrim".

Her spirituality and life were marked by the vision of the church as the Body of Christ and hence as *one*. All who live out the gospel are brothers and sisters in Christ and members of one and the same Body of Christ. This is why the Lord's supper in the Reformed Church is offered to all who are baptized. Sr Antoinette found it hard to understand that the discipline of certain churches should refuse "communion" to their "brothers and sisters". When they recognize one Lord and one baptism, and profess their faith in the same creeds of the first centuries, why then can they not all take communion at the same table? What is inter-communion? Cannot the Body of Christ have many members and respect the diversity of ministries?

As early as 1935 she expressed her faith in these terms:

> The universal church is the church which is the incarnation of the Body of Christ. We are not able to see God's work: we are still looking for our prayer to be granted, when in fact he is already there. For we have to learn to discern. God is at work. Humanly, practically, we can already perceive the universal church, the unity of all the churches.
> It is where Christ is incarnated.
> Where there is the Word — and everyone understands it to the best of their ability.
> Where there is the Lord's Supper — and everyone receives it with their best.
> Where there are the sacraments — because they are the means of grace.
> Where there are the signs of the Spirit — which can be recognized by their fruits.
> Where there is the real presence — in each sincere believer, however weak.
> Is not this in itself a fairly full and precise definition of the church?
> The unity of the church does not have to be created, but recognized. We have to recognize it.[5]

In such a vision of the church, writes Suzanne de Diétrich, the diversities and successive reformations are not necessarily divisions. What breaks the unity of the church, surely, are the divisions within each church, and between these churches. What makes it so difficult, really, is the fact that we all dream — arrogantly — of building a powerful institutional or dogmatic unity. This is a subtle temptation, the temptation of great souls — the very temptation which our Lord himself knew. "I will give you the whole world." "Winning the world to give it to God!... That has been the church's temptation throughout the ages."[6]

In France the separation of church and state in 1905 put an end to the long and often oppressive political and ideological supremacy of the Roman Catholic Church. After the Russian Revolution in 1917, many Orthodox families emigrated to France. Alongside the small Protestant community, this new religious minority came to add its own touch of colour to the Christian scene in France.

The experience of the second world war brought Christians in France back to the essentials of their faith. At the same time, the *Résistance*, in which French Catholics,

Protestants and Orthodox worked side by side with Jews and atheists, created an ecumenism on the ground parallel to the progress being made at the theological and dogmatic level.

The ecumenism practised by Sr Antoinette and the Pomeyrol community was entirely a product of this climate. Firmly rooted in the French Reformed Church, the community had Lutheran and Calvinist sisters from the very beginning and was surrounded by "companions" of different nationalities and confessions. However, Sr Antoinette never sought unity for unity's sake, but always out of a desire to deepen her life in Christ. Starting in the 1940s, she invited people to Pomeyrol for ecumenical Bible studies.

After the war ended, reconciliation between France and Germany was a matter of deep concern to Sr Antoinette, despite the lack of understanding and even hostility she encountered in some quarters. All too soon came the events in Algeria and another war (1954-62). At the request of the French ecumenical aid agency CIMADE, the tiny community of Pomeyrol agreed to let one of its members go to Algiers, where she lived a life of prayer and absolute poverty among the local Algerian villagers, who adopted her with affection and respect. The friendly relations between the Pomeyrol sisters and the Muslims in Algeria and their attention to Islam in France date from this period.

Deep links of fellowship and mutual spiritual aid were also formed with the neighbouring Catholic religious communities of Eygalière and the Visitation. The Pomeyrol community actively observes the Week of Prayer for Christian Unity and seeks contacts with the Catholics in the village. Its retreats are attended by both Catholics and Protestants. Every year the sisters request hospitality from another community, Protestant or Catholic, for a week of communal retreat, in which the diversity of the sisters' gowns reflects the diversity of their traditions. "Ecumenism is not an intellectual activity, but a spiritual one," Sr Antoinette often said. Communities of prayer are thus one form of the ecumenical movement; they are not simply the custodians of their own tradition.

The sisters have also participated in international and interconfessional meetings since 1970. In 1983 a sister was a delegate of the French Reformed Church to the WCC assembly in Vancouver, an opportunity to forge ties of fellowship and discover the riches Christians have to offer one another. During such visits Sr Antoinette always gave her sisters time to meet the local church of whatever tradition — Protestant, Catholic or Orthodox. In their fourth novitiate year, once they are familiar with Protestant communities of prayer, the novices of Pomeyrol are sent to live for six weeks in a Catholic convent with sisters of the contemplative tradition so that they can get to know their great liturgical life.

These rich relations with Roman Catholics can by no means be taken for granted in the south of France, where Protestants were persecuted for centuries. This was brought home to Sr Antoinette during a visit to villages between Nîmes and Arles with Sr Chantal, a Benedictine nun. Sr Chantal had been deeply moved when she had visited the ruins of the chapel at Domessargues in the course of her research into the history and origins of her order. She had the idea of restoring this chapel to its vocation as a place of prayer for the village. As the village was partly Catholic and partly Protestant, it had to be restored by everyone and for everyone. At first Sr Antoinette was doubtful about the venture, but then she said, "the Lord took hold of me. He was opening up a field of work for us which quite clearly went in the direction we wanted — working among the people of God at the grassroots, among a group of people who had been spiritually abandoned but who were nevertheless interested and open to the adventure of faith." With a Belgian priest, Fr Philippe Liessens, and with the help of Sr Danielle of Pomeyrol, work camps were organized over a number of years with Catholic and Protestant young people who bore a lively and joyful Christian witness among the local people. As a result, the people of the villages themselves set up a small ecumenical reception group in each village. Now the church is used for worship by the two communities in turn.

At the beginning of the 1960s, Sr Antoinette began to ponder the fact that the Feast of the Transfiguration was not observed in the Reformed Church. She invited some Orthodox speakers to reflect with the community on this feast, and this gave rise to an annual Transfiguration retreat (1-6 August), which has become a significant event on the French ecumenical scene. For a whole week young people, couples, children, parents, teenagers and grandparents gather together for prayer, worship and praise. Often the speakers return to take part in subsequent retreats and long-standing cooperation has developed with Orthodox and Catholic theologians and clergy. Everyone joins in preparing each celebration of the eucharist, especially the music, according to one of the three traditions of the church, respecting the tradition and the discipline of each so that no new schisms are created.

Starting in 1967 a new adventure began for the community. Two Yugoslav friends, one a Serbian Orthodox and the other a Baptist from Croatia, invited them to Zagreb to help with their ecumenical problems. Private contacts began to develop among Protestants, Orthodox and Catholics. In 1985 the international meeting of religious comunities was held in Zagreb, attended also by clergy and lay-people from what was then Yugoslavia and leading to many more meetings among the churches of the three confessions. A Pomeyrol sister continued to visit monasteries and parishes and was involved, among other things, in the rebuilding of an Orthodox monastery at Lepavina in Croatia. She organized work camps with the metropolitan of the diocese and young people from the Evangelical Church of Württemberg in Germany, so that ecumenical inter-church aid developed. Despite the outbreak of civil war Sr Ursula has untiringly continued her work of visiting and listening to the people in the parishes of former Yugoslavia, in all their diversity.

Throughout her long life of attending to others Sr Antoinette never ceased to learn from them. She welcomed homeless vagrants and prominent theologians alike at Pomeyrol, sharing her table with the same open heart. She displayed the same attitude in spontaneous encounters as well as in organized meetings with members of the different Christian confessions.

The offering of your life,
though you knew not what it would become.
A cloth little by little
woven around you,
without pattern or subtle design.

In this cloth you are a thread,
a splash of colour...
deep blue? bright red?
the thread of linen grey, perhaps?
the third colour, most important of all,
the weavers say.

The neutral grey of everyday,
the grey which lends beauty to the
blue and the red.
The grey which makes harmony,
a colour all its own and glad to be,
bringing joy, not rivalry.

And what of those who cannot
join with us in the weaving, or will not?
There is a place for everyone.
Each separate thread
mingling makes a whole...

Each thread, however bright,
can disappear, woven in with others.
Yet it is there, not far
though hidden from our sight...
Today your thread in turn
is woven through the warp.

When its colour is no longer seen,
then we shall see the beauty of the whole,
your thread of colour woven in
with all the others, mingling till it disappears.

The warp which is the base remains,
constantly renewed, and between its stretching threads
the fabric grows.

This is not vain offering
but creative strength,
joy, calm and serene,
the tapestry of love. [7]

The universal church — a tapestry of love! God is the weaver. A pattern of communion (*koinonia*) into which the churches are woven together with their ministers and their witnesses who have committed themselves to God's work. Antoinette Butte is one of these; her ecumenical pilgrimage has made her a thread woven into the tapestry of love.

The important thing for her was not to complete the work but to be part of it. To be, within the catholicity of the church, through her membership of the French Reformed Church, a hidden thread bringing out the colours God has given to the other churches. It is not a matter of engaging in ecumenism but of being ecumenical. It concerns the fulfilment of Christ's prayer "that they all may be one" (John 17:21).

Sr Antoinette herself said of her vocation that it was "a calling to prayer in the church. To attain to the fullness of the church's life through meditation and prayer... because unity is already given us in Christ and we simply have to recognize it and practise it." [8]

NOTES

[1] *Semences*, meditations, letters, testimonies, Editions Oberlin, 1989, p.36.
[2] *Ibid*.
[3] *L'incarnation, la Sainte-Cène, l'Eglise* ("The Incarnation, the Holy Supper and the Church"), Librairie Fischbacher, 1936.
[4] W.A. Visser 't Hooft, *Memoirs*, Geneva, WCC, 1973, p.131.
[5] *L'incarnation, la Sainte-Cène, l'Eglise*, p.199.
[6] Suzanne de Diétrich, *L'heure de l'offrande*, Neuchâtel/Paris, 1935, p.51.
[7] *Semences*, pp.169-70. Extract from a poem dedicated to Antoinette Butte for her 80th birthday.
[8] Article written in 1974, published in the French Protestant journal *Réveil*.

BIBLIOGRAPHY

Works by Antoinette Butte:

Le chant des bien-aimés, 2nd ed., Oberlin, 1984.
"La communauté de Pomeyrol", *Foi et vie*, no. 6, 1977, re-ed. Pomeyrol, 1988.
L'incarnation, la Sainte-Cène, l'Eglise, Fischbacher, 1936.
L'offrande, office sacerdotal de l'Eglise, Oberlin, 1965.
Pauvreté, beauté, amour, joie, introduction for people attending retreats, Pomeyrol.
Petite liturgie quotidienne, 4th ed., Pomeyrol, 1981.

Works on Sister Antoinette:

Semences, meditations, letters, testimonies, Oberlin, 1989.

Sarah Chakko
1905–1954

SUSANNAH HARRIS-WILSON

Sarah Chakko was one of the outstanding women India has produced. She possessed the rare combination of saintliness and humour; and the impression she left on those who met her was a lasting one, attested to by the abundant tributes to honour her after her death.

She was born in 1905 in Trichur, Cochin, South India, the fourth of ten children. Her parents belonged to the Syrian Orthodox Church, and its life and worship were a vital part of the Chakko family's spiritual development. The ancient rites were full of movement and colour — lighted candles, swinging censors, fragrant incense, the brightness of the priests' robes. The children listened spellbound to the ancient chants and stood reverently with their elders during a service lasting two hours or more. The richness and beauty of the Orthodox liturgy left a deep imprint on Sarah's mind.

There was another significant aspect of the church: it was the ancient church of a minority, with no money, little leadership and no theological colleges. Much of the credit for its survival from the time of St Thomas to our own day goes to the women of the church, who transmitted the faith in their families. Chakko herself said that her only theological training came by way of her mother's reading the Bible aloud in their home. From the continued sound of the Scriptures around her, she absorbed their teachings.

Chakko's father was for many years head of police and later head of the excise department in Cochin. Deeply concerned for the Christian community in India, he helped to found Union College in Alwaye, one of the country's first indigenous ventures in Christian higher education.

At home, Chakko helped her oldest sister Mary look after the other children, and when Mary went away to college Chakko became known as the "little mother" in the home. Even so, she had other independent ambitions; and, wishing to be a doctor, she begged her father to send her to the boys' school, where better science courses were offered. Though her family was tolerant and liberal, this her father would not allow.

Despite the heartbreak, Chakko's youthful stubbornness thus learned its limits; and, from this early acceptance of obedience, she learned also to let go of dreams and wait to see what life would offer in their stead.

She was sent instead to a local government school run for high-caste Hindu girls. This was followed by a course in Madras at Queen Mary's, a government college for women, where she studied history. When she received her degree in 1925, she decided that she wanted to become an educator. Her father disagreed, insisting that a woman's place is in the home and that she carry out his plan for her marriage. But she was determined to dedicate her life to teaching, completely sure of what God wanted her to do. After a battle of wills over several months, her father was eventually persuaded to allow her some practical experience of teaching in the Bentinck High School of the London Missionary Society in Vepery, Madras.

This seems to have been just what Chakko required to confirm her in her vocation. The principal was one of the most progressive educators in India, serving for the barest pittance of a salary. Life for both staff and students was utterly simple. After two years' practice teaching, Chakko went to Presidency College, Madras, to obtain her master's degree, and in 1930 she was appointed to teach history at Isabella Thoburn College, an American Methodist foundation at Lucknow, North India.

As well as teaching history, Chakko involved herself in every aspect of college and community life at Lucknow. For her, punctuality was as important as classroom studies; and the enthusiasm, alertness and control of a team game were appropriate training for life itself. So, too, in college dramatics, she understood the need to draw a character into oneself before one could project it convincingly. The community included not only teachers and students, to whom she was available, but also the college servants and their spouses and children, whom she treated as equals in the college family since they were equals in the sight of God.

One of the heads of department at Lucknow University, commenting on her enormous influence over his men students, remarked:

> No other educationist in India possessed a personality and sense of dignity and self-respect like hers. Though a strict disciplinarian, instead of awe she inspired respect, admiration and confidence in the minds of students. The fact that [her] college was almost the only institution in this town which functioned regularly during the strike and consequent closure of the university last year was sufficient testimony of her ability, her tact and her administrative capacity.

Chakko's range of interests and activities led her into a variety of geographical and cultural environments and gave her contact with an even greater variety of men and women. In 1937 she studied at the University of Chicago, where she received a master's degree in education, and at the University of Michigan. But underlying everything was a strong commitment to the central vision of being a Christian educator in India. She had a concern to create a spirit, a culture and a place which was not only Christian but truly Indian and expressive of an Indian understanding of Christianity. This deep gratitude towards her own cultural heritage equipped her well for her pioneering ecumenical and international role.

Her first such activity was in the Student Christian Movement of India, Burma and Ceylon. In 1933 she was an Indian delegate at the SCM area conference in Java, and in 1936 she went to a conference of the World Student Christian Federation in San Francisco. Even after her appointment as principal of Isabella Thoburn College, she continued to give a great deal of time and interest to the SCM. In 1947, for example, she was one of a small team sent by the Indian SCM on a mission to university students of China. At the same time, she served on the national committee of the YWCA of India, Burma and Ceylon and in 1947 was one of the vice-presidents of the World YWCA.

However active she became outwardly, it is clear that, as an observer notes, "her public life was fed by springs of private and personal devotion which... sustained and controlled her" and which were rooted in her Syrian Orthodox origins. If her *role* was a delegate to or chairman or secretary of one of these bodies, her *identity* was with the Orthodox community. During her years in Lucknow she had worshipped in a Methodist church, since there were no Syrian Orthodox churches there. But she felt the lack of her own ritual and ceremonies very keenly. Invited to attend the WCC's first assembly in Amsterdam, Chakko made it clear that the only way she was prepared to go was as a Syrian Orthodox. When Methodist Bishop G. Bromley Oxnam wrote back saying that she was chosen to represent not the Methodists but the younger churches, she protested that her church was hardly "young", being 1600 or 1700 years old. Before she accepted the invitation to the assembly, she consulted her Orthodox bishop, who gave her permission to attend.

For the WCC's second assembly (Evanston 1954), the Syrian Orthodox Church named her as an official delegate. Delighted, she noted proudly that such an appointment "establishes the principle that a woman *can* work in an official capacity in the Orthodox Syrian Church. There has never been any rule against it, but it has never been done."

It was entirely in character for her to take a leave of absence from Isabella Thoburn to be in Amsterdam and Geneva during the formative years of the WCC, and in particular to assist in the early days of the Commission on the Life and Work of Women in the Churches.

In Chakko's lifetime feminism had not yet surfaced in its contemporary form, and for her the "woman's question", when it arose, was not an isolated issue and never a "cause". In her student days Chakko had been known as a champion of causes, especially on behalf of underdogs. At Isabella Thoburn she came to realize the futility of fighting one's way through life, even on behalf of others: "I realized that a time will come when fighting will be of no use, but a time will never come when love will be of no use." The fact that love was her incentive in any advocacy of change, her sense that love made certain demands for wholeness, softened the edge of any criticisms she had to make and made it possible for men to accept them. Madeleine Barot summed up this gift and power:

> Sarah never lost her genuinely feminine character, and was thus able to prove in a particularly brilliant way, by her own personal manner, what a woman can achieve — this despite the fact that she belonged to one of the most tradition-bound of the Christian churches, in one of the countries where woman is most sheltered.

Chakko did voice criticisms when she had them. They arose from her evident belief in the contribution women had to offer both church and society. Certainly she made it clear that she expected men to behave with more maturity and charity than they often did. In the diaries of her travels in post-war Europe there is an implicit rebuke of the institutional church's blatant neglect of women, their needs, and their aspirations:

One is very much intrigued by the concept of "woman" underlying church and public life in Europe. In countries where women have political rights they are not found in any significant numbers in places of trust and responsibility. In some churches where women were ordained to the ministry during the war and did serve their congregations effectively, a reaction seems to have set in, and women ministers are asked to confine their service to women and children.

All this is very puzzling to one who has come from a land where the Christian conception of womanhood has served as a dynamic in social and public life. The church in many so-called "mission lands" pioneered women's education, gave them their rightful place in society, and offered them opportunities of service. Many of the European missionary women workers find in these lands greater opportunities for creative service than in their own home countries.

Women themselves found something in Chakko which drew out of them a fuller and more confident life. The freedom with which Chakko inspired other women always carried with it a larger vision of responsibility and self-giving; and while it encouraged wholeness, it never gave room to cold ambition or self-pity. The growth into humanness was Chakko's achievement. For her the motivating image was to become more fully ourselves. She saw clearly that this meant giving up a certain kind of power and recognition: "Don't ever expect the reward for service to be expressed in gratitude or appreciation by those among whom you work. The reward lies in what service does to you yourself — the richness, the sympathy, the humanness it brings you."

Chakko rejoiced in the "givens" of her life: her own sex, her own culture, her own religious tradition. Largely through her witness, the WCC women's department was characterized by a vision of reconciliation and cooperation between men and women rather than being just another women's desk over against all the activities in which men were engaged.

In her work for the WCC, Chakko had the opportunity to travel widely. Even after her return to Isabella Thoburn in 1951, when she already knew that her health was impaired, she found her ministry outside India at least as demanding as her work for the college. She made official visits to churches throughout Europe, America and North Africa, seeking always to encourage and evaluate and educate a wider women's ministry. She was asked to chair international conferences, to address conventions and to deliberate at executive sessions.

In August 1951, Professor T.C. Chao of China, one of the WCC presidents, felt it necessary to resign from the Central Committee on political grounds. Chakko was chosen to succeed him "in recognition of her exceptional service to the whole ecumenical movement". Furthermore, at her insistence, the final Central Committee meeting before the Evanston assembly was held in Asia — at Isabella Thoburn College, in January 1953.

Over Christmas 1952, the World Christian Youth Organizations held a world conference at Kottayam, near Chakko's home in India. She chaired the Indian planning committee for this event and welcomed the delegates, expressing the hope that they would "come face to face with all kinds of challenges, from the ancient faiths and from modern ideologies, that from this learning we may become the channels through whom the message of Christ our Lord reaches those who hunger and thirst after the things of God". Within days of the close of this youth conference, Chakko was welcoming the dignitaries and leaders of the churches in her own college at Lucknow.

The following months were filled with college duties and preparations for the Evanston assembly. In January 1954 she was busy with her duties as educational inspector in Lucknow. Roshan Jehan Begam, principal of Karamat Hussein Girls' College, recalls the gracious way she conducted the inspection and her remarks upon leaving: "I am going on leave for a month, at the end of February." "To fly to another country?", someone asked. "No, I have cancelled all invitations. I am going to see my mother and to sleep at home."

On January 25 she was taking part in a game of basketball with the students. In the interval, she sat down to rest — and died of a heart attack.

At her death Chakko was accorded the kind of public recognition she believed no one should expect. Journalists — from the *The Times* of London to small secular and religious magazines around the world — regarded her passing as newsworthy. W.A. Visser 't Hooft noted that "there were not only letters and telegrams from well-known church leaders, but from very simple people, e.g. from the owner of the residence where Chakko used to live in Geneva". Chakko's funeral took place the day after she died, yet over one thousand people attended — obviously most of them from Lucknow. The fame and the cosmopolitan style of Chakko's final year had not in any way diminished her commitment to Isabella Thoburn and the daily tasks which her call as an Indian Christian educationist imposed.

The eucharistic quality of Sarah Chakko's life, her pronounced thankfulness for what was given to her to be and do, is expressed in the closing paragraph of the annual report she prepared for the governors of the college in the week of her death:

> For me personally, the year has been one of great enrichment. The state of my health, which made it imperative that I stay put for a period of time, made it possible for me to concentrate on details of work in the college. I have found in this chance of concentration a fullness of satisfaction denied me before.
>
> It has been a constant joy to work on complex human problems with groups of dedicated colleagues who are also one's personal friends... The teamwork of the group is something that each one of us will ever cherish. In the absence of a physical education instructor, the informal contact with the students on the playing fields has been invaluable... All through the year, through happy times and difficult times, I have felt the touch of God transforming our problems into opportunities and beckoning us onward to greater usefulness. I thank God for his gift of work and the fellowship of the saints.

Shoki Coe (C.H. Hwang)
1914–1988

JOHN S. POBEE

Shoki Coe was a pioneer in the ecumenical discussion of contextual theology. He made his contribution to the world and the ecumenical movement on the basis of a solid academic background. He studied philosophy at Tokyo University, significantly during the Japanese occupation of his own country — Formosa, now Taiwan. Between 1937 and 1947 he studied theology at Cambridge University, working thereafter at the School of Oriental and African Studies. He did further theological studies at Union Theological Seminary, New York, in 1959 and 1960. His thinking was very much influenced by the writings of Søren Kierkegaard and Karl Barth.

From 1949 to 1965 he was principal of Taiwan (Presbyterian) Theological College. From there he moved to the Theological Education Fund (TEF), a service of the WCC Commission on World Mission and Evangelism, first as an assistant director (1965-70) and then as director (1970-77), succeeding James Hopewell. After his retirement, he served for two years as a consultant to the Programme on Theological Education, the successor body to TEF. He also served on the advisory committee which carried out the evaluation of the first mandate of the TEF.

Shoki Coe was a person who keenly discerned the signs of the times. He was conscious that the 1940s were revolutionary times, and that the changes in old orders described in words like modernization and industrialization were also important for theology. "The task", he wrote, "is how we can serve our churches constructively so that they may in turn act responsively and creatively in the new situation emerging in our land." [1] This was his way of articulating the missionary vocation of the churches.

His understanding of the missionary vocation was a multi-faceted one. A primary element was his conviction that, contrary to contemporary perceptions of mission as a one-way stream from North to South or West to East, and the resultant "beggarly mentality", each place has a missionary vocation and responsibility: "The home base now is everywhere and as we recognize this in every country, the missionary task takes on new perspective." [2]

Second, the missionary vocation is about living the Christian faith with imagination and courage. For example, he wrote that "we must not be tied to the thought that we shall always be a small minority nor always live in isolation from each other."[3] It was this he saw as giving contextuality its importance for the life of the church. It is a search after "a new living language of Christian faith".[4]

Third, Shoki Coe believed that the missionary vocation has to be lived out with an ecumenical perspective and urgency. Applied to his own country, the ecumenical perspective meant asking "how the body of Christ might become more visible in Formosa today and tomorrow in spite of the existing divisions among the church. In practice this meant, how could we take joint action in mission at serious strategic points, so that we might be obedient to the living Lord of the church now?" Obedience to the Lord is and should be our ultimate concern.[5] But alongside the vision of ecumenism he understood clearly that the problem "is the nature of our 'togetherness'".[6] The ecumenical vision is about crossing national and denominational boundaries. It is about integration of each and all and therefore getting rid of every trace of "the Invisible Man". It is about consensus and mobility.

It was natural for Shoki Coe to come to the staff of TEF. As principal of Taiwan Theological College he had brought to theological education and the churches prophetic and charismatic gifts and initiated important movements in the life of the church. Indeed, he was to become the personification of the mutual influence that TEF and theological training centres in the third world would come to exercise on each other. His book *A Rethinking of Theological Training for the Ministry in the Younger Churches Today* not only criticized "church-directed ministry", that is, clergy-oriented and one-person ministry, but also proposed a "world-directed ministry".

Moreover, it was Shoki Coe who contributed the term "contextualization" to the vocabulary of theological education. On the analogy of the idea of "demythologizing" popularized by Rudolf Bultmann, the great German New Testament theologian, he put forward the proposal that a "de-contextualization" of Western church and theology was a precondition for a "re-contextualization" by the so-called younger churches. Making a distinction between indigenization and political opportunism, he stressed that the incarnation process is indispensable for theology in the younger churches and, therefore, for contextualization.

Although by vocation a theologian, educator and churchman, Shoki Coe had keen political sensitivities. This was a natural consequence of his thoughts on "world-directed ministry". The nationalist government of the Kuomintang, led by General Chiang Kai-Shek, saw the Presbyterian Church and Taiwan Theological College as potential centres of Formosan feeling. Soon the issue arose of whether one who believes in Jesus Christ must necessarily be an anti-communist. The litmus test issue became the question of whether or not the People's Republic of China, with its communist government, should be accepted as a member of the United Nations. The World Council of Churches, of which the Presbyterian Church of Taiwan was a member, had publicly supported acceptance of China. As a consequence, the Taiwan government, under pressure from the USA, tried to force the Presbyterian Church to withdraw from the WCC. Shoki Coe's role in exposing the real reasons for the church's withdrawal letter of July 1970 enabled the WCC to postpone any decision.

The courageous stances which Shoki Coe took on social issues did not endear him to the nationalist government. For security reasons, his family left Taiwan in 1959, and he went into "voluntary exile" in 1965. During this period, particularly after his retirement, Shoki Coe was one of the founders of the Formosan Christians for Self-Determination, of which he became the unofficial leader. It is significant that the movement retained the word "Formosa" in its name, for it underscored the search of the island people for independence from Chiang Kai-Shek and the Kuomintang. The aim of the movement was and is to give visible demonstration of the Christian view of human rights on the island and to work towards a free and just government and society.

But although Shoki Coe was involved in politics, and unashamedly so, he was not a politician. He was first and foremost a Christian and a theologian who allowed his faith and theology to influence his life in church and in the state. Would that many a church person and theologian might emulate his example!

Shoki was a very human, very loving person, rooted in the world and yet mindful of things transcendent. He had tremendous energies; and was well-known at commission meetings for keeping late hours during which he dispensed stimulating conversation (with refreshment) to all and sundry. His wife was a tough ally and supporter of his activities.

NOTES

[1] C.H. Hwang, "Into a New Era Together", in R.M. Orchard, *Witness in Six Continents*, London, Edinburgh House Press, 1963, p.113.
[2] *Ibid.*, p.117.
[3] *Ibid.*, p.116.
[4] *Ibid.*
[5] *Ibid.*, p.112.
[6] *Ibid.*, p.116.

Ioan Coman
1902–1987

ION BRIA

One of this century's great Orthodox theologians and outstanding figures in Romanian society and European culture was the patrologist and philosopher Ioan Coman. Renowned as the author of a classic three-volume treatise on patrology, he was also a witness to his cultural heritage alongside such great Romanian scholars as Nicolae Iorga, Vasile Pârvan and Mircea Eliade. But above all it was the personality of Ioan Coman, combining erudition, a vocation to the priesthood and moral values, which makes him stand out as an exemplary incarnation of the genius of Romanian Orthodoxy and emphasizes his importance to the ecumenical community.

Romanian theology benefitted greatly from Coman's vast ecumenical horizon.[1] Lecturing as professor of patristics in Bucharest he had the figure of a prophet, speaking with gravity, joy and emotion. Insisting firmly on the need for a solid academic formation of priests and theologians, he was one of the great teachers and scholars who brought a high academic level and prestige to the Theological Institute of the old Bucharest University after it was integrated into the structure of the church in 1948. He was a professor at the Institute from 1944 to 1970 and dean from 1954 to 1961.

In 1946, Coman was one of the influential participants in the Second Congress of Orthodox Faculties in Athens, where he presented a paper on "The Church Presence in the World". In 1948, he wrote an important paper on "The Orthodox Church and the Ecumenical Movement", presented by the Romanian delegation to the Inter-Orthodox Conference held in Moscow in July 1948.[2] The conference decided not to be represented at the first assembly of the World Council of Churches in Amsterdam a month later. As a matter of fact, Coman was the only Orthodox theologian who defended the ecumenical movement in this difficult period, saying that the unity question concerns the "ecclesiology" of all churches.

His teaching, writing and preaching promoted the encounter between theology and culture, theology and poetry.[3] Widely read in classical Greek and Latin, he also held a doctorate in history of religions from Strasbourg University. Coman believed that theology has something in common with aesthetics and philosophy. His lectures to the students and the poetical sermons he delivered in St Spyridon Church in Bucharest remain one of the premier examples of Romanian church oratory in our times.

The fruits of Coman's research in patristics are compiled in his three-volume treatise on patrology,[4] which constitutes an excellent introduction to the projected 100-volume collection of the writings of the church fathers now being translated and published in Bucharest. The first Romanian-language handbook on the subject to use modern methods of theological research, its dominant feature remains its identification of the ecumenical spirit of the church fathers. Based on this open character of the patristic tradition, Coman criticized those who try to isolate the Orthodox tradition.[5]

Of the major ecumenical implications of Coman's theology, the most important contribution is perhaps the theology of *Logos* placed at the centre of biblical and Eastern thought. The ancient church began the reading of the New Testament with the prologue of St John's gospel (at the midnight liturgy of Easter). The importance of this tradition is that it shows that the incarnate Word is one and the same person with the *Logos* who created the world. The *Logos spermatikos* (Creator) is identical with the *Logos prophorikos* (the historical, incarnate Word) and the *Logos agoristis* (the Redeemer). The history of creation and the history of salvation are inseparable. The image of the Pantocrator reveals this identity.

Another strong emphasis of his theology was christocentric anthropology.[6] Coman emphasized the healing of the human being through positive ascetical virtues, but also by communion with a living community. The world is the place for all, a city of justice and freedom.[7] Christian spirituality is demanding. It requires tenacity and courage, particularly to reveal human situations and conditions which directly contradict the values of the gospel. In this connection, Coman recalled the example of St John Chrysostom, who paid the price for criticizing the sin of rapacity and unjust imperial laws.

Part of the theology of *Logos* is the theology of culture. On the basis of his familiarity with the history of religions and Byzantine and European philosophy, Coman proposed a working principle in the gospel and culture encounter: he favoured restoration of secular wisdom (*logos*) through transcendence (*epektasis*) and transfiguration (*theosis*).

Ioan Coman was the founder of a new discipline: ancient Romanian patristics. During a patristics congress in Oxford he introduced this important chapter of the history of Romanian theology. Due to his research in this field, we know better the ancient roots of Romanian theology, expressed by several ecclesiastical witnesses from Dobroudja, near the Black Sea. There is a theological tradition from that region which goes back to St John Cassian (4th century), about whom Coman wrote: "We esteem that the Romanian Church should canonize him, under the name Cassian the Romanian from Scythia Minor."[8] He described the character of Romanian Orthodox Christianity as determined by two factors: the Latin language and culture on the one hand, and Eastern doctrine and liturgy on the other hand.

Coman made a substantial contribution to modern ecumenical theology. Besides his study on *Orthodoxy and the Ecumenical Movement* for the 1948 Moscow conference, he is well-known for his research on the notions of Tradition and reception in the doctrinal decisions of the ecumenical councils.[9] He also wrote on the relationships between Orthodoxy and the Old Catholic Church. The principle of ecumenicity which he formulated is organically related to the method of *oikonomia*. There was no trace of alienation, sectarianism or excommunication in the minds of the church fathers; therefore, there is no patristic reason to criticize without discernment the doctrine and practice of other Christian confessions. Part of ecumenicity is recognition of the diversity in culture, history and spirituality. The ecumenical community is built on honesty, competence, discernment and love.[10]

The "appeal to the fathers" constitutes a point of reference for understanding both church history and the doctrine of the faith. Ioan Coman liked to speak about the "*symphonia* of the fathers", the living dialogue between all parts of the universal church. After a conciliar-dialogical period in the history of the church follows a period in which a confessional-monological method prevails. If the Orthodox theologians adopted a conservative, polemical attitude after the great separation between East and West, it was because they did not accept that the doctrine of the universal church could be formulated separately by one part of the *oikoumene*, outside of a dialogue between East and West.

During the period of the ecumenical consolidation of Christianity, the church fathers identified the great convictions of church unity. Coman summarized the contribution of the patristic tradition to the ecumenical efforts of today as follows:

> (1) The calculation of the Christian era, which was adopted by the whole church; (2) a new vision of world history, based on hope, prayer, creative work, spiritual development (*epektasis*); (3) the recognition of the nations and peoples, for whom the church created languages and literature; (4) the promotion of a religious ecumenism, through the ecumenical and regional councils, exchange of letters and visits, circulation of works and concepts; (5) the fathers have a veneration for peace, the mother of all virtues; they are against violence, war, and crime; (6) they created a new literary gender of *philokalia* (love of beauty); (7) the human being is made in the image of God: a patristic humanism is based on two forces — *Logos* and *agape*.[11]

Coman has reminded us that there is a philosophical component and element in Eastern theology. He drew attention to the ecumenical mind of the church fathers, which should inspire the present-day ecumenical movement and dialogue. Above all, we are forever grateful to him for the irenic quality of his works and heritage — his irenic theology, humanism and ecumenism.

NOTES

[1] A tribute to Coman by the faculty of the Theological Institute in November 1982 was published in *Romanian Orthodox Church News*, no. 4, 1982, pp.41-43.

[2] Cf. *Actes de la Conférence des Eglises orthodoxes* (1948), vol. 2, Moscow, 1952, pp.2-86.

[3] Initial biographical and bibliographical studies of the heritage of Ioan Coman include those by Stefan Alexe, *Studii Teologice*, 1-2, 1973, pp.98-114; Ioan Caraza, *ibid.*, 7-10, 1981, pp.542-46; and Ioan Ramureanu, *ibid.*, 1-2, 1982, pp.79-80. Examples of his articles show the range of his interests in patristic theology and philosophy, history of religions, Byzantine culture, classical Greek literature and the history of Romanian theology and spirituality; cf. "The Dacian-Roman Patristic Spirituality" (3rd-7th centuries), *Biserica Orthodoxá Romaniá*, 7-8, 1973, pp.565-89; "Theologians and Theology in Scythia Minor (4th-6th centuries)", *ibid.*, 7-8, 1978, pp.784-96; "The Patristic Literature in the Danube Region (4th-6th centuries) as the Origin of the Dacian-Roman and Romanian Culture and Literature", *ibid.*, 7-8, 1981, pp.775-81.

[4] *Patrologia*, 3 vols, Bucharest, Biblical Institute, 1984-89; a one-volume version was published in 1957.

[5] Cf. "Aspects of St John Chrysostom's Ecumenism", in *Telegraful Roman*, 33-34, 1986.

[6] Cf. "L'éthos humaniste des Pères", *Contacts*, nos 78-79, 1972, pp.177-203; "Eléments d'anthropologie dans les œuvres de St Justin", *ibid.*, no. 84, 1973, pp.317-37.

[7] Cf. "The World According to Orthodox Patristic Teaching", in *The Sofia Consultation Report*, Geneva, WCC, 1982, pp.61-64.

[8] *Ortodoxia*, 4, 1978, p.565.

[9] Cf. "The Doctrinal Definition of the Council of Chalcedon and its Reception in the Orthodox Church of the East", *The Ecumenical Review*, vol. 22 no. 4, 1970, pp.363-82.

[10] Cf. "St Basil the Great and Atarbies: Between Calumny and Honesty, Ignorance and Discernment, Isolation and Ecumenicity", *Mitropolia Banatului*, 9-10, 1983, p.555.

[11] *Patrologia*, vol. 1, pp.5-6.

Leslie E. Cooke
1908–1967

THEO TSCHUY

From 1955 until his premature death in 1967, Leslie Cooke was director of the World Council of Churches' Division of Inter-Church Aid, Refugee and World Service. He provided leadership in this important area of ecumenical involvement during the crucial period when the churches' participation in European reconstruction after the second world war and the integration of millions of refugees from the East drew to a close, and the worldwide ministry to the vast regions beyond Europe began to open up: the Middle East, Asia, Africa, Latin America and the Caribbean.

This transition was delicate for various reasons. The WCC itself was of recent origin. Would its precarious structures be able to manage this expansion? The Cold War, which had already divided Europe into two armed camps, was expanding throughout the rest of the world. Any ecumenical aid to churches in an emerging non-aligned or socialist nation could easily give rise to charges of "leftism" if not "pro-communism". Moreover, as European churches regained their economic strength in the 1960s, diplomatic finesse was needed to reassure US and Canadian churches that their role in ecumenical inter-church aid was still essential, even though they no longer contributed 80 percent, as they had during the immediate post-war period. Finally, as the Division extended its work into the third world, careful dialogue was necessary with the missionary agencies, boards and societies grouped together in the International Missionary Council (after 1961 the WCC Division on World Mission and Evangelism). As mission churches became autonomous, would there not be a danger of new dependency through inter-church aid? In this multiple dialogue Cooke further developed his ecumenical creativity and refined his convictions, continuously mindful of the rapidly evolving world situation.

Cooke's spiritual home was British Congregationalism, which also gave the ecumenical movement such noted leaders as A.E. Garvie, Norman Goodall, Douglas R. Horton and Henry Smith Leiper. In their youth both of Leslie Cooke's parents had been formal members of the Church of England. As a young working man from Brighton, his father had a conversion experience and joined the Plymouth Brethren.

> Then he met my mother and took her to the Plymouth Brethren meeting, and she said to him when they came away, "Bob, if you are going to marry me you will have to find a different church, because I am not going to sit among the damned while you sit among the elect." So they decided to find a Congregational church and they were both happy in it. That is how I came to be a Congregationalist.[1]

In his biographical sketch of Leslie Cooke, Norman Goodall wrote:

> While still a schoolboy he became powerfully conscious of a call to the Christian ministry. This eventually led him to Lancashire Independent College, Manchester, where he was greatly stimulated by its principal — Alexander Grieve — a teacher of great and original intellectual gifts, as independent in spirit as in his churchmanship. Here Leslie took his B.A. degree (Manchester University) in 1930, and his B.D. in 1933. In later years he received the honorary degree of D.D. from Chicago Theological Seminary (1949) and Victoria College, Toronto (1950). Mount Allison College, New Brunswick (Canada) awarded him an Ll.D. in 1954.[2]

His transition from his parents' rigid view of verbal inspiration to a wider understanding of the Bible did not proceed without some jolts. While his own understanding of the Bible broadened under the cultured and gracious understanding of his minister, he later admitted that when he went to college he experienced a shock by his introduction to lower and higher criticism. Entering the ministry with what he described as "a certain competence in handling the critical apparatus", he arrived at positive biblical affirmations primarily on the basis of pastoral experience and further reflection. This inner struggle provided depth to his preaching. He became a first-rate speaker in the great tradition of Anglo-Saxon rhetoric, and many churches requested his services. Even after his move to Geneva, he used his rare free moments for biblical exegesis and preparing sermons.

Steeped in biblical theology, Leslie Cooke saw world poverty and human injustice as perversions of God's creative intentions. He held that the encounter of modern biblical criticism with human reality would lead to an unprecedented mental change within Christianity. Arriving in New York on a wartime journey in 1944, he chastized a US censor who, on checking his belongings, remarked caustically: "Only sermons, only a Bible — OK." That man, Cooke mused later, apparently had never read or understood a radical text like Mary's Magnificat.[3] His social and political analyses were infused by his biblical knowledge, which enabled him to see the signs of the times in the expectation of God's coming kingdom.

Leslie Cooke was ordained in 1933 and ministered to a small Congregational church in Gatley, Cheshire. There he married Gladys Evelyn Burrows in 1936. The marriage was childless. As pastor of the large Congregational church in Warwick Road in Coventry, he witnessed the brutal air raids on this beautiful mediaeval city in 1941 and 1942. His own church was so severely damaged that it had to be torn down. Amidst the chaos he provided pastoral care to the wounded and dying and, together with the Anglican bishop and the mayor of Coventry, he organized relief and sought shelter for the homeless. For the first time the combination of his pastoral and organizational talent came to the fore. Out of this partnership with the bishop grew the Chapel of Unity, with the Cross of Nails, in the restored Cathedral. Years later, after

Cooke had moved to Geneva, he cherished the invitation to share in the dedication of this chapel.

In 1948, at the age of 40, Leslie Cooke became Minister Secretary of the Congregational Union of England and Wales. As Goodall wrote:

> During the next seven years he gave himself with zest and great competence to a task which he believed to be imperative, namely, bringing the Congregational churches in England and Wales into greater cohesion with one another without impairing the spiritual authority and integrity of the local church. The pursuit of this aim was far from easy, and it was made all the harder by the conditions of life in Britain during the immediate post-war decade. [4]

Cooke's style of leadership and alertness to new developments inevitably brought him into early contact with both the British Council of Churches and the World Council of Churches. He was a delegate to the WCC assemblies in Amsterdam (1948) and Evanston (1954) and was elected to both the Central and Executive Committees. Before Evanston he chaired the Committee on Structure and Functioning. His contributions in debate, his administrative sense, his conduct of worship and his gift for good companionship ensured that he would sooner or later be called to an international ecumenical position of great responsibility. In fact, during the Central Committee meeting in Lucknow, India, in 1953, W.A. Visser 't Hooft, the WCC general secretary, approached Cooke and, after much hesitation he took leave of the Congregational Union and came to Geneva in 1955 to head the Division of Inter-Church Aid and Refugee Service.

There Leslie Cooke found a challenge equal to his great capacities. Under his leadership the division grew to become one of the largest non-governmental organizations in the world. But Cooke was far too perceptive to permit the division to be nothing more than a Christian charitable organization. He insisted that the giving churches must learn how to provide aid across and not simply within confessional boundaries. Much as the Apostle Paul had collected funds for the "poor in Jerusalem", that is, for the Jewish-Christian mother church from which he had become theologically estranged, Cooke kept reminding the churches that ecumenical sharing must always be accompanied by sound biblical and theological reflection. Referring to Ecclesiastes 9:7 he once said:

> We have a gospel the dominant theme of which is the establishing of a community. We have a social gospel because our gospel is about a society and for society. It is no accident that the symbol of membership in the divine community is to partake of the broken bread... The Christian knows that if men are to have bread with laughter, then this concern must be a concern that men shall secure their bread in justice and freedom. [5]

Increasingly, however, Leslie Cooke's ecumenicity did not limit itself to the worldwide Christian community, but began to include all of humanity. At the third WCC assembly (New Delhi 1961) he had the name of the Division of Inter-Church Aid and Refugee Service changed to Division of Inter-Church Aid, Refugee and World Service. With great trepidation he contemplated United Nations' forecasts in 1960 that the world's population would double from 3000 million to 6000 million by the end of the century. Would human suffering increase correspondingly?

Cooke visited Asia several times during his first years as director of the division. He confessed:

I have not yet found an anaesthetic against the hideousness of the sufferings of the multitudes who dwell in Asia. Everywhere you go you may see the sunken eyes, the hollow cheeks, the taut lips of the hungry ones. Ours is a suffering world. Sometimes the suffering is caused by man's inhumanity to man. Revolutions and wars drive men from their homes to crowd the highways with refugees and leave in their wake burning cities and villages... The richer nations are getting richer and the poor are getting poorer. [6]

If the ecumenical movement pooled its intelligence and material sources, it might make a significant breakthrough in helping to reverse the tide. Under Cooke's leadership the division contributed to the financing of the Rapid Social Change studies coordinated by the WCC's Division on Church and Society. Cooke was convinced that the root causes of under-development had to be analyzed seriously for any useful ecumenical action. Out of this grew the idea to create a semi-autonomous body within the division called SASP (Specialized Action for Social Projects). It was to gather some of the best minds to sponsor a number of strategically placed "demonstration projects" which would provide stimulus throughout the developing countries. This attempt ultimately failed. The projects were usually too large for the local churches to handle. Moreover, it became clear that neither better technical assistance nor more finances sufficed to change deep-rooted structural distortions in the third world, especially those which had resulted from the impact of European colonialism. Leslie Cooke would be the first to admit that he, too, had to undergo a continuous learning process.

During a 1966 visit to Brazil and Chile, Cooke became aware of the newly emerging structure/dependence debate in Latin America. One of its principal insights was that "conscientization" or awareness-building is an indispensable first step towards self-reliant human development. New approaches from below, so to speak, were required to heal the broken world community. Cooke's concluding comments at the June 1966 global consultation in Swanwick on inter-church aid reflected his new insights, but also his anxieties:

We shall have to face a great deal of misunderstanding in the churches. There will be many who have been generous in their giving for relief who will become hesitant, if not resistant, when they realize that our aim is to change the status quo. They will think that the church has gone leftist or socialist or communist. There will be those among the rising generation, and the churches of the developing countries, who are radical, who will say: "At last the churches are with us — they have espoused our cause, they have joined the revolution." Then there will come a moment when to the word "revolution" we will have to add the word "reconciliation", and these heralds of the new dawn will be disappointed and disillusioned as they see that the church cannot deploy into the long lines to face the enemies of change for violent battle. We shall face grave misunderstanding. [7]

Despite his many international travels, Leslie Cooke took time to involve himself in local church life at the Church of Scotland congregation in Geneva, feeling the need to keep his own spiritual life active. He often preached there and was a member of the choir. On the job, Cooke always found time for pastoral care of his staff. Each staff member was made to feel free to approach the director about work or personal problems. He had a great ability to understand and handle an international group of people; in turn, he was able to count on the unquestioned loyalty of his spirited and diverse team.

Not long after the Swanwick consultation, the landmark 1966 Geneva World Conference on Church and Society took place. It put the vast North-South confrontation squarely within the centre of the ecumenical fellowship, presenting it with an unprecedented challenge. Just as Cooke had predicted, the ecumenical fellowship was to be rudely torn between the poles of "revolution" and of "reconciliation". During the following years several highly vocal protest movements arose — Black Theology in the US, Latin American liberation theology, minjung theology in Korea — against poverty and under-development. Related to these were the protests against the Vietnam war and the European youth revolt of 1968. One of the WCC's responses was the creation of the Programme to Combat Racism, which turned out to become a watershed in ecumenical history.

Leslie Cooke did not see any of this. We do not know how he would have reacted and how he might have led the Division of Inter-Church Aid, Refugee and World Service to face these unprecedented challenges. One of his speeches gives a glimpse of what one might call an unfinished reflection:

> The trouble with the Christian church is this: that it is now frightened to recognize and acknowledge the revolution which it started. And it is becoming a violent revolution because we abandoned it when we ought to have been making it a non-violent revolution. And there are others with other philosophies, secular and atheistic, who walk in to claim the fruits of a revolution in the beginning of which they had no part whatever. It was a Christian revolution.[8]

During the autumn of 1966 Leslie Cooke undertook a journey to Canada and the United States in order to explain the evolution of ecumenical thought to church leaders there. At that moment he did not seem to realize that his frequent headaches were not the result of work pressure or uncertainty over his future — the Congregational Union of England and Wales wanted him to fill one of the large London pulpits — but of a malignant tumour. He collapsed during a speech in New York City. Rushed to hospital, he lingered between life and death for several more months. On 22 February 1967, Leslie Cooke died at the age of 58.

NOTES

[1] Leslie Cooke, "A Responsible Church in a Changing Society", in *Bread and Laughter*, Geneva, WCC, 1968, p.112.
[2] Norman Goodall, "Leslie Edward Cooke — A Biographical Sketch", in *ibid.*, p.17.
[3] "The Biblical Revolution", in *ibid.*, p.144.
[4] *Op. cit.*, p.18.
[5] "Bread Is Made for Laughter", in *ibid.*, p.103.
[6] "A Responsible Church in a Changing Society", in *ibid.*, p.109.
[7] "Beyond Co-operation to Community", in *ibid.*, p.118.
[8] "A Responsible Church in a Changing Society", in *ibid.*, p.111.

BIBLIOGRAPHY

Works by Leslie Cooke:

Faith Stakes a Claim, London, Independent Press, 1949.
"Implications of Ecumenical Loyalty", in *The Ecumenical Review*, vol. V, no. 4, July 1953, pp.349-57.
"Toronto 1950", in *The Congregational Quarterly*, vol. XXIV, no. 1, 1951, pp.39-48.

Paul Couturier
1881–1953

RENÉ BEAUPÈRE

Born on 29 July 1881 in Lyons into a family of industrialists, Paul Couturier received an ordinary formal education, ending with the traditional training in a major seminary. Ordained priest in 1906, he worked towards a degree in the natural sciences at the Catholic faculty in Lyons and in October 1909 began to teach science at the Institution des Chartreux, a Catholic college in Lyons — a vocation which was to last for more than 40 years.

In 1920 Couturier met Albert Valentin, a Jesuit and a director of retreats for priests. Some years later Valentin encouraged Couturier to take an interest in the Russian immigrants of whom there were then more than ten thousand in the Lyons area. While not neglecting the Catholics, for whom he had created a place of worship, Couturier developed a certain sympathy with the Orthodox. He became very attached to Seraphim of Sarov, the most popular saint in Russia, and adopted the formula coined by Metropolitan Platon of Kiev: "The walls of separation do not reach to the sky." Victor Carlhian, a lay friend of Abbé Couturier who came from a background more open than his, helped to broaden his horizons and expand his intelligence and his heart.

In 1932 Couturier spent some time in the Benedictine monastery of Amay-sur-Meuse (now Chevetogne) in Belgium. There he discovered the thinking of its founder, Dom Lambert Beauduin, and the testament of Cardinal Mercier: "to unite, we must love each other; to love each other, we must know each other; to know each other, we must meet each other".

While Couturier was already aware of the periods of prayer set aside for Christian unity in January and at Pentecost, it was at Amay that he gained a greater grasp of the problems and limits of the 18 to 25 January Octave, which had been founded in 1908 by two Anglicans whose aim was to ask God to guide the Anglicans back to the See of Rome. In 1933 he introduced a three-day version of this Octave (20-22 January) in Lyons, "for the return of separated Christians to the unity of the church". Despite this somewhat ambiguous formulation, he foresaw a need to redirect this prayer by opening it up more widely to both the will of Christ and to all Christians, not merely Catholics and Anglicans. In 1934 the Russian Metropolitan Eulogius authorized his clergy in France to take part in the Octave of Prayer the next year. At the end of 1935 Couturier published an article on the "psychology of the Octave of Prayer" which was to have a wide influence. [1]

In 1936 his friend Laurent Rémillieux, another priest in Lyons, brought Couturier into contact with the Fraternité St Jean, a group of Reformed pastors from German-speaking Switzerland who had taken up the cause of prayer for Christian unity. This was the origin of the Groupe des Dombes which, beginning in 1937, brought together French and Swiss pastors and priests in an annual retreat for prayer and theological dialogue. In 1939 he made contact with W.A. Visser 't Hooft; and in the autumn of 1940 he was visited by Frère Roger Schutz, whom he in turn visited at Taizé in July 1941. During the same period he made and strengthened contacts with French Reformed pastors in Lyons and elsewhere, including Wilfred Monod and A.-N. Bertrand.

These "external relations" with persons from all Christian denominations did not prevent him from giving much of his time and the little money he had to making the January Week of Prayer in its more universal form more widely known in France and beyond. To do this he produced brochures, tracts and posters, brought in speakers and preachers and engaged in an ever-growing correspondence with people from all the churches. With some of his correspondents, above all certain women, he created what he called the "invisible monastery", a spiritual communion of persons who, without knowing each other, nevertheless prayed for Christian unity in a convergent manner. Some of them were to offer their lives to the cause.

Couturier's precarious health had been aggravated by two months' imprisonment in Lyons by the Gestapo. He was poor; he worked alone, though with some support provided by his disciple and spiritual heir, Marist Father Maurice Villain. He died on 24 March 1953 at the age of 72. At his funeral, homage was rendered by Cardinal Gerlier, his archbishop and protector, Roland de Pury, on behalf of the French Reformed Church, the brothers of Taizé and the World Council of Churches, and Alexandre de Weymarn, editor of the WCC's *Ecumenical Press Service*, to which the abbé was a regular correspondent. His grave in the Loyasses cemetery in Lyons has become a place of pilgrimage for people of many churches.

* * *

Yves Congar once wrote that Paul Couturier gave ecumenism its "heart of love and prayer". His contribution was decisive. "It was he who, spiritually, founded that immense movement which, today, bears the ecumenical hope of the world."

It was Couturier who suggested the formula that was to enable all Christians to come together in prayer while excluding any efforts towards proselytism: "That we may see the visible unity of the kingdom of God desired by Christ, by the means which he wished". At the same time, he recalled with conviction the basis of this prayer: it is not I who pray, it is Christ who, in me, repeats his high priestly prayer found in John 17: "Father, that they may be one..."

Abbé Couturier insisted that the Octave of Prayer is "something spiritual which everyone lifts up in the sincerity of his soul, the Orthodox remaining Orthodox, the

Anglicans Anglican, the Catholics Catholic". Thus there is no question of one or the other Christian "converting" to another Christian church: unity is not a question of a return but of a regrouping. Moreover, as the term "universal prayer" suggests, the point is that all Christians, even if they cannot pray together (something which at the time seemed almost impossible), can at least pray in a convergent manner. (The awkward neologism which he originally coined for this — "parallel elaboration" — was fortunately replaced by the term "spiritual emulation".

> The essence of the question is to promote ecumenical prayer in all Christian groups, a prayer which will echo our intimate suffering in the horrible sin of division. We have all sinned. We must all humiliate ourselves, and pray without ceasing and constantly call for the miracle of total reunion... Catholic prayer, Orthodox prayer, Anglican prayer or Protestant prayer is not enough. We need them all and all together.

Throughout his life, Abbé Couturier hoped to hear a call to such prayer emanating jointly from the highest authorities of the Christian churches.

For Couturier Christ's prayer for unity in John 17 is the prototype of all prayer for unity. In what he called his "spiritual testament", he wrote:

> My confidence in you, O Christ, thrusts me into your heart, where I find your prayer: "Father, that they may be one... so that the world will learn that you sent me. Father, that they may be perfectly one." My prayer as a sinner is your prayer, and your prayer is my only consolation... How will unity come about? What are the obstacles which we must overcome? That is your business; my faith can only command me to pray with you, in you, so that your unity may come about, the unity which you always wanted, the unity you sought, the unity which you prepared...
>
> This way of praying is simple and faithful. It is a centre of convergence where, under the sign of charity, all the prayers for unity of the true sons of Love and of all true Christians — despite their separation — can flow together in the heart of Christ.

Although completely orthodox, this formula frightened some carping theologians. But Couturier insisted:

> With a great stroke of the wings, this type of prayer flies above all demarcations and brings us all to rest in the heart of our Christ. This flight is in no way negative. It in no way means a reduction, or forgetting, of our respective beliefs which for each of us are more important than ourselves. This affirmation of a rising-above is true for the Protestant, the Anglican, the Orthodox just as much as for a Catholic; it is exact, no matter the way each person's faith allows him to envisage the problem of Christian unity.

Couturier stressed the importance of integrating our prayer into that of Christ:

> Christ wishes us to be in him in this prayer because we are part of his life, all of us who are Christians. And he can no more, simply because he wanted it, bring about Christian unity without us, than he can save us, because he wanted to, without us. We can all make our own Paul's words: "I fulfil in my prayer in him for unity what is missing from his prayer."
>
> Down through time, Christ's universal prayer, in the hearts of Christians, and in which he pleads with his Father for their unity, will flow and spread throughout the whole Christian body. God only hears the secret, incessant murmur of prayer through souls, fraternities and cloisters... Visible Christian unity will be achieved when the praying Christ will have found sufficient Christians from all traditions to pray freely with him to his Father for unity. The silent voice of Christ should swell with all the voices of the baptized... The problem of Christian unity is, for all of us, a problem of directing our internal lives.

* * *

Abbé Couturier never claimed to be a theologian. Yet as we have seen he was one of the founders of the Groupe des Dombes, and from 1937 to 1952 he took part in its annual meeting of priests, pastors and professors of theology. In these gatherings he did not play a "starring" role, but rather provided spiritual support to the dialogue. As one who sought a "theology streaming with prayer", he had no hesitation about calling for silent prayer at times when this dialogue deteriorated into sterile debate or became extremely tense.

Faithful to its founder, the Groupe des Dombes continued its work where it began, in the Cistercian abbey of Notre-Dame des Dombes, near Lyons, although over the years it held several meetings in the Protestant centres of Grandchamp and Taizé. Despite the fact that it is a non-official group which chooses its own members, it has earned a high degree of respect in the ecumenical field.

For a long time it lived a "hidden life". Not until 1956, after the death of Couturier, did it begin to produce at the end of each meeting a memorandum in the form of theses ("on this we are agreed"; "this requires further discussion") for internal use. Its first publication, *Vers une même foi eucharistique?*, is dated 1972. Since then it has gone on to study ministry, the episcopate, the ministry of unity within the church universal, and the Holy Spirit, the churches and the sacraments. [2] More recently it has discussed the need for a conversion of the churches [3] and Mary in the design of God.

Inspired by a discussion with Abbé Couturier's cousin, Fr Robert Clément, Maurice Villain suggested to his spiritual master in 1944 the need to create a forum not for a small specialized group like the Groupe des Dombes but for all Catholic priests working in the "spirit of emulation", in order to help them to get to know each other, exchange experiences and look for ways of approaching non-Catholics. Held in July, these meetings soon came to represent an intra-Catholic dialogue on the issues that would be discussed during the Dombes retreat in September. The Catholic speakers tested their thinking on their confrères and profited from their comments. In addition, these meetings left ample room for ecumenical information and formation. While aimed at and led by Catholic priests, already in the second year half a day was devoted to dialogue with a representative from another church; and this custom has continued. As his own health permitted, Abbé Couturier took part in this group until 1951.

* * *

As an oblate of the Benedictine monastery of Amay-sur-Meuse, Abbé Couturier added the name Irénée (Irenaeus) to his Christian name Paul. A number of his tracts and brochures are signed with this simple Christian name. As the name suggests — and like the great bishop of Lyons whom it recalls — Paul-Irénée Couturier was a man of peace and reconciliation. We still live out, spiritually, the mission which God entrusted to him in the twilight of his life to call all the disciples of Jesus to pray together for their unity.

Since 1966, the documents for the Week of Prayer from 18 to 25 January have been prepared by a joint committee of the WCC's Commission on Faith and Order and the Pontifical Council (formerly the Secretariat) for Promoting Christian Unity in Rome. As for the Groupe des Dombes, it continues its work under the direction of two co-presidents, Catholic and Protestant, elected by their peers.

NOTES

[1] "Pour l'unité des chrétiens: Psychologie de l'Octave de prière du 18 au 25 janvier", *Revue apologétique*, December 1935; cf. his further reflections in "L'universelle prière des chrétiens pour l'unité chrétienne", *ibid.*, November-December 1937.
[2] These documents are compiled in *Pour la communion des Eglises*, Paris, Centurion, 1988.
[3] Cf. *Pour la conversion des Eglises*, Paris, Centurion, 1991, English tr., *For the Conversion of the Churches*, Geneva, WCC, 1993.

BIBLIOGRAPHY

Works by Paul Couturier:

A collection of tracts for the Week of Unity 1938-1953.
"Psychologie de l'Octave de prières" and "L'universelle prière des chrétiens pour l'unité chrétienne", in *Revue apologétique*, December 1935, November and December 1937.
Various brochures including *Testament spirituel*, *Prière et unité chrétienne*, 2nd ed., 1952.
The major aspects of his works have been collected in Maurice Villain, *Œcuménisme spirituel: Les écrits de l'abbé Couturier*, Paris, Casterman, 1963.

Works on Paul Couturier:

Geoffrey Curtis, *Paul Couturier and Unity in the Church*, London, SCM, 1964.
The Life and Work of Abbé Paul Couturier, Haywards Heath, UK, Holy Cross Convent, 1959 (this is not a translation of Fr Villain's book).
Maurice Villain, *L'abbé Paul Couturier: apôtre de l'unité chrétienne*, Paris, Casterman, 1957.

Dorothy Day
1897–1980

JIM FOREST

> *What I want to bring out is how a pebble cast into a pond causes ripples that spread in all directions. Each one of our thoughts, words and deeds is like that.*
>
> Dorothy Day

Dorothy Day was a person of stunning contradictions: devout Catholic and avowed anarchist, activist and contemplative, journalist and prisoner, political radical and theological conservative. Intending to found a newspaper, she ended up founding a movement. A passionate advocate of community, she was a part-time hermit. A member of a church that since time immemorial (until Pope John XXIII and the Second Vatican Council) gave little support to conscientious objectors, she dared to imagine that one day it would recover its more ancient identity as a peace church.

She was born in Brooklyn, New York, on 8 November 1897. The daughter of a journalist, she became a reporter for New York's socialist daily *The Call* at the age of 18. A year later she joined the editorial staff of *Masses*, a radical magazine suppressed by the government following the entry of the US into the first world war. Soon after her 19th birthday she was one of a group of feminists arrested at the White House for protesting the exclusion of women from political affairs. Her time in jail proved to be a religious awakening.

After her release, Dorothy Day became a nurse in a Brooklyn hospital. She realized she wanted to serve those who suffered, not only write about them. But a love affair led her away from her work and back to a bohemian life in Greenwich Village in Lower Manhattan. The affair ended with an abortion; the man she lived with moved on.

Just after the war she was briefly married to a New York literary figure and went with him to Europe where she wrote her first book, an autobiographical novel. Back in the US, she joined the staff of *The Liberator*, a communist magazine in Chicago. In 1922 she was arrested and jailed again, this time in one of the government's "anti-red" raids. She went back to reporting, first for a Chicago newspaper then for one in New Orleans. In 1925, with her novel published and the film rights sold to Hollywood, she returned to New York, where she fell deeply in love with an anarchist. The pregnancy that resulted was the turning point in her life.

That she should be carrying a child again seemed to her a miracle. The abortion five years earlier had left her feeling not only profoundly ashamed but fearful that she might never conceive again. The second pregnancy filled her with a sense of God's mercy. She found that whenever she went walking, she was praying, and the prayers were entirely of joy and gratitude. "How can there be no God when there are all these beautiful things?", she would ask her common-law husband. As the months passed, she decided she wanted her child baptized in the Catholic Church; and then she realized she wanted to become a Catholic herself. To the man she lived with, however, the Catholic Church was one of the world's most oppressive structures. Their relationship disintegrated.

Her daughter Tamar was baptized in July 1927, and Day herself, now a single parent, was baptized in late December. Then began her six-year search for a vocation that could bridge her radical political convictions with her new-found religious commitment.

In the spring of 1933, in the midst of the Great Depression, Day founded *The Catholic Worker*, initially intended to be a monthly. The idea had been proposed to her by a remarkable French immigrant, Peter Maurin, a former Christian Brother who lived a life of the utmost simplicity. The paper sold, and still sells, for a penny a copy. It was aimed at ordinary people, many of them out of work. Her first editorial said *The Catholic Worker* would show its readers that the Catholic Church is concerned not only with spiritual welfare but material welfare.

The paper caught on. Within a few months there were thousands of readers. Almost as quickly, what had been only a paper became a movement. First in New York, then in other cities, Catholic Worker communities were formed. They were both places of welcome for homeless people (the houses are in the down-and-out areas like New York City's Bowery) and centres for organizing a "green revolution": social change brought through non-violent means.

Dom Helder Camara once said, "When I give bread to the hungry, they call call me a saint. When I ask why the hungry have no bread, they call me a communist." Though Day never joined any political party, she was often called a communist. She was also dismissed as "impractical" because of the non-institutional approach of her hospitality to people living ragged lives on the street. "Those who cannot see the face of Christ in the poor are atheists indeed," she said more than once.

A social worker visiting the Catholic Worker house in New York asked Day how long her guests were "allowed" to stay. She answered: "We let them stay forever. They live with us, they die with us, and we give them a Christian burial. We pray for them after they are dead. Once they are taken in, they become members of the family. Or rather they always were members of the family. They are our brothers and sisters in Christ."

For centuries before the founding of *The Catholic Worker*, there had been no avowedly pacifist movement in the Catholic Church. Perhaps more than any Catholic since St Francis, Day began a process within Catholicism that put Jesus, rather than the just-war theologians, at the centre of the church's social life.

Dorothy Day was often imprisoned for her activities in peace, civil rights and labour demonstrations. One of my favourite photos of her, taken in 1973, shows her holding the dress she wore during her last imprisonment, after being arrested in California with Mexican-Americans who were struggling to form a union. All the women imprisoned with her signed their names on the rough prison garment, making it a treasure to her.

At the centre of Day's faith was her certainty that we are saved not because we are clever or are often found in religious buildings but because of our loving response to "the least". The Catholic Worker way of life is to practise daily "the works of mercy" of which Jesus speaks in Matthew 25: feeding the hungry, giving drink to the thirsty, clothing the naked, taking in the homeless, caring for the sick, being with prisoners. This same teaching led Day to oppose all systems that cause suffering. "We see that the works of mercy oppose the works of war," she said. Often she quoted St John of the Cross: "Love is the measure by which we shall be judged."

Day stressed what she called "the little way". Big changes were only won by countless little changes. On the refrigerator door in one Catholic Worker house, I found this text from Dorothy:

> Paper work, cleaning the house, dealing with the innumerable visitors who come all through the day, answering the phone, keeping patience and acting intelligently, which is to find some meaning in all that happens — these things, too, are the works of peace, and often seem like a very little way.

When Dorothy Day died on 29 November 1980, the event was widely marked in the US, not only by Christians of every stripe but by people of many other religious traditions and those outside any religion. Many regarded her as one of Christianity's great reformers and a modern saint, though she herself sometimes said: "Don't call me a saint — I don't want to be dismissed so easily." She never hesitated to talk about her faith: "If I have achieved anything in my life," she commented, "it is because I have not been embarrassed to talk about God."

After the funeral, an editor of *The Catholic Worker* was asked whether the movement would be able to continue without its founder. "We have lost Dorothy," said Peggy Scherer, "but we still have the gospel."

The most extraordinary monuments to Day are eighty houses of hospitality stretching from Los Angeles to Amsterdam (and now just beginning in Oxford), places of welcome that not only offer a caring response to the homeless and runaways but are centres of work for a non-violent and sharing society.

"It is the living from day to day," she once commented, "taking no thought for the morrow, seeing Christ in all who come to us, and trying literally to follow the gospel that resulted in this work."

BIBLIOGRAPHY

By Dorothy Day:
The Long Loneliness, New York, Harper & Row, 1992.

Works on Dorothy Day:
Robert Ellsberg, ed., *Dorothy Day: Selected Writings*, Maryknoll, NY, Orbis, 1992.
Jim Forest, *Love Is the Measure: A Biography of Dorothy Day*, Maryknoll, NY, Orbis, 1994.

Suzanne de Diétrich
1891–1981

HANS-RUEDI WEBER

"If you were a boy, what would you study now?" Suzanne de Diétrich was 15 years old and already an orphan when that question was asked. She was born in January 1891 into a rich aristocratic family in Niederbronn, in the north of Alsace. Since they already had four girls, her parents had hoped that the last child would be a boy to follow the father into the large family foundries. Suzanne answered: "It would have to be engineering." "Well then, why not!" was the reply — and the decision.

There was no doubt that Suzanne, as she would later be known to several generations of students throughout the world, had the intelligence. Until the age of fifteen she had never gone to school, but her tutor had given her a good general education. Personally, Suzanne would have preferred to study the classics and as a child she had already learned the Greek alphabet. Now, however, an engineer

from the family business taught her algebra and technical drawing, and off she went to Lausanne to the industrial college and the university's school of engineering. Soon she was at the head of her class. Only the large drawing board created problems. Like her father and three of her sisters she suffered from an hereditary disability: she was very small and had to walk with the help of two canes.

During her studies in Lausanne she came into contact with the Student Christian Movement (SCM). After the weekly forty-eight hours of mathematics, physics and technical drawing, she relaxed by preparing and leading Bible studies with other students. This created a dilemma for her: should she become one of the first women electrical engineers in the French-speaking world, or should she go back into the family factories and use her skills there? Or, on the other hand, should she continue to do what really fascinated her and work as a volunteer among the many foreign students who came to French universities?

The first world war solved that problem. Alsace was occupied by the German army, and most of the French SCM leaders were mobilized to serve on the battle front. Suzanne volunteered to work mainly among girl high school students, and what began as a two-year commitment developed into a lifetime vocation. Her extensive and moving correspondence with the SCM leaders and students at the front shows how she became the pastoral confidante of these soldiers, many of whom never returned from the battles. During this time she also developed her friendship with Suzanne Bidgrain, another remarkable French ecumenical pioneer who later edited the first ecumenical hymnary, *Cantate Domino*, a book which has been of major assistance in the ecumenical education of successive generations of students.

From 1920 onwards Suzanne de Diétrich became more and more involved in the work of the World Student Christian Federation (WSCF). She was an active member of its Executive Committee, and served from 1928 to 1932 as its vice-moderator, together with T.Z. Koo from China. In 1936, W.A. Visser 't Hooft asked her to join him as a colleague at the WSCF headquarters in Geneva, where she also worked for the World YWCA on a part-time basis. Despite her physical disability, Suzanne now became a great traveller, visiting and inspiring student groups all over Eastern and Western Europe, the Indian sub-continent and in North and South America.

During the 1930s Suzanne, stimulated by the theology of Karl Barth, was deeply involved in the search for a new understanding of the Christian message. She did so with her scientifically trained mind, her sensitivity as a woman and the special competence of a lay person. She herself never became a Barthian; her favourite Christian authors were Blaise Pascal and the representatives of that peculiar school of thought which originated in the *Ban de la Roche*, an isolated mountain valley in the Vosges — Johann V. Oberlin, Christophe Dieterlen and Tommy Fallot — who combined a very earthly biblical spirituality with a great concern for social-ethical questions and an openness to Christians from different denominational families that was amazing for the 19th century. They liked to call themselves "reformed Catholics". It is no surprise that Suzanne's friends included such outstanding Protestants as Marc Boegner and Catholics as Yves Congar. To this, she added a deep sensitivity to the worship and spirituality of the Orthodox churches, which she gained from her many Orthodox friends, especially Paul Evdokimov. She once wrote: "I always live Good Friday in close communion with my Protestant and Easter Day in close communion with my Orthodox friends."

Suzanne's main task in the WSCF became training Bible study leaders and writing hundreds of study outlines on texts and themes from the whole of biblical literature. In the 1930s she also collected and edited liturgies and prayers for the ecumenical prayer books, *Venite Adoremus I* and *Venite Adoremus II*, which came to be used among a public far wider than the Student Christian Movements.

Together with H.L. Henriod, she served as the secretary for the WSCF ecumenical commission. In 1932 the two of them organized a residential ecumenical retreat in Mouterhouse, one of the country houses belonging to the de Dietrich family, on the theme of "Incarnation". There outstanding Protestant, Catholic and Orthodox thinkers, mainly from Europe but with a few representatives from Asia and North America, learned to live, think and pray together. In the inter-church climate of the time such a gathering still had to take place discreetly without publicity.

The second world war brought new tasks. WSCF general secretary Robert Mackie went to Toronto in 1940 to work from there, in order to keep relationships open with North and South America and as far as possible to maintain contacts with Asia and Southern Africa. Suzanne stayed at WSCF headquarters in Geneva. Using often ingenious ways to circumvent censorship, she kept open the mutual information and fellowship between Christian student groups in the nations at war in Europe and between the occupied countries and those which were still free. What remains of the extensive correspondence between Suzanne and Robert Mackie from 1940 to 1945 demonstrates how the WSCF universal network of friendship remained intact to a far greater extent in the second world war than in the first.

The Geneva base involved Suzanne in collaboration with the "World Council of Churches in Process of Formation", with European student relief work and with the work of the French youth movements. After visiting Alsatian refugees in central and southern France in October 1939, she became the principal initiator of CIMADE, the refugee service of the combined French Protestant youth movements. With travel severely restricted by the war, she finally found time to write the books which had long been maturing in her mind.

In the autumn of 1946 the Ecumenical Institute at Bossey, near Geneva, was founded. The horrors of the war had upset many life projects. Young people in particular were asking: "What shall we do now?" At the front, in prisons and detention camps, Christians like Dietrich Bonhoeffer and Hendrik Kraemer had met deeply committed Marxists and secular humanists who challenged their faith. Reading the Bible in this frontier-context gave them a new vision of the vocation of God's people in the world. The Ecumenical Institute was created to help this questioning post-war generation of Christians to gain a new vision of their calling, and especially of their ministry to the laity. Broken fellowship between enemy nations and separated denominations had to be healed. New leaders of the ecumenical movement at the local, regional and universal level needed training. No better team than that of Hendrik Kraemer and Suzanne de Diétrich could have been found to provide inspiring leadership to this venture. Since Kraemer was unable to come before 1948, Suzanne served as acting programme director during the initial phase.

Until her retirement in 1954, Suzanne remained in Bossey, using all her rich gifts and experiences to enable both lay and ordained people to study the Bible in the light of the great issues of their time and their society, to introduce representatives of different confessions and cultures to ecumenical spirituality and worship and to help pastorally those who felt disorientated in such intensive ecumenical gatherings.

Retirement meant that Suzanne once again became a world traveller. She was much in demand as a Bible study leader in North and South America, and then also in Africa. She kept in contact with the work of the WCC, especially its Department on the Laity, and with all that was going on in the field of biblical exegesis and theology. Living in Paris she was also much involved in the life of a local parish, in the ecumenical training camps organized by CIMADE, the *Equipes de recherches bibliques*, and the Commission for International Affairs of the French Protestant Federation. As long as she was in Paris, she led a weekly Bible study in her apartment.

During the last two years of her life Suzanne lived in the deaconesses' home in Strasbourg, where she died on 24 January 1981. She is buried in the cemetery of Windstein in a beautiful valley near Niederbronn. Several of the barons and baronesses de Dietrich are also buried there, but Suzanne's grave is not in the impressive row of aristocratic tombs. She lies among the common people, beneath a simple flat stone with the symbol of the cross and the inscription: *Mon âme bénit l'Eternel*.

* * *

Suzanne de Diétrich is best remembered as the pioneer of ecumenical Bible study. In a small pamphlet written in 1966, *Discovering the Bible*, she described the kind of voyages of discovery she enabled people to undertake:

What if the Bible is the "best-seller" of all books in the whole world — does this mean that it is really *known*? Wherein lies its *uniqueness*? How can this old book become a living message for our time — for you and me?

Each generation has to rediscover the biblical message if it is to become truly its own...

The first thing the word of God does for us... is to unmask us, to reveal to us there is one before whom hiding is of no avail.

The crucial experience of the men of God in Israel was not so much to "know God" as to be *known of him*. This discovery filled the psalmist with reverence and awe (see Psalm 139). The Samaritan woman meeting Jesus goes through a similar experience: here is one who reads through her soul! A precondition for reading the Bible effectively is our readiness to expose ourselves to a Word which strips us naked and forces us to see ourselves as we really are. Only then can God's healing power reveal itself and his forgiveness take its full meaning. Only then can we grasp the deepest of all mysteries: there is One who cares, One who loves me and accepts me as I am.

Here we come to our first conclusion: the uniqueness of the Bible lies in the fact that the men of God who speak there have had a living encounter with the holy God; through the Word we are called to share in this encounter. We too are called; the promises made to them hold true for us, the commandments given to them require our faith and obedience, a new life is offered to every one of us. If the Bible does not lead to such an encounter, it remains a sheer chapter of past history. It does not become the word of life it is meant to become.

We certainly do not hear God's voice immediately every time we open our Bible. Many passages leave us cold. We frequently have to listen for a long time, to search for the meaning of words and images foreign to our way of thinking and speaking, before a passage comes alive to challenge our will and our heart.

Because it pleased God to reveal himself to men of flesh and blood who lived in a given time and place in history, we have, in order to understand what they meant to say to us, to know something of the circumstances in which they lived, the language they spoke, their traditions. Here study is required (happily we have today a number of simple and clear wordbooks and commentaries to help us)...

This being said, let us remember that, in the deepest sense, the real encounter with God remains his secret. The Bible shows us from first to last that the initiative always belongs to God. It is he who stepped into *his story*, rescued a few obscure tribes and called them to be *his people*. It is he who called the prophets and appointed them to be "his mouth". It is he who, at the appointed time, sent his Son to save a lost mankind. And it is his Holy Spirit who opens our hearts and minds so that we may understand and believe...

Bible study will consist of honest search and humble listening. God surely wants us to use the best scholarship available so that we may understand the Scriptures better. But they will be opened to those only who are ready to obey. In biblical language *knowledge* implies *commitment*. Jesus tells us again and again that only those who do God's will shall know who he is.

The pamphlet then gives practical advice on where and how to begin such study. It further stresses the importance of the Old Testament and leads on to the witness of the New Testament. The closing paragraph reads:

We live today in a world fraught with social, political, racial tensions. It is in this world that God calls us to witness to his message of justice and redeeming love. The Bible confronts us with a long range of men and women who have gallantly fought God's battle against all the forces of evil — in their own souls, and in the surrounding world. We need their company in order to learn from them the secret of a victorious life.

Suzanne did not propose brilliant new hypotheses of biblical interpretation. Her strength and special contribution consisted rather in the clarity with which she summarized the insights of the foremost exegetes of her time. She checked such insights critically and interiorized them through prayer. She also attempted to apply them to the questions of the present world. Above all she was deeply concerned to listen to all the voices speaking in the Bible, to discover inter-relationships between the Old and the New Testament and thus to present the biblical message in its rich variety as a whole.

The same wholeness characterized her contributions in the fields of ecumenical service and witness. She had little patience with people who wanted to separate Bible study from risky social and political involvement. People who made a show of piety but did not live by faith and grace, and those who simply enjoyed theological discussions without incarnating them in concrete and costly decisions found no favour with her.

This is how she envisaged ecumenism: in the meeting of Christians from different confessions, nationalities and cultures, "there always will be crisis if one does not content oneself with superficial friendships, if the ecumenical dialogue is taken seriously. One inevitably inflicts suffering on one another, for what is at stake is the truth of God which each one sees from a different point of view." Again, "ecumenism must be lived and suffered. We confront impossibilities. And it is through such impossibilities that we are ever again led to the cross of Christ, to this certainty which we all have in common, namely his victory over sin and death."

Wholeness also characterized Suzanne's greatest contribution, namely her own presence, which made a deep impact on most of those who met her. Not that she was perfect. She could have sudden outbursts of anger, sometimes making too great demands on people, or being too impatient with her own weaknesses and those of others. Yet this was all part of her personality. The love of the Bible was not separated from her love of beautiful trees and of children. Her continuing honest search for truth was combined with much humour. Her passion for justice and her concern for those suffering both materially and spiritually went together with her passion for playing Scrabble (and she did not like to lose!). She rejoiced when others discovered in Bible study approaches and new insights into the meaning of a text which she herself had not yet seen. All this formed a whole, including even her own infirmity, which she accepted with a remarkable courage to live.

Sometimes in the midst of a discussion Suzanne would become strangely silent, as if she were involved in another dialogue, bringing in prayer before God what was being said here on earth. Thus she held together time and eternity.

BIBLIOGRAPHY

As an author Suzanne de Diétrich was, first and foremost, a letter writer. Her worldwide correspondence, together with her published and unpublished manuscripts, is at present being collected in the Suzanne de Diétrich Archives of the National Library in Strasbourg.
Suzanne also wrote hundreds of Bible study outlines, most of which have never appeared in print.
Her first and last major books are meditations on passages from the synoptic gospels and on John's gospel: L'heure de l'offrande, Neuchâtel/Paris 1935 (English tr. Behold Thy King, London, 1938) and L'heure de l'élévation, Neuchatel, 1966 (English tr. And He Is Lifted Up, Philadelphia, 1969).
Suzanne's gifts as a story-teller are evident in her history of the first fifty years of the World Student Christian Federation: Cinquante ans d'histoire, Paris, 1948 (English tr. 50 Years of History, Geneva, 1993).

Besides many articles and brochures Suzanne published commentaries for lay people on the Letter to the Philippians, on Matthew's Gospel and on the Letters of John. Some of these writings as well as the following better-known books have been published in several languages (among them English, Spanish, German, Dutch and Scandinavian):
— *Le dessein de Dieu*, Neuchâtel/Paris, 1945, 12th ed. Paris, 1992; translated into 12 languages; English ed. *God's Unfolding Purpose*, Philadelphia, 1961.
— *Le renouveau biblique*, Neuchâtel, 1945, an expanded version of the earlier handbook *Rediscovering the Bible*, Toronto, 1942.
— *The Witnessing Community*, Philadelphia, 1958.
— On the basis of new developments in biblical scholarship and new experiments in Bible study leadership Suzanne later rewrote and expanded the above-mentioned classic handbook: *Le renouveau biblique: hier et aujourd'hui*, 2 vols, Neuchâtel, 1969.
A fairly complete bibliography of Suzanne de Diétrich's published writing has been prepared by Christian Barbery and published in the Bulletin de la Société de l'Histoire du Protestantisme Français, (vol. 137, 1961, pp.599-609).
A major biography by H.-R. Weber is *The Courage to Live*, Geneva, WCC, 1995; French, Paris, Les Bergers et Les Mages, autumn 1995.

Paul Evdokimov
1901–1970

OLIVIER CLÉMENT

Paul Evdokimov was born on 2 August 1901 in St Petersburg. After studying in Kiev, he left Russia in 1921 for Constantinople, arriving in France in 1923. In 1942 he earned a doctorate in philosophy at the University of Aix-Marseille. From 1943 onwards he worked with CIMADE, the ecumenical organization set up to help displaced persons and refugees during the war, directing a centre for refugees in Bièvres, near Paris, and a CIMADE students hostel in Sèvres and Massy. Active in the ecumenical movement, he was a member of the board of the Ecumenical Institute in Bossey from 1950 to 1968, and he was one of the professors of the first Bossey graduate school (1953-54). From 1953 onwards he taught theology at the Orthodox faculty of St Sergius in Paris. He died on 16 September 1970 in Meudon, France.

In Paul Evdokimov's personal history, ecumenism was initially a succession of experiences and gestures which filled his exile with a sense of pilgrimage towards the heavenly Jerusalem:

> Finding yourself a young emigrant in the West constitutes a turning point in your life, a break in the conditions of your existence, but it does not destroy your spiritual continuity.
>
> As an adolescent I was enthralled by the genius of Dostoevsky and soaked myself in it. As I trod the French soil, the paved streets of Paris, stopping in the shadow of the old churches, I reverently recited his words: "For a Russian, Europe is just as precious as Russia; every one of its stones is sweet and dear to his heart..." Exile was an opportunity for pilgrimage to the sanctuaries. I urgently wanted to get to know Western Christianity, its treasures, miracles and saints. My mind opened up quite naturally, with a fresh naiveté, to an ecumenism that was still very vague. [1]

For the young refugees under his care in Sèvres he spelled out lucidly the providential significance of exile:

> The break in one's empirical ties with one's country, one's national setting, causes profound suffering, but this suffering makes the person more profound and, in the end, it lends great

lightness in the midst of all the earthly weights; it allows the pilgrim's freedom of judgment, a much more objective evaluation of the goods of this world, a more immediate grasp of spiritual values. This kind of thinking is easily tinged with eschatology; it sets its sights on the ultimate... Impatience with limits is a spur to discover the explosive vocation of the church in this world... and the struggle for existence, which is so hard for the sufferer, makes us almost hypersensitive and imperatively shapes within us a vision of the church comprising the salvation of the whole world. [2]

In a contribution to the 1964 Week of Prayer for Christian Unity, Evdokimov said, "We can paraphrase the words of the gospel and say: seek the salvation of the world and unity will be given to you as well, freely, as a final grace of the ministry of salvation."

Already during his first years of study at St Sergius between the wars, he had begun to discover that "conscious Orthodoxy" and "shared Orthodoxy" must be two sides of one and the same coin. At early meetings of the ecumenical movement he was struck by "something that was both infinitely simple and infinitely great... I saw several bishops, who were very firm about their dogmatic and canonical limits, suddenly become 'impatient about the limits' as they realized the limitlessness of the presence of God..." [3] This, he wrote (paraphrasing Pascal), was "the ecumenical fact speaking to the heart", not to the heart of sentimentalism but to that of spiritual knowledge:

Faithfulness to the Orthodox truth which gave me birth and, on the other hand, attention to our Lord's high priestly prayer, attention to history... were an imperative challenge to discover their meaning jointly with all of Christendom, to see what we could do, and what we could become together. Kierkegaard's statement rang strikingly true: it is not the path that is impossible but the impossible that is the path, and we had to set out on it. [4]

The impossible as the path implies grace and miracle and our being open to them in common prayer. First in Protestant and then in Catholic churches, attracted by the spiritual friendship that linked him with pastors and priests, Paul Evdokimov shared in the prayer of the other, hoping through it to uncover and actualize the praise of the undivided church to which Orthodoxy bears humble witness whenever it transcends its historical limitations. In attending Protestant services he hoped to be present "as an Orthodox, which means not as an individual but as a witness aware of what he bears within himself, as a custodian of the whole, unbroken history of the church since apostolic times", thereby in some way integrating the worship "with the sacred history of the church beyond rupture and separation. An integration of this kind remains a mystery, indefinable theologically and still less canonically, but it is none the less mystically real for those who experience it." [5]

Between 1956 and 1958 Evdokimov spent several weeks each summer in Provence near the hermitage of Dom Célestin Charlier who had enlisted him as a contributor to the journal *Bible et vie chrétienne*. Every Sunday the Evdokimovs attended mass celebrated by Fr Charlier in an ancient chapel he had restored himself.

He baked a large host himself and broke it during the eucharistic canon. His slow speech could be understood by everyone; his flowing, genuinely liturgical gestures overflowed with heavenly content. The power of this witness through the liturgy attracted a previously de-Christianized crowd. We were witnessing the miracle of Western Christianity, touching the naked, pure reality transmitted through the centuries, divested of the heavy burden of average Catholicism... I felt at ease, transported into being an Eastern pilgrim visiting the

Christian West as it was before the schism. Faced with the eucharistic advent of Christ, nothing prevented me from being one with this priest, his parish and his mass. This foretaste of unity that is possible, one of the most striking in my life, is still alive. Naturally, I could not receive communion. But this pain in the midst of joy seemed to hold a promise, an ardent, epicletic hope. [6]

Prayer entails commitment, and Paul Evdokimov was led to make some very significant ecumenical gestures.

In the reception centre he directed just after the war, the German group, impressed by the discussions and Bible studies he was leading, asked him to organize joint prayers or some kind of "worship":

> These souls needed to be provided with familiar, well-known, habitual elements. I selected some biblical readings and some prayers from a Protestant book of worship. I had a deep feeling that in my humble way I was exercising the Orthodox priesthood of all believers as a "priest, king and prophet" according to the patristic definition. In these very special circumstances, where the ecumenical voice was speaking, I had been called to lead these souls into the presence of the Lord, to a state of prayer, through the grace of God. [7]

At Sèvres he encouraged the students of many different nationalities and confessions to build an ecumenical chapel together, where prayers were offered each evening "for Christian unity, for peace and that all may bear one another's burdens". From that time onwards, daily life regained its calm at their common evening prayer, based on the Orthodox vespers and led most often by Evdokimov himself, in this chapel where everyone felt at home. As he told the students, "the test we face daily is to examine and look with trembling to see whether the spiritual chapel in the depths of our souls and our community life as a whole correspond to the building of bricks and stones, to the Presence which animates it." The chapel provided "an open space in which every priest and every pastor can recognize the living characteristics of his own faith and can conduct his own worship in true ecumenical freedom and love".

One of Paul Evdokimov's joys was how this undertaking helped to move the young refugees from being "displaced persons" to "the Christian universalism in which all people by the same title are exiles in search of the heavenly city". Indeed, one of the students wrote, "We are all 'displaced persons' in an atheist world... It turned out that by pure grace we had built the landing place that we lacked, the threshold of a new, true dwelling place."

* * *

Prayer and gestures enriched Evdokimov's thinking and he was one of the first to attribute a theological and spiritual status to ecumenism.

At the outset, ecumenism discovered "the radiant presence of God in the disunited parts of Christendom". Human sin has broken Christian unity but God has undertaken a counter-action. Hence "the mystery of disunion" which requires us "to recognize the real and therefore saving presence of Christ in others", to recognize the "ecclesial reality" of others. [8] As Evdokimov said in an address at Meudon, God's counter-action

> changes surface appearances from within. The ravages of the separation that was a dangerous threat to the very being of the church are thus checked... We are well aware where the church is, but fortunately we do not know where the church is *not*; who can limit or restrain the action of God's grace, which is all that matters for the salvation of

humankind? The visible, canonical boundaries of the church do not coincide with its invisible, charismatic boundaries. The mutual acceptance at least of the sacrament of baptism is already a confirmation or acceptance... of the action of the Holy Spirit beyond the... canonical jurisdiction of the church.

So it is important to live and think no longer against the other but "from the one to the other" in a "life-giving dialogue". First, this demands "mutual repentance": ecumenical reflection "requires transparency and purity of heart, its maximum ascetic purification". By means of this catharsis ecumenism "ceases to be an enterprise of conversion or the occasion for sentimental soft-heartedness". Observing that there is "a certain relationship" between spiritual attitudes and sacraments, Evdokimov went so far as to speak of an "ecumenical baptism". "It means dying to any spirit of imperialism, any attempt to impose our way of thinking, believing or living at any price."[9]

In this way Christians are brought together again in love, a truly ecumenical analogy to the "kiss of peace" in the Orthodox liturgy: "Let us love one another so that with one mind we may confess the undivided Trinity." Ecumenical love has a share in the trinitarian love which is the foundation of the church. It describes the spiritual realm where the Spirit can blow. If "the Holy Spirit is the great teacher of the church", as Cyril of Jerusalem wrote, the church with its charismatic structure is above all a "perpetual Pentecost".[10] Prayer for unity takes the form of an epiclesis; it implores the Father to send his Spirit to consume the superficial divisions and reveal the profound unity of the Body of Christ.

True ecumenical theology has to be contemplative because the contemplatives seek "the 'lived reality' of God in liturgical experience, the testimony of the praying and hence teaching church... The monastic communities are ecumenical places par excellence."[11] Being contemplative, this theology is necessarily concerned with the salvation of the world, its eschatological transfiguration. "The most urgent appeal for unity comes from the lost world, from its groanings, from its infernal dimension. It is striking that it is the saints who feel guilty for the hardened state of a world turned in on itself."[12]

The search for the salvation of the world and the search for Christian unity are inseparable. The salvation of the world requires Christians to offer together to those who are hungry, "not the ideological stones of systems, nor the theological stones of scholastic handbooks", but rather a truly eucharistic word which radiates both "the bread of the angels", the bread of the resurrection and of eternal life, and, "according to Origen's beautiful expression, the heart of a human brother offered as pure food".[13]

* * *

Evdokimov believed that Orthodoxy has a unique part to play in the ecumenical dialogue and the ecumenical service of humankind. Well aware of the historical problems of his church, he nevertheless knew that these conceal a providential reserve of mystery and adoration. The eucharistic unity of the church enables catholicity, spiritual fullness, "to enter our very being like a spring from which we come and draw our life". This free communion is the basis of the absoluteness of the individual: "The disorder... makes us suffer, but... at the same time it safeguards the uniqueness of every face and of its destiny."[14]

The contribution of Orthodoxy, for Evdokimov, is basically the living continuity of the Tradition ever since the Apostles and the Fathers, the testimony — foundation of everything — of the undivided church: "The East knew neither a Reformation nor a Counter-Reformation and it has preserved the undivided Tradition until today."[15]

"We are all united in front of a closed Bible," Evdokimov said. "As soon as we open it, our interpretations differ."[16] Orthodoxy has maintained the ecclesial and spiritual hermeneutics of the undivided church contained in the Fathers' reading of the Bible and the liturgy. Only the Spirit which rests on the sacramental body of Christ can constitute the "canon within the canon" of Scripture, to use an expression from contemporary exegesis. "The convergence we seek between Truth and Life can only be found by discovering the Tradition of the Fathers."[17]

Thus Orthodoxy invites other Christians to be reintegrated "into the one common stock". It calls them "to re-establish their links with their original kinship by breaking out of closed confessional economies". This in no way implies a "return" that would deny the creativity of the Spirit in the development of their churches, but rather a going back to draw on the original sources which are inseparable from the ultimate. "For theologians this means a conversion to the patristic style. Going back to the Fathers means going ahead, not imitating them but creating with them, in faithful continuity with their Tradition... It is a call to go beyond every 'fundamentalism'... towards the gushing spring of the living water of the Holy Spirit."[18]

* * *

Evdokimov concentrated initially on ecumenical dialogue with Protestants. Just before and just after the second world war the ecumenical movement was being structured into a council of churches which made possible encounter between the Protestant and Anglican world and the Orthodox; at the same time, Protestants in France were offering generous, disinterested hospitality to the Russian diaspora. Evdokimov occasionally took part in the discussions of Faith and Order and, as noted above, was closely involved with the Ecumenical Institute in Bossey. In his dialogue with Protestants and his work with CIMADE, he underlined the pneumatological and charismatic aspects of Orthodox ecclesiology, while emphasizing that these were rooted in the sacramental life of the church, so that prophetic speaking was not in conflict with the sacrament but presupposed it. His Orthodox testimony helped certain Protestant theologians and spiritual leaders to discover the mystery of the church, which assisted them in their own dialogue with Rome.

After meeting Dom Charlier, Evdokimov had several books published by Catholic publishers and won some faithful readers among French Catholics, especially contemplatives. He was invited to the Second Vatican Council, and from 1967 onwards he taught at the Higher Institute for Ecumenical Studies at the Catholic Institute in Paris. Gradually this experience, at a time when Catholicism was undergoing an enormous transformation, led him fully into a dialogue with the Catholics with a view to a union which could now become possible, a union which, far from rejecting the Protestants, would allow Rome to accept *its* Reformation: not by relativizing the mystery of the church — a temptation which many Catholics face today — but by entering into it in greater depth.

In the "postface" to his book on Christ in Russian thought, Evdokimov underlines that the Orthodox diaspora makes possible direct contact between the West and Orthodoxy today. "Returning together to the sources in the Tradition of the Fathers enables Westerners to discover their 'Eastern soul' and Easterners 'Western reason' with its dynamic universalism."[19]

The witness of Orthodoxy in the Western context today is first of all to freedom within communion, the inseparable union of mystery and liberty.

Second, Orthodoxy could render the service of counteracting the "new theologies" which threaten to undermine the very foundation of the faith, not with the obscurity of fundamentalism but with the experience of the resurrection, the liturgical experience which gradually permeates the inner being of the liturgical person. Beyond all knowledge, the ultimate meaning is to be found in the experience of those who, according to an old saying, "give their blood in order to receive the Spirit" — those who, during Easter night in Russia, respond joyfully to the hostile shouts of "God is dead" by saying, "almost as eye-witnesses" that "Christ is risen!"[20]

Third, at a time when the "death of God" seems to entail that of humankind, Orthodoxy persistently affirms the great mystery of divine humanity, of the God who became man so that man can become God. "Not the 'God alone' of a triumphalist, outdated theology, nor the 'man alone' of a worn out, flagging atheism, but a theology of the God-Man, of the cosmic Christ, giving back to nature and to humankind their ontological status of the Eighth Day, can speak to the people of today and respond to their thirst."[21]

In a very short statement which we wrote together in 1955, to announce the programme of a new Centre for Orthodox Studies in France, we said:

> The West of today is no longer a geographical area because its machines and mental mechanisms have invaded the universe; it is still a spiritual area, that of relentless humanity in the face of death... In this way the West opens the eyes of the Orthodox to their true riches, namely their true duties. This diverse unity which the West is seeking, this religion of faces which it senses beyond loneliness and despair — is this not what Orthodoxy means by the very mystery of the Trinity revealed... in free communion between persons...? The loving knowledge for which the world of reason pleads through its separations and which gnosticisms and drugs promise in a false peace of the impersonal — is it not... the sense of inwardness which culminates not in the dissolution of the individual but in a deifying face-to-face? And can this feverish exploration of the world from the atom to the nebulas, this totalization of humankind and its planet from prehistory to the crypts of the soul, lead to anything other than hell or Christ, the conqueror of hell, to the deified flesh of the one whose transfiguration is only waiting for us freely to adhere to it in order to reveal its universality?

NOTES

[1] "Quelques jalons sur un chemin de vie", in *Semences d'unité*, 1965.
[2] *Ibid.*
[3] *Ibid.*, p.14.
[4] *Ibid.*
[5] *Ibid.*, p.18.
[6] *Ibid.*, p.19.
[7] *Ibid.*, p.17.
[8] *Ibid.*, pp.20-21.
[9] *Ibid.*, pp.20-24.
[10] Quoted in *L'Esprit-Saint dans la Tradition orthodoxe*, Paris, Cerf, 1969, p.109.
[11] *Ibid.*, p.30.

[12] "Quelques jalons...", p.22.
[13] *L'Esprit-Saint...*, p.109.
[14] *L'Orthodoxie*, Neuchatel/Paris, Delachaux & Niestlé, 1959, p.41.
[15] *L'Esprit-Saint...*, p.107.
[16] E.g. "Quelques jalons...", p.23.
[17] *L'Esprit-Saint...*, p.106.
[18] *Ibid*.
[19] *Le Christ dans la pensée russe*, Paris, Cerf, 1970, p.215.
[20] *Ibid.*, pp.215-16.
[21] *Ibid.*, p.216.

BIBLIOGRAPHY

Works by Paul Evdokimov:

Le Christ dans la pensée russe, Paris, Cerf, 1970.
L'Esprit-Saint dans la Tradition orthodoxe, Paris, Cerf, 1969.
L'Orthodoxie, Neuchâtel, Delachaux & Niestlé, 1959.
"Quelques jalons sur un chemin de vie", in *Semences d'unité*, Paris, Cerf, 1965, pp.83-94.

Works on Paul Evdokimov:

Olivier Clément, *Orient-Occident, Deux passeurs: Vladimir Lossky et Paul Evdokimov*, Geneva, Labor et
    Fides, 1985.

Georges Florovsky
1893–1979

EMILIANOS TIMIADIS

I knew him from Oberlin Faith and Order (1957 ff) ... saw him often in Princeton

Georges Florovsky, the son of a priest, was born in Odessa in 1893. He graduated from the Faculty of Philosophy in the Crimea and taught for several years in public schools there before becoming sub-dean of his old university. In the political upheaval following the Revolution, he left Russia for Bulgaria. From 1921 to 1926 he was invited to lecture on the philosophy of law in Prague and thereafter was appointed professor of patrology at the St Sergius Orthodox Institute of Theology in Paris. He was ordained priest in 1932.

Between 1926 and 1948 Florovsky developed contacts with all the Catholic and Protestant ecumenical circles then in existence, notably with Karl Barth; and in 1934 he published a definitive comparison of ecclesiological streams in the West with those in Orthodoxy. Here he differentiated

the charismatic structure of the Orthodox understanding of ecclesiastical Tradition and the mystical character of the church as the Body of Christ from what he saw as the arbitrary, subjective and revolutionary teaching and interpretation of Protestantism, which undermines the catholic conscience and the oneness of the apostolic faith.

Florovsky became an eloquent and active spokesman for the Orthodox faith in many conferences and bilateral dialogues in Europe until 1948, when he put down his roots across the Atlantic, having been appointed professor of theology at the Orthodox Seminary of St Vladimir in New York. He was also a visiting professor at Columbia, Boston, Holy Cross, Harvard and Princeton and a guest professor at a number of other academic establishments.

From the ecumenical perspective Georges Florovsky was important as one of the most brilliant pioneering heralds of Orthodoxy to the West, revealing the inestimable treasures of our common faith, and pointing out the shortcomings and excesses of Western rationalism and determinism, Protestant exclusiveness and isolation and Roman claims to infallibility, with the inevitably resulting legalism.

Free from any narrow and restrictive theological formalism, Florovsky introduced a new and original patristic synthesis between the positive elements of the ancient Greek philosophy and culture on the one hand and the wisdom of the Cappadocian Fathers on the other. He saw ancient Greek philosophy as antechamber to and instructor for Christianity, and thus as rendering enormous service for our understanding of modern technology, secularism and other non-Christian ideologies or religions. Churches therefore become really ecumenical by seeing the many positive values of entering into dialogue with them. Such an approach enables them to see their partners not as hostile adversaries but as the heirs of certain treasures and, step by step, to be encouraged to reach the fullness of truth. The unity of humanity is a long process calling for continuous encounter.

Moreover, Florovsky avoided the trap of romantic neo-Christianity, a 19th-century current associated with Vladimir Soloviev (1853-1900), who established a philosophical system that sought to bring about a close association between Christianity and Platonism, thus unconsciously seeking to put more emphasis on gnostic perception. Among Soloviev's followers were Sergei Bulgakov (1871-1944), Pavel Florenskii (1882-1943) and Nicolas Berdyaev (1874-1948). Imbued with Platonism, all these theologians were forging a universal synthesis for a new version of Slavophile Russian Orthodoxy, to which they turned after a brief flirtation with Marxist socialism.

The temptation for the young Florovsky was great, for this was a time when many theologians were seeking to construct a Christian *Weltanschauung* at the root of the Western influence on Russian religious thought. Romanticism and Idealism became the points of reference for many people — influenced not only by Plato and Plotinus, but also by Meister Eckhart, Spinoza, Paracelsus, Hegel and Boehme. They saw the cosmos as an epiphany, a revelation of God, the being in which he realizes himself, unfolding in time, and eventually reuniting with the Absolute at the end of the cosmogonic-theogonic process. Moreover, they saw Christ as Sophia incarnate. Sophia, the feminine element in the divine, associates with Christ in time as she had in eternity.

There is no doubt that the personal experiences of these thinkers were essential to their new consciousness, their total commitment to Christianity and their hope to free their church from the bonds of the Constantinian era and help it to meet the challenge of atheistic materialism.

What some of these Russian thinkers brought along when they fled to the West was not Orthodox philosophies but rather a Russian version of German idealism. While some condemned this new current for its pretentiousness and for construing its own ideas as fixed ecclesiastical truths, Florovsky lamented the absence of a credible and reliable Christian philosophy in their writings. For this reason, he denounced them as strangers to Orthodoxy and said their opinions were the result of deliberate subjectivism, of a fondness for "theologizing".[2]

Amidst all this turmoil, Florovsky succeeded in holding the line and maintaining his balance. For the ecumenical family he was the first true interpreter of many controversial terms: *eros, agape*, the wisdom of God (*sophia*). He thus helped to prevent a proliferation of the crypto-gnostic views of Russians which were beginning to discredit the true mystical-ascetic teaching. He called attention to the contradictions created in Florenskii's theology by adopting the Augustinian idea that the Spirit is the unity of the love of the Father and the Son for each other, decrying such paradoxical theories as arbitrary and individualistic, placing their own conclusions above everything else and thus departing from the *symphonia* of the one undivided church.

How Orthodox teaching would have been misjudged by Western churches if such uncontrolled views had prevailed, without the corrective balance of the teachings of the true patristic tradition! Florovsky offered an undefiled, authentic picture of Orthodoxy as it entered the arena of ecumenical debate.

Florovsky addressed ecumenical bodies, confessional assemblies, the observers' forum at the Second Vatican Council and his mostly Protestant students at Harvard and Princeton with both well-founded arguments and amazing openness. Even his contacts with the most uncompromising integrists were never marked by aggressiveness or fanaticism. At the WCC's first assembly (Amsterdam 1948), pleading for a return to patristic thought, he highlighted the vacuum of the modern West, its permissive culture, its estrangement, rupture and isolation from the Tradition and, as a result, from the oneness of the church and from the fathers of our common faith.

Within the Commission on Faith and Order, he significantly pointed to the urgent need to study the theme of Tradition and traditions as it related to the nature of the church. In so doing, he was explaining what remains permanent and unchangeable despite the vicissitudes of history and what is subject to change and reformation. This became an agonizing challenge to the Reformation, by pointing out to Reformers past and present where *Reformatio* should stop — by remaining within the church, the place of security, renewal and spiritual growth — if it was not to deteriorate into *deformatio*.

Lucid, objective, deeply rooted in patristic-ascetic spirituality, critically minded, a richly gifted scholar in philosophy and theology, fully aware of the colossal expectations the West had of Orthodox thought, Georges Florovsky became an instrumental interpreter of Tradition in a new way. Always open, available, present at most ecumenical gatherings, often as the delegate of the Ecumenical Patriarchate, he participated in nearly all the important ecumenical gatherings in the 1950s and 1960s.

Thus he contributed enormously to setting the WCC on solid foundations and promising orientations. Georges Florovsky must certainly be considered one of the architects and builders of the World Council of Churches, an organization which is deeply indebted to him. He deserves the gratitude of all the servants of unity for his ongoing efforts towards the full unity of divided Christendom with an objective and faithful *martyria* of the Orthodox heritage in all its forms.

NOTES

[1] "The Catholicity of the Church", in E. Mascall, ed., *The Church of God*, London, SPCK, 1934.
[2] Cf. *The Path of Russian Theology* (Russian ed.), Paris, 1937, p.495.

BIBLIOGRAPHY

Works by Georges Florovsky:

Bible, Church, Tradition: An Eastern Orthodox View; Christianity and Culture; Creation and Redemption; Aspects of Church History; Ways of Russian Theology; vols I, II, III, IV and V of collected works, Belmont, MA, Nordland Publ. Co., respectively 1972, 1974, 1976, 1975, 1979.
"The Ethos of the Orthodox Church", in *The Ecumenical Review*, vol. 12, 1959-60, no. 2, pp.183-98.

Franklin Clark Fry
1890–1968

[handwritten: Baroted]

WILLIAM H. LAZARETH

[handwritten: I knew him first at meetings of the U.S. Conference of the WCC, at Buck Hill Falls, PA.]

Franklin Clark Fry was born in Bethlehem, Pennsylvania, on 30 August 1890, and died on 6 June 1968 in New Rochelle, New York. His father and grandfather were pastors, and he was a descendant of Heinrich Frey, a Swiss-German mechanic who had arrived in the colony of Pennsylvania about 1670.

He attended Hamilton College in Clinton, New York, where he was elected to the scholastic honour society Phi Beta Kappa. Following his graduation in 1921, he spent a year at the American School of Classical Studies in Athens, before attending Philadelphia Lutheran Seminary. In June 1925 he was ordained by the Lutheran Synod of New York and New England, and served as pastor in Yonkers, New York (1925-29), and Akron, Ohio (1929-44).

In 1930 he was appointed secretary of the Commission on Evangelism of the United Lutheran Church, a post he held until 1938. From 1934 to 1942 he served as a member of the denomination's Board of American Missions, and in 1942 he was elected to the Executive Board. From 1934 to 1938 he was also a member of the Board of Directors of Wittenberg College and held many board and committee posts in the Ohio Synod. The 1944 convention of the United Lutheran Church in America elected him as president to succeed Frederick H. Knubel, who had led the church since its founding in 1918. Fry held this position until 1962, then became president of its merged successor body, the Lutheran Church in America, where he served until his death.

Fry's ecumenical activity began in 1936 with membership of the national preaching mission and national Christian mission of the Department of Evangelism of the Federal Council of Churches. When the FCC was succeeded in 1950 by the National Council of Churches of Christ in the USA, Fry served as the chairman of its Policy and Strategy Committee. He was also one of the organizers of the Lutheran World Federation at Lund, Sweden, in 1947, thereafter serving as its treasurer (1948-52), first vice-president (1952-57) and president (1957-63).

In the World Council of Churches, Fry was vice-chairman of the Central and Executive Committees from 1948 to 1954 and chairman of both from 1954 to 1968. That unique recognition was richly deserved. Fry's exceptional skills as parliamentarian (Visser 't Hooft once wrote that Fry "knew all there is to be known about the technique of chairmanship"), drafter and diplomat, nurtured by a profound knowledge of the Holy Scriptures and the history of Christian doctrine, equipped him for decades of trustworthy ecumenical leadership throughout the world.

Germany awarded Fry its *Grosses Verdienst-Kreuz* in 1953 in recognition of his leadership in post-war reconstruction; Austria, in 1955, gave him its *Grosses Silbernes Ehrenzeichen mit Stern*. He was granted an astonishing 34 honorary doctoral degrees, including three from institutions outside the United States.

Fry was a gifted speaker, annually addressing literally hundreds of church, civic, educational and political groups (including as chaplain of the 1956 national convention of the Democratic Party). His 1956 presidential address to the convention of the United Lutheran Church in America unfolds some of the key ideas of this ecumenical pilgrim:

Unity is a gift from God. We do not create or achieve it. Here is the most fundamental fact of all, a truth which we need to understand clearly with our minds and hold firmly and obediently in our hearts. Like all the undergirding axioms of the Bible and of life itself, it is very simple. It is so simple that Christians often fall into irretrievable error by overlooking it; by not realizing that unity is as directly his gift as life, strength, love, joy, hope, yes even forgiveness. God is its source. Unity is a reflection of his nature. Whatever else the often used and sometimes abused text from John 17 means, it teaches that when our Saviour prayed, "That they all may be one; as Thou, Father, art in me, and I in Thee, that they also may be one in us," he spoke not only of the standard of unity, nor of its goal, but equally of its origin.

Unity is in Christ and, reciprocally, through Christ being in us. St Paul's haunting phrase "in Christ" is as practical as it is mystical. In it the secret of the unity of the church is unfolded a vital step further. All true oneness among Christians not only goes back to him; it flows from him. It is because we have one Lord that we also have one faith and one baptism. Every syllable in his classic declaration, "I will build my church," is heavy with meaning, but the first person singular looms high over all. The living, the being and the unity of the church are all in the "I".

One of the favourite dictums of Martin Luther was, "The Word constitutes the church". That is only another way of saying that Christ is its unitive principle. He is the one who is in the Word, and is its perfect embodiment. He makes the Lord's supper a sacrament by being really present in it. As he sends life coursing out from himself to all the members of his body, he binds them together. Well St Paul exclaims, "The bread which we break, is it not the communion of the body of Christ? For as it is one bread, so we being many, are one body, for we are all partakers of that one bread." To be in Christ is to be caught up by him into the new redeemed humanity, of which he is the head. It is to be with many brethren in the community of his resurrection.

Leading into unity, as well as into truth, is the work of the Holy Spirit. We Lutherans have tended to emphasize truth; sometimes we place such exclusive stress upon it that the other pole of the Spirit's magnetism has been obscured. Insistence upon agreement in doctrine as a precondition for church fellowship is the distinguishing mark of Lutherans among all Protestants, and should never be relaxed. Allegiance to Christ as the truth rules out indifference, or even a casual attitude, to the truths about him that have been revealed. Here we stand and we shall not renounce our conviction.

The Spirit, with equal dynamism, leads to the church. It is no coincidence that at the very hour when he descended, the church began; a Christian community was born, which because it was a community had unity as one of its inherent features. It is more than an accident of language that the word "church" appears in the New Testament in only two meanings, denoting the local congregation and a single universal church of God. The many, separated "churches" of today do not fit in the New Testament vocabulary, not only because they did not come into existence until a later period of history; the very idea of them would have been a jar to the apostles and evangelists who wrote as they were inspired by the Holy Ghost. "Is Christ divided?" was an absurdity to the mind of St Paul. The dividedness of the church does violence to the Holy Ghost who lives in it.

Unity, as a concept, is glorious. There is a reflection of God in it and a vital principle for his church. A matching, equally important value in it that we must not overlook is in what it does. Unity is not an ethereal, Platonic idea that floats high in the air; it has a practical mission in this world. God never gives any of his blessings simply for our own enjoyment, merely for us to keep to ourselves. Health is not for idleness but for productive work. Forgiveness is not to enable us to relax in a glowing feeling that we are the sons of God but to send us out to be little Christs to our neighbours. The peace in our hearts is to radiate out to all mankind. When nations containing many Christians with God's peace in them are not peaceful, unbelievers do not know what to make of it. They keenly sense the inconsistency and point the finger of shame. To be grateful and obedient, Christians must act on their gifts. "Ye are a royal priesthood," St Peter exclaimed in his first epistle, and then went on to say why: "that ye should show forth the praises of him who hath called you out of darkness into his marvellous light." Even God's old chosen people, unlike the other nations of antiquity, did not think of him as only a tribal deity, but recognized that the promised Messiah was to rule over all of humanity. All peoples would catch hold of their cloaks in order to ascend into the mountain of the Lord. Above the whole orchestra of the Holy Scriptures sounds Christ's own high priestly prayer: "That they all may be one... that the whole world may believe."

Unity is not an end in itself. Through it, at its best, God gives new life to Christians, a new glow to the gospel, a new flowering to the church, and a new and clearer witness to his Son.

BIBLIOGRAPHY

Although a talented writer, Fry's printed productions were limited to a vast volume of reports, newsletters, constitutions and a variety of official documents. He contributed sermons to *Great Sermons by Young Preachers* (1931), *Sermons on George Washington*, 1932, *From Throne to Cross*, 1940, *A Faith for These Times*, 1942, *Calling on All Christians*, 1942, *Best Sermons*, 1947-48.

Works on Franklin Fry:

R.H. Fischer, ed., "Franklin Clark Fry: A Palette for a Portrait", in *The Lutheran Quarterly*, supplementary no., vol. XXIV, 1972.
Mr Protestant, Philadelphia, United Lutheran Church in America, 1960.

Germanos of Thyateira
1872–1951

GEORGES TSETSIS

When a delegation from the Episcopal Church in the USA visited Constantinople in April 1919 to discuss plans for a world conference on Faith and Order with the Ecumenical Patriarchate, its itinerary included the renowned theological school on the island of Halki in the Sea of Marmara. There the delegation had a lengthy discussion with the dean, Germanos Strinopoulos, Metropolitan of Seleukeia. Their subsequent report of this encounter would prove to be prophetic:

> He is a keen and alert theologian and chairman of the special committee of the Holy Synod appointed to study the symbols and confessions of the Anglican Church and of the Protestant churches. He will doubtless occupy a foremost position in the World Conference matters. [1]

Developments in inter-church relations, the evolution of the ecumenical movement between 1920 and 1938 and the subsequent foundation of the World Council of Churches in 1948 bore out this assessment of Metropolitan Germanos and the role he would play.

Born in 1872 in Delliones, a village in Eastern Thrace, Germanos Strinopoulos enrolled in the Theological School of Halki in 1889, graduating with distinction in 1897, after submitting a dissertation on "The Ecumenical Church as Infallible Judge on Matters Concerning the Faith". In 1899 he was sent to Europe by the Ecumenical Patriarchate to further his theological knowledge. He studied at Strasbourg, Lausanne and Leipzig, where he was granted a doctorate in 1903 for a thesis on the philosophical theories of Hippolyte. Returning to Constantinople in 1904, he was appointed professor at Halki and became dean in 1907, a position he held until 1922. He taught dogmatics, symbolics, New Testament and catechetics. In 1912 the Holy Synod elected him titular Metropolitan of Seleukeia, but he retained his leading position at the school. Finally, in 1922, he was promoted Metropolitan of Thyateira. From his episcopal see in London he had jurisdiction over the Greek Orthodox diaspora of Western and Central Europe and served as personal representative of the Ecumenical

Patriarch to the Archbishop of Canterbury. Metropolitan Germanos passed away in London on 23 January 1951.

Germanos Strinopoulos had his first contact with the ecumenical movement as the representative of the Ecumenical Patriarchate at a conference of the World's Student Christian Federation in Constantinople in April 1911. Here he met several exceptional Christian leaders, including John R. Mott and Nathan Söderblom, who would later be his devoted co-workers in the ecumenical movement.[2]

N,ß

Metropolitan Germanos' decisive ecumenical contribution came in 1919, when the Church of Constantinople took the historic initiative of issuing an encyclical inviting world Christendom to establish a "League (*koinonia*) of Churches". This encyclical was the natural follow-up to two encyclical letters issued by the Ecumenical Patriarch Joachim III in 1902 and 1904, in which he pleaded for Orthodox unity and at the same time suggested the initiation of fraternal relationships and dialogue between the Orthodox East and the Roman Catholic and Protestant West, the Anglicans and the Old Catholics in particular.

On 10 January 1919 the Holy Synod of the Ecumenical Patriarchate decided to issue this new encyclical, following a statement by the *Locum Tenens* of the Ecumenical Throne, Metropolitan Dorotheos of Broussa, arguing in favour of a "*koinonia* of the churches":

> I think the time has already come for the Orthodox Church to consider seriously the matter of its union with the different Christian churches, especially with the Anglican, the Old Catholic and the Armenian churches. As the most significant announcement and recommendation for the union of the different nations in a League of Nations have come from the great Republic of the United States of America in the Western world, so I believe that the equally significant announcement and recommendation for the study on the approach and the union of the different Christian denominations in a League of Churches ought to come from the Great Church of Constantinople in the East. Our church therefore should take this initiative and, after a thorough study of the whole matter, she should give the signal for the union of all churches in Christian love.[3]

After an exhaustive discussion, the Holy Synod appointed the faculty of Halki, headed by Germanos as its dean, as a special commission to propose appropriate action. Many people, among them Visser 't Hooft, believed that Germanos played a key role in drafting the text, which was presented to the Holy Synod on 19 October 1919 and adopted with only some minor changes in wording. It was then forwarded "Unto all the Churches of Christ Wherever They Be" in the form of an encyclical letter in January 1920.   (1920)

N,ß,

In August of the same year, Metropolitan Germanos made his entry on the ecumenical scene when he travelled to Geneva for the meeting of the preparatory committee for the world conference on Faith and Order — and quite unexpectedly became involved in the preparations for the first world conference of the Life and Work movement.

The August 1920 meeting of the Life and Work preparatory committee was to have taken place without the participation of the Orthodox Church. Despite the strong stand taken by the Archbishop of Canterbury, Randall Davidson, that the conference ought to be "genuinely ecumenical", involving both Roman Catholic and Orthodox, and the conviction of Archbishop Nathan Söderblom that "to convene an ecumenical conference of Protestant churches involved a contradiction in terms",[4] the Swiss Protestant churches were in favour of common action whose primary aim would be to "unite

Protestants", and some persons within the Federal Council of the Churches of Christ in America, which was responsible for organizing the conference, opposed sending invitations to the Roman Catholic and Orthodox churches.

Apparently, however, Söderblom, who chaired the preparatory committee, disregarded the Federal Council's stand and cultivated the idea of associating the Orthodox in the Geneva meeting in one way or another. Taking advantage of Metropolitan Germanos' presence in Geneva for the Faith and Order meeting, Söderblom invited him, Metropolitan Nicholas of Noubia (Patriarchate of Alexandria) and Archimandrite Chrysostomos Papadopoulos (Church of Greece), to attend the Life and Work meeting as visitors. Metropolitan Germanos, responding to Söderblom's invitation, attended a session, where he spoke at length about the intimate relationship between the aims pursued by Life and Work and the goals set out in the 1920 encyclical. Thereafter Söderblom, "holding in his hand the encyclical, addressed the representatives of the Orthodox Church, emphasizing the similarities existing between the encyclical and the new plan, and proposed that the Orthodox Church be invited to participate in its preparation".[5] As Söderblom himself testified later, "it was a historic moment when the Orthodox churchmen entered the room in Geneva where the Universal Christian Conference on Life and Work was founded".[6]

This represented the beginning of the challenging and fruitful presence of the Orthodox Church in the ecumenical movement — a presence which has now lasted for seventy years. According to N. Karlström, "it was undoubtedly a bold stroke on Söderblom's part to invite the Orthodox churchmen to the Life and Work conference without previous discussion or authorization. It was a step taken in faith, and later developments have fully confirmed the wisdom of what was then done. Protestant and Orthodox churchmen entered into such a realistic experience of fellowship in the faith, as is the mainstay of Life and Work."[7]

At the world conferences on Faith and Order (Lausanne 1927, Edinburgh 1937) and Life and Work (Stockholm 1925, Oxford 1937), Metropolitan Germanos was the leader of and spokesman for the Orthodox delegations. As a member of the Committee of Fourteen (seven members from Faith and Order and seven from Life and Work) mandated to form a world council of churches, he played an active role in the Utrecht conference (1938), where decisions about the merger of the two movements into one World Council of Churches were taken. It was natural that he should be included in the Provisional Committee of the "World Council of Churches in Process of Formation" as vice-chairman.

At the inaugural assembly of the WCC (Amsterdam 1948), Metropolitan Germanos was quite naturally leader of the delegation of the Ecumenical Patriarchate and coordinator of the work of the Orthodox delegations. As W.A. Visser 't Hooft wrote, "He did everything that could be done to create relations of confidence between the Orthodox delegations and the delegations of other churches."[8] The assembly elected this ecumenical pioneer as one of the six presidents of the WCC, a position he held until his death in January 1951.

Metropolitan Germanos' forty years of devotion to ecumenical *diakonia* can be easily interpreted in the light of an address he gave in 1925 at the Stockholm conference of Life and Work. Explaining the reasons which prompted the Ecumenical Patriarchate to issue the 1920 encyclical, he spoke of his concept of church unity:

> Besides the narrower notion of unity which brings together the members of any single communion and makes of them one body, there is another wider view of unity. In that wider

unity, all who accept as a fundamental doctrine the revelation of God made in Jesus Christ, and who confess him as their Lord and Saviour, should not consider themselves as strangers one to another, still less as enemies, but as fellow-heirs and of the same body and partakers of his promise in Christ by the gospel (Eph. 3:6). [9]

Metropolitan Germanos was convinced that mistrust among churches can be overcome only when each church acquires a better understanding of the historical conditions under which other churches have developed. The ecumenical movement, he believed, is the ideal platform on which to build such mutual acquaintance. Certainly he was more than loyal to his own church and to its theological tradition. But he did not see loyalty to one's own tradition as an obstacle to cooperation between Christians of different denominations. On the contrary, he believed that "loyalty to one's own communion may even be conducive to cooperation when, together with the spirit of wider unity, the feeling is cultivated that each church is bound, in common with other churches, to strive for the solution of problems far beyond the power of any single church". [10] It was for this reason that he pleaded with his ecumenical partners at the 1927 Faith and Order world conference not to forget "that apart from all the points that divide us one from the other, there exists a common bond which binds all... and that is faith in our common Saviour and Redeemer, our Lord". [11]

Nearly seven decades later Metropolitan Germanos' conviction still preserves its freshness and relevance for the ecumenical movement.

NOTES

[1] *Report of the European Deputation to the Commission on the World Conference on Faith and Order*, 1919, p.7

[2] B. Sundkler, *Nathan Söderblom: His Life and Work*, Lund, 1968, p.98.

[3] See *Ekklesiastiki Alitheia*, 39, 1919, p.277; see also W.A. Visser 't Hooft, *The Genesis and Formation of the WCC*, Geneva, WCC, 1982, p.1.

[4] N. Karlström, "Movements for International Friendship and Life and Work, 1910-1925", in N. R. Rouse & S. Neill, eds, *A History of the Ecumenical Movement, 1519-1948*, 4th ed., Geneva, WCC, 1993, pp.535 and 538.

[5] Archbishop Germanos, "The Ecumenical Patriarchate", in *The Ecumenical Review*, vol. 1, 1948-49, p.88.

[6] N. Söderblom, *Mobilising the Forces of the Church*, off-print from *Goodwill*, 15 July 1926, p.88.

[7] Karlström, *op. cit.*, p.538.

[8] W.A. Visser 't Hooft, *Memoirs*, Geneva, WCC, 1973, p.255.

[9] Metropolitan Germanos of Thyateira, "Methods of Cooperation and Federative Efforts among the Churches", in G.K.A. Bell, ed., *The Stockholm Conference 1925*, London, 1926, p.628.

[10] *Ibid.*, p.629.

[11] "The Call to Unity", in H. Bate, ed., *Faith and Order: Proceedings of the World Conference, Lausanne, August 3-21, 1927*, London, SCM, 1927, p.23.

BIBLIOGRAPHY

Works on Germanos of Thyateira:

Anglican Commemoration of the Twentieth Anniversary of Archbishop Germanos' Arrival in London, London, 1943.

Gennadios of Heliopolis, "Metropolitan Germanos of Thyateira", in *Orthodoxia*, 26, 1951, pp.39-42.

V. Istavridis, *The Interorthodox and Interchristian Work of Germanos Strinopoulos Prior to his Promotion to the Metropolis of Thyateira*, Patriarchal Press, Istanbul, 1959 (in Greek).

A. Tillyrides, "Archbishop Germanos Strenopoulos and the Ecumenical Movement — Unpublished Documents", in *Texts and Studies*, vol. I, Thyateira House, London, 1982, pp.69-184.

W.A. Visser 't Hooft, *The Genesis and Formation of the World Council of Churches*, Geneva, WCC Publications, 1982.

Josef Lukl Hromádka
1889–1970

JOSEF SMOLIK

Josef L. Hromádka was born on 8 June 1889 in Hodslavice, Czechoslovakia, and died in Prague on 26 December 1970. Appointed professor of systematic theology at the John Hus Faculty in Prague in 1920, he remained there — except during the second world war — until 1964. Politically a strong supporter of the democratic ideals of Tomás Masaryk, the first president of Czechoslovakia, Hromádka first became known ecumenically as the recipient of the famous letter in which Karl Barth encouraged the Czech people to oppose Nazism. In 1938, just before the outbreak of the war, Hromádka went to the United States to teach at Princeton Theological Seminary, where he stayed until 1947.

It was Hromádka who was chiefly responsible for the unification of Lutherans and Reformed within the Evangelical Church of Czech Brethren. He attended the 1928 conference of the World Alliance for Promoting Friendship through the Churches and the Edinburgh world conference on Faith and Order in 1937, and was a member of the Faith and Order Commission until 1961. At the WCC's Amsterdam assembly in 1948, Hromádka defended the socialist experiment in a famous exchange with US Presbyterian (and later secretary of state) John Foster Dulles. Hromádka served three terms as a member of the WCC Central Committee.

During the Cold War, Hromádka founded the Christian Peace Conference (CPC) in an effort to prevent an escalation of East-West tension and to overcome the danger of nuclear war. Under his leadership, the CPC contributed to détente and eventually was to prepare the way for the development of democracy in Central and Eastern Europe. During Czechoslovakia's "Prague Spring" of 1968, Hromádka was actively involved in seeking to build "socialism with a human face". After the intervention of Warsaw Pact troops in August of that year, he protested that "the moral weight of socialism and communism has been shattered for a long time to come". At his funeral, WCC General Secretary Eugene Carson Blake called him "a man of hope":

For 21 years he was the strongest force in Eastern Europe in persuading his fellow churchmen to support, in faith and hope, their revolutionary socialist governments and societies. During these same 21 years he was the outstanding moral interpreter to the West of the vision of justice and peace that has inspired the best in the socialist nations.

Hromádka's message drew on the story of Israel and the story of Jesus of Nazareth as testified to by the prophets and apostles. The biblical stories take place within human history as "history-making factors", but they are simultaneously "beyond history". God's word is addressed to us in them as a "challenge which sheds new light upon our life from the cradle to the grave, opens our eyes to the perspective of the ultimate victory of the crucified and risen Lord and makes us realize his solidarity with other men, with the most destitute, miserable and filthy human creatures". Here is a challenge "to surrender our life to the Lord of the universe and history, the Lord present in the deepest depth of human misery, corruption and hopelessness".

In a certain sense, what the Apostle Paul said of himself in 2 Corinthians 2:2 can be said of Josef Hromádka: he resolved that he would think of nothing but Jesus Christ nailed to the cross. But Hromádka's situation was of course different from Paul's. Longing for the living charismatic communities to be found in the congregations of Paul's day, he encountered instead a church which was weary and tradition-bound, a church which he himself described as "spiritually lazy". "While so many people of the world are working hard, even to the point of exhaustion, many of our Christians only sit in their churches, moralize and pass judgments upon the world. This is what I call spiritual laziness... There is among Christians very much frustration due to the lack of love and expectation, resulting in defeatism and frustrated pessimism." The fire of faith had lost its original heat and the so-called Christian nations had fallen victim to the "spirit of scepticism and cynicism which permeates the area of traditional Christian society".

What is the message of the church of Christ in such a situation? What is its mission? For Hromádka, the testimony of Scripture is a powerful challenge which, although coming from beyond, penetrates so deeply into our personal lives, the life of the church and all that occurs in the world that it transforms everything. The most profound and basic transformation takes place on the personal level, when the individual has a revelation of "the unfathomable depth of divine grace, when by his unconditioned free mercy God unveils the majesty of the divine holiness and righteousness and makes us to live in penitence and forgiveness of sin".

Christians in the traditional churches need to ask themselves whether they really do believe. We may recite the Apostles' Creed or the Nicene Creed during the liturgy, but we go to the heart of these confessions of faith only when they penetrate into our personal life, transform our relationship to God and to our neighbour and shape our basic attitude. "We cannot understand what faith in Jesus Christ means unless we are fully engaged in all the difficulties, struggles, failures and victories of our present time." Convinced that our faith "must be relevant to ordinary daily life", Hromádka was sharply critical of the internal "rottenness" of a faith that uses ritual and liturgy as a means of escaping from our responsibilities in the world.

The horizon of faith is universal. Faith in Christ cannot be reduced to the personal relationship between the individual soul and God. On this universal, ecumenical horizon, Hromádka saw two immensely important problems in relation to the mission of Christians and of the church: the problem of secularization and the problem of the poor. His message is directed primarily to the church and people of the "Christian civilization" of the West, which bears the main share of responsibility for the situation throughout the world today. Seriously disturbed by the "disintegration of the historical unity of the Christian church and of what we call Christian civilization", he was even more disturbed by the question of "whether the Christian church, in all her historical manifestations and institutions, has preserved a creative ability to write a new chapter of history".

Hromádka had the courage to look reality in the face. He saw how the process of secularization permeates all areas of life through the scientific and technical transformations of our day. The secular meaning of the gospel was one of Hromádka's central themes. The radical secularization confronting his own church in a country with an atheistic ideology led him to reflect on *The Gospel for Atheists* (the title of one of his books), and also led him in the 1960s to devote a good deal of attention to Christian-Marxist dialogue. The question of whether the Christian message can hold its ground against the tide of secularization sweeping through the "Christian" nations in particular was one that he took seriously. He observed how the churches allowed themselves to be isolated and pushed to the margins of society by the process. He had no illusions about this. Yet he was still able to say:

> Secularization is for me no calamity. It may be providential, it may be a blessing if we understand its true meaning... Speaking about the providential and beneficial aspect of secularization I have in mind the fact that the Bible, both in the Old and in the New Testament, is a radical and continuous ferment of secularization — a struggle against superstition and magic, against gods and demons, against any mythical effort to create our own God according to our human pattern.

An understanding of the secular meaning of the gospel can help to reveal the true basis of faith.

The second burning issue for Hromádka was that of social justice, the problem of the poor. The gospel's preferential option for the poor became an urgent challenge for him long before the phrase became a standard item in the ecumenical vocabulary. It was a problem he encountered already as a theology student in Scotland, when he came into contact with slum life in Edinburgh. His friend Paul Lehmann recalled how Hromádka, speaking about his participation in the First Presbyterian Church in Princeton, "suddenly paused, and then with some exclamatory surprise at this discovery declared: 'But I do not find any poor people in this congregation! Where are they?'" The question of the poor, of where they were in society and in the church, never gave Hromádka any peace, which explains his lively interest in movements which struggled for social justice and also in the socialist experiments in Central and Eastern Europe. The latter he saw as a challenge to enter into a dialogue about the spiritual and moral foundations of Western democracy. He saw dialogue — and certainly not either a cold or a hot war — as the only means of resolving issues.

The ecumenical movement was for Hromádka a forum for discussions among Christians and churches throughout the world, and for the struggle for mutual understanding, peace, social justice, the elimination of the nuclear threat and the unity of the church. It was a community of pilgrims, *Communio Viatorum* — the title of a review which he founded. It was in discussions within the ecumenical movement that communities were formed which acted as models for what Christianity in this world ought to be: the leaven of a new age.

Hromádka was not subject to any illusions. He did not try to conceal from himself the crisis of both the world and the ecumenical movement. He was able to look history in the face because, with Jesus of Nazareth, he had descended to the depths of God's judgment and had found in the risen Christ a hope which would never fade. He believed that God's "yes" to the world, affirmed in the resurrection of Jesus Christ from the dead, is stronger than all the powers of evil.

We conclude our portrait of this ecumenical pilgrim by citing two passages from Hromádka's writings. The first comes from 1957:

> Our generation faces a situation almost totally different from that of the last 150-200 years. Many of the non-Christian nations are very old, with a highly developed ancient culture, older than the nations of Western civilization. They can look back to many treasures of poetry, literature, moral wisdom, philosophical thoughts and spiritual experience. However, in the years of European and American expansion they were weakened in their growth and creativity. Western science and critical thought, Western technical achievement and economic prosperity have produced in them a kind of inferiority complex and backwardness. Politically and internationally, they were driven to the margin of modern civilization.
>
> The self-complacency, self-righteousness and self-assurance of the so-called Christian nations have grown out of proportion to the real dignity, to the real human grandeur of Western nations. The nations of Asia (and more and more also in Africa) are coming of age. They are dropping their complex of backwardness. They are realizing their own dignity and a tremendous possibility of their own self-determination, freedom and prosperity. Hand in hand with this new historical situation is the revival of their spiritual, religious and philosophical heritage. We find ourselves at the point in human history when we have to face a provoking question of whether non-Christian nations are morally and spiritually not superior to the nominally Christian nations, whether our Christian decadence is not linked to the human renaissance of the peoples who until recently were looked upon as spiritually and mentally ignorant, who were considered dependent for the whole future on the leadership of the West...
>
> How much of moral misery and material destitution was prompted by contact between white invaders and the poor, miserable, Oriental man and, primarily, woman. To avoid any misunderstanding, I wish to stress many aspects of the political, social and spiritual influence on the part of the West that proved to be beneficial to the non-Christian nations. However, the present vitality of the people must disturb our attitude of pride and self-complacency. The future of Christian civilization depends on the vigour and integrity of our Christian self-examination, self-criticism and penitence on the one hand and, on the other, on our readiness to listen to what is going on in the non-Christian world, to open our eyes and ears to its expectations and aspirations.[1]

The second is taken from a lecture given by Hromádka at the 1962 European conference of the World Student Christian Federation in Graz, Austria:

> Let me repeat what is the essential and most relevant aspect of the gospel: the Son of Man, the Man of Sorrows, came to this world in order to give himself to man for his true humanity, for his liberation and redemption. He did not come to organize an exclusive religious group or sect or church institution. He came to the bottom, to the depth of humanity, beyond all boundaries of race and culture, of religion or social or political order. Everything in him was concrete, real, nothing purely abstract and impersonal.
>
> However, in his concrete personal and spontaneous attitude to man — man with his sin and error, with his weakness and powerlessness, with his ordinary hope, work and aspirations — he broke down all the divisions between races and nations, cultures and political institutions, and revealed the ultimate dignity and destiny of man in spite of all darkness and confusion, of all the terrible crimes and destitution, in spite of all frustration

and unbelief, hopelessness and despair. Jesus Christ as we know him from the gospel is inclusive, not exclusive. He is the divine *Yes* and the divine *Amen*. It is a wonderful divine *Yes* to man in his guilt and misery. We have to understand it in its simple reality, in its secular dress.[2]

NOTES

[1] From "The Present Age and the Crisis of Christian Civilisation", in M. Opocensky, ed., *The Field Is the World: Selected Writings of Josef Hromádka, 1918-1969*, Prague, Christian Peace Conference, 1990, pp.324ff.
[2] From "Hope for Man", in *ibid.*, p.338.

BIBLIOGRAPHY

Works by Josef Hromádka:

Doom and Resurrection, London, SCM, 1945.
The Field Is the World: Selected Writings of Josef Hromádka, 1918-1969, M. Opocensky, ed., Prague, Christian Peace Conference, 1990.
Thoughts of a Czech Pastor, London, SCM, 1970.

Works on Josef Hromádka:

D. Neumarker, *Josef L. Hromádka*, Munich, Kaiser, 1974.
J. Smolik, ed., *Von Amsterdam nach Prag: eine ökumenische Freundesgabe an Josef L. Hromádka*, Hamburg, Herbert Reich, 1969.

Akanu Ibiam
1906–

MODUPE ODUYOYE

One would have to look far and wide to find someone anywhere in Africa who, during the independence decade of the 1960s, moved from being headmaster of a school to governor of a region. But the invitation to be the first Nigerian governor of the Eastern Region came to Francis Akanu Ibiam while he was principal of Hope Waddell Training Institution in Calabar.

One would also have to look far and wide in Africa to find a fully qualified medical doctor working as the principal of a secondary school. Again, Francis Akanu Ibiam was the exception. In 1957 the Church of Scotland Mission called him away from his post as missionary doctor in charge of its hospital at Abiriba to be the first Nigerian to head Hope Waddell Training Institution, their premier secondary school, where Ibiam himself had his own first three years of secondary schooling.

As principal there, Francis Akanu Ibiam was at the height of his missionary and ecumenical career. He had been president of the Christian Council of Nigeria from 1956 to 1958. To all intents and purposes he was the host of the All Africa Church Conference in Ibadan in January 1958, where the decision was taken to form the All Africa Conference of Churches. Having founded the SCM in Eastern Nigeria in 1937, he was elected the first national president of the Student Christian Movement of Nigeria at its first national conference in Onitsha in December 1958.

Upon completing his medical studies in Scotland in 1936, Ibiam had written to the Board of Foreign Missions of the Church of Scotland that he wanted to become a missionary doctor, preferably among his own people in Igboland in Nigeria (he was only the third Igbo to qualify as a medical doctor). His application created some perplexity in the circles of the Church of Scotland Mission: it was one thing to receive applications for missionary assignments in Africa from English or Scottish candidates — or, indeed, even from people of African descent from the Caribbean. It was something else to receive one from a well-qualified African who wished to be sent home as a lay missionary among his own people. Ibiam for his part could not understand why his British SCM colleagues could qualify as missionaries to Nigeria while he could not. Declining job offers with the British colonial civil service in Nigeria, he eventually got what he wanted: the Church of Scotland accepted him as a missionary and assigned him to medical work in Itu. As a result, from 1936 to October 1960, Ibiam worked as a Church of Scotland missionary doctor in his home country and grew to be a leading elder of the Presbyterian Church of Nigeria.

In 1939 Ibiam took another step which was unusual for an Igbo man at that time: he married a Yoruba woman, Eudora Olayinka Sasegbon, whom he had met while completing his secondary education at King's College, Lagos. After her secondary education at Queen's College, Lagos, she trained as a dispenser and midwife in England at the time her future husband was doing his medical studies in Scotland. The couple formed an ideal combination for the pioneering Christian mission in Abiriba; and the work they did won Ibiam a British knighthood in 1951. From then on, until he renounced the title during the Nigerian civil war, we heard news of the work of Sir Francis Ibiam in Abiriba, away from the limelight of Lagos or even of Enugu.

When D.C. Nwafo, dean of the School of Medicine of the University of Nigeria, wrote Ibiam's biography, he entitled it *Born to Serve*. Ibiam's spirit of serving and not counting the cost became legendary. What Albert Schweitzer did in Lambarene, Francis Ibiam did in Abiriba. Indeed, in his early days as a missionary doctor he rode around on a bicycle.

Ibiam was elected to the presidium of the World Council of Churches at its third assembly (New Delhi 1961). Four years later, as governor of Eastern Nigeria, he hosted the WCC Central Committee meeting in Enugu. He was also elected to the presidium of the All Africa Conference of Churches at its first assembly in Kampala in 1963. He was one of the elders selected by the AACC to intervene in the civil war in Sudan. Once, returning from a peace mission to the Sudan, his plane landed in Lagos. Since this was a time when the federal government of Nigeria was already in conflict with "Biafra", Ibiam was asked if he had not been anxious about what would happen to him as an Igbo leader landing in federal territory. He said he had no anxiety at all, for "if anyone had touched me in Lagos, that person would have been lynched". So sure was he of his pan-Nigerian credentials in a country of ethnic allegiance.

Ibiam is a simple and straightforward man for whom life is religious and moral. A lover of sport (he captained the soccer team at Hope Waddell and at King's College and played soccer and hockey for the University of St Andrews), he nevertheless urged the government to ban Sunday football matches. When Igbo people returned from Northern Nigeria in September 1966 with bruises and corpses, he reacted in righteous indignation against the brutality and supported the view of Colonel Odumegwu Ojukwu that there was no longer any place for the Igbo in the Federation of Nigeria. He did not resign his governorship; in fact, it is said that he composed the Biafran national anthem, giving it a hymn tune. During the civil war he campaigned for recognition of the Republic of Biafra, a name which he is said to have suggested. When the British government supported the federal side in the civil war, he renounced his British knighthood and dropped the English name Francis. Ever since then he has been known as Akanu Ibiam.

Ibiam's undoubted status as a community leader led to his nomination for a seat on the legislative council of colonial Nigeria in 1947 and to the governorship in 1960. In 1983 he was elected the Eze Ogo Isiala I of Unwana, his home town on the Cross River. As soon as he became a traditional ruler, the Imo State Council of Chiefs elected him their chairman. In 1990, still active at 84, he led Igbo chiefs to request the federal government to create two more states in Igboland, and the government created Enugu State and Delta State.

His condition for accepting the office of traditional ruler was that his coronation be performed during a Christian service, with the Rev. Dr Inya Ude of the Presbyterian Church placing the crown on his head. For Ibiam is not a man to compromise his Christian principles. He has preached Christ by the example of his life and work — as one who serves — for fifty years. He has never been a politician seeking votes: he has always been a statesman.

Ibiam was the founder and first president of the Bible Society of Nigeria, which replaced the British and Foreign Bible Societies in 1966, and has supervised the second round of Bible translations into Nigerian languages going on at present. The first translations were missionary translations; this series is sponsored by local committees with the participation of Catholic, Protestant and Pentecostal churches. In 1979, when Adeolu Adegbola constituted the Board of the Centre for Applied Research in Religion and Education, he invited Akanu Ibiam to be one of the two patrons. In this role of patron — he is also life patron of the Student Christian Movement of Nigeria — Ibiam has moved already in his lifetime into the role of "ancestor", providing lasting inspiration to all who would follow him who came "as one who serves".

Like John R. Mott, Ibiam is a "layman extraordinary". I have no evidence that he ever developed a theology of the priesthood of all believers: his Presbyterianism took care of that and he simply lived it. But he definitely thought deeply about what it meant to be a missionary. His ecumenical pilgrimage, therefore, followed the missionary trail. A total commitment to the vocation of missionary doctor tied him to acting locally. That he was thinking globally at the same time is evident from the fact that he founded the SCM in Eastern Nigeria not from a seat in an institution of higher learning but from a location in a rural missionary medical outpost. As a missionary doctor in rural South-Eastern Nigeria, he found in the teachers in the surrounding missionary schools the "students" he needed to continue the fellowship he had enjoyed in the University of St Andrews. If Nigeria in the 1950s had one of the most active SCMs within the World Student Christian Federation, it is thanks to Ibiam, who would not wait until Nigeria had its first university college before planting the student ecumenical movement in Nigeria. This demonstrates his belief in social development from the grassroots up; yet this deep commitment to the grassroots did not prevent Ibiam from becoming chairman of the council of the University of Ibadan or governor of Eastern Nigeria or one of the presidents of the World Council of Churches.

Today Akanu Ibiam lives in Unwana. There he can be found guiding his people as their chief — their most respected son, their most esteemed father. The title "Eze Ogo" means a noble of eagle rank (high chief). His concern for the welfare of that little place is total — completely ecumenical, non-sectarian, non-partisan. The Federal Polytechnic at Unwana is named the Akanu Ibiam College of Technology; the sports stadium of the University of Nigeria in Nsukka is the Akanu Ibiam Stadium; in Enugu there is the Lady Ibiam Women's Conference Centre.

For his 80th birthday in 1986, I drove from Ibadan with a greeting card signed by members of the Ibadan SCM senior friends group to present it to him in Unwana. Somewhere beyond Owerri the police on traffic duty stopped me and asked me for my automobile documents. One of them was missing. Normally I would have been booked and asked to report the following day, and the following day, and the following day. After some delay, during which I was thinking of ways of escaping from the grip of these law enforcement officers, I went to the car and took out the large greeting card and told the constable: "Look, I am going on a pleasant mission. I don't want this type of thing to ruin the pleasure. I have come all the way from Ibadan to deliver this to Dr Ibiam." He looked at it, went and conferred with his boss and came back and said, "You may go."

I had a similar experience during the tense period in 1966 prior to the Nigerian civil war. Colonel Ojukwu had advised all Igbo people to return to Igboland and all Nigerians from outside to leave the Eastern State. As general secretary of the Nigerian SCM, I had an invitation to visit the SCM of the University of Nigeria in Nsukka. The permit I needed to enter the Eastern State had not arrived. But I had written to Ibiam and had received his reply that I should come anyway. At the Asaba-Onitsha bridge, the police asked for my permit to enter the Eastern State. I had none, but I said, "I have to visit our branch of the SCM at the University of Nigeria in Nsukka. The students are waiting for me. I have a letter from Sir Francis Ibiam." When I produced the letter, I was allowed to drive across the bridge and I showed that letter all the way to Nsukka. At the bridge, on my way back, the soldier said; "What are you doing here at this time?" When I told him why I was on the other side, he said: "I advise you not to come back." And I told him, "If the students invite me again, and if I have a letter from Sir Francis, I will come back again."

BIBLIOGRAPHY

By Akanu Ibiam:
"Thirty Years as a Missionary Doctor", in *The Nigerian Christian*, August 1972.

Works on Akanu Ibiam:
Agwu Kalu, *Dr Ibiam: The Challenge of His Life*, Aba, Presbyterian Church of Nigeria, 1986.
D.C. Nwafo, *Born to Serve: The Biography of Dr Akanu Ibiam*, Lagos, Macmillan Nigeria, 1988.

John XXIII
1881–1963

TOM STRANSKY

Angelo Giuseppe Roncalli began his pilgrim-age on 25 November 1881, born of very poor farmers at Sotto il Monte on the Italian slopes of the Alps. Throughout his life he would refer to the poverty of his youth with affection, though seldom with nostalgic romanticism: a small house complex for the close-knit extended family; rarely fewer than thirty people around the table, on which there was "never bread, only a dish of polenta, and home-made cake only at Christmas and Easter"; "clothes and shoes for going to church had to last for years and years"; share-cropping work in the fields from morning to night (half of the produce to the landowners). Too many in too small a space, but Roncalli liked to recall the Lombardy proverb: "God blesses big pots more than small ones."

Roncalli confessed that he could never re-member when he did not want to be a priest. The village pastor at first discouraged him: "Angelino, you see how high and sharp this collar is. It digs into the neck and sometimes really hurts." Angelo would wear it. Shortly before his twelfth birthday he entered the junior seminary in nearby Bergamo, then the major seminary, concluding his studies in Rome's Apollinari in 1904 with a doctorate in theology and priestly ordination. His 82 years would be filtered through a single vocation — seminarian, priest, archbishop-diplomat, cardinal patriarch, pope. [1]

In the diocesan seminary of Bergamo, he began in 1906 to teach church history — his life-long intellectual passion. Roncalli was never disposed to float in a sea of ideas and systems of thought, preferring to walk about the grounds of history with women and men who had incarnated ideas and ideals. [2] The saints were his friends. From them "one must take the substance, not the accidents, of their virtues... I must not be the dry, bloodless reproduction of a model, however perfect" (Journal, 1903). His diary and letters repeat his favourites: Joseph ("my chief protector"), Isidore, Francis de Sales ("my model... oh, if I could really be like him"), Gregory the Great ("one of the most brilliant jewels of the Roman pontificate"), Bernard of Clairvaux, Charles

Borromeo, Phillip Neri, John Berchmans ("my patron saint"), Ignatius Loyola, Thomas Aquinas; above all, Mary.

In 1910 he became full-time secretary to the bishop of Bergamo, Giacomo Radini-Tedeschi. A pastoral reformer, especially in the area of Catholic social action, he always remained for Roncalli "my bishop", and the two of them were so strong-minded in the defence of the rights of the working class that they were suspect in some Vatican circles as "too socialist".

As a young priest Roncalli devised detailed "rules of life" according to a tradition-stamped model which he continued to observe even when pope: rising at 5.30 in the morning for at least 15 minutes of "mental prayer", Mass, chapel visits to the Blessed Sacrament, rosary, reading a chapter from the *Imitatio Christi* of Thomas à Kempis and evening examination of conscience; weekly confession and monthly counsel from a spiritual director; and an annual retreat when he went through a check-list to spot faults and back-slidings.

In 1915 after Italy stumbled into an unpopular world war, Roncalli was called up for military service as a chaplain in Bergamo's army hospitals. This raw experience at the beds of wounded and dying young men led the ex-chaplain in 1920 to preach: "War is and remains the greatest evil, and one who has understood the meaning of Christ and his gospel of human and Christian brotherhood can never detest it enough. It would be naive to expect very much from war as a contribution towards the moral progress of people."

In May 1919 Pope Benedict XV issued the encyclical *Maximum Illud* on the new demands of missionary activity in the much-changed postwar world. One of its fundamental principles was that every Catholic is called to support worldwide missionary activities by prayer, sacrifice and finance. To develop this consciousness in Italian Catholics, Benedict called Roncalli to Rome as the first national director of missions. The assignment widened his vision of the church, as did his foreign travel for consultations with mission organizations in France, Belgium, Germany and the Netherlands.

There are no private or public indications that ever plotted his steps up the ecclesiastical ladder, yet his horizons continued to broaden. In 1925, newly conse-crated archbishop, he left Italy as the first Vatican diplomat to Bulgaria. In his retreat notes before his episcopal ordination (March 1925) he wrote, "I have not sought or desired this new ministry; the Lord has chosen me, making it so clear that it is his will and that it would be a grave sin for me to refuse. So it will be for him to cover up my failings and inadequacies. This comforts me, brings tranquillity and confidence." He could say the same thing at every future change in church positions. The episcopal motto he chose for himself was *Obedientia et Pax*. The path to peace lay through obedience.

Most Christians in Bulgaria belonged to the Bulgarian Orthodox Church (then in schism with Constantinople); the minority were Catholics, both Latin (48,000) and Byzantine Slav (14,000); and there was also a sizeable Muslim population. Before Roncalli left Rome, the Vatican secretary of state, Cardinal Pietro Gasparri, informed him that "the situation in Bulgaria is very confused... Everyone seems to be fighting with everyone else: the Muslims and the Orthodox, the Greek Catholics and the Latins, the Latins with each other. Could you go there and find out what's happening?" Roncalli soon discovered his superior's description to be an understate-ment.

Here the archbishop began his ecumenical apprenticeship among the Orthodox laity, clergy and hierarchy.[3] He took the initiative to visit the Ecumenical Patriarch Basil III in Constantinople in March 1927. He reflected on the visit in a letter to a friend: "What a great thing it is to understand and show compassion... How times have changed! Catholics are impelled by charity to hasten the return of the brethren to the unity of the one fold... by charity — this rather than by theological discussion."

The theme is charity, the language is of "return". Roncalli's ecclesiology was solemnly articulated in Pope Pius XI's *Mortalium Animos* (1928): "There is only one way in which the unity of Christians may be fostered, and that is by promoting the return to the one true church of Christ [the Roman Catholic Church] of those who are separated from it." Home is Rome. And for Roncalli, the charity of Catholics was the precondition for the return.

The Bulgarian ministry was not easy. Roncalli's private notes in 1930 record his "uncertainty... about the exact scope of my mission in this country". The "difficulties and trials" of the first five years had brought "no consolation save that of a good conscience and the rather sombre prospect for the future", which convinced him that "the Lord wants me all for himself along the royal road of the holy Cross". He loved to quote St Francis de Sales: "I am like a bird singing in a thicket of thorns." During his retreat in 1935 he asked himself: "What has Msgr Roncalli been doing during these monotonous years at the apostolic delegation? Trying to make himself holy and with simplicity, kindness and joy opening a source of blessings and graces for all Bulgaria, whether he lives to see it or not." *Obedientia*, yes, but one suspects that he was constantly warring within himself to reach the *pax* during the ten hard and rather lonely years in Bulgaria.

Roncalli then moved further east, spending the ten years from 1935 to 1945 in Istanbul as Apostolic Delegate to Turkey and to Greece. He had direct responsibility for the bewildering variety of 35,000 Catholics in and around Istanbul: "Latins" of various nationalities — French, Italian, German and Austrian; and Eastern Catholics of various "Uniate" churches — Armenians, Chaldeans, Syrians, Maronites, Melkites, Bulgarians and Greeks.

After only three weeks in Istanbul Roncalli concluded the Octave of Prayer for Christian Unity with an appeal for greater harmony and unity among Catholics: "The church is not bound to this or that nation, but to all nations... In Jesus' church there are no first- or second-class citizens." Disunity among Catholics, indeed among all Christians, was a "laceration of the divine plan". He saw his ministry first to unify his own flock, then to seek good relations with the 100,000 or so Eastern Orthodox who clustered around the Ecumenical Patriarch Photius II. Soon he realized that he should enlarge "good relations" to include not only the observant Muslims but also those "Young Turks" who were trying to break the Islamic power of the caliph and mullahs in Ataturk's ruthless creation of a thoroughly secular state.

Roncalli quickly became known for his diplomatic skills amid hostile nationalities, governments and religious factions, and for his practical charity towards various social groups. He personally met with many Orthodox laity and prelates in Turkey and in Greece. He attended the funeral of Photius II in January 1936, and that same month first met with his successor, Benjamin, who later arranged for Roncalli's visit to the monasteries on Mount Athos in Greece. Greece he experienced as an even greater challenge than Turkey, writing to his mother in May 1936: "There are so many things to fix in this country; but since the people are all Orthodox and are frightened of the

Holy See and the Pope, one has to act slowly, cautiously and with extreme sensitivity."

Yet his life was far less monotonous, far more upbeat than in Bulgaria. During his annual retreat in December 1937, he noted that his usual routine now allowed him only two hours of undisturbed work, at night. And he resolved: "The exercise of pastoral and fatherly kindness, such as befits a shepherd and father, must express the whole purpose of my life as bishop. Kindness, charity: what grace is there! 'All good things came to me along with her' (Wisdom 7:11)."

His diplomatic style was modelled on the gospel, not Machiavelli: "Above all I wish to render good for evil, and in all things try to prefer the gospel truth to the cunning of human politics." Such a method, without guile in practice, laid a firm foundation for the next phase of his diplomatic activity during the grim years of the second world war. Turkish neutrality made Istanbul a meeting-place for all contending sides. In diplomatic and humanitarian work, in particular among prisoners of war and refugees, especially Jews, Roncalli tried to remain faithful to the resolution in his 1940 journal: to be "above all nationalistic disputes". He saw his mission as "a teacher of mercy and truth" with "principles and exhortations from my lips and encouragement from my conduct in the eyes of all — Catholics, Orthodox, Turks and Jews". He admitted to himself that God gave him "a natural inclination to tell the truth, always and in all circumstances and before everyone, in a pleasant manner and with courtesy, to be sure, but calmly and fearlessly. Certain small fibs of my childhood have left in my heart a horror of deceit and falsehood."

As the war was drawing to a close, Roncalli preached on Pentecost 1944 that "we all can find plausible reasons for stressing differences in race, religion, culture or education". Catholics in particular like to mark themselves off from others — "our Orthodox brothers, Protestants, Jews, Muslims, believers or non-believers". But "in the light of the gospel and of the Catholic principle, this logic of division does not hold. Jesus came to break down all barriers. He died to proclaim universal brother-hood. The central point of his teaching is charity, that is, the love which binds all to him as the elder brother, and binds us all with him to the Father." He prayed for "an explosion of charity".

Late in 1944 Roncalli left Turkey for Paris, as the Vatican nuncio to France. "Once again my motto *Obedientia et Pax* has brought me a blessing," he wrote in his 1945 retreat. His primary task was to heal the divisions between the victorious followers of De Gaulle and the discredited compromising bishops of the Vichy regime. He had frequent contacts with Orthodox, Protestant and Catholic promoters of church unity, especially with his old friend Lambert Beauduin, the Benedictine liturgist and ecumenist. He was also the Holy See's first permanent observer to UNESCO, headquartered in Paris.

His retreat notes from the end of his third year as nuncio revealed that the 66-year old was simplifying his spiritual reading habits. Serious devotional books were becoming a distraction. "I am now quite content with the Bible, *Imitatio Christi* and Bossuet's *Méditation sur l'Evangile*. The holy liturgy and sacred scripture give me very rich pasture for my soul." He resolved to be even more attentive to chapel visits to the Blessed Sacrament, the devotional Way of the Cross, the breviary's office for the dead and the frequent recital of the penitential psalms. And he affirmed what is best suited to "my own temperament and training": "I leave to everyone else the superabundant cunning and so-called skill of the diplomat, and continue to be satisfied with my own bonhomie and simplicity of feeling, word and behaviour."

In 1953 Pius XII appointed Roncalli as archbishop of Venice. Diplomatic titles and life-style were gratefully left behind. In May, after two months as cardinal patriarch of the island and the surrounding mainland, he wrote in his retreat jottings: "Providence has brought me back to where I began my priestly ministry — pastoral work, ministering directly to souls... To save souls and guide them to heaven — that is the church's final purpose... The arc of my humble life... rose in my native village and now curves over the domes and pinnacles of St Mark's." Happily Roncalli resumed what fitted him best — direct pastoral ministry, especially with the working class. He initiated reconciliation with anti-clerical socialists. His 72 years and "the short time left to me tempt me to slacken my efforts... I will not give in. The Lord's will is still my peace."

On his visits to Rome, required by his membership of three curial congregations, he felt not even a tinge of envy towards his colleagues on the Tiber. He quoted a former patriarch of Venice, Giuseppe Sarto (later Pope Pius X): "I prefer to be a cardinal in the forest than a cardinal in a cage."

When Pius XII, pope since 1939, died on 8 October 1958, Cardinal Roncalli found immediate comfort in the image: "We are not on earth to be museum-keepers, but to cultivate a flourishing garden of life and prepare a glorious future." He packed two bags for the conclave, but would never return to Venice. On 28 October his fellow cardinals elected him pope — intentionally, it appears, to have a lull with an elderly, mere transitional person at the helm: Roncalli was 77.

John XXIII had different hopes. Only three months into his pontificate, on 25 January 1959, the last day of the Octave of Prayer for Christian Unity, and without prior consultation, he announced his intention to convoke "an Ecumenical Council for the Universal Church". The idea was "a spontaneous inspiration which hit us as a sudden and unforeseen blow in the humility of our soul".[4] The Second Vatican Council would become Roncalli's major achievement. He called it a "new Pentecost."

Included in Pope John's initial hopes for the event was "an invitation to the separated communities to seek again that unity for which so many souls are longing in these days throughout the world". He gradually clarified his intention, perhaps even to himself, by shifting from a "reunion council" to one of the internal renewal of the Roman Catholic Church. The language is still "return", but the "true home" needed to be more of a home.

In June 1960 John XXIII established the Secretariat for Promoting Christian Unity (SPCU), with the elderly German Jesuit biblical scholar, Cardinal Augustin Bea, as its president (the same age as the pope), and Monsignor Jan Willebrands from the Netherlands as its secretary. The fledgling SPCU arranged the first face-to-face meeting since the Reformation between a pope and the head of another Christian communion: in December 1960 John XXIII met with Archbishop of Canterbury Geoffrey Fisher. The visit set the precedent for what have since become normal acts of Christian courtesy.

Under Pius XII the most public symbol of Rome's deliberate distance from the ecumenical movement had been the refusal to have Roman Catholics present in any role, no matter how "unofficial", at the two first assemblies of the World Council of Churches — Amsterdam (1948) and Evanston (1954). But Pope John now approved the SPCU delegation of official observers to the third assembly in New Delhi (1961), and he later invited the Orthodox, Anglican and Protestant churches to delegate observers to Vatican II. He eliminated anti-semitic expressions in the Good Friday liturgy, and initiated the placement of Catholic-Jewish relations on the council's agenda.

His annual retreat notes in the period preceding the opening of the Council reflect his thoughts and feelings:

> The maxim "know myself" suffices for my spiritual serenity and keeps me on the alert... The whole world is my family. This sense of belonging to everyone must give character and vigour to my mind, my heart, my actions (*December 1959*). The course of my life over these two years... shows a spontaneous and whole-hearted intensification of union with Christ, with the church and with the heaven which awaits me (*December 1960*). I feel like St Martin who "neither feared to die, nor refused to live"... Everyone calls me "Holy Father" and holy I must and will be... Charity is the virtue which comes most easily to me; yet even this sometimes costs me some sacrifice and I feel tempted and roused to show an impatience from which, unknown to me, someone may suffer... Now more than ever, and as long as I live, and in all things: *obedientia et pax* (*August 1961*).

In September 1962, a month before he would formally open Vatican II, he intended his private retreat "to fix my thoughts on spiritual matters", with an ordered six days: Monday, faith and hope; Tuesday, charity; Wednesday, prudence; Thursday, justice; Friday, fortitude; Saturday, temperance. He admitted that he "was the first to be surprised at my proposal [of a Council], which was entirely my own idea... After this everything seemed to turn out so naturally in its immediate and continued development... We are now on the slopes of the sacred mountain."

By 11 October, when he formally opened the Council, "good Pope John" had already won the affection of Catholics and non-Catholics alike. He did so by doing what he did best: being himself. Transparently wide-hearted and affable, humble about his own gifts and limitations, he diminished the cult of the aloof pontifical personality, self-imprisoned in the Vatican. As bishop of Rome, he restored the neglected tradition of visiting the city's parishes, hospitals, schools and prison.

John XXIII's principal contribution to Vatican II was not its content but its spirit and conduct, best expressed in his opening address: a contagious confidence that the Roman Catholic Church needed serious *aggiornamento* (updating) in order to be faithful, an optimism about the action of God in the world as seen in "the signs of the times", and a conviction that the church should "use the medicine of mercy rather than severity" and that since error is best dissipated by the force of truth, dialogue cannot begin or end with mutual fulminations.

Two days later, 13 October, the 38 delegated observers from almost all the other Christian communions met with Pope John. He asked them to read what was in his heart more than in his familial words. He briefly outlined his own life with its providential encounters with other Christians. He calmly confessed that "never in my soul has been a desire to be directed to such a function or such a ministry. My response has been always my motto: '*Obedientia et Pax!*' and '*Blessed be the Lord day after day, the God who saves us and bears our burdens!*'" (Ps. 68:19).

Although he did not attend the general deliberations during the first session of Vatican II, he did intervene at a critical point to support the desire of the majority for a completely new draft on revelation and scripture and empowered Cardinal Bea's SPCU to be a co-drafter. Some historians have suggested that this act marked the end of the Counter-Reformation.

During that session, the pope never even hinted, publicly or privately, what his doctors had bluntly told him in mid-September: he had inoperable stomach cancer and his months were numbered. In that same autumn, the world came to the brink of nuclear war over the Cuban missile crisis between the United States and the USSR. These circumstances prompted the dying pope to begin what would become his last will and testament — *Pacem in Terris*, the first-ever papal encyclical addressed not to the church alone but also "to all people of good will".

The papal letter advocated human freedom and dignity as the basis for a world order of peace with justice, and it proposed that a proper philosophy of law should be based on the necessary conformity between human legislation and the will of God. The pope pleaded for an end to the arms race, the banning of nuclear weapons and the negotiating of a general disarmament. True to his own disposition and experience, he believed that "the signs of the times" were more positive than negative, and that even enemies "could be domesticated, brought within the range of civilized discourse, reminded of their humanity".

On Holy Thursday, 11 April 1963, when he promulgated *Pacem in Terris*, the pope talked simply about it to the assembled diplomatic corps: "This is the day on which the lips of Christ pronounced the words, 'Love one another' (John 15:12). For what I wanted to do above all was to issue an appeal to love for the people of this time. Let us recognize the common origin that makes us brothers, and come together!"

The long ceremonies of Holy Week were a torture. His journal records: "I came through Ester well enough, though with considerable pain... *Pacem in Terra* [sic] acclaimed more than ever... Unbroken pain that makes me seriously wonder about my chances." He would have none. He knew he would not see the Council's conclusion. To a close cardinal-friend he said: "Now I understand what contribution to the Council the Lord requires from me: my suffering." And to another he confided: "At least I have launched this big ship — others will bring it into port."

On the early evening of the Monday after Pentecost, 3 June 1963, his life slipped away. The "mere transitional pope" had in less than five years launched a new era in Roman Catholicism, indeed in modern Christianity.

NOTES

[1] Already in 1895 Roncalli began entries in a diary which he entitled *The Journal of a Soul*. This life-long spiritual discipline followed the recommended tradition of frequent recording for only his eyes and God's: graces received and resolutions made (especially during the annual retreat), pious sighs of spontaneous prayer and striking maxims gleaned from readings. In 1961 he reluctantly permitted his secretary, Loris Capovilla, to publish the journal posthumously, because church historians "will want to know everything I have written; my soul is in these pages". From the first entry to the last (1963), his journal — and private letters — reveal the pilgrimage of one who never felt awkward with his traditional Italian Catholic piety, in fact so "conservative" that many reviewers were puzzled that such a spirituality could produce such a "modern person".

[2] For example, he never published theological analyses of the Council of Trent, but over the years he patiently edited and published in five thick volumes (1936-57) the records of the episcopal visitations of St Charles Borromeo, archbishop of Milan from 1565 to 1584. Borromeo was tirelessly committed to carry out Trent's pastorally reforming decrees in catechetics and preaching, liturgy, seminary training and religious life among the priests, religious and laity of his sprawling diocese. "If I could inspire the souls of our clergy with the example of St Charles," Roncalli wrote in 1909, "it would do much to increase their eagerness for apostolic work, to the greater spiritual advantage of the whole diocese."

[3] Accompanying him at first as temporary secretary was Dom Constantine Bosschaerts, recommended by his Benedictine prior Dom Lambert Beauduin.

[4] In his retreat notes of August 1961 he wrote that when he became pope at the age of 77, "everyone was convinced that I would be a provisional and transitional pope. Yet here I am... with an immense programme of work in front of me to be carried out before the eyes of the whole world, which is waiting and watching."

BIBLIOGRAPHY

Loris Capovilla, personal secretary and confidant to Angelo Roncalli in Venice and in the Vatican, is the literary executor of Pope John's papers. He edited *Il Journale dell'Anima* (Roma, 1964), and included more materials (1967) for the English version, *Journal of a Soul*, tr. Dorothy White (London, 1980 [revised]). Archbishop Capovilla, besides publishing *Pope John's Letters* (Rome, 1978), opened all the archives for Peter Hebblethwaite's research on his *Pope John XXIII* (London, 1985), with extensive bibliography.

Alexis Kniazeff
1913–1991

GENNADIOS LIMOURIS

The life of Alexis Kniazeff was closely linked with the community of Russian immigrants exiled in France and in particular with the Orthodox Theological Institute of St Sergius in Paris.

Born on 16 April 1913 in Baku, on the shores of the Caspian Sea, Kniazeff spent only a brief period of his childhood in his native land due to the Russian Revolution. In 1923, at the age of ten, he came to France, first to Nice, where there was a large Russian community, and later to Paris. In Nice the young Alexis met Alexander Eltchaninov, an elderly Russian priest whose spirituality and strong personality had a great influence on his commitment and faithfulness to the Orthodox Church and his decision to serve the church for the whole of his life.

Although Kniazeff eventually became a French citizen and was even involved in the politics of his new country, his heart remained forever Russian. He admired the Russian imperial family, in particular the family of the last czar Nicholas II for their martyrdom; and he was an irreconcilable anti-communist. He never returned to his native country, despite many invitations, saying that he did not want to visit "the land which was spoiled by communists". Even so, he followed with particular interest the political situation in Russia, always prayed for "a new political revolution and democratic change" and for many years wore two watches so he would always know what time it was in Paris and in Baku. This was an "expression and a sign" of his heart which remained forever "the Russian heart of a little child".

In 1924 his family established itself in Neuilly, near Paris, and the young Alexis continued his studies at the Lycée Pasteur and later at the Faculty of Law in Paris. After several years of working for insurance companies, he decided in 1938 to study theology at St Sergius and to commit himself entirely to the service and diakonia of the church.

At St Sergius he met such eminent Russian professors as Sergei Bulgakov, Kassien Bezobrazov and Cyprian Kern. He began his own teaching career there in 1942 by giving courses in dogmatics, but he felt a new vocation after meeting Antoine Kartacheff, who instilled in him a love for the Old Testament. Fr Alexis became a unique specialist in Orthodox circles, and for almost fifty years, until his death in 1991, he taught Old Testament, canon law, Hebrew, hagiology and Mariology. Ordained a priest in 1947, he later received all the honorary grades of the church (archpriest, protopresbyter). In 1965 he became dean of the St Sergius Institute and rector of the St Sergius parish, both positions he kept until his death.

After Kern's death, Fr Alexis continued, in collaboration with the famous Roman Catholic liturgist Fr Pierre-Marie Gy, to organize and convene the annual *Semaine d'études liturgiques* (Week for Liturgical Studies) at St Sergius, which continues until today as one of the major ecumenical gatherings in Paris. During this ecumenical week specialists in liturgical matters from various countries and different Christian churches and denominations meet to study various aspects of liturgy and liturgical texts from an ecumenical point of view. Fr Alexis used to describe it as "the annual meeting of the ecumenical friends of the St Sergius Institute". As records of this event report, "at the opening of the conference, when Fr Alexis called the roll of participants and referred to those friends who had passed away during the year, he was always very moved and tears came to his eyes, saying that 'we have lost one or two more of our old friends, but new ones have joined us'".

Primarily, though, Fr Alexis was a pastor of the soul. In addition to his pastoral responsibilities at the institute and in the parish, he served tirelessly for more than thirty years as the chaplain of the *Action chrétienne des étudiants russes* (youth camps of the Christian Association of Russian Students), teaching catechism, presiding over worship services and preaching every day.

Besides his doctorate, which he received from St Sergius in 1954, he was awarded honorary degrees by St Vladimir's Theological Seminary in New York and the Orthodox Theological Faculty of Presov, Slovakia. He spoke English, French, German, Greek, Hebrew and Russian.

Although he seldom travelled abroad, particularly in his later years, Fr Alexis had a special interest in the ecumenical movement. He was one of the Orthodox observers at the Second Vatican Council and was an active member of various ecumenical bodies in France: *Association œcuménique pour la recherche biblique* (Ecumenical Association of Biblical Reasearch), *Association chrétienne française des études bibliques* (French Christian Association of Biblical Studies), *Bibliothèque œcuménique scientifique des études bibliques* (Ecumenical Scientific Library of Biblical Studies), the Orthodox Brotherhood of France and others.

For many years he lectured on Orthodox theology at the Ecumenical Institute of Paris. He participated in ecumenical meetings and conferences in France and was invited to lecture by Roman Catholics and Protestants. He had many close friends among the great pioneers in the ecumenical movement.

His greatest involvement in ecumenical circles in France was his active collaboration in the ecumenical translation of the Bible, the *Traduction œcuménique de la Bible* (TOB). As an expert in the Old Testament and the Hebrew language, his participation in this significant masterpiece was highly valued.

But Fr Alexis was not simply a scholar and professor. He was also an open-minded person with a vast knowledge of many issues. His law studies at the famous university of the Sorbonne had given him a particular way of thinking and analyzing theology, and he never abandoned his personal theological and scientific research.

Yet his great passion was teaching; and hundreds of students became his faithful disciples, among them future patriarchs, pastors, lay theologians, faithful of God and servants of the Orthodox Church from all around the world: Greeks, Serbians, Lebanese, Russians, Americans, Romanians, Ethiopians, Arabs, Japanese and others.

Fr Alexis had a particular love for confessing and for celebrating the divine liturgy. The altar was for him a source of spiritual nourishment, and he always recommended to new priests that they worship daily, as he did, not only as a matter of liturgical education, but also as a spiritual link with the church and its theology. He had an extremely wide knowledge of liturgical texts and church order, and he told his students that he drew his theological thinking from the liturgy and the altar through his meditation on liturgical prayers and texts.

A profound and remarkable preacher, Fr Alexis was always faithful to the gospel message, and his words flowed out of a deep and rich knowledge of the Holy Scriptures and liturgical and hymnological literature. He sought to transmit the gospel lesson to the hearts of the people by bringing in the contemporary situation and relating the message to the problems that humanity presently faced.

A fitting illustration of this is from his homily on the Old Testament story of Jonah:[1]

Here we have a man trying to hide from God, trying to escape from the face of the Lord. He plans his escape by way of the sea, on board ship. It is an attempt not without a certain charm, like a children's game. But, at the same time, it is also a striking archetype of the human adventure, the "sign" of Jonah.

Jonah's escape route runs up against the unyielding limits of nature itself. When the sea refuses to give the runaway any chance of refuge, Jonah risks the ultimate "leap". The value of the "sign" is, above all, in the way it marks the limits of this final estrangement — the belly of the fish, the monster, the last stage in the flight from God, the pit, the depths of hell. "The waters closed in over me; the deep surrounded me; weeds were wrapped around my head at the roots of the mountains. I went down to the land whose bars closed upon me for ever" (Jonah 2:5f.).

And there, faced with those mystical frontiers in the chaos of the belly of the fish, Jonah comes to the end of his flight — and the end is, of course, God. In the belly of the great fish Jonah discovers that he is precisely in the place where he had no wish to go to. But now he knows what it is that he had denied and what it is that he had been seeking in his flight. He has marked out a way: Jonah is now a pointer, a "sign".

The human adventure of running away from God takes on many forms. There are many ships, many routes, and all of them have the same childlike naiveté, the children's game. And they always come up against the same unyielding boundaries of nature. Even though not all dare to push their flight to the furthest point, the illusion of having reached the extremities follows every attempt at escape. That is why the belly of the great fish, that limit where revelation takes place, the experience of the depths of the abyss, is never the necessary end of the flight. It remains only a "sign".

In the memory of the church the "sign of Jonah" recalls the event of Easter Eve. The sign prefigures Christ. Those who follow humankind to its final limits of flight come to the furthest depths of humankind's distance from God, to take into the divine life the response of humankind's revolt at their extreme point, in the abyss. Three days and three nights in the heart of the underworld like Jonah — a "Trinitarian" time, always present and non-dimensional — at the supreme limit of self-abandonment.

And this descent into hell is the resurrection. Christ tears Adam and Eve out of the hell of punishment and death; the keys of Hades are destroyed; the bonds of the condemned are loosened. All these inexpressible things, foreshadowed by the "sign", are expressed in Byzantine iconography.

Thus Jonah becomes the archetype not only of our flight, but of our salvation as well. "This generation… asks for a sign, but no sign will be given to it except the sign of Jonah" (Luke 11:29). A God unapproachable in the exaltation of his splendour is a God whose greatness is irrelevant to humankind who knows by experience the depths of hell. However splendid his manifestation, however objective the sign which imposes acceptance and submission, it is not enough to remain human in their ignorance. And that is why, although the objective silence of God is often the pretext for our flight, such a "sign" will not be given.

If humankind is to recognize the divinity of God, it must feel it to be co-extensive with their own deepest exigency. In this dimension of death, of the plumbing of the depths of the underworld, the boundlessness of God's love appears. A God "disfigured with injuries" is yet "in all things victorious". Humankind becomes like Jonah, following the tracks of Jonah's flight, transforming their escape into encounter and koinonia. The unyielding frontiers of nature are abolished by a love which is beyond any dimension; God and the abyss of humankind's despair become "one body". Jonah becomes one with the belly of the great fish. This "sign" is indeed the sign of salvation.

NOTE

[1] This text is written on the basis of notes I took during my studies at St Sergius in 1974.

BIBLIOGRAPHY

Fr Alexis wrote innumerable theological articles, sermons, interviews and other contributions (published in many French and Russian journals). His master works are the two publications on *L'Institut Saint-Serge: de l'académie d'autrefois au rayonnement aujourd'hui 1925-1975*, Paris, Beauchesne 1974, and *La Mère de Dieu dans l'Eglise orthodoxe* ("The Mother of God in the Orthodox Church"), Paris, Cerf, 1990.

Hendrik Kraemer
1888–1965

ALAIN BLANCY

Hendrik Kraemer was a genuine self-made man, owing to his personal, passionate endeavour to become both a fighter for a great cause and a go-between across frontiers. His way was not solitary but personal in all respects. He never left indifferent those who crossed his path.

Born in Amsterdam into a poor emigrant family from Germany, he was soon orphaned. After being shifted about in the wider circle of family and friends, some of them committed socialists, he finally ended up in a narrowly religious Reformed orphanage. At 14, searching for the meaning of life, he began to read the Bible for himself and indeed even put forward a plan to transform the house into a community.

These two early influences moulded his life and behaviour. At the age of 12 he prophesied: "I shall be a Christian or a socialist." He had only to change the "or" into an "and" to enable him to state much later: "I have become both: socialist as a Christian, and Christian by the grace of God." His Christianity would never be introverted, backward-looking or narrowly church-centred. He never separated church and world. At the end of his career he settled in the centre he helped to create in Driebergen, the Netherlands, shortly after the second world war, named after its programme *Kerk en Wereld* — "church and world".

The circumstances of his youth meant that Kraemer did not receive a normal secondary school education. When he was 16, a missionary from Papua New Guinea awakened his own missionary vocation, and a year later he entered a missionary training school to prepare for service in Indonesia, then a Dutch colony. He taught himself the Latin he had missed. At the end of the course, however, he did not pass his final examinations, having failed dogmatics, never his favourite subject. With zeal — and this time with excellent results — he resumed his studies at the University of Leiden, now in the field of linguistics, concentrating on Indonesia. Again, because of a shortage of qualified teachers in certain fields, he taught himself the missing courses.

Meeting men such as J.H. Oldham and John R. Mott drew Kraemer into a more immediate form of missionary activity in the Student Christian Movement, of which he soon became a prominent leader in his own country. This enabled him to move from a more pietistic faith to a committed, pioneering witness in church and society, an in-depth struggle with the immediate challenges of the world on his own doorstep. Consequently, he would never be simply an "export" missionary, doing nothing about the effect of foreign mission on his home church, so badly in need of renewal. It also prevented him from being merely a representative of the West in the East. Kraemer could be open to unexpected innovations and to the God-given directions to be found in any given, often confused, religious, social or political scene, confused as it might be.

The first world war made him feel the extent to which God tries the Christian church in the crucible of the world's turmoil, preparing for a spiritual combat through the birth-pangs of a new world. The Christian's task is to read the signs of the times, and instead of giving way to relativism and indifference, to mobilize new energies for social renovation. Kraemer learned to combine a deep rootedness in the faith with great openness to others. In theology and church practice, he never fell prey to either narrow orthodoxy or a wishy-washy liberalism. Tradition and modernity are in tension, but they are inseparable. Witnessing to one in the other, and listening to the challenge of the latter to actualize the former was his outstanding personal and public endeavour. A dispute, in writing, with a fellow woman student, led Kraemer to discover his future life companion, Hyke van Gameren. Another indication of the vocation of reconciler was aroused by his failed attempt to bridge the gap created by the war in meeting first with British and then with German student groups.

His tireless study, travel and visits to student groups badly affected his health. Depression followed and thereafter his life was plagued by insomnia. And yet this health problem, like so many other trials, strengthened rather than weakened his work.

Kraemer never followed the normal path: as a missionary, he became a linguist; as a theologian, he remained a layman; as a churchman, he became involved in the world; as a committed Christian, he became a man of dialogue; as a scholar, he was known as a barefooted wandering guru; as a Dutchman, he gained universal insight into the Christian calling through missionary work.

* * *

Hendrik Kraemer never in fact became a missionary. His assignment in Indonesia was to counsel missionaries in the face of the crisis arising from the yearnings of the growing nationalist movement for independence, a fact largely ignored by the European-led churches, and to supervise new Bible translations. He soon became aware of the real plight of the missions in Indonesia. On his way there he had spent a few months of study in Paris with the Islam specialist Massignon. He also spent four months at the Al-Azhar University in Cairo, and soon became recognized as an open-minded orientalist.

This was to become an outstanding feature of Kraemer: first to listen, then to understand, finally to be in empathy with his partners. Sensing the nationalists' antagonisms to the European colonial power and the confusion of mission with colonialism, he endeavoured to liberate the gospel from its Western cultural captivity. This meant taking seriously not only the local situation but also the issues to be faced, helping to find solutions from the point of view of the gospel, in and at the service of people's true liberation.

For more than six years Kraemer travelled throughout Indonesia visiting local missions and parishes. His primary interest, however, was to respond to the challenge of Islam, a challenge abandoned by a mission facing setbacks. He discovered that religion is not a simple belief or other-worldly orientated hope, but a life-encompassing cultural reality which structures the totality of people as individuals, a nation and a state.

The gospel must work from the inside out in any given culture if it is to produce its liberating power. Each people has a right and duty to inculturate the gospel according to its own culture. In order to do this there must be a twofold shift: the mission churches should themselves become independent, and their leadership should be well trained in local seminaries and theological schools. These two goals became Kraemer's lasting endeavour. As a result, these churches would be prepared for the war and post-war situation after the missionaries had been expelled and the countries had gained their independence.

During his first furlough, Kraemer went to Jerusalem for the 1928 conference of the International Missionary Council. The issue at stake was how to handle the command to "evangelize the world in this generation" in the face of a divided mission. The question of the value of the other religions in comparison to Christianity arose. Kraemer made the point that the gospel is not a value but a historical reality related to the incarnate one who alone is the Way, the Truth and the Life.

On his way back, Kraemer visited India, where he gained insight into the differences between stern Islam and the softer Hinduism, each of which was having to come to terms in its own way with the impact of modernism on tradition, for which nationalism was the outlet. Nationalism, however, could not be an end in itself; Kraemer wanted to move from this outer condition of freedom to an inner conviction of God's mandate in and for a new situation.

Back in Indonesia he resumed his twofold task as visiting counsellor and overseer of Bible translations, promoting both the education of locally trained theological leadership and the spread of national and foreign Christian literature in translation.

A conflict concerning Bali, an island which the Dutch colonial government closed off to any foreign mission in order to preserve its culture (and the growing tourist interest in its folklore), shed light on Kraemer's efforts to ensure that only indigenous mission should be permitted and supported. He did not believe that mission should destroy local culture; on the contrary, he wished to see culture prosper under a new sign, that of Christ's gospel. He knew that the unavoidable Western influence would, in any case, disrupt old ways. He wanted people to be aware of this and to cope with it in a responsible way. Here again he took the middle road between an idealization of the past and the ideology of the future, between falling prey to worn-out tradition or to dazzling modernism.

Behind his combat was the conviction that religion aims only at human self-achievement, not at living under the grace of the God who is ever-present and active in history. Salvation will come neither through religion nor through culture but to both through God's revelation and action in history, as manifested in the gospel of Christ. But to grasp what the gospel is and provides, one must first become aware of one's own plight and endeavour. Not in the weakness but in the strength is the point of contact for God to come in. No one is the object of the gospel without becoming its subject. This precondition means that mission must labour hard in order to become acquainted with the partner's position.

* * *

Returning from Indonesia in 1935, Kraemer was asked to write the preparatory document for the 1938 world missionary conference in Tambaram, India, in 1938. An experienced mediator was needed between the different streams of theology and missiology. More than ever, the key issue was the value of religion. Is Christianity just another religion among several? How could relativism, which would cast off mission, be overcome? Kraemer had barely a year to carry out this work. In between, however, he made a trip to the USA and attended the second world conference on Life and Work in Oxford in 1937. Thus Kraemer was prepared for writing his most famous book, *The Christian Message in a Non-Christian World*.

For Kraemer the non-Christian world encompassed secularized Europe as well as the religious East, and the Christian message is the gospel's call in a time of crisis. The crisis of the world is the crisis of the church. The answer lies not in theology but in revelation, and revelation erupts in history. Totalitarian systems, whether secular or religious, are anthropocentric in scope; the Christian message by contrast is in essence theocentric, yet it is at the service of humankind. There is no confusion between God and humanity, but God is the only one to care for human salvation. Mission is only to bear witness to God's deeds. Religions are a yearning for what they do not grasp; their restlessness is a sign of God's leaven working in them.

Only gradually did Kraemer's vision begin to trickle down in church and in mission. After further travels in South Asia, he was called to be professor of history and phenomenology of religion at the University of Leiden, a position he held for the next ten years. Once again he was almost a barefoot professor, more on the move making contacts with the base than in his study. Knowledge was only conceivable in relation, thinking in dialogue, theologizing in an effective environment. Theology is science only if it is also prophecy, that is, at the service of him who is beyond all science. Kraemer's empathy for religions, however, never led him to fall prey to syncretism. Indeed, he fought to have the neutral faculty of religious sciences, as it was called, stand up to its consciously Christian witness. At the same time, he rejected the solution of creating a separate church seminary. He never wanted to avoid a confrontation between theology and science.

The outbreak of the war and the occupation of Holland by Nazi Germany led to the closing of Leiden University when the faculty protested against the introduction of the "Aryan paragraph", resulting in the dismissal of Jewish professors. Kraemer sided unhesitatingly with those who were persecuted. The church was called to demonstrate openly what it believed, whom it obeyed and to whom its faith witnessed.

Aware of the low spirits of his divided home church and its unpreparedness to respond properly to the challenge, Kraemer saw a new mission field opening up, similar to the one in Indonesia. His aim was to rebuild the church from bottom up, from the local congregation up to the synod. He entered and transformed an existing church renewal movement, inspiring it with both a sense of mission and of ecumenism. Yet once again his voice failed to break through the walls thrown up by a self-satisfied church leadership bogged down in narrow organizational issues. The apostolate to a world in distress commanded by God did not move the masses, still less their leaders.

The "Rebuild the Church" movement was inspired by the Confessing Church in neighbouring Germany. The future of the church depended on whom it served: God or Baal. This was the sole issue to be faced. Kraemer understood that recovery could come only from below and from the vast reserve of the laity, emphasizing that he himself was a layman.

During the war Kraemer, together with a number of other prominent Dutch leaders, were taken into custody as possible hostages. This was another trial which he turned to positive use. His encounters with other leaders of the resistance from church and society led to lasting friendships and cooperation. One of the fruits of this was that after the war he joined the Socialist Party whose leader he had met at that time.

The renewal movement changed its title to "Ecclesial Edification". A complete network was set up not only to put pressure on the synod but also to encourage parishes to become involved in forms of training and other action. Kraemer knew that the battle must be fought on the ground, yet despite his passionate involvement, he always avoided becoming involved in petty disputes or hidden underground activities. His combat was open when necessary, but he could hold back patiently for long periods.

As in Indonesia, Kraemer travelled back and forth throughout the Netherlands to arouse parishes from their lethargy and turn them once again into real communities, a witnessing koinonia.

At the end of the war, Kraemer and Eykman created the Driebergen institute *Kerk en Wereld*. Its aim was to break down walls between church and society and, more pointedly, between Christianity and socialism or, in church terms, between the former orthodoxy and liberalism. Kraemer fought against the individualism that was so dear to Protestants. For him the social responsibility of the church's message was of prime importance. He took the side of Indonesian independence, despite outright opposition from the church and the government. He knew not only of the power of nationalism but also of its right to exist. He knew that God will not abandon a people come of age, nor will he resign from his task as the Master of history, even within independence. God's ways are not our ways. The first victory to be won is over oneself, one's own pride and false superiority. It was the same message in the Netherlands as in former colonized Indonesia.

* * *

The variety of experience Kraemer had accumulated made him an ideal candidate for his final major assignment: director of the newly created Ecumenical Institute in Bossey, near Geneva. W.A. Visser 't Hooft had had a vision of this institute as a place of confrontation and reconciliation between churches torn apart or severed from society, and in 1946 he called on his well-known compatriot to bring this vision to life. Together with the remarkable French ecumenical pioneer Suzanne de Diétrich, Kraemer entered into a lasting teamwork in which the reconstruction and reconciliation of badly damaged churches, first in post-war Europe and soon worldwide, could take place.

Laity was the first target at Bossey, but leadership could not be ignored; and Kraemer never dreamed of playing one off against the other. Bossey would offer the opportunity for confrontation between laity and clergy, faith and science, church and society in a combination of study, community life and prayer. This was a vision taken directly from the experience in the field and the struggles in real situations which Kraemer had lived through and fought through.

The "equipping of the saints", as the letter to the Ephesians puts it, was at the core of Kraemer's endeavour to renew and unite churches in their God-given mission in and to the world. The task of enabling people, churches and nations to mature was central to this task. For this reason theologians and scientists, clergy and lay people, male and female, people of East, West, South and North were on an equal footing at Bossey. The international, interdisciplinary and inter-religious scope was never to be forgotten.

To be sure, nothing can ever succeed totally. Kraemer knew of the weight of the human heart, its laziness, its fear of going on. While he never gave way to resignation, his own experiences of failure made him aware of the limits — which were also the stimuli — of a never-ending battle. Despite — or perhaps precisely because of — his hard work and stern commitment, he had acquired the necessary sense of humour. First and foremost, however, this lay person had a deep sense of pastoral care, which he never refused to anyone in need, tending to anticipate those who were in need of it thanks to his long, widespread human knowledge.

Retirement in 1955 in no way represented a retreat. Up to the end, while living in Driebergen, Kraemer went on writing, visiting and speaking. A follow-up book to the Tambaran conference, *Religions and the Christian Faith* (1956), grew out of a lectureship in Geneva. Last but not least, we should mention his book on his principal concern: *A Theology of the Laity* (1958).

* * *

A few excerpts from Kraemer's best-known work. *The Christian Message in a Non-Christian World*, give some of the flavour of the rich and provocative thinking that emerged along his own "ecumenical pilgrimage":

> The Bible offers no religious or moral philosophy, not even a theistic or Christocentric one. It is rebellious against all endeavours to reduce it to a body of truths and ideals about the personality of God, the infinite value of man, the source of ethical inspiration... The intense religious realism of the Bible proclaims and asserts realities. It does not intend to present a "worldview", but it challenges man in his total being to confront himself with these realities and accordingly to take decisions... The essential message and content of the Bible is the living, eternal-active God, the indubitable Reality, from whom, by whom and to whom all things are (pp.64-65).
>
> The Christian faith stubbornly refuses to be treated as a specimen of religious specula-tion, a set of ideas about God, man and the world, which affords an explanation of the world and life... Not the mystery of his being or essence is revealed, because that remains God's exclusive domain, but his redemptive will towards mankind. God's saving will becomes manifest in divine action, in what is revealed in the Christian faith. Therefore it is quite natural that the God who wills and acts is the God who commands, and that the appropriate correlate to the divine command is human obedience... The mystery of God's essence as is demonstrated in all ages and all religions is to be concealed... the mystery of the divine will, as lies in the nature of the case, has to be announced. The missionary command and urge in Christianity thus bursts forth from the heart of God (p.73).
>
> The problem of the independent autonomous, indigenous church became a burning issue in the wake of the rising tide of nationalism. The spirit of nationalism and the awakening of Oriental self-consciousness caused an acute awareness of the "foreign-ness" of Christianity

and of the way it had taken shape hitherto in the various mission fields... The problem of the church since then has always been conceived in terms of the problem of the indigenization of the church... It is universally felt as true that the main task which faces the "younger churches" is that of becoming truly indigenous to the various nations in which they live and work. It is also almost universally expected that if the "younger churches" find a vital relation to their cultural, social and political environment, they will no longer be considered by their overwhelmingly non-Christian environments as factors of de-nationalizing propaganda, but as the bearers of a supra-national eternal God.

The prophetic religion of biblical realism is, in contrast to the other soteriological religions, not anthropological but theocentric. This causes a radical difference. The well-known Asiatic soteriologies by their anthropocentric and eudaemonistic character all evince a strong world-denying tendency. Historical Christianity more than once has come under the influence of this same tendency, but even then its innate world-affirming tendency has often broken through triumphantly. The best illustration is West European monasticism and its activist, cultural tendencies.

Because the real centre of Christianity is God, the living, the Creator and the Redeemer of the world and of man, its ethos, although deeply personalist, cannot adequately be described by this term, and its attitude towards the world and its spheres of life must necessarily be positive and not negative. God is the God of history. History is not a reproduction of the cyclic course of nature, but God's will is the transcendent force and the end of history. The kingdom of God, the reign of God in a fellowship of redeemed men, is the end of all human history, of which only God knows how it is to be realized (p.428).

The only way to get in our modern age... a new and vital grasp of the relevance of God to this de-religionized everyday world is to live by the dynamic word of prophetic religion which we have called the world of biblical realism. Its dominant conception is that God, the Creator and Redeemer, is the great Initiative-Taker and the absolute in all things. This is the only way to prevent that fatal isolation of the domain of God and of religion, which so easily becomes a fact by the tendency to treat religion as a set of detached dogmas which, as is erroneously presumed, pertain exclusively to the life of the soul and the domain of private opinion. It is, too, the only way to counteract the pull of the pagan attitudes in religion, everywhere evident in nascent Christianity, the tendency to manipulate religious ceremonies for achieving material ends... Our Christian festivals must become great moments of dramatic force in the yearly life... The great acts of God are celebrated in these festivals. The great themes of sin and victory over sin, of death and the triumph of life, of God's immediate concern with man and the world and of his abiding activity in the life of men, pervade them. Everywhere in the world there is much opportunity to mark these times in vivid and expressive ways through the great wealth of means for religious expression that have been inherited from the pre-Christian past (pp.440-41).

BIBLIOGRAPHY

Works by Hendrik Kraemer:

"Anknüpfung", in *Die Religion in Geschichte und Gegenwart*, vol. 1, Tübingen, 1957.
"Buddhismus, Hinduismus, Konfuzianismus, Synkretismus", in *Weltkirchen-Lexikon, Handbuch der Ökumene*, Stuttgart, Kreuz, 1957.
The Christian Message in a Non-Christian World, London, Edinburgh House, 1938.
"Christianity and Secularism", in *International Review of Mission*, vol. 19, no. 74, 1930, pp.195-208.
From Mission Field to Independent Church: Report on a Decisive Decade in the Indigenous Churches in Indonesia, The Hague, Boekencentrum, 1957.

"L'Islam, une religion, un mode de vie: L'Islam, une culture"; "La responsabilite des laïcs dans l'Eglise et dans le monde"; "Qu'est-ce que l'evangélisation dans le monde moderne?", in *La revue de l'evangélisation*, Paris, 1960.

"Mission und Nationalismus", in the series *Die Sammlung der Gemeinde*, vol. 8 (German), Basel, Missionsbuchhandlung, 1948.

Religions and the Christian Faith, London, Lutterworth, 1956 (expanded French ed.: *La religion chrétienne et les religions non-chrétiennes*, Delachaux & Niestlé, 1956).

"Spiritual Currents in Java", in *International Review of Mission*, vol. 13, no. 49, 1924, pp.101-108.

"Synkretismus II", in *Die Religion in Geschichte und Gegenwart, op. cit.*, vol. VI.

A Theology of the Laity, London, Lutterworth, 1957.

World Cultures and World Religions, London, Lutterworth, 1960.

About Hendrik Kraemer:

A.Th. Van Leeuwen, *Hendrik Kraemer, Pionier der Ökumene*, Basel, Basileia, 1962.

Vladimir N. Lossky
1903–1958

GENNADIOS LIMOURIS

Vladimir Lossky, one of the most eminent twentieth-century Russian theologians in the West, was born in 1903 in Göttingen, where his father Nikolai, a well-known philosopher, was teaching at the university. As a child, he lived in St Petersburg, and he attended university there. His family was exiled to Prague in 1922, and he worked there with N.P. Kondakov, an expert on Byzantine archaeology and art. In 1924 he settled in Paris, where he spent the rest of his life, apart from the war years, when he joined the French Partisans. In 1928, he married Madeleine Schapiro, and they had four children.

J.-L. Swiners, Paris

Lossky studied mediaeval history at the Sorbonne with the well-known Professor F. Lot and was greatly influenced by the lectures of the French philosopher E. Gilson. His friendship with Fr Eugraph Kovalevsky introduced him to the Brotherhood of St Photius, which he later joined, and which stimulated his idea of a vocation of being a witness to the West — in particular France — of a universal-catholic Orthodoxy, capable of re-appropriating the traditions of French Christianity into the Orthodox perspective of a "unionism" in relation to Roman Catholicism.

The Orthodox Theological Institute of St Denis was founded in 1945 in Paris. Vladimir Lossky taught dogmatics and church history there and later became its dean. In 1953, due to the non-canonical status of his friend Fr Kovalevsky, who had broken with the Moscow Patriarchate and was dreaming of a small "French Orthodoxy", Lossky decided to leave St Denis and to concentrate for the rest of his life on various ways of making an Orthodox witness in the areas of science and Western thought. He died on 7 February 1958 from a heart disease.

Outwardly, his life was that of a man of academic interests, unmarked by startling events except insofar as it was influenced by the cataclysmic happenings of his time. As a thinker and student, he moved with remarkable ease in a number of different fields. Well-read in patristic and mediaeval theology, both Eastern and Western, he was at the same time vitally interested in the currents of contemporary thought and life.

For more than 25 years, his particular interest and the priority in his research was the person and thought of Meister Eckhart. His study of Eckhart, together with the editing of certain of Eckhart's texts, was virtually completed by the time of his death. It is appropriate that such a great part of his work should have been devoted to a Western writer, for Vladimir Lossky was a person at home in both the East and the West, and he was especially gifted in interpreting the one to the other. He was moreover deeply convinced that there was nothing specifically "Eastern" about Orthodoxy.

Above all, Vladimir Lossky was a theologian, not in the sense of someone whose profession is to study the history of Christian doctrine — he delighted in proclaiming that he was not and never had been a "theologian" in that sense — but in the sense in which the word was used by fathers of the church. The intensely lived quality of his theology did not for an instant preclude a great intellectual integrity and accuracy. Rather it demanded it. No one could have been more precise — at times one felt tempted to say pedantic — about the use of words and the details of scholarly enquiry. The suggestion that the Orthodox tradition is misty and unclear was unthinkable for him. To arrive at that knowledge which is beyond knowledge, the most complete intellectual discipline and integrity is necessary. The knowledge of God demands the whole person, and in Vladimir Lossky it found a philosophical and historical intellect of the very first quality.

His tiny study overlooking the roofs of Paris was lined with editions of the church fathers and books of more recent theologians. Everything spoke eloquently of the labour which he had put into "mastering the Tradition", in order that he might so live in the Tradition as to become a living witness to it in our century.

For a man of his temperament and interests, the temptation to live in the past could have been great. Yet one was always conscious that when Vladimir Lossky spoke, the truths with which he was dealing were not past but present realities. He could not handle theology as though it were of abstract or historical interest only. For one who spent so much of his life in the work of historical scholarship, he was amazingly contemporary and not at all donnish. He was awake to what was currently being thought and written and responsive to the latest developments in the arts or literature. He was a person who, in all the parts of his life, lived with the whole of himself. The gulf between "religion" and "life" simply did not exist. He had overcome it without in any way ceasing to be fully human. He was equally free from any form of religious affectation or pietism, or from any of those inhibitions which make the lives of so many Christian people meticulous, faded and grim.

His ecumenical activity was limited — partly because of his short life — to his participation in the conferences of the Fellowship of St Alban and St Sergius with Orthodox and Anglican theologians, and in conferences in France in particular. Several young Anglican theologians became not only his friends but also his disciples; and they translated his *Théologie mystique de l'Eglise d'Orient* into English.

Many have characterized Vladimir Lossky as a great theologian who offered his mystical theology of Orthodoxy to the ecumenical movement "silently", through the new generation of theologians, Orthodox and non-Orthodox. This was due to the remarkable clarity and penetration of his thought, a feature not common among Orthodox or other theologians. Indeed, although there was nothing "Latin" about his theology, his mind always seemed to display some of the more admirable Latin, and indeed French, characteristics, particularly the determination to avoid any kind of ambiguity or obscurity. When reading his masterworks, it is not always easy to discover what a given Orthodox thinker may really have held about a difficult theological question, but there was never any doubt in the case of Vladimir Lossky's own thought. Yet one always knew with him that what mattered was the truth, not its verbal formulation. No one was less a slave to words than he.

Then there was his courteous but persistent adherence to the traditional positions of the Orthodox Church. Many Orthodox thinkers who come into contact with the West seem anxious to soft-pedal the classical formulations in the interest of ecumenical understanding. Not so Lossky. He would never admit that the *filioque* was a matter of indifference; on the contrary, he was inclined to trace from it all that he considered to be distorted or displaced in Western theology, not least the authoritarian papacy. But there was nothing obstinate or truculent about his loyalty to Orthodox tradition; no one could have been more modest, humble or willing to learn from others.

In the best sense of these often devalued terms, Vladimir Lossky was a layman and a churchman. No one would have hated more the thought of being celebrated as a "great man", in the sense that the world understands that phrase. Lossky knew too well that human greatness does not lie in the inflation of the individual and personal ego, but in the renewal of the whole person by participation in the life of God. Like every true servant of God, he points us not to himself, but to the holy undivided Trinity in whose "image" (*eikon*) we are made.

* * *

Lossky believed that the frequent infractions of church unity in our time, the casual attitude towards schisms as "a temporary, but inevitable evil", the scornful attitude of some towards canons as no more than external administrative prescriptions, rather than as the living expression of church unity administered by the hierarchy — all these lamentable phenomena conceal in their depths a false perception of the church.[1] They involve a weakening of the unity of divine and human elements in the church if not a denial of its living flesh, a "disincarnation".

This Protestant spiritualism on Orthodox soil gives rise to a certain callousness towards the concrete and historical character of the Body of Christ. There remains only the liturgical aspect of this Body, of the church as a sacramental structure (and here the divine and the human are usually confused in an ambiguous concept of the "theandric" nature of the church). For many, the awareness of the church as *ecclesia*, with its canonical and hierarchical structure, with the responsibility for its unity and independence that devolves above all on the hierarchy and subsequently on each of us, has vanished.

If the church in its day-to-day concrete and historical manifestation is not the very Body of Christ, summoned to exist in the historical conditions of the contemporary world, then everything becomes relative and indifferent. Then schisms do become only a temporary phenomenon to be overcome "some day" — as they are indeed already overcome in the "invisible church". The injustice of hierarchical powers and their deviation from sound teaching will need to be reviewed at some stage by a competent council, but for the present they may be tolerated.

If we leave all these aside and turn to the church, says Lossky, particularly to the church in such conditions as cause it to live its life with an exceptional sense of responsibility, and ask what has changed since the period of the early church, we would have to reply: nothing but the external forms and circumstances of the church's life, in other words nothing but that which ought to change with the times so that the church will always be capable of accomplishing its task, the salvation of the actual world in which it lives. The plenitude of its powers remains undiminished. If that is something we do not see or do not wish to see, this testifies only to our blindness, lack of spiritual vigour, despair. Such despair causes us to evade our responsibility fully to engage ourselves in the service of the church.

To this service we are called at the present moment and in the present circumstances, without waiting for "normal" times. There are no normal times before the parousia. The church can accomplish today what it ought to accomplish because "today's trouble is enough for today" (Matt. 6:34).

Vladimir Lossky's involvement in the ecumenical movement was a service of contributing theologically to the better understanding of Orthodox teaching and Orthodox tradition in the wider ecumenical world. During his lifetime the ecumenical movement was in the process of involving new churches, which had a particular bearing on their relationships and theological negotiations. Lossky himself died before all the Orthodox churches were able to join the World Council of Churches — which only happened at the New Delhi assembly in 1961.

NOTE

[1] The following paragraphs are based on some passages from his article "Ecueils ecclésiologiques", in *Messager de l'Exarchat du patriarche russe en Europe occidentale*, no. 1, 1950, pp.16-28.

BIBLIOGRAPHY

Lossky's published work is small in quantity, but great in value: a few articles and pamphlets and his short, but immensely important book on *The Mystical Theology of the Eastern Church* — important because among all the many books that have been written on Orthodoxy for the instruction and education of Western Christians, none so lucidly and accurately pinpoints the theological issues. And then in the background of all his works there is the great unpublished research work and study on Eckhart which had preoccupied him for so many years: a book which somehow never seemed to get finished.

"The Byzantine Patriarchate", in *Sobornost*, 3, summer 1948, pp.108-12.

"La conscience catholique: Implications anthropologiques du dogme de l'Eglise", in *Contacts*, 452, 1963, pp.76-88. English tr. in *St Vladimir's Theological Quarterly*, 14, 1970, pp.187-95.

"Darkness and Light in the Knowledge of God", in *The Eastern Churches Quarterly*, 8, winter 1950, pp.460-71.

"Le dogme de l'immaculée conception and 'Lourdes'", in *Messager*, 24, 1955, pp.227-35. English tr. *The Theology of Image*, in *Sobornost*, 22, winter 1957-58, pp.510-20.

"Dominion and Kingship: An Eschatological Study", in *Sobornost*, 14, winter 1953, pp.67-69.

Essai sur la théologie mystique de l'Eglise d'Orient, Paris, Aubier, 1994. *The Mystical Theology of the Eastern Church*, Naperville, IL, Alec R. Allendo, Inc., 1957, and London, James Clark and Co., 1957. German tr. Graz, Verlag Styria, 1961. Russian tr. in *Bogoslovskie Trudy*, 8, 1972, pp.7-128.

"Foi et théologie", in *Contacts*, 13, 1961, pp.163-76.

A l'image et à la ressemblance de Dieu, Paris, Aubier-Montaigne, 1967.

La procession du Saint-Esprit dans la doctrine trinitaire orthodoxe, Paris, Setor, 1948. English tr. in *The Eastern Church Quarterly*, 7, suppl. issue, 1948, pp.31-53.

Redemption and Deification (English tr.), in *Sobornost* 12, winter 1947, pp.47-56.

"La théologie de la lumière chez Saint Grégoire de Thessalonique", in *Dieu vivant*, 1, 1945, pp.94-118.

Théologie négative et connaissance de Dieu chez Eckhart, Paris, J. Vrin, 1960.

Tradition and Traditions, English tr. in *The Meaning of Icons*, Boston, Book & Art Shop, 1952, pp.13-24; see also *Explanation of the Main Types of Icons*, pp.69-126.

Visions de Dieu, Paris, Delachaux et Niestlé, 1962. English tr. *The Vision of God*, Clayton, WI, American Orthodox Press, 1963, and London, Faith Press, 1963. German tr. *Schau Gottes*, Zürich, EVS Verlag, 1964. Russian tr. of chapter 8 in *Messager de l'Exarchat russe en Europe Occidentale*, 61, 1968, pp.57-68; chapter 9 in *Messager de l'Exarchat russe en Europe Occidentale*, 63, 1968, pp.151-63; both printed in *Bogoslovskie Trudy*, 8, 1972, pp.187-203.

Robert C. Mackie
1899–1984

HANS-RUEDI WEBER

There he sits, quite as if he had all the time in the world, listening to someone seeking advice and guidance — perhaps a fellow executive with a difficult decision to make, perhaps a secretary who is finding it difficult to work together with a supervisor, perhaps a gardener or cleaning woman who is having financial problems or a family crisis. Robert Mackie welcomes them all into his office with some cheerful remarks to make them feel at ease. Then he listens, asks a question here and there and finally says: "Well, listen, I think that..." It would usually be good advice, because Robert — as his many friends called him — had a remarkable gift of discerning a person's strengths and weaknesses and the real opportunities, dangers and impossibilities in a given situation. When the person had left, he would not put the whole matter out of his mind but would pray about the issue, which often led him to initiate a fresh conversation with the person.

This was the man behind the many high offices entrusted to him. He himself took such leading positions seriously only insofar as they served God's purpose. Born on 30 April 1899 at Bothwell, near Glasgow, he decided to follow his father's vocation. After completing his M.A. at Glasgow University, he studied for the ministry at Trinity College, Glasgow, and was ordained a minister of the United Free Church of Scotland in 1925.

Already as a student Robert Mackie became involved in the British Student Christian Movement (SCM). After ordination he was asked to become the SCM Scottish secretary and married his predecessor in this post, Dorothy Steven. From 1929 to 1938 he served in the general secretariat of the British SCM. Already he was taking part in meetings of the World's Student Christian Federation (WSCF), where he came to learn the difficult art of understanding and communicating across barriers of language, confession and culture, an art which was indispensable in his many subsequent international work assignments: treasurer of the WSCF (1935-38); general secretary of the WSCF (1938-48) as successor to W.A. Visser 't Hooft; chairman of the WSCF (1948-53), again following Visser 't Hooft; associate general secretary of the World Council of Churches and director of its Division of Inter-Church Aid and Service to Refugees (1948-55). After his return to Scotland he continued ecumenical work, for local ecumenism for him was no less important than worldwide involvement. He became one of the main artisans of such innovative ecumenical ventures as the "Tell Scotland" campaign with its "Kirk Weeks" and the Scottish Churches House in Dunblane. Thus he served the ecumenical movement until his death on 13 January 1984.

If one were to characterize Robert C. Mackie in terms of the New Testament lists of "gifts of grace", several would immediately come to mind. Not the extraordinary ones which quickly catch the eye and the ear: speaking in tongues, prophecy, working miracles (though balancing budgets in periods of economic crisis was often little short of miraculous!). His life, work and writing were not particularly marked by new and exciting theological insights or an outstanding gift of interpretation. He was not good at languages, and it was his wife Dorothy who had this gift. However, if the gift of grace of *hermeneia* includes not only the ability to interpret from one language to another, but also to interpret different people to one another, from one thought-structure and deep conviction to another, then Robert Mackie had a superlative measure of this gift. This made him such a good moderator of meetings, especially since it went hand-in-hand with a large dose of humour, a gift which, though not mentioned in Paul's list of *charismata*, certainly belongs there.

His very special gifts of grace for use in the service of the church universal and to the glory of God were those of "the *exhorter*, [exercised] in exhortation; the *giver*, in generosity; the *leader*, in diligence; the *compassionate*, in cheerfulness" (Rom. 12:8). He had also received the great and often under-estimated gifts of *antilepsis* and *kybernesis*, mentioned in 1 Corinthians 12:28. The former refers to the art of administration and, according to Greek papyri, was a technical term for banking; the latter comes from the world of seafaring and refers to the art of piloting and giving direction.

For such "gracious" administration and leadership two further gifts mentioned in 1 Corinthians 12 were endowed upon Robert Mackie in abundance: the "utterance of wisdom" and the "discernment of spirits" — the rare ability of identifying the specific possibilities in crisis situations and the specific vocations of people. For this reason he was often sent to regions where delicate political or ecclesiastical problems had arisen, in order to help people and organizations see more clearly what was the will of God. Through such gifts he also became a pastoral counsellor to many people at crucial moments of their lives.

Let me illustrate this with a personal memory. As a young SCM secretary, I had to decide which direction to take for my further life: pastoral ministry in Switzerland or service as a missionary overseas. I had no specific missionary vocation, but at the same time, I had great doubts about my pastoral gifts. So, like many others, I turned to Robert. How he understood my English — then practically non-existent — seems to me still a miracle, yet I felt understood. After a while Robert smiled and said, "Well, H.R., I think you are an *exportable* Swiss!" That settled the matter. In all such counselling, managing and administrative leadership Robert was never overbearing nor did he become a dry administrator or a scheming manager; he remained a pastor. As such he radiated warmth and created confidence. He could, however, become quite stern, almost pitiless, whenever he detected dishonesty, pride and self-seeking ecclesiastical power politics.

During Robert Mackie's main period of work in the WSCF and the WCC, there were three people with whom he worked together intimately — his wife Dorothy and his colleagues W.A. Visser 't Hooft and Suzanne de Diétrich.

With Robert away for so many months of the year on intercontinental travel and endless meetings, it was not easy for Dorothy to keep up a welcoming home in a foreign country for the many guests, and at the same time create a homely atmosphere both for their son Steven and the often overworked husband and father. This, however, she did. She was fully behind Robert in his work, and often helped with translations and editing. Above all, when Robert came home discouraged, sometimes irritated and himself in need of advice, she was there. Later, during Dorothy's long illness prior to her death in 1974, Robert was able to return some of this selfless availability and service. For many months he set all other work aside and became Dorothy's full-time nurse.

The team of Visser 't Hooft and Robert Mackie shaped much ecumenical history both through the WSCF and the WCC. Though it was usually Visser 't Hooft who stood in the forefront and had the bright ideas, it was Robert who often had to find people and money for translating ideas into policies, to see to the details of plans and ensure that a new step forward was not endangered by administrative chaos. Much of the delicate correspondence which the WCC general secretary was required to send was first submitted to Robert for advice. Visser 't Hooft would also seek Mackie's counsel on major personnel and policy issues. When the WCC (then still in the process of formation) had to consider the effect of the Munich crisis in 1938 on international Christian affairs, Visser 't Hooft asked Mackie to come to Geneva for consultations. When money became available to set up the Ecumenical Institute, the two of them visited possible sites around Geneva, and it was their joint decision that it should be located at the Château de Bossey near Céligny.

Mackie's collaboration and deep friendship with Suzanne de Diétrich bore much fruit during the second world war. When the frontiers of Europe were closed in June 1940, it was decided that Suzanne should stay in the WSCF Geneva office while Robert, as general secretary, should work from a country whose frontiers to the rest of the world were still open. Yet the Mackie family left too late and were caught up in the stream of refugees and the advancing German troops in France. For several weeks nothing was heard from them, and they seemed lost. Finally, they were able to reach Canada via Portugal. Commenting on this in a July 1940 letter to an English friend, Suzanne wrote:

> I am so thankful that the experience of Robert's trip was not too bad a one, but Robert is the type of man who would win every heart everywhere and would convert the devil himself to better feelings, if the devil could be converted... Robert's amazing gift of understanding and sympathy helped me as nothing else could do... to be brave and face the worst during those awful weeks of June.

Throughout the war the team of Robert Mackie and Suzanne de Diétrich kept alive the worldwide network of friendships which had grown up through the WSCF. Through correspondence and travels Robert, from his base in Toronto, maintained contacts with the student movements in North and South America, Asia and South

Africa. Suzanne kept open the lines of communication with the SCMs in Eastern and Western Europe across the barriers of enmity, suspicion and closed frontiers. Together with many of their friends, they organized continuous spiritual nurture for students fighting on the various fronts or languishing in prison camps. Soon they began to look to the future, to plan for peace and to become involved in World Student Relief.

The letters between Robert and Suzanne from 1940 to 1945 are a strange mixture of business correspondence planning for regular publications and relief action in several continents, mutual reporting on events and opinions in their very different worlds and very personal reciprocal support in faith and hope. There were differences in viewpoints and sometimes sharp disagreements, but the bonds of friendship and mutual trust were kept intact.

Mackie's August 1943 correspondence with colleagues in Europe about the nature of the war is instructive. Visser 't Hooft and others felt that this war was completely different from previous ones and that the spiritual issues were so clear that the general secretary of the WSCF ought to take a clear stand on the side of the Allies. In a statement on "The War and the Policy of the Federation", Robert Mackie responded that he always felt a strong tension between his personal political feelings and his inevitably more detached position as a WSCF officer. He warned his colleagues in Geneva not

> to identify the war with its European or Middle Eastern phase. Many of the deductions naturally made in Europe do not fit the Far East, or even the Russian front. This is not just a war between Nazism and Democracy with Christian foundations. We need a variety of categories in which to think... Is it not true that there are several wars being fought?... The spiritual issues are very apparent, but there are imperial, commercial and racial issues also... Every country I think of has its own peculiar angle on the war, and I do not know for what group we might, by lack of caution, make things difficult when next we meet.

Here Mackie's main contributions to ecumenical spirituality shine through: a truly worldwide view; thinking and planning ahead with a great sensitivity to diverse positions; struggling in the first place to understand and not to condemn. This was accompanied by a deep conviction that Christian fellowship grows more through mutual help and service than through verbal statements. Thus he constantly ensured that, in addition to unity and mission, selfless service remained an integral part of the ecumenical movement. In 1940 he helped to set up the European Student Relief Fund and, in 1943, World Student Relief as a joint venture of the International Student Service, Pax Romana and the WSCF. When he became director of the WCC's interchurch aid and refugee service in 1948, most of its assistance was still going to European churches and to refugees who were mainly white. By the time he left in 1955, the division was extending its services to all continents. His last director's report to the 1955 WCC Central Committee meeting was a moving plea that the widening of WCC service to needs in Asia and Africa should be based not on the power of money but on the resources of faith "which we ultimately derive from the compassion and the righteousness of God". In the fellowship of the WCC, he insisted,

> there can be no hint of patronage due to size or history. In all our churches there is the same story of human weakness and divine strength. We all stand under the judgment and mercy of the cross of our Lord Jesus Christ. And in our World Council there has grown up a will to bear one another's burdens. [1]

The work of the Division of Inter-Church Aid and Service to Refugees later expanded so quickly that it sometimes seemed in danger of becoming a huge, autonomous service programme, isolated from the rest of the WCC's life and work. It is therefore salutary to recall how Robert Mackie in 1955 envisaged this widening service. First of all he pointed to the centrality of the Christian mission:

> There is always a danger of thinking that our "know-how", our fraternal visits, our surpluses (God forgive us!) will save the world. That is not true. The only thing that saves the world and answers the fundamental human need is the gospel. The World Council of Churches and the International Missionary Council are together pledged to unfaltering obedience to the Great Commission.

But this pledge did not mean looking back "longingly to the great days of the missionary enterprises".

> We must see whether God is calling us to a new form of response in our day... We are trying to work out again the nature of the service of Christians to one another and to their fellow men. We are building a path amidst many pitfalls.

In order to do this, Mackie emphasized the great importance of maintaining the link between action and reflection, ecumenical service and ecumenical studies. He therefore welcomed the WCC's decision to launch a study on "Common Christian Responsibility towards Areas of Rapid Social Change". He knew that

> relief action may often be damaging, leading to further pauperization, unless it is wisely handled. At a very practical level the churches and missions, and the Division itself, need sound economic and social advice. This network of enquiry and reflection will be invaluable to all relief work, and that relief work will prevent this study from the danger of remaining academic.

The widening of ecumenical service also had implications for Christian unity:

> The Division does not depend on large funds, though some ability to meet emergencies quickly is essential. The Division relies solely upon the will of the churches to cooperate. The Division does not ask for financial power: it asks the churches to coordinate their mutual service. Therefore, this whole work is a living test of unity, and a humble instrument in creating unity.

NOTE

[1] *The Ecumenical Review*, vol. 8, 1955, pp.8-17.

BIBLIOGRAPHY

Robert C. Mackie was not a writer of books, though he is the author of many thousands of pages. Much of his extensive correspondence is preserved in the archives of the WSCF and the WCC in Geneva. There, too, are the many reports and minutes which he wrote in the course of his ecumenical work assignments. We probably come closest to Mackie's real person, wisdom and wit in his editorials and "Editor's Travel Diaries" in *The Student World*, which he edited from 1938 to 1949. It is typical of Mackie that he edited more books by others, or contributed to symposia, rather than writing books himself.

Among his contributions to the works of others are, for instance:

"Introduction" to Suzanne de Diétrich, *Cinquante ans d'histoire* (history of the first fifty years of the WSCF), Paris, 1948, pp.5-7.

"Introduction" to Ruth Rouse, *The World's Student Christian Federation*, London, 1948, pp.11-21.

Robert C. Mackie, ed., *Christians and Atomic War: A Discussion of the Moral Aspects of Defence and Disarmament*, London, 1959.

Robert C. Mackie & Charles C. West, eds, *The Sufficiency of God: Essays in Honour of W.A. Visser 't Hooft*, London, SCM, 1963, pp.7-16.

Robert C. Mackie, *Witness and Service to All*, London, BCC, 1964.

Layman Extraordinary: John R. Mott, London, Hodder & Stoughton, 1965, pp.11-69.

A short profile of Robert Mackie by Christian Berg and Marie-Jeanne de Haller was published in the series *Ökumenische Profile: Gestalten der Einen Kirche aller Welt*, no. VI/3, Berlin, pp.9-16.

A major biography of Robert C. Mackie, by Nansie Blackie, is in preparation and will probably be published in Scotland by Hansel Press under the title *With Love and with Laughter*.

Max Josef Metzger
1887–1944

GERHARD VOSS

KNA-Bild, Frankfurt

"God needs people to run ahead and herald the day! But they have to die before the day comes." These words of Peter Lippert, a Jesuit priest and well-known radio preacher, apply to Max Josef Metzger. It was on 17 April 1944 that he had to die. The life of a tireless campaigner for peace and advocate of ecumenism was at an end when the death sentence pronounced six months earlier by the Nazi People's Court under Roland Freisler was carried out.

Max Metzger came from a teacher's family in Baden. He was born in 1887 in a small town in the Black Forest. After completing his secondary schooling, he studied philosophy and theology in Freiburg im Breisgau and then in Fribourg in Switzerland, where he met students from a number of European countries. As a student he became involved in social work and so came to know the misery that is frequently linked to alcoholism. After receiving his doctorate and being ordained as a priest in 1911, he spent several years as a curate. During the first world war he served for some time in France as an army chaplain.

Against this background, the rest of Metzger's life was governed by the single keyword "peace": peace between the peoples, peace and social justice within each society, so that human beings would no longer have to drown their misery in alcohol, peace between Christians.

In October 1915 the young cleric became general secretary of the Alliance of the Cross, a Catholic temperance organization in Graz. In this new position Metzger undertook an absolutely astonishing variety of activities. He expanded his association's headquarters, founded a publishing house, a "League for World Peace" and a "People's Hospice for the Reform of Life and Society". He lectured widely, established contacts with individuals and groups in many countries, wrote many letters and published numerous articles and brochures.

A versatile, talented man with an open and sensitive heart and a passionate temperament, Metzger came across to some people as brash, inordinately ambitious and volatile. He was an indefatigable agitator, firebrand, fanatic, radical and individualist. In the pursuit of his aims he was ruthless, most of all with himself. He rejected everything mediocre. In a poem he wrote in prison in 1944 we read:

> "The normal" is something shameful, I claim;
> "Standardized" humans? — a gruesome thought:
> The Creator named *me* by my own special name
> When he called *me* to live the life I've got.

Cautious evaluations were not in Metzger's nature. He simply wanted to force in the coming of the kingship of Christ. "Christ must reign!" (cf. 1 Cor. 15:25) were the words that occupied his whole being and drove him on.

A fundamental experience for him, he wrote in an essay in 1931, was distress with the church as he found it in reality. He felt bitter about its general superficiality, its overemphasis on form and organization, letter and tradition, and its complacent self-righteousness. He noted a frequent lack of vigour in the life of this "communion of saints". His guiding image was "the Roman Catholic Church which, in a genuinely universal, world-unifying way binds the peoples together, gathers in all truth from all the Holy Spirit's scattered seeds and combines it in a divine synthesis, the worldwide Fellowship of Peace of Christ's League of Nations". He wanted to be "a Protestant Catholic, a Catholic Protestant... at one and the same time truly Protestant *and* Catholic".

In an appeal in 1920 Metzger quoted the words from Jesus' high-priestly prayer: "that they may all be one" (John 17:21). In these words he saw the profoundest expression of the peace for which he was struggling: all were to be one as the Father and the Son are one in the mystery of the living, triune God. Metzger's work for peace brought him into contact with Protestant pacifists throughout Europe. These links were perhaps what stimulated him to think not only about world peace and peace in society but also peace between the confessions. Increasingly he sought theological discussion with Christians of other confessions.

Although Roman Catholics were forbidden by the Vatican to participate in the first world conference on Faith and Order in Lausanne in 1927, a Protestant friend of Metzger's in Rome secured permission for him to be an unofficial observer, and the Bishop of Fribourg, as the competent authority, gave his consent. What impressed Metzger most of all in Lausanne was the common prayer of the 500 representatives of so many different confessions gathered there. The conference stimulated him to identify himself even more with the ecumenical movement — despite opposition in many quarters.

In Graz there was a desire to be rid of the troublemaker. Many of the devout regarded him as ecclesiastically unreliable, and some even thought he was a communist or fellow-traveller. The episcopal authorities therefore called for his transfer back to his home diocese of Freiburg. Metzger saw no chance of continuing his work there. But he found an opportunity in Meitingen near Augsburg, where he was able to take over a home for recovering alcoholics. He transferred the office of his association from Graz to Meitingen, where he established in 1928 the mother house of the Society of Christ the King of the White Cross (known today as the Institute of Christ the King).

A year after the Lausanne conference Pope Pius XI published his encyclical letter *Mortalium Animos*, on the promotion of true religious unity, stating that only return to the Roman Catholic Church could lead to unity:

The unity of Christians cannot be otherwise obtained than by securing the return of the separated to the one true Church of Christ from which they once unhappily withdrew. To the one true Church, We say, that stands forth before all and that by the will of its Founder will remain forever the same as when He Himself established it for the salvation of all mankind.

Max Metzger stayed his course despite the pope's warnings against the "ensnaring hope", "error" and "coaxing words" of those who were striving for unity at that time. In the context of his labours for peace he worked increasingly towards peace between the confessions. Towards the end of 1938 he founded the Una Sancta Fraternity, "in which Catholics and noble-minded people of different faith pray together for the unity of the church in the Christian world and systematically build bridges of mutual understanding and a genuinely fraternal attitude of mind". He was an important counsellor and animator for the Una Sancta groups that came into existence in those years.

At the end of 1939, while temporarily in prison, he wrote a prophetic letter to Pope Pius XII, signing it Brother Paulus, as he now called himself. It is not known whether this letter ever reached the pope. The letter recalled that at the time of the Council of Trent, the view was held that a root and branch reform of the church was necessary; and the Protestants were invited to the Council, though they did not come. The time was now ripe to repeat the Tridentine attempt. In preparation for a Council, Brother Paulus proposed that the pope select twelve men he could trust — well-known personalities, of proven theological learning and firm in the faith — who should attempt an initial approach to leading representatives of the separated ecclesial communions. His proposal was realized roughly twenty years later when Pope John XXIII established the Secretariat for Promoting Christian Unity led by Cardinal Bea.

At Pentecost 1939, Protestant and Roman Catholic Christians met in Meitingen for the first Una Sancta meeting. The appeals, which at first appeared irregularly under the heading "Una Sancta", became the "Una Sancta Circulars"; and from them developed the ecumenical journal *Una Sancta*, which is still published by the Una Sancta Association of the Meitingen Institute of Christ the King and the Ecumenical Institute of the Benedictine Abbey of Niederaltaich.

Initially, Metzger could envisage church unity only as a return to the Roman Catholic Church, but his ecumenical ideas evolved. To overcome confessional complacency and self-sufficiency, he encouraged discussion wherever possible, breaking down entrenched fronts and deep-rooted mistrust and dispelling the suspicion that Roman Catholic ecumenists were simply offering a subtler version of their church's old absolute claims. While he hoped for the coming unity as the work of the Holy Spirit, he insisted that we must painstakingly prepare for that work. In 1941 Brother Paulus framed a number of conditions for ecumenism in terms very similar to those of Vatican II in its Decree on Ecumenism two decades later:

Each party must lovingly strive to understand the other in the concern by which it believes it must abide on the basis of the gospel; in so doing the one party must beware of evaluating the language of the other by its own terminology; rather each party must study in advance the other's language and mode of expression, in order to be able to understand at all what the other means by the words it uses. Interconfessional semantics is not the least of the presuppositions for fruitful encounter.

With Vatican II, which regarded the ecumenical movement as a work of the Holy Spirit in which all Catholics should cooperate, the small, almost invisible mustard seed

— which is how Max Metzger saw his work in 1930 — became a vigorous plant. What he sowed by his words, his work and his life has germinated.

Metzger had given much thought to the shape of Germany after the war, and he set forth his ideas in a memorandum to Swedish Lutheran Archbishop Eidem of Uppsala, who was to pass it on to authoritative representatives of the Allied powers. The courier was to be a Swedish woman, Dagmar Imgart, whom Metzger had known for years as a loyal member of the Una Sancta movement. On 29 June 1943 she visited Metzger in Berlin, and he handed the memorandum over to her. Shortly afterwards two officials of the Gestapo came and found it when they made a search. Metzger and the woman were at once arrested. Dagmar Imgart was in fact an agent of the Gestapo, and she had been corresponding with Metzger on their instructions for years.

In the proceedings against Metzger in the People's Court Roland Freisler focussed on the words "Una Sancta" and bellowed, "Una Sancta! Una Sancta! Una! Una! Una! that's what *we* are! And there is nothing else!" The *Führer* did not want people who thought for themselves. Everyone had to believe only in him. Max Josef Metzger, the fervent and tireless campaigner for peace, paid for his struggle with his life. The Nazi dictatorship tried to confine religious life to the church and the sanctuary. Max Metzger wanted to break out of that confinement; he wanted peace for everyone and peace among Christians. For us today his ecumenical pilgrimage raises the question: how do we make use of the opportunities we have in constitutional democratic states for peace among the nations and among divided Christians, for the growing together of human beings and for the ecumenical movement?

* * *

In an essay in a 1931 issue of the quarterly journal *Religiöse Besinnung*, Metzger eloquently set forth his ecumenical ideals:

We could not conceive of the true church of Christ without the fundamental and actual universality of the church, without its catholicity. But... we often perceived only a hierarchical, liturgical, legal catholicity, and not really the vital catholicity which alone can make the whole church a deep communion of faith, that is, a transcending fullness of life, an ecumenical "bond of love". When the war came, tearing apart the *corpus Christi mysticum* and causing its members to slaughter one another, our hearts bled...

And we were deeply depressed that the apostolic church often contented itself with the apostolicity of the hierarchical succession, but did not display the strength of the apostolic faith and love which would have carried the cross of its Lord, the king of peace, before the "Christian" rulers of the world and forced them to halt the bloodshed. And this drove us to apostolic action.

Not to sterile, negative criticism of the church and its members! Not to the attitude of the "catholic reformer" but to that of the *poverello* who wanted to rebuild a church inwardly undermined by its external splendour, power and indulgence, by purely and simply beginning with his own people to live out anew the life of the poor, crucified Christ and preaching him wherever they went... What we had before us was the *una, sancta, catholica et apostolica ecclesia*, which truly realized the *corpus Christi mysticum* in the world.

The *one* church, one in dogma and in hierarchical organization, but above all one through the living Spirit of Christ its Lord who quickens all its members and all they do. One without the narrow-mindedness which constantly comes to the fore when human dogmatism takes over at the expense of humble service of Christ and the burning desire to forward God's kingdom on earth.

The *holy* church, which uses all the means of holiness in the Lord's rich treasury of grace, but without falling into an over-literal sacramentalism which forgets the old Catholic truth of the *sacramenta propter homines* and by external service of the sacraments all too easily neglects the deep spiritual transformation of the human person.

The *catholic* church, which in a truly universal way unifies the world and binds its peoples together, gathering in all the truth from all the scattered seeds of the Holy Spirit and binding them together in a divine synthesis, the worldwide fellowship of peace of Christ's league of nations.

The *apostolic* church, which permeates all members of the mysterious body of Christ with Christ's Spirit and leads them all to fulfil an apostolic function in the actual building of Christ's kingdom on earth.

This was the image we had — and still have — before us and which our Institute of Christ the King seeks through its work to make a reality. That seems to us to be Protestant-Catholic, Catholic-Protestant ecumenical work.[1]

A week before his execution, Brother Paulus wrote and set to music the following poem, on Easter Monday 1944:

Christ the Lord — he is risen!
transfigured in body and in glory.
Freedom! Peace! a time of joy!
In each land proclaim the story!
Sing in triumph, for the foe
is quelled — the Lord has stood his ground:
The Saviour heals the scars of sin —
through him today salvation we have found.

Christ the Lord — he is risen!
Rejoice, though given over to death;
He, the victor over Satan,
frees from hell's enslaving breath.
Never more in the new body
life decaying in the grave,
Free, with joy in holy life,
lift your heads high, you are saved!

Christ the Lord — he is risen!
the firstborn of his heavenly host.
All have found life and salvation
at the altar of his cross.
You who died with him are raised
today: and what he gained for you
through the very death he braved
is the glory, which is yours![2]

NOTES

[1] *Religiöse Besinnung*, vol. 3, no. 3, 1930-31, pp.121f.
[2] From Max Josef Metzger, *Gefangenschaftbriefe*, 2nd ed., ed. Hannes Bäcker, Meitingen, Una Sancta Bücherei, 1948, p.293.

BIBLIOGRAPHY

Works by Max Josef Metzger:

Für Frieden und Einheit. Briefe aus der Gefangenschaft, ed. Meitinger Christkönigsschwestern, Meitingen-Freising, 1964.

Gefangenschaftsbriefe, ed. Matthias Laros, Meitingen, 1947.

Gefangenschaftsbriefe, ed. Hannes Bäcker, 2nd ed., Meitingen, 1948.

Zwei karolingische Pontifikalien vom Oberrhein, Freiburg im Breisgau, 1914, dissertation.

Works on Max Josef Metzger:

Werner Becker, "Max Josef Metzger", in W. Becker & B. Radom, *Ökumenische Menschen*, Leipzig o.J., 1969, pp.39-59.

Paulus Engelhardt, *Max Josef Metzger. Bruder Paulus*, eds Victor Conzemius & Peter Meinhold, Freiburg, Switzerland, Hamburg, 1980.

Augustin Kast, "Dr. Max Josef Metzger. Gründer der Christkönigsgesellschaft", in *Die badischen Martyrerpriester. Lebensbilder badischer Priester aus der Zeit des 3. Reiches*, 2nd ed., Karlsruhe, 1949, pp.56-65.

Marianne Möhring, *Täter des Wortes. Max Josef Metzger — Leben und Wirken*, Meitingen-Freising, 1966.

Franz Posset, *Krieg und Christentum. Kath. Friedensbewegung zwischen dem Ersten und Zweiten Weltkrieg unter besonderer Berücksichtigung des Werkes von Max Josef Metzger*, Meitingen-Freising, 1978.

P. Robert Quardt SCJ, "Hingerichtet. Max Josef Metzger 1887-1944", in *Unsterbliche Christusjünger. Vierzig Priestergestalten*, Celle, 1951, pp.159-63.

F. Siegmund-Schultze, "Max Josef Metzger", in G. Gloede, ed., *Ökumenische Profile*, 1, Stuttgart, 1961, pp.354-70.

John Meyendorff
1926–1992

THOMAS HOPKO

When John Meyendorff attended the fourth assembly of the World Council of Churches in Uppsala in 1968 as a delegate of the Ecumenical Patriarchate of Constantinople, he was 42 years old, an internationally renowned historian and theologian, already designated moderator of the WCC Faith and Order Commission and nominee to the Central Committee. Coming to Sweden from his summer residence in Canada, he brought his Russian Orthodox cultural heritage, his Baltic Lutheran-Greek Orthodox ancestry, his German surname, his French upbringing, education and citizenship, and his scholarly and priestly ministry in the United States. He was seated under the standard of Turkey.

John Meyendorff was born of aristocratic, artistic Russian émigré parents in Neuilly-sur-Seine, France, in 1926. He attended French schools, completed his theological education at the Orthodox Theological Institute of St Sergius in Paris in 1949 and earned a doctorate of letters from the Sorbonne in 1958 for his pioneering work on St Gregory Palamas, the fourteenth-century Byzantine monk, bishop and theologian.

After being ordained to the priesthood, he came to the United States in 1959 to join the faculty of St Vladimir's Orthodox Theological Seminary in New York as professor of patristics and church history. After the death of his close friend and co-worker Fr Alexander Schmemann, he was elected dean of the seminary in 1984, a position he held until his retirement in July 1992, a few weeks before his own sudden death from pancreatic cancer.

Upon his arrival in the US, Meyendorff also joined the faculty of Harvard University's Byzantine Research Center, Dumbarton Oaks, in Washington DC, where he taught until 1967 and subsequently served as board member and director. From 1967 until 1992 he was also professor of Byzantine history at Fordham University in New York. He lectured occasionally as visiting professor at other universities and theological schools and served terms as president of the American Patristics Association and of the Orthodox Theological Society of America.

In addition to his teaching and administrative work, Meyendorff was a priest, pastor and spiritual father to countless people, including many theological students, pastors and church workers whose minds and spirits he informed and inspired by his teaching, direction and personal example.

John Meyendorff was active in ecclesiastical affairs from his earliest years as acolyte in the Russian Orthodox cathedral in Paris, and later as a theological student at St Sergius Institute and a founding member and first president of Syndesmos, the international organization of Orthodox youth movements. He participated over the years, particularly in North America, in countless church meetings, councils and delegations. Besides editing *St Vladimir's Theological Quarterly*, he was for many years general editor of *The Orthodox Church*, the official newspaper of the Orthodox Church in America, the former Russian Orthodox Missionary Metropolia in North America to whose attainment of self-governing (autocephalous) status in 1970 he contributed greatly.

It seems almost impossible that the quantity and quality of scholarly books and articles by John Meyendorff came from one person. Like his lectures and seminars, these written works are full of ecumenical considerations and implications. Besides speaking and writing extensively on the specific ecumenical issues and concerns in which he himself was directly involved, he was always keenly aware of the ecumenical significance of historical events and theological controversies and developments in their particular context, and for subsequent generations.

By his heritage and very nature, Meyendorff was a person with a thoroughly ecumenical mind and spirit. He despised the private, petty and provincial in human life. He loved the universal, the catholic, the all-inclusive, the truly "great". Always and in everything he desired to come to a knowledge of the truth, which in his opinion is alone capable of bringing sinful, divided people into unity with themselves and others, and most importantly with God himself.

Meyendorff's ecumenical witness always went in two directions. Within the Orthodox Church he testified to the absolute necessity of ecumenical involvement and participation, insisting that fidelity to Orthodoxy is in no way compromised by ecumenical activity. And within the ecumenical movement he testified to traditional Orthodox convictions about the nature of God's unity for the world, for the church, for ecclesial communities and for Christian believers, thereby bearing the cross of *martyria* to the Orthodox faith which he firmly believed to be the very substance and content of the "visible unity" God gives to creation in Christ and the Spirit in the church, the foretaste of the communion of everyone and everything in God in the age to come.

Meyendorff insisted that members of the Orthodox Church are necessarily ecumenical in attitude and action by virtue of their calling, faith, baptism and participation in the mysteries of Christ in the catholic church, since in the church they experience everyone and everything as already united to God through Christ and the Holy Spirit. This experience produces the passionate desire and labour to have this God-given unity ever more perfectly realized by members of the church and ever more fully actualized among divided Christians in separated ecclesial communities. These communities remain united in various degrees, despite their many and varied disagreements and differences, through their profession of faith in Christ, their worship of the tri-personal Godhead, their commitment to the authority of canonical scriptures, their mutual acceptance of a certain shared history and their desire to be visibly united in God, the Holy Trinity, in God's one holy church.

Meyendorff was willing to question and evaluate the methods and means of ecumenical involvement and participation. He would eagerly enter into discussions about ecumenical tactics and goals — including even the debate over whether membership in the WCC and other ecumenical agencies and organizations is always the best way of ecumenical witness. But he never questioned the basic conviction that ecumenism is an essential element of Christian faith and life.

In a paper shortly after the Uppsala assembly, Meyendorff expressed his deepest ecumenical convictions:

> I very deeply feel that ecumenical dialogue and ecumenical action in the world are possible only if one agrees that the gospel was preached so that [human persons] may live a new and eternal life, so that the world may be changed and transfigured. We will certainly not contribute to this change unless we are able to offer something radically different from what the world knows already. Now the world certainly knows about bureaucratic structures, as well as about social revolution, but it lacks "the Spirit of Truth whom the world cannot receive because it neither sees him nor knows him". The temptation to use means and categories which the world knows has always been with Christians...
>
> The future of true ecumenism lies in asking together true questions instead of avoiding them, in seeking the unity God wants instead of settling for substitutes, in invoking the Spirit of God which is not the spirit of the world. Councils, assemblies, conferences and consultations provide the opportunities for doing so and should not therefore be altogether discarded. However, they will not create unity because unity "in Christ" is not man-made; it is given in the church and can be only discovered and accepted. [1]

About the same time, struggling as he constantly did with the critical ecumenical issue of what is truly essential to Christian (and human) being and life, and what is incidental and secondary, Meyendorff concluded an essay on the meaning of tradition with these words:

> The establishment of a clear distinction between Holy Tradition as such, and the human traditions created by history, is probably the most essential aspect of contemporary theology, especially when it wants to be ecumenical. The very reality of Tradition, a living and organic reality manifesting the presence of the Spirit in the church, and therefore also its unity, cannot be fully understood unless it is clearly distinguished from everything which creates a normal diversity inside the one church... Therein lies a very urgent problem for contemporary Orthodoxy, especially in connection with its ecumenical responsibility and involvement... The union of all is the fundamental aim of ecumenical activity and thought. The obvious Orthodox responsibility is to show where this union can become a reality and how it can be realized. The claim of the Orthodox church to be already the *Una Sancta* must be substantiated in the empirical reality of its life so that it may appear also as the *Catholica*... But all these efforts [of ecumenists] will bring forth fruit only if they end upon an encounter, not only with each other, but also with the Lord in the Spirit of Truth. To be truly "ecumenical" is to be ready at every moment for this encounter, which will come on a day and at an hour when we least expect it. [2]

NOTES

[1] *Witness to the World*, Crestwood, NY, St Vladimir's Seminary Press, 1987, p.22.
[2] "Living Tradition", in *The Orthodox Church*, 1987, pp.25-26.

BIBLIOGRAPHY

Works by John Meyendorff:

The Byzantine Legacy and the Orthodox Church, Crestwood, NY, St Vladimir's Seminary Press, 1982.
Byzantine Theology, New York, Fordham UP, 1974.
Byzantium and the Rise of Russia, Cambridge UP, 1981.
Catholicity and the Church, Crestwood, NY, St Vladimir's Seminary Press, 1983.
Christ in Eastern Christian Thought, Washington, Corpus Books, 1969.
Imperial Unity and Christian Division: The Church 450-680 A.D., Crestwood, NY, St Vladimir's Seminary Press, 1989.
Living Tradition, Crestwood, NY, St Vladimir's Seminary Press, 1978.
Marriage: An Orthodox Perspective, Tuckahoe, NY, St Vladimir's Seminary Press, 1970.
The Orthodox Church: Its Past and Its Role in the World Today, New York, Pantheon, 1962.
Orthodoxy and Catholicity, New York, Sheed & Ward, 1966.
A Study of Gregory Palamas, 1959.
St Gregory Palamas and Orthodox Spirituality, New York, St Vladimir's Seminary Press, 1974.
"Vision of Unity", in *The Orthodox Church* (journal), 1987.
"Witness to the World", in *The Orthodox Church* (journal), 1987.

John left his Faith and Order leadership because he felt (i) the WCC was being influenced too much by social rather than theological ideas and (ii) in order to concentrate on his scholarship and writings.

The last ecumenical task John and I shared was the joint Orthodox – NCCC group to negotiate the return of the Orthodox into membership into NCCC. At our last meeting he said to me: "We have done good work."

Charles Moeller
1896–1986

JAN GROOTAERS

By his very ancestry Charles Moeller seems to have been destined to excel in ecumenical dialogue. His great-great-grandfather Nicolas Moeller was a Scandinavian Lutheran who migrated to Germany, where he became one of the group surrounding Princess Amelia of Gallitzin and the celebrated "Münster Circle" (1779-1806), a centre of Roman Catholic renewal and of a genuine ecumenism before that term existed. When they came to Belgium in the middle of the 19th century, the Moeller family soon became part of the upper middle class of Brussels and in each generation they provided the Catholic university in the country with a professor.

Charles Moeller's training and education prepared him for the great ecclesiological and ecumenical turning-point which the Roman Catholic Church was to experience with the liberating pontificate of John XXIII. The Belgian theologian seems to have been predestined from his early days for the part he was later to play in the Second Vatican Council and the ecumenical movement.

The doctorate he undertook after his ordination in 1937 led Moeller to take a particular interest in patrology, specifically in the Christological and trinitarian controversies of the fifth and sixth centuries. His thesis on "Neo-Chalcedonism" (1942) represented a foundation on which he built thirty years later in his conversations with the Coptic Pope Shenouda III, leading to a declaration on the "common faith" signed by Shenouda and Pope Paul VI in 1973, the first reconciliation between Rome and Alexandria since the Council of Chalcedon in A.D. 451. [1]

From those years of study onwards, Moeller took an interest in the spirituality and recent theology of the Orthodox church. As a young man, he regularly visited the "monastery of unity" at Chevetogne, where Dom Clément Lialin, a Russian monk and great friend of Fr Georges Florovsky, helped to introduce him to Orthodoxy. These visits gave rise in 1945 to a series of *Journées de Chevetogne* ("Chevetogne Theological Sessions"), a virtual laboratory for dialogue and ecumenical research with an interconfessional and international outreach.[2] Already during the pontificate of Pius XII, the main approaches for a return to doctrinal basics were being discussed, which Vatican II was suddenly to bring to the fore a decade later. Moeller was responsible for organizing these sessions each autumn and for drawing out the final conclusions from them — each time producing a kind of theological fireworks whose brilliance surprised and dazzled his listeners. The choice of themes treated demonstrated the extraordinary perceptiveness of the organizers: Bible and Ecumenism (1950), Tradition and Dialogue (1951), Schism (1952), Grace and Ecumenism (1953), Baptism and the Church (1955), Holy Spirit and Church (1956). At the same time, strong links of friendship were being forged in various quarters, foreshadowing the close cooperation at Vatican II and in the ecumenical movement after the Council.[3]

Adding distinctive colours to those first years of Moeller's teaching was his enthusiastic interest as a theologian in the intellectual guides and moral mentors in contemporary literature. When Moeller was appointed lecturer (1949) and then full professor (1954) at the Higher Institute for Religious Studies at Louvain, he was already well-known to a youthful public for his critical studies of contemporary novelists and poets whose work enabled him to identify the main religious quests that exercise the modern mind. This original work, which involved a direct experience of the contemporary ethos, paved the way for his personal contribution to the drawing up of Vatican II's Constitution *Gaudium et Spes*, especially the two key chapters on "The Dignity of the Human Person" and the "Proper Development of Culture".

Moeller's important involvement as an expert in the work of Vatican II came not only in his well-known role in drawing up the great constitutions of the Council and the Decree on Ecumenism (*Unitatis Redintegratio*) but also in his discreet work on other documents such as that dealing with relations with other faiths. Moeller himself referred to these latter efforts as "toiling below deck". One of his great merits was rescuing difficult texts that had run into an impasse, including a draft on the church's presence in the modern world — a task from which many ecclesiologists in the previous stage had preferred to distance themselves.

While an important delegation of observers from the World Council of Churches established a permanent link between Geneva and the Council, Moeller was also a very valuable liaison officer. It is mainly due to him that the Montreal world conference on Faith and Order (1963) influenced the Vatican II text on Divine Revelation, and the WCC's New Delhi assembly (1961) is reflected in *Gaudium et Spes* (especially no. 92).[4]

Soon after the Council Moeller felt called to comment on the documents that had been promulgated and to show their practical importance. Having personally experienced the beginnings of the renewal and then having shared in its birth-pangs during Vatican II, he quite naturally came to be the historian of and commentator on the conciliar event and later to collaborate directly in the post-conciliar reform of the curia and the implementation of Vatican II from Rome. This meant seven years with the Congregation for the Doctrine of the Faith (1966-73) and seven happier and more fruitful years in the Secretariat for Promoting Christian Unity (1973-80), where he worked together with another veteran of the *Journées de Chevetogne*, Cardinal Willebrands, to translate Vatican II's ecumenical renewal into the living reality of the relations between churches and between Christians.[5]

* * *

Diversified and busy as it was, Moeller's life nevertheless displays remarkable continuity if one looks closely at the sources of his inspiration. His ecumenical concern was clearly one of the main pivots of its unity.

From adolescence onwards the stages in his vocation were marked by the discovery of liturgy as a living experience and of monastic life in several Benedictine abbeys. After having himself taken part in a monastic novitiate, he entered the seminary of the diocese of Malines (1935). His mentor was Dom Lambert Beauduin, founder of Chevetogne and pioneer of what could then not yet be called Catholic ecumenism, who was currently "in exile" in the region of Paris. The years which led to Moeller's doctorate in theology in 1942 were an initiation into Byzantine Christology as an extension of Greek patristics.

Moeller belonged to the high church trend found in 19th-century Catholicism in J.A. Möhler and J.H. Newman and in the 20th-century liturgical movement — with its return to patristic sources and the theology of the local church and the episcopate. The inspiration of Moeller and his fellow-workers drew on deep and lasting roots in that innovative tradition.

Nourished by a prayerful, reflective reading of the Bible, at home with the Eastern church fathers, well acquainted with the councils of the first few centuries, concerned for a revitalized liturgical life and involved in the ecumenical movement before it went by that name, Charles Moeller was unequivocally in line with a spirituality that drew on the wellsprings of the first millennium, in other words, of a Christianity prior to the great divisions in the church. Such a spirituality is clearly far removed from the particular — not to say particularist — "developments" of the Middle Ages in the West, which contributed to hardening the schism with the East and preparing the way for the Reformation.

Thus well before the election of Pope John XXIII, Moeller was equipped for a future no one could yet imagine. In Vatican II Moeller found a task to match his capacities. Granting that his vocation never led him to make a structured synthesis of theological thought, and that he consequently did not come into the class of the "great theologians", his personal qualities ensured that he would become a documentary craftsman of the first rank, and at the Council, amidst the tensions of a frequently stormy gathering, he accomplished tasks which precisely the "great theologians" could not manage.

These qualities — his intellectual curiosity, his ability to draw together scattered elements of a discussion and his long experience of dialogue — were well suited to the requirements of work at the Council, which could only be done by a team. Some may have suspected Moeller of a kind of intellectual dilettantism, but those debates in the Council which ventured away from the beaten track of textbook theology needed just such "dilettantes", with their boldness, creative spirit, erudition and flexibility.

A significant feature of Moeller's fundamental ecumenism was that he soon went beyond the bounds of the high church tendency of which we have spoken. After his considerable share in the work of drawing up *Gaudium et Spes*, he developed a great interest in the problems of society and social justice. This manifested itself in sustained cooperation with the WCC's Church and Society department and even a distancing from his friends whose relations with Geneva were limited to Faith and Order matters. He was personally involved in the preparations for the world conference on Church and Society (Geneva 1966), where he himself gave a masterly presentation, and for the WCC assembly in Uppsala in 1968.

During these somewhat euphoric transitional years, which marked a kind of "honeymoon" in relations between Geneva and Rome, Moeller developed a novel ecumenical scheme around the polarity between retrospective, backward-looking ecumenism (which seeks to eliminate inherited doctrinal divergences over Christology, ecclesiology and eschatology) and forward-looking ecumenism (which looks for a common approach to the urgent questions society is asking and will increasingly ask of the churches).[6] The originality of this updating of ecumenism lay in the attempt to establish the link between the social and doctrinal fields — a polarity which continues to constitute a problem for the World Council today.

While continuing to be concerned with exploiting the wealth of teaching of the church fathers and the great councils of the past, Moeller remained steadfast in his concern to listen to the clamant demands of present-day human beings. Here, it seems, is one of the chief lessons the great figure of Charles Moeller the ecumenist is still teaching us today.

* * *

In a published interview in 1983, Moeller reflected on ecumenism and diversity:

Ecumenism is not a department for specialists. If it were only that it would not be worth an hour's trouble. Rather it is a dimension that must run through the whole of theology, the whole of pastoralia, the whole of Christian education, and must lead to cooperation in confronting the great problems of the church in the world, for instance hunger and peace. On all these points we are both united and divided, in an imperfect communion. Thus to do ecumenical work means studying together Christian divisions and what causes them and answering new questions in a forward-looking way.

This is the spirit in which, at Tantur (Jerusalem), we have implemented the idea of Lutheran Professor Skydsgaard, an expert at the Council, which Paul VI took up again. There an academic community lives in fellowship with a community of monks and their celebrations. I have travelled all over the world to make that ecumenical institute known and to make it possible, for it should be an institute where one constantly and immediately realizes the scandalous absurdity of the divisions among Christians... From the Institute's terrace, overlooking Jericho, you see on the one hand the ruins of the town and on the other the remains of the fortress of Machaerus. That reveals where our conflicts lead, including our conflicts about doctrine — to a torn world, a lacerated Jesus. One cannot fail to see it — just as one cannot fail to see it also at the [Church of the] Holy Sepulchre...

Diversity is possible and beneficial precisely in so far as we are faithful to the truth. Johann Adam Möhler discovered that through the Romantic movement in Germany and the Greek fathers... He stressed that heresy was nothing but the presentation of a partial truth of faith in isolation. This we keep forgetting, and so we replace harmony with ideology. One cannot keep hold of the truth without tension. Möhler made use of that principle — which in my view is of central importance — to reflect on church unity. Unity cannot be established by reducing everything to the lowest common denominator. Everyone, wherever they happen to live, can find the path towards koinonia in diversity...[7]

NOTES

[1] *Documentation catholique*, vol. 70, 1973, pp.510-16.
[2] On the *Journées de Chevetogne*, see D.O. Rousseau in *Au Service de la Parole de Dieu*, Gembloux, 1969, pp.451-85; and E. Lanne, "Les semaines œcuméniques de Chevetogne", in *In Memoriam Mgr Charles Moeller*, pp.53-58. Reports of the *Journées* appeared in *Irénikon*, 1950, 1951, 1952; *L'Eglise et les églises*, Chevetogne, 1954; and *Grâce et œcuménisme*, 1957.
[3] Cf. Lanne, *op. cit.*, p.57.
[4] Cf. J.L. Leuba, in *La révélation divine*, ed. B.D. Dupuy, Paris, Cerf, 1968, pp.478ff.; C. Moeller, in "Das Zweite Vatikanische Konzil", in *Lexikon für Theologie und Kirche*, III, Freiburg, Herder, 1968, p.589n.
[5] On the end of the post-Vatican II "ecumenical springtime", see Moeller's comments in *Osservatore Romano*, 19 January 1974, cited in *Documentation catholique*, vol. 71, 1974, p.246.
[6] Cf. Moeller, "Perspectives postconciliaires en théologie et catéchèse", *Lumen Vitae*, vol. 21, no. 4, December 1966, pp.665-82; "A la veille de l'assemblée d'Upsal", *Irénikon*, 1968, no. 2; "Perspectives théologiques après le Concile", in *Au service de la parole de Dieu*, pp.367-93.
[7] "Au carrefour des lettres et de l'Eglise", *La Foi et le Temps*, no. 6, 1983, pp.511-24.

Martin Niemöller
1892–1984

HANS HAFENBRACK

Martin Niemöller was born on 14 January 1892 in Lippstadt, Westphalia, where his father was pastor. After finishing school in 1910 he became a cadet in the imperial navy; and from 1912 until the end of the first world war he was a naval commander. In 1919 he married Else Bremer. After planning to emigrate and spending some time as a farm worker, he studied theology in Münster because "faith in Christ makes people new, free and strong". From 1924 to 1930 he was the executive secretary of the Home Mission in Westphalia and from 1931 pastor of St Annen in Berlin-Dahlem.

In 1933 Niemöller founded the "emergency alliance of pastors", which would be the forerunner of the Confessing Church. After Adolf Hitler received a group of church leaders in the Reich chancellory in Berlin on 25 January 1934, Niemöller was banned from preaching. On 1 July 1937 he was arrested and tried; and from 1938 to 1945 he was Hitler's "personal prisoner" in the concentration camps of Sachsenhausen and Dachau. In 1945 he was moved to the Tyrol where he was freed by German, then US forces.

Niemöller was instrumental in the Stuttgart Declaration of Guilt by the Evangelical Church in Germany in October 1945 and became president of the church's office of external affairs and a member of its council. From 1946 he made hundreds of ecumenical visits to almost all the countries in the world. From 1947 to 1964 he was president of the Evangelical Church in Hesse and Nassau, and from 1961 to 1968 he was a president of the World Council of Churches. He died on 6 March 1984 in Wiesbaden.

During his lifetime honorary doctorates were conferred on him by universities all over the world. He also held the Lenin gold medal, the gold medal for peace of the German Democratic Republic, and the grand cross of merit of the Federal Republic of Germany.

Niemöller has no doubt become the best-known German Protestant in this century. In the words of the president of the Bundestag, Eugen Gerstenmaier, "There was a time when two German Protestant theologians were famous all over the world. One was Martin Luther and the other Martin Niemöller." His arrest by the Nazis in 1937 was reported by press agencies all over the world and church bells tolled in Britain. Deeply affected by the news, a young West Indian Methodist, Philip Potter, took the decision to study theology. Even his opponents in church politics within the Evangelical Church in Germany — who were never lacking — agreed about Niemöller's pre-eminence. The Bishop of Berlin-Brandenburg, Otto Dibelius, his opponent in the struggle for the restoration or renewal of the church after the second world war, wrote that Niemöller's name would live on "long after we have been forgotten".

Niemöller's life has not been forgotten for three reasons. First, his long journey from nationalistic, militaristic patriotism to radical pacifism reflects and exemplifies the human turmoils of this century. Second, as the founder of the Confessing Church and the "personal prisoner" of the *Führer*, he became the symbol for the rest of the world of church resistance to Nazi totalitarianism. Third, after 1945 he was the first positive product to be exported from an ostracized Germany. On his numerous world travels he became the ambassador of the "other Germany", a father of the ecumenical movement and a pioneer of international understanding.

It was a long way from patriot to pacifist, from wartime commander to messenger of peace, and Niemöller's path along it showed the many contradictions which made him a controversial figure in Germany. In the first world war this pastor's son fought for the German Reich as a submarine commander, refusing in 1918 to obey the order of a British officer to hand over his ship to the victorious powers. He was married on Easter Sunday 1919 wearing the uniform of the imperial navy. In 1920 he commanded a nationalist battalion of the First Westphalian Brigade in the fight against the first German democracy. From the concentration camp in Dachau he volunteered for the front in Hitler's army — an action which after 1945 caused even his friends to shake their heads.

After 1945 Niemöller became the standard-bearer of the German peace movement. He turned into a radical pacifist after the atomic physicist Otto Hahn explained to him in 1954 that human beings could now wipe out the human race with weapons of mass destruction. A speech in Kassel in 1959 unleashed a storm of indignation against him in both church and state: "Mothers and fathers should know what they are doing when they let their son become a soldier. They are letting him be trained as a criminal." Federal Chancellor Konrad Adenauer stigmatized him as a "rabble-rouser". In the anti-communist mood of the Cold War he was branded as a "tool of Moscow".

But Niemöller was no politician — and friends like Karl Barth said that he was no real theologian, either. The only thing that makes Niemöller's radical change of heart understandable is that he was a biblical rigorist — something that no political pragmatist can grasp. "What would Jesus have said of this?" is the fitting title of a remarkable film made shortly before Niemöller's death in which he took stock of his life in several long interviews. As a small boy he had read a text on the wall of a room where his father was visiting one of his parishioners, a working man who was dying: "What would Jesus say of this?" That question became the central guiding principle in his life. It explains his radicality, and the controversy and admiration that surrounded his life.

The transition from defender of the popular alliance of throne and altar to spearhead of the Confessing Church struggling for its autonomy was, if anything, still more problematic. In his autobiography *From U-boat to Pulpit*, published in 1934, there is still no trace of the change of heart. Niemöller approved the Nazis' seizure of power in 1933, read Hitler's *Mein Kampf* and voted for the Nazi party. Even as the chairman of the "emergency alliance of pastors", the core from which the Confessing Church grew, he assured the *Führer* in a loyal address of his "true allegiance".

The Niemöller whom Adolf Hitler met on 25 January 1934 along with other Protestant leaders was a completely changed man. On his lapel he wore his first world war decorations and in his pocket, in case it was needed, he had the order of the "Turkish Crescent" awarded for sinking enemy ships off Saloniki. But in his heart the ex-naval captain carried a torpedo trained against the Nazi effort to reduce the church to religious matters only.

Hitler never forgave Niemöller for having the last word at this meeting. To Hitler's demand that the church mind its own business and leave it to him as *Führer* to look after the German people, Niemöller replied: "To that I must say we as Christians have a responsibility for our people, laid on us by God; neither you nor any power in the world can take that responsibility away." This marks the turning point in Niemöller's life. His courage cost him eight years in the concentration camps of Sachsenhausen and Dachau. At the same time his courage made it possible after 1945 for German Protestantism to point to its political responsibility with the Barmen Declaration of 1934. For Niemöller it came to be the epitome of the Evangelical doctrine.

The *Führer*'s personal prisoner really had nothing to reproach himself for. But after the liberation in 1945 Hitler's victim became the unwavering preacher of guilt. He insisted that the Stuttgart Declaration include the words Dibelius had wanted removed: "We accuse ourselves..." From him, too, came the sentence, "We say with great sorrow: through us endless suffering has been brought to many peoples and lands." With this Declaration he opened the way into the ecumenical movement for the Evangelical Church in Germany. Later Niemöller was to speak of his personal guilt in sentences which went round the world and which are still highly relevant today: "When the Nazis came for the Communists, I said nothing — I wasn't a Communist; when they locked up the Social Democrats, I said nothing — I wasn't a Social Democrat; when they took away the Catholics, I didn't protest — I wasn't a Catholic. When they came for me, there was nobody left to protest."

On hundreds of visits as the head of the office of external affairs of his church, he preached reconciliation in almost all the countries of the world. His favourite destinations were the United States and the Soviet Union. In the ecumenical movement Niemöller represented a new German church. He was a member of the Central Committee of the World Council of Churches, chairman of the Finance Committee and one of the presidents.

In his own country the controversy surrounding him continued unabated. He was an outsider in Adenauer's Germany and in his church, which withdrew from him the direction of the office of external affairs. His verdict was bitter and not entirely fair: "I have suffered more under the church since 1945 than under the whole of National Socialism." He provoked everyone who chose to honour him. The Federal Republic, which honoured him with its highest order, he described as a changeling "sired in Rome and born in Washington". When receiving the gold medal for peace, he described the German Democratic Republic as a "colony" of the East. To the representatives of the Soviet Union, honouring him with the Lenin medal, he began his provocative toast with the words, "Dear Soviet friends, our Lord Jesus said... "

Niemöller's importance for the ecumenical movement is clear. He called the churches to "prophetic witness in the world", as the former WCC general secretaries Philip Potter and Willem Visser 't Hooft wrote on the death of the German theologian in 1984. One central idea shaped his life. Written on one of his postcards from the concentration camp were the words "The gospel is attack". By that he meant first and foremost the church's responsibility in the world. Because of that he fought against a conservative understanding of the classic Lutheran two-kingdom doctrine, which with the National Socialists had degenerated into the cynical interpretation: "The earth is ours, heaven for the Christians and the sparrows."

Niemöller put more and more emphasis on living out the Christian faith, on discipleship. Accordingly, in his last interview he expressed the opinion that he found it more than doubtful whether the "Christian West" had brought any progress at all to humanity in the 2000 years of its existence. Worse still, it had given it "nothing Christian" at all apart from human self-justification.

With his message of reconciliation Niemöller became a "pastor to the churches of the whole world". More than anyone else he had helped his own country to resume its place in the community of nations. World traveller that he was, he did more for this than anyone else in Germany. One biographer of Niemöller worked out that he had been everywhere except China, Tibet, Afghanistan and Albania.

Later, in Potter's words, Niemöller once again played the role of reconciler. His numerous visits to the countries of the main protagonists in the Cold War built bridges. Not least, his visits to the Soviet Union helped to bring the churches of that country into the ecumenical movement.

Karl Barth called his friend a "credible witness to Jesus Christ". He was a true servant of the gospel. Important to him above all else was the question which clearly set the keynote of his life: "What would Jesus say of this?"

BIBLIOGRAPHY

Works by Martin Niemöller:

From U-boat to Pulpit, Constable 1934.
Letters from Prison in Moabit, 1975.
Sermons in Dahlem, 1936-37.
Five volumes of talks and sermons from the years 1945-76.

Nikodim (Rotov)
1929–1978

KIRILL OF SMOLENSK AND KALININGRAD

In the 1960s, when a "thaw" in Soviet domestic policy was combined with the most severe persecution of the church, I was at school in St Petersburg (then Leningrad). Truth to tell, as the son of a priest I was close to a nervous breakdown. I was hounded by the press; indeed, a front-page newspaper article once asked: "What shall we do with this young man, who is excellent in school subjects but goes to church?" I was summoned to the teachers' councils to be admonished and warned that unless I joined the Komsomol, I would be expelled from school and denied any role in future life.

Just at this time a new metropolitan came to Leningrad. All of us thought at first that he was yet another protegé of the secular authorities, for he was only 32. A stout man of average height, full of energy but repulsive to the people — that is how he seemed at first sight. A couple of days after Nikodim's arrival in Leningrad my father came home from church and said: "Just as we are criticizing the new metropolitan, do you know what he has done for a start? He has had the censorship of sermons lifted!" Up to that time, priests in Leningrad had to present the text of every sermon to the dean or to the local commissioner for religious affairs before preaching it. Things changed with the arrival of Metropolitan Nikodim.

The coming of the new metropolitan to Leningrad brought changes in my own life as well. Had I not met him, I would have joined the company of dissidents. But Metropolitan Nikodim, while fully admitting the justice of criticism of the existing regime — criticism which was part of my own family upbringing — used to say to me: "The church ought to seek ways of asserting its physical presence. It must take into account the historical reality in which it exists. It is important to maintain a dialogue with the world around, including the ruling powers. This dialogue will bring victory to those who prove to be spiritually stronger and better equipped and whose convictions are deeper."

Today, more than 15 years after his death, Nikodim has become an almost mythical character. Many church leaders charge that he compromised, as if they hope themselves to be found innocent of doing so. Some refer to him as a "KGB general", as if this would make them holier. When it comes to discerning the spirits, however, the gospel says: "You will know them by their fruits" (Matt. 7:16). What are the fruits which this now-departed servant brought to Christ?

He was born Boris Rotov in the village of Frolovo, in the Ryazan region, on 15 October 1929. His parents had no attachment to the church, but the boy, thanks to the unfathomable ways of the Lord, was drawn to God from an early age. After two years at the Ryazan Teachers' Training Institute, he left his native town for Yaroslavl, where his church service began. There at 17 he became a deacon and a monk, taking the monastic name of Nikodim. He began to work at the bishop's house in Yaroslavl under Archbishop Dimitry (Gradusov), who had ordained him. He was barely 20 when Archbishop Dimitry raised him to the rank of hieromonk (monk-presbyter).

The future metropolitan began his pastoral ministry at a small parish in the village of Davydovo, moving from there to the ancient Russian towns of Pereslavl-Zalevssky and Uglich. At the beginning of 1952, Nikodim was appointed to the staff of the cathedral church of Yaroslavl as secretary to the archbishop and, in 1954, acting rector. He continued his theological education at the Leningrad Theological Seminary and Academy by correspondence and completed it in 1955.

Nikodim's involvement in the church's external relations began in 1956 when he was assigned to the Russian Orthodox mission in Jerusalem. Shortly thereafter he was appointed head of the mission and was promoted to the rank of hegumen and then archimandrite. While in the Holy Land, he wrote a theological paper on the history of the Russian Orthodox mission in Jerusalem, for which he was awarded a degree in theology in 1959.

In March 1959 Archimandrite Nikodim was appointed head of chancellery at the Moscow Patriarchate and shortly afterwards vice-chairman of the Department for External Church Relations as well. In 1960 he became chairman of the Department, a post he was to hold until 1972. On 31 May 1960, at the Trinity-St Sergius Lavra, he was consecrated Bishop of Podolsk. At the end of that year he was transferred to the see of Yaroslavl. In 1963 he was appointed metropolitan of Minsk and then of Leningrad. In 1974 as Metropolitan of Leningrad, he became Patriarchal Exarch to Western Europe. Between 1960 and 1963, he also headed the Publications Department of the Moscow Patriarchate; and from 1961 until his death he chaired the synodal Commission on Christian Unity.

In 1970 Metropolitan Nikodim received the degree of master of theology for a dissertation on the life and work of Pope John XXIII. The senate of the Leningrad Theological Academy awarded him a doctorate in theology for his theological works as a whole. He also received honorary doctorates from the Theological Academy of Sofia, Bulgaria, and from a number of Protestant theological faculties.

Metropolitan Nikodim's involvement with the World Council of Churches is well known, but his ecumenical activity was not confined to that alone. Above all, he was a devoted intra-Orthodox ecumenist, who did much to strengthen the spiritual unity within Orthodoxy. He headed the Russian Orthodox delegations to the pan-Orthodox conferences of 1961, 1963, 1964 and 1968; and as chairman of the special theological commission of the Russian Orthodox Church for the pan-Orthodox Council, he never abandoned the idea of the Council. Better than many others, he realized that the Orthodox churches, which have not convened their supreme doctrinal and canonical legislative body since the 8th century, urgently needed to reflect on the new realities and draw authoritative conclusions with regard to them in conciliar agreements.

His search for reconciliation among Christians in one faith and fraternal love also led Metropolitan Nikodim to work to overcome the division between the Russian Orthodox Church and the Russian Orthodox Church in America. The autocephaly (independence) granted to the latter, as well as the autonomy granted to the Orthodox Church in Japan, can be attributed principally to Metropolitan Nikodim's efforts. He was also concerned about the division among the Orthodox in Russia itself and, thanks to his efforts, in 1971 the local council lifted the anathema on the "Old Believers" and recognized them as Orthodox Christians.

The opening of theological dialogues and bilateral relationships between Russian Orthodox and the non-Orthodox churches also owed a great deal to Metropolitan Nikodim's initiative. He attended the closing ceremony of the Second Vatican Council in 1965, which opened the way for dialogue between the Russian Orthodox and Roman Catholic churches. The division between the Catholic and Orthodox churches caused him special pain and, while appreciating the complex problems which divide them, he was eager for the day of blessed unity. He was no less anxious to achieve understanding and unity with the Oriental Orthodox churches and with the churches of the Reformation. Under his leadership theological dialogues were opened with many of the latter, for example, the Lutheran churches in West and East Germany and Finland.

In 1961 Metropolitan Nikodim headed the Russian Orthodox delegation to the WCC's third assembly in New Delhi, where the church became a member of this international ecumenical organization. Twice more he headed Russian Orthodox delegations to WCC assemblies — at Uppsala (1968) and Nairobi (1975). From 1961 to 1975 he was a member of the WCC Central and Executive Committees, and from 1975 until his death he was one of the WCC presidents. Actively involved in the many activities of the WCC, he greatly appreciated this forum of world Christianity as a meeting place of different traditions, offering all Christians an opportunity to come to know one another better and to move closer to confessing the one faith in order to fulfil Christ's prayer for unity of his followers (John 17:21).

There are people — few of whom knew Metropolitan Nikodim — who now say that he undertook his ecumenical activity on assignment from the secular authorities seeking to create in the West the illusion that there was religious freedom in the former Soviet Union. While it is true that the Soviet leaders hoped to improve their international image through the external contacts of the Russian Orthodox Church, it was in vain, for it was precisely this possibility of international contacts that made the church feel stronger and more sure of itself and enabled it to stop repressive action by the authorities by drawing the attention of public opinion abroad to our troubles. Many representatives of the church, when visiting foreign countries, secretly handed over information about the persecution of the church to Western Christians, while the arrival of a foreign delegation at a church or monastery in the USSR might well save that building from profanation. Once when the authorities decided to close the Leningrad Theological Academy, after refusing students permission to live in the city, Metropolitan Nikodim simply opened a department for Asian and African students. The presence of foreigners at the Academy frightened the authorities and the Academy soon resumed its activities.

Fighting for the rights of the church was not, however, the only — and perhaps not even the most important — advantage won by Russian Orthodoxy through its first moves into ecumenism. The wall between Russian Christians and the rest of the world was virtually impenetrable during the three decades of the Stalin era. Forcibly separated from both world Christendom and the life of its own nation, the Russian Orthodox Church was in danger of turning into a ghetto made up of clergymen and old women. By the early 1960s, church circles were dominated by people who had resigned themselves to the prophecy of the Marxist authorities that religion would "wither away". Such people lived as if they had no wish to hinder the process, as if their only wish was to pass away themselves as quickly as possible. Liturgical life in the parishes attended to only the people's elementary religious needs; and daily routine proceeded according to the proverb "near is my shirt, but nearer still my skin". The memory of the spirit of mission, of communal life, of liturgical, theological and social creativity was virtually extinguished. In that situation of spiritual asphyxia a break-through to brothers and sisters living in freedom offered us a possibility of spiritual renewal and delivered us from the threat of theological provincialism, in addition to preparing us for the changes which would take place after the fall of the totalitarian regime.

It is often said that Nikodim was ahead of his time. In all likelihood, this was true. But I think it was through his efforts that the Russian Orthodox Church has found itself prepared to meet the challenges of today. Precisely through the ecumenical and other external church contacts that began under his leadership, the church has succeeded in nurturing a noticeable if not numerous group of theologians and church leaders who have shown themselves ready, like the late metropolitan, realistically, competently and wisely to meet the new challenges in relation to our internal life: inter-denomina-tional relationships, the social teaching of the church, the problems of humanity and society in a Christian perspective. Some people today ask whether the Russian Orthodox Church should have devoted so much attention to South Africa when it could not speak up about its own internal problems. But what the church learned from the experience of the inter-ethnic conflicts in apartheid South Africa now helps us approach similar conflicts in our country with greater wisdom and foresight than the secular specialists in the country.

A major interest of Metropolitan Nikodim was modern Russian ecumenical theol-ogy, which took shape under his leadership and inspiration. For him and his followers the search for Christian unity was organically connected with faithfulness to Orthodoxy and the conviction that the basis of our future unity is to be found in the ancient undivided church, with its spirit of brotherly love, founded on one common faith and respect for diversity, provided it did not distort the teaching of Christ rooted in the good news. Return to the spirit and the faith of the early Christians, a fresh look at existing traditions and opinions of every particular church and distinguishing what is authenti-cally inherent to the church and what is brought about by current developments could indeed lead us to the genuine "unity of the Spirit in the bond of peace" (Eph. 4:3).

Metropolitan Nikodim was fully aware that the witness to our faith in the ecumenical movement would not be easy. He told the Uppsala assembly:

> It has been clear to the Orthodox mind from the very beginning that the cooperation with the World Council and all the more so our joining its membership will inevitably mean our immersion into the element of Protestantism, or, if you want, some kind of *kenosis*, inasmuch as the voice of the Orthodox witness at ecumenical gatherings and in the documents of the World Council is to be almost always drowned in the choir of diverse, but essentially Protestant opinions.

But this realism did not prevent Metropolitan Nikodim from believing that the Lord was blessing the dialogue that had been opened and would help its participants to find brothers and sisters in one another through obedience to his will. As he said in concluding his report in Uppsala:

> Looking upon all the difficulties and complexities on our way together to Christian unity with optimism and hope, inspired by the love of the God-Man, Jesus Christ our Lord, and anxious to multiply his faith and love all over the world, we shall steadily go forward, furthering the ecumenical movement, because in front of us, as a good pastor, he is going, the Saviour and Restorer of the world, who makes all things new, who is the Way, the Truth and the Life.

To this day, Metropolitan Nikodim's ecumenical activities continue to arouse mistrust among some Russian Orthodox clergy and lay believers in the Russian Orthodox Church. I am sure that this mistrust is born of ignorance both of what all the ecumenical efforts of Orthodoxy are really about and of Metropolitan Nikodim's personality. He was a son of his church, believing that the Lord himself had called him to serve the unity of Christians. Aware that many people rejected ecumenism out of sheer ignorance, he dedicated much effort to establishing systematic ecumenical education, thanks to which a whole generation of theological students in the Russian Orthodox Church learned about the history and doctrinal principles of non-Orthodox denominations and about their relations with the Orthodox Church.

But it is not only as an administrator and public ecclesiastical figure that Metropolitan Nikodim's flock and his fellow bishops and presbyters remember him. For those of us who consider ourselves his disciples, he was the highest example of pastoral zeal, dissatisfaction with himself, constant search, selflessness and ardent ministry to God. Like St Paul, he could have said of himself: "Beloved, I do not consider that I have made it my own; but this one thing I do: forgetting what lies behind and straining forward to what lies ahead, I press on towards the goal for the prize of the heavenly call of God in Christ Jesus" (Phil. 3:13-14).

He was a wonderful preacher. Although most of his sermons — delivered spontaneously, but notable for their logic and many quotations, for he had a vast memory — are not extant, many were published in the *Journal of the Moscow Patriarchate*, like the one in 1968 from which this is taken:

> A Christian, the servant of God, does not fear the omnipotence of God, as he knows with awesome happiness that he can audaciously call upon God as his heavenly Father. It is with humility that he feels the imperfection of his human nature, which could become omnipotent if human will joined with divine grace. "I can do all things in him who strengthens me," said St Paul. The Christian humility with which it is natural for a Christian to look at himself is not a passive feeling which weakens a man. It does not lead to inactivity and indifference in life. On the contrary, humility is a very active principle which allows human conscience to see a real picture of inner imperfection, and a man can completely and impartially appraise himself and his inner, spiritual state, which is always far from the ideal towards which a Christian yearns and from the potential power of spirit which a Christian draws in his sonship of God, in the inexhaustible source of the grace of the Holy Spirit, which always heals that which is infirm and completes that which is wanting.

He was a real archpastor, a spiritual father to both clergy and laity. As the ruling bishop of three dioceses — Leningrad, Novgorod and Olonets — to which the West European Exarchate was added in the last years of his life, he often visited parishes, received visitors and fairly, though sometimes very emotionally, resolved many conflict situations. He had a particular interest in the Leningrad Theological Seminary, as I know very well through my work as Rector there since 1975.

Metropolitan Nikodim was an expert in Orthodox traditions, especially the liturgical tradition. He knew many of the psalms, prayers and canons by heart. He himself compiled inspired liturgical texts. Fascinated with the beauty and wisdom of Orthodox liturgy, he reflected deeply on how to bring an understanding of it to people today. He knew the Old Church Slavonic language perfectly, but translated many liturgical texts into Russian and gave his blessing to the reading of the Holy Scriptures in Russian in some churches. At the same time, he was aware that Russia's complicated problem of liturgical language and forms would not be solved by administrative decisions, and he never opposed those who wished to adhere to traditional liturgical statutes.

He lived by prayer, by divine services, by the eucharist. Sometimes he celebrated over one hundred divine services a year. Occasionally he would come to the cathedral church to sing together with the choir during the service. If there was no opportunity to celebrate in one of the city churches, he celebrated liturgy in the private chapels in each of his residences. He carried liturgical vessels with him on all his trips and celebrated the eucharist at ancient holy places or even at meetings and conferences.

Partaking of the body and blood of Christ was a necessity of his life. I remember many moments when Metropolitan Nikodim, weakened by hard work and the ill feelings aroused by certain actions on the part of the authorities, found himself spiritually revived after holy communion. He advised all of us, his disciples and his flock, to take holy communion as frequently as possible. The wish to celebrate the liturgy and to take holy communion was especially strong in the last years of his life when he suffered from serious heart disease. When his illness confined him to bed, an altar was placed by his bedside. When he regained some strength, he would go to his private chapel — against doctor's orders — and celebrate the eucharist. After holy communion his strength was renewed.

Even so, his health was gravely imperilled by his heart condition. From 1974 onwards, he gradually turned over his church and public duties to his disciples. Five heart attacks, one after another, kept him from his work for long periods of time. On 5 September 1978, during a visit with the newly-elected Pope John Paul I at the Vatican, Metropolitan Nikodim died suddenly of a heart attack.

At the monastic cemetery of the Alexander Nevsky Lavra in St Petersburg stands a black gravestone with a high, typically Russian eight-pointed cross. Metropolitan Nikodim's disciples come to this grave each year on the anniversary of his death and on Easter to pray for the rest of the deceased hierarch in the eternal mansions of the heavenly Father. But besides bishops, theologians and his former colleagues, ordinary parishioners also come, remembering the solemn divine services conducted by Metropolitan Nikodim, his sermons, his inspired face on which both an intense spiritual and intellectual activity and a profoundly tragic element were imprinted.

Those who visit his grave try to grasp the meaning of the words inscribed on the gravestone in accordance with the Metropolitan's will. Taken from old Orthodox liturgical texts, these words sum up the meaning of this man's standing before God, this man who was "a burning and shining lamp" (John 5:35):

> O Lord, as a man I have sinned; have mercy on me, as the God full of competence, seeing the feebleness of my soul.
> O Jesus, the God of my heart, come and unite me with thee for ever.

BIBLIOGRAPHY

Texts by Metropolitan Nikodim published in the Journal of the Moscow Patriarchate:

"About the Ways to Christian Unity", 1965, no. 11.

Address at the opening of the third pan-Orthodox conference, Rhodes, 1965, no. 2.

"Christian Responsibility for a Better World", address at the fourth All-Christian Peace Assembly, Prague, 1972, nos 1-2.

"Concerning a Rapprochement between the Chalcedonian and Non-Chalcedonian Theology", 1970, no. 4.

"Dialogue with Roman Catholics on Modern Christian Social Thought", address to the 1966 Geneva world conference on church and society, 1966, no. 9.

"The Holy Eucharist: The Sacrament of the Life of the Church", 1974, no. 8.

"On the Tasks of Modern Theology", 1968, no. 12.

"Peace and Freedom", 1963, no. 1.

"Peace Ministry of Churches in the World Which Launched out on a Way to Perfection", 1964, no. 1.

"The Russian Orthodox Church and the Ecumenical Movement", 1968, no. 9; also published in *One Church*, no. 6, 1968.

"The Russian Orthodox Church and the World Council of Churches", 1960, no. 4.

"Tradition and Contemporaneity", 1972, no. 12.

An English translation of Metropolitan Nikodim's thesis *John XXIII: The Pope of Rome* was published by Pro Oriente, Vienna, 1984.

Daniel Thambyrajah Niles
1908–1970

ANS J. VAN DER BENT

D.T. Niles was a key leader of the ecumenical movement for four decades, a bridge-builder between the churches in the East and the West and a powerful evangelist in the multi-religious and secular world of his day. The slim, white-robed son of Asia, with an instinct for the right word on an important occasion, took as his text for the opening service of the first assembly of the World Council of Churches (Amsterdam 1948) Moses' question when God called him: "Who am I, that I should go?". Twenty years later, at the opening service of the fourth assembly in Uppsala, he stood in the place that Martin Luther King, murdered four months earlier, was to have occupied in the cathedral. With freshness and power he expounded the assembly theme: "Behold, I make all things new". None would have guessed from his appearance and his manner that he was sixty years old.

When in 1962 Niles published his book *Upon the Earth: The Mission of God and the Missionary Enterprise of the Churches*, Lesslie Newbigin wrote in the preface:

> When the study plan on "The Word of God and the Church's Missionary Obedience" was developed, there was never any doubt who should be asked to write this book. D.T. Niles combines in a unique manner the insights and experiences that were needed for the job. He is both a theologian and an evangelist. There are theologians who can write about evangelism but have not the gift of so presenting Christ to men that they find in him their Saviour. And there are effective evangelists whose theology is an easy target for attack. Niles is an evangelist who is also a profound thinker, a theologian who can commend his Saviour effectively to others. Moreover, he is at home at both ends of the foreign missionary operation as it is normally understood. He knows the "feel" both of older and younger churches from inside and he can speak with authority to both. And, finally, his ministry is both local and ecumenical. Perhaps this is his most important qualification to speak to us at this moment.

The son of a distinguished lawyer and the grandson of a much-loved pastor and poet, D.T. Niles was born on 4 May 1908 in Tellipalai, in what was then called Ceylon.

After school and college in Jaffna, he studied theology in Bangalore, India, from 1929 to 1933. He was frequently in Europe and North America and gained a remarkable mastery of the English language, especially of English poetry. Nevertheless, he remained a son of Asia, never quite at ease if he was away from his own land for any length of time. In 1936 he was ordained to the ministry of the Methodist Church and for three years served as a district evangelist.

For a time he served in Geneva as evangelism secretary of the World YMCA. Returning to his own country, he was general secretary of the National Christian Council from 1941 to 1945. Niles was a determined, resourceful and patient advocate of the church union scheme in his nation. He was also involved in interfaith dialogue, which made him "see how essential it is for a Christian to think Christianly of other faiths". From 1948 to 1952 he was chairman of the WCC Youth Department and from 1953 to 1959 executive secretary of its Department of Evangelism. From 1953 onwards he was also co-chairman, with Philippe Maury, of the World Student Christian Federation, and planned and carried through an energetic programme on "The Life and Mission of the Church". He was deeply involved in the WCC's Evanston, New Delhi and Uppsala assemblies (1954, 1961 and 1968). In 1959 and 1960 he served as Henry Emerson Fosdick Professor at Union Theological Seminary in New York. When he resigned his position as general secretary of the East Asia Christian Conference in 1968, he was made its chairman. That same year he was elected to the WCC presidium. In 1970 he went to the Christian Medical Hospital in Vellore, India, for treatment and later an operation for cancer. There he died on 17 July of that year.

Loyal Methodist though he was, D.T. Niles was uneasy about the world confessional bodies. "It is my conviction", he said, "that denominations and confessions throughout the world have a function to perform of the utmost importance... To put a structure around any particular tradition is to make it indigestible." And again: "The church in its encounter with the world, and its service to the world, and its witness in the world, has in many places heavy institutions, and has adopted intricate procedures of work. To put it another way, the church has prepared for trench warfare but found itself faced with an enemy whose methods were much more flexible."

Despite these strong convictions and opinions, which he held passionately, D.T. Niles remained until the end of his life a gifted evangelist, a genuine revivalist and a brilliant missionary in the most humane sense of the word. At a memorial service for him vice-moderator Ernest Payne of the WCC Central Committee recalled:

> Dr Visser 't Hooft... was at first somewhat concerned about the events which led to the formation of the East Asia Christian Conference. But when he came back from Prapat in 1957 he declared: "Its motivation was wholly positive. The whole content of the discussion was the evangelistic calling of the church in Asia." That was D.T.'s constant aim and purpose. The Lord God had indeed given him "the tongue of a teacher and skill to console the weary" (Isa. 50:4)... He had the gift of interpretation. He was a most impressive preacher and Bible expositor, able to hold congregations in almost any land.

D.T. Niles was profoundly influenced by dialectical theology, especially by Karl Barth, whose radical Christocentricity, he said, "demonstrates the impossibility of including Jesus Christ in any theological understanding except as such understanding is grounded in him alone and arises out of an acceptance of him only as Lord". He was also greatly indebted to W.A. Visser 't Hooft for his Christocentric universalism and "the life-and-death nature of the church's struggle with all forms of syncretism". From Hendrik Kraemer, he said, he learned "to approach other faiths and to enter into them as a Christian", and Paul Devanandan taught him "to see and understand the Christian faith from the vantage ground of other faiths".

Yet throughout his life Niles continued to cherish several doctrinal emphases of Methodism: the emphasis on "experimental religion", the need for a "personal encounter with Jesus Christ" and "personal decision and commitment"; the indispensability of "holy living"; the centrality of the Bible, reflected in the deep rooting of all his writings in scriptural Christianity; the emphasis, evident in his ecumenical concern, on the "universality of the will of God for salvation"; and the emphasis on the doctrine of "prevenient grace", which played a significant role in his theology of dialogue.

At the same time, Niles was profoundly aware that the Christian faith must find indigenous expression in each place. He defined an indigenous church as one that is "national in its expression, spontaneous in its growth and local in its colouring". He was convinced that the process of indigenization in India and Sri Lanka must be different from that of Christianity in the West, where, generally, Christianity was first accepted as a state religion and then races, cultures and nations were gradually Christianized. In India and Sri Lanka the process was reversed: "in the East, the church as a Christian institution has to be nationalized".

Along with an astonishing range of public responsibilities and an almost ceaseless succession of journeys to all corners of the earth to preach, lecture and conduct university missions, D.T. Niles wrote a large number of English verse translations of Asian hymns, which are still sung today at many ecumenical gatherings.

Of him, his friend Bishop Kulendran said: "He went to the Bible not to pick up a verse but to think with the biblical writers." Lesslie Newbigin called him "an ecumenical statesman, a strategist whose long-term planning did much to influence ecumenical development and also a skilful tactician who could change a situation with a brilliant and unexpected move. He could outwit his opponents, but he did not make enemies. Central to his whole life was the giving and receiving of friendship." Typical of the man are these words from one of the last sermons he preached:

> When I am dead, many things will be said about me — that I held this and that position and did this and that thing. For me all these are irrelevant. The only important thing that I can say about myself is that I, too, am one whom Jesus Christ loved and for whom he died.

Indigenous theology is always situational or contextual theology. Its response to the gospel is made from within a particular historical situation and by a particular involvement in it. Because of this, M.M. Thomas has written, the articulation and formulation of faith "at the level of a living situation is often partial, fragmentary and unsystematic". According to C.L. Furtado, "systematization and comprehensiveness of theology cannot be made the primary criterion of evaluating this theology. Its adequacy must be judged in the light of the mission of the church of which it is the servant". That sums up well the primary concern of D.T. Niles for winning a hearing and explains his evangelistic effectiveness.

BIBLIOGRAPHY

Works by D.T. Niles:

A Testament of Faith, London, Epworth, 1972.
That They May Have Life, London, Lutterworth, 1952.
Upon the Earth, London, Lutterworth, 1962.

About D.T. Niles:

Christopher L. Furtado, *The Contribution of Dr D.T. Niles to the Church Universal and Local*, Madras, Christian Literature Society, 1978.

Nikos Nissiotis
1924–1986

MARIOS BEGZOS

A philosopher of religion and an internationally renowned Eastern Orthodox theologian, Nikos Nissiotis was a key figure in the 20th-century ecumenical movement. After studying theology, philosophy, psychology and sociology in Athens (1942-47), Zurich (1948-49, under Emil Brunner and Carl-Gustav Jung), Basel (1951-52, under Karl Barth and Karl Jaspers), and Louvain (1952-53), he received a doctorate in theology in Athens in 1956. His thesis was on "Existentialism and the Christian Faith".

In the ecumenical movement he was a leading figure at the Ecumenical Institute and Graduate School in Bossey near Geneva (1956-74), associate general secretary of the WCC (1968-74) and moderator of the Commission on Faith and Order (1977-82). He first taught as a professor at the theological faculty of the University of Geneva
(1962-74), serving as director of the Bossey graduate school from 1966 to 1974. He then became professor of the philosophy of religion in the theological faculty of the University of Athens (1965-86). As a visiting professor he lectured in universities all over the world and received honorary doctorates from Paris, Aberdeen, Bucharest and Geneva. He was president of the *Académie internationale des sciences religieuses* in Brussels (1984-86) and a member of the editorial board of various international journals (*Concilium, Journal of Ecumenical Studies, Ecumenical Review, Ökumenische Rundschau*).

Nissiotis was also an active and well-known sportsman and a leading member of the Olympic movement. A member of the Greek national Olympic committee from 1975, he served on the International Olympic Committee in Lausanne from 1977. He died in an automobile accident as he was returning to Athens from an Olympic institute where he often lectured to young athletes.

The originality of the intellectual achievements of Nikos Nissiotis rests on two main elements. As a philosopher of religion he introduced existentialism critically into the modern Greek-speaking world, and as an ecumenical theologian he strongly represented the Orthodox tradition to the Western ecumenical community. He is the only modern Greek theologian to have studied under the leading representatives of all the major European intellectual movements in the post-war era: Emil Brunner and Karl Barth (dialectical theology), Carl-Gustav Jung (depth psychology) and Karl Jaspers (existentialism). Nissiotis remains the world's most outstanding Orthodox theologian since the 1960s.

The starting point of his theological reflection was a personalist interpretation of the Greek patristic tradition: "The Christian God is a personal God... Person is the key biblical concept in the relation between God and man."[1] The main feature of his ecumenical contribution was an emphasis on the doctrine of the Trinity and especially pneumatology. Convinced that "the doctrine of the Trinity is the foundation on which Orthodoxy stands and from which the life and theology of the church have developed",[2] he took his direction from pneumatology: "The most important and difficult task for theology was and is to penetrate ever more deeply into doctrine of the Trinity on the basis of pneumatology",[3] or to put it more clearly, "Pneumatology is at the centre of Christian theology and is related to all aspects of faith in Christ... Pneumatology does not mean discourse about the Holy Spirit, but the reality of the Paraclete as the logos, the Word made flesh in us."[4]

In his view, Western Christian theology has always tended towards one-sidedness and has remained distant and estranged from pneumatology. In the Roman Catholic tradition he saw a so-called "unitarian Patromonism",[5] a one-sided emphasis on the Father to the neglect of the Son and the Spirit. The end result of this theological attitude is the precedence of the institutional over the charismatic, the lack of personal freedom and church totalitarianism. On the other side, he saw Reformation theology, in reaction against this approach, emerging with the danger of "Christomonism", the primacy of Christ as opposed to the Father and the Holy Spirit.[6] Further consequences of Protestant Christomonism are a one-sided emphasis on the charismatic at the expense of the institutional, the reinforcing of individualism and even pietism in Christian life and the dissolution of creative freedom into unlimited licence. In this way Christianity dissolves "either into mass collectivism of church institutions or into fragmented individualism".[7]

The Orthodox contribution to the Christian ecumenical fellowship lies precisely in the fact that pneumatology transcends the boundaries of Roman Catholic "Patromonism" and Protestant "Christomonism". The Holy Spirit "is a principle of unity, a unifying principle. He does not work simply as an organizer, but as a renewer and as such as a comforter".[8] In this sense, "we may say that within the Trinity unity is neither static nor purely functional. It is hypostatic... The idea of hypostatic unity precludes any type of monism focussing on one of the persons (whether Patromonism or Christomonism)."[9] Nissiotis sees Orthodox ecclesiology as the outcome of this pneumatological Christology: "The church, the mystical body of Christ, is a type, an *eikon* (image) of hypostatic unity; everything static and ontological in it becomes existential and dynamic through the life-giving strength of the Holy Spirit."[10]

The originality of Nissiotis' philosophy of religion was not only that he was the first to introduce existentialism along the lines of Kierkegaard and Jaspers into the modern Greek-speaking world, but that he also made a critique of it. He did not accept the existentialist elucidation of human existence without critical reservations. Nissiotis valued existentialism as a signal against the conformity of Christians in the post-war era, but at the same time he was fully aware of the limits of this philosophical definition of the human being. With the help of the personalist tradition of Greek patristics, Nissiotis criticized the latent individualism in existentialism, its polarization of the human person and society and the peculiar psychologism in the existentialist analysis of borderline situations.

In both his theology and his philosophy Nissiotis had the gift of combining faithfulness to the tradition of the past with openness towards the future. The dialogical and the dialectical were unquestionably the constant features of Nissiotis' thinking. As he said already in his doctoral thesis, "Philosophy is a constant dialogue with the other."

NOTES

[1] Nissiotis, *Die Theologie der Ostkirche im ökumenischen Dialog*, Stuttgart, Evangelisches Verlagswerk, 1968, pp.29,47.
[2] *Ibid.*, p.19.
[3] *Ibid.*, p.28.
[4] *Ibid.*, p.64.
[5] *Ibid.*, p.22.
[6] *Ibid.*, p.23.
[7] *Ibid.*, p.27.
[8] *Ibid.*, p.30.
[9] *Ibid.*, p.31.
[10] *Ibid.*, p.32.

BIBLIOGRAPHY

Works by Nikos Nissiotis:

Studies, Geneva, 1962, 1964, 1966, 1968, and Athens 1982: comprising 200 articles in Greek, English, German and Franch.
Die Theologie der Ostkirche im ökumenischen Dialog, Stuttgart, Evangelisches Verlagswerk, 1968.
Three monographs on the philosophy of religion in Greek: *Existentialism and the Christian Faith*, Athens, 1956; *Prologema of Theological Epistemology*, Athens, 1965; *Philosophy of Religion and Theological Philosophy*, Athens, 1965.

Works on Nikos Nissiotis:

M. Begzos, *Logos als Dialogos. Ein Porträt von Nikos Nissiotis*, Thessaloniki, 1991, in Greek with detailed bibliography.
O. Clément, "Prolégomènes à la gnoséologie théologique de N. Nissiotis", in *Contacts*, vol. 18, 1966, no. 56, pp.301-14.
S.P. Schilling, *Contemporary Continental Theologians*, London, SCM, 1966.

Joseph Houldsworth Oldham
1874–1969

PHILIP POTTER

W.A. Visser 't Hooft, the first general secretary of the World Council of Churches, used to say that the ecumenical movement owed more to Joseph Oldham than to any other of its pioneers. No one has disputed that. Surprisingly, apart from biographical articles in two or three dictionaries and a few tributes after his death, there is no substantial biography or portrait of this extraordinary man of God. Kathleen Bliss, who worked closely with him during the last thirty years of his life, died without being able to produce the official biography she had been commissioned to write. One of the difficulties with such an enterprise, she explained, was that Oldham did not write a diary or keep letters. Clearing up his last home, he made a bonfire in the garden of his papers. When Kathleen Bliss, who was present, remarked that several doctoral theses were being consumed in smoke, Oldham replied: "Thank God for that. I can't help feeling there's something wrong when young people are more interested in resurrecting this sort of stuff than in looking to the future."

Who was this man who was always looking to the future and enabling so many things to happen? Joseph Houldsworth Oldham was born into a devout Christian family in Bombay, India, on 20 October 1874. His father was a colonel in the Royal Engineers, but the family decided to leave the fashionable part of Bombay to live in a missionary bungalow near the poorer people, and Oldham spent his very early years playing with Indian children. When his father retired in 1881, the family went to Scotland, where Colonel Oldham became a well-known lay evangelist, leading and participating in evangelistic campaigns. Joseph Oldham thus grew up in a family atmosphere of prayer and nourishment from the Bible, of a passion for communicating the good news of Jesus Christ and living with and accepting people of other races and classes as made and beloved by God.

Graduating from Edinburgh Academy at the head of his class in 1892, Joseph Oldham went to Trinity College, Oxford, during a period of great religious ferment in all British universities, led among others by the US evangelist Dwight L. Moody. Out of this revival two movements had grown, and Oldham became involved in both: the Student Volunteer Missionary Union (SVMU), and the British Colleges Christian Union (BCCU), later called the Student Christian Movement (SCM). When the great Christian student leader John R. Mott visited Oxford in spring 1894, he noted in his diary that Oldham, who served as his guide, was a "likely lad".

That summer Oldham went with a college friend, Temple Gairdner, to the British student summer conference at Keswick, where the US student and missionary leader Robert Speer spoke on the new SVMU watchword: "the evangelization of the world in this generation". That night Gairdner wrote in his diary: "Never heard anything like it. Oldham and I walk up the road and give ourselves to God." At the January 1896 BCCU conference in Liverpool, Oldham signed a card pledging: "It is my purpose, if God permit, to become a foreign missionary." Later in 1896 he began a one-year term as general secretary of the BCCU and the SVMU. In 1895 Mott had persuaded the North American, British, Scandinavian, German and Oriental (Japan and China) SCMs to form the World's Student Christian Federation (WSCF) — the first international, inter-confessional body of its kind. Oldham was deeply involved with all these developments, and was to be a leading shaper of what was to be the ecumenical movement. So the years 1892 to 1897 were crucial years in the life and future service of Oldham. He used to say, "The Student Christian Movement taught me to think." It is even more pertinent to say that he taught generations of students and others to think and to act on their thinking.

Oldham was sent by the Scottish YMCA in 1897 to work in Lahore among students and young Indians employed in government offices. In 1898 he married Mary Fraser, the sister of one of his closest friends at Oxford. But Oldham, whose health was never robust, contracted typhoid fever and had to return home after less than three years. Even so, in that short time, he helped to form the Indian Student Christian Movement and made lasting friendships with Indians. One of them, S.K. Datta, who later became a student, church and national leader, said of him: "He left no buildings or institutions, but he builded mightily in the hearts of a few men."

The next years, 1901 to 1904, Oldham spent studying theology at New College, Edinburgh. During this time he and his wife also studied at Halle University in Germany under the famous missiologist Gustav Warneck. Mary Oldham, an accomplished linguist, helped him to gain a working knowledge of German and French and was a partner in all his activities, including the production of his numerous memoranda and books, the first of which, *Studies in the Teaching of Jesus*, was published in 1903 and used by student groups for the next thirty years. After his studies, Oldham was a ministerial candidate and chair of the theological department of the SCM. He did not receive a call to be a parish minister, and instead became the mission study secretary of the United Free Church of Scotland in 1906. Soon he was well known in the student and missionary world for his devotion, scholarship and administrative competence.

Then Mott came to Edinburgh and persuaded Oldham to be the organizing secretary for the World Missionary Conference to be held there in 1910. Oldham threw himself into the task with the Christian commitment, intelligence, wisdom and sense of purpose for which he became renowned. He organized a series of study commissions which produced preparatory volumes on various aspects of the Christian world mission. The success of this gathering of more than a thousand representatives of missionary societies and of churches in mission countries was largely due to Oldham's unobtrusive but tireless labours. When the conference decided to have a continuation committee, he was appointed its secretary. The modern ecumenical movement was born. By 1912 a new quarterly journal appeared — *The International Review of Missions* — with Oldham as editor. In his first editorial he stated his understanding both of the missionary task and of the *Review*:

> In the kingdom of God truth is apprehended, not by those who stand by as spectators, but by those who do and serve. The task of evangelizing the non-Christian world is most intimately related to that of meeting the unbelief and intellectual perplexity so widespread at the present time, and only by attempting both tasks together can the church hope to accomplish either... In boldly claiming the allegiance of every race and nation to Christ, in confronting all thought and all life with the gospel, Christian faith will become aware of the depth and strength of its inner resources, and receive fresh confirmation of its truth. Its most convincing vindication will be its world-conquering power.

N.B.

The outbreak of the first world war was a grave challenge to the Christian world. With characteristic courage and forthrightness, Oldham wrote:

> When the war is viewed in the light of God's intention for the world, it appears as hideous sin... The war is a signal and crowning proof of the refusal of the Christian nations to be ruled by the law of Christ... The intellectual classes of Europe have to a large extent turned their back upon Christ... The whole commercial system of the West is based largely on the principle of securing advantages at the cost of someone else; and it is noteworthy that conflicting commercial interests have been one of the chief influences that have fostered national antagonisms... The situation in Europe drives home the question whether a wholehearted acceptance of Christ's teaching is not the only sound basis on which society can be built... If a new and better civilization is to be built, he must be the cornerstone...

In assessing the driving forces leading to this catastrophic conflict Oldham made no judgment on one side over against the other — remarkably, given that the churches often reflected the jingoistic nationalism of the first world war. In fact, when German missions in Africa and Asia were closed and missionaries interned, Oldham struggled for equitable treatment, and during the debates on the Versailles Treaty, he success-fully secured the exemption of German mission properties from the "war debts" conditions being imposed on Germany. This and later struggles in the political arena for the sake of fairness and sanity led to his being described as "a wily, slippery saint" and "the arch-intriguer for good".

After the war, Oldham steered the Edinburgh continuation committee to set up a more permanent body which would draw the churches of the Reformation together in working out common strategies for mission and enabling the churches in mission lands to develop their own selfhood and missionary purpose in their own cultures. At the meeting of the continuation committee in 1920, Oldham went further. While he recognized the importance of an international organization to represent the home bases of missions, he declared: "It is becoming less and less possible to discuss missionary matters without representatives of the churches in the mission field, and any organiza-tion that may be created will probably have before long to give way to something that may represent the beginning of a world league of churches." So in 1921, the International Missionary Council was created with Mott as chairperson and Oldham as secretary. At its inaugural meeting he obtained the Council's assent to do a study on racial discrimination around the world. This was based on his experience in Asia, but especially in his dealings with missions in Africa.

Indeed, one of the major areas of Oldham's creative contribution was in the relations of white and black in Africa. During the first world war he wrote in his wide-ranging, prophetic book on *The World and the Gospel*:

> The problem with which we are confronted in Africa is one of the great issues of history. Have we eyes to see its immense significance? Shall the African peoples be enabled to develop their latent powers, to cultivate their peculiar gifts and so enrich the life of humanity by their distinctive contributions? Or shall they be depressed and degraded and made the tool of others, the instrument of their gain, the victim of their greed and lust?

The first test came in 1919, when the colonial government in Kenya tried to authorize the use of forced labour of black men, women and children on European settler farms. The missionaries and others on the spot felt helpless to prevent this action, but Oldham took up the struggle, challenging all the responsible persons in church, community and state he could reach in London and mounting a determined campaign in the press. The order for forced labour was dropped and the governor was recalled to England. Oldham, however, knew that this was not enough. He pursued the matter and in 1923 got the British government to make a policy statement that "the interests of Africans must be paramount".

In 1924, Oldham published his findings on racism, after collecting massive evidence from different parts of the world, especially in Africa. His book *Christianity and the Race Problem* is regarded as the most influential he ever wrote. He declared:

> As Christ was sent by the Father, so he sends his disciples to set up in the world the kingdom of God. His coming was a declaration of war — a war to the death against the powers of darkness. He was manifested to destroy the works of the devil. Hence when Christians find in the world a state of things that is not in accord with the truth which they have learned from Christ, their concern is not that it should be explained but that it should be ended. In that temper we must approach everything in the relations between races that cannot be reconciled with the Christian ideal.

It would be 45 years before concerted action along these lines was taken on a world scale, when the Programme to Combat Racism was set up by the World Council of Churches.

Oldham never stopped at specific protests or actions. He always went deeper. There could be no future for Africa in a highly complex, exploitative world economy unless its people had the possibilities of appropriate education and of developing their capacities according to their own cultural genius. This could happen only if there was cooperation between Christian missions and the governments on the basis of well-researched needs and of the resources both local and from public bodies and private foundations. One result was that the British government established an advisory committee on Education in Tropical Africa in 1923 and published a policy paper on the subject in 1925. Oldham himself studied deeply the aims and methods of Christian education with special reference to Africa. The fruit of his reflections appeared in 1931 in a book he wrote with his colleague, Ms B.D. Gibson, *The Remaking of Man in Africa*. In the process, Oldham was instrumental, together with others, in creating the International Institute of African Languages and Cultures and starting a scientific journal *Africa*. He secured also the cooperation of leading linguists and anthropologists.

What motivated and upheld Joseph Oldham in all these activities and struggles? At least parts of the answer can be found in *A Devotional Diary*, first published in 1925 and in its sixteenth edition in 1947. Here is one of his reflections:

To live is to meet life eager and unafraid, to refuse none of its challenges, to evade none of
its responsibilities, to go forth daily with a gay and adventurous heart to encounter its risks,
to overcome its difficulties and to seize its opportunities with both hands.
    *Grant to us, O Lord, the royalty of inward happiness and the serenity which comes from
living close to thee. Daily renew in us the sense of joy, and let the eternal Spirit of the
Father dwell in our souls and bodies, filling every corner of our hearts with light and
courage, so that, bearing about with us the infection of a good courage, we may be diffusers
of life, and may meet all ills and cross accidents with gallant and high-hearted happiness,
giving thee thanks always for all things.*

It was this attitude of mind and heart which characterized Joseph Oldham throughout
his long and most fruitful life. One of his favourite sayings was "we must dare in order
to know". Oldham had the rare gifts of concentrating on one issue or situation at a time
and of being able to discern the signs of the times.
    After the first world war, he perceived that secularism was the most radical
challenge to the Christian message. Secularism conceived people and things as being
removed from any reference beyond themselves and thus making idols of themselves
and of things. Oldham persuaded the International Missionary Council to make this a
major subject at its meeting in Jerusalem in 1928. He asked the crucial question: "What
is the true diagnosis of the sickness of our civilization? What is the word of salvation?"
The emergence of totalitarian systems in Russia, Germany, Italy and Japan, and the
increasingly dominant role of technique and the machine occupied his mind. The Life
and Work movement invited him to its meeting in 1934, where he expounded this
concern. This led to his being made chairperson of the Study Commission of Life and
Work. Soon he developed a theme for the forthcoming (1937) world conference on
Church, Community and State. As always, he gathered a remarkable group of lay
persons eminent in various fields like economics, education, international law and
relations, as well as theologians. It was during this time of intensive preparation that the
saying went around that "for Oldham the road to the kingdom of God went through the
dining room of the Athenaean Club in London". He used every stratagem to get lay
people in particular to participate in what he described as "the life-and-death struggle
between Christian faith and the secular and pagan tendencies of our time".
    That the 1937 Oxford conference became a landmark in church history owed a
great deal to Oldham. Significantly, the slogan which came out of this meeting was
"Let the Church be the Church". In a chapter on the church in his 1952 book *Life is
Commitment*, Oldham recalled a conversation in 1936 with Paul Tillich, in which he
had said to the German theologian: "You know, Tillich, Christianity has no meaning
for me whatsoever apart from the church, but I sometimes feel as though the church as
it actually exists is the source of all my doubts and difficulties." Oldham then went on
to summarize what the Oxford conference was trying to say as he reflected on it during
and after the second world war, and in the light of all the initiatives he took to promote
the formation of the World Council of Churches:

    In the first place, if Christianity is the revelation of the depths of the personal and of love as
    the ultimate meaning of the universe, it can find expression only in a community... Christ is
    not Christ without the community of love which he founded...
        The church is indispensable, secondly, as the society which has to do with people's
    ultimate concern. Our ultimate concern is about our fundamental being and the meaning of
    our life and destiny... Take away the church with its centres of worship, and life becomes
    wholly this-worldly and loses immeasurably in depth.

Thirdly, the church is necessary because Christianity is essentially the proclamation, not of a demand, but of fulfilment. It is not the insistence on love as an ideal to be striven after, but the joyful news that God *is* love and that we know this because it has been manifested in history. Grace and truth *came* by Jesus Christ. The church is the witness to that revelation and the continuing embodiment of that new life. Take away the church and Christianity itself disappears...

Fourthly, the church is the guardian of the new message and proclamation, and has to see that they are preserved in their purity and power and protected against error, misrepresentation and emasculation.

The church is most true to its own nature when it seeks nothing for itself, renounces power, humbly bears witness to the truth, but makes no claim to be *possessor* of truth, and is continuously dying in order that it may live.

Immediately after the Oxford conference, Oldham played a leading role in drafting the documents which would bring together the world movements on Life and Work and Faith and Order to form the World Council of Churches.

The deteriorating political situation, which eventually led to another world war, found Oldham ready to promote instruments by which Christians could wrestle with the critical issues posed to the church to be Christ's faithful witness and servant. Within a few weeks of the beginning of the war, Oldham launched and edited the *Christian News Letter*, which appeared weekly and later fortnightly until 1945. He also created the Christian Frontier Council as a forum for people in every walk of life to wrestle with how they could live on the frontier towards the kingdom of God. Oldham put it in a sentence: "In its heart and essence the Christian decision is the decision to live in the actual world of nature, history and society by the power of faith, hope and love."

This is how Joe Oldham lived and witnessed as an unassuming lay disciple of Christ, one whose calling it was to invite the community of the church to strive for "a responsible society". This concept of "a responsible society" was the last of his many contributions to ecumenical thinking. He wrote a long essay on it in a volume on *The Church and the Disorder of Society* in preparation for the inaugural assembly of the World Council of Churches in 1948. He is also credited with drafting the two paragraphs on "The Responsible Society" which were eventually adopted by the assembly:

Man is created and called to be a free being, responsible to God and his neighbour. Any tendencies in state and society depriving man of the possibility of acting responsibly are a denial of God's intention for man and his work of salvation. A responsible society is one where freedom is the freedom of men who acknowledge responsibility to justice and public order, and where those who hold political authority or economic power are responsible for its exercise to God and the people whose welfare is affected by it...

Man is not made for the state but the state for man. Man is not made for production, but production for man. For a society to be responsible under modern conditions it is required that the people have freedom to control, to criticize and to change their governments...

In remembrance of this gift of God for our times and in the communion of the saints, we can make our own the prayer which Joseph Oldham wrote in his *Devotional Diary*:

O thou who art heroic love, keep alive in our hearts that adventurous spirit which makes us scorn the way of safety, so that thy will be done. For so only, O Lord, shall we be worthy of those courageous souls who in every age have ventured all in obedience to thy call, and for whom the trumpets have sounded on the other side; through Jesus Christ our Lord.

BIBLIOGRAPHY

Works by Joseph Oldham:

Christianity and the Race Problem, London, SCM, 1924.
A Devotional Diary, London, SCM, 1925.
Life Is Commitment, London, SCM, 1953.
New Hope in Africa, London, Longmans Green, 1955.
The Question of the Church in the World of Today, London, Edinburgh House, 1936.
Real Life Is Meeting, London, SCM, 1942.
The Remaking of Man in Africa, with B.D. Gibson, London, Oxford UP, 1931.
The Resurrection of Christendom, London, Sheldon, 1940.
White and Black in Africa, London, Longmans Green, 1930.
Work in Modern Society, London, SCM, 1950.
The World and the Gospel, London, United Council for Missionary Education, 1916.

Albert Cook Outler
1908–1989

JOHN DESCHNER

Al and I shared birthdays.
He was a mentor to me.

Albert Cook Outler was born into a Methodist parsonage in the US state of Georgia on 17 November 1908. After studying English literature at Wofford College and psychology of religion at Emory University, he received a doctorate in 1938 from Yale University, with a dissertation on Origen. From 1938 to 1945 he taught at Duke University; then he held the Timothy Dwight Chair in Theology at Yale from 1945 to 1951. Thereafter he became professor of theology in the Perkins School of Theology, at Southern Methodist University, Dallas. He died on 1 September 1989.

An ordained and active Methodist elder, Outler was a frequent delegate and leader at world, general and jurisdictional Methodist conferences. He became the leading figure in the Doctrinal Study Commission which followed the Evangelical United Brethren-Methodist merger, and played similar roles in the denomination's Commission on Ecumenical Affairs and the quadrennial Oxford Institute of Methodist Theological Studies.

John Messina Studios, Dallas, Texas

As an ecumenist Outler was active primarily in Faith and Order and in the Consultation on Church Union (COCU). He was a leading participant at the third world conference on Faith and Order (Lund 1952), and was vice-chair of the fourth world conference (Montreal 1963). He chaired the North American section of the Faith and Order Study Commission on Tradition and Traditions (1953-63) whose work undergirded the New Delhi statement of 1961. He was also a frequent participant in and contributor to national and international bilateral dialogues. At the same time, he was a leading figure in the most creative period of COCU's development, especially in shaping its theological consensus in the 1960s.

He was a very active delegated observer and commentator in all four sessions of the Second Vatican Council, a contribution which was recognized by his election as president of the American Catholic Historical Association. Moreover, he served as president of the American Society of Church History and of the American Theological Society, and was a fellow of the American Academy of Arts and Sciences.

By the 1970s Outler was giving major attention to creative bridge-building initiatives with conservative evangelicals, especially within the United Methodist Church. In this his extraordinary knowledge and competence as a historical scholar and eloquent interpreter of the Wesleyan tradition made him a central authority in virtually all quarters of the United Methodist Church, a role whose principal contribution was his critical editing of the first four volumes (the sermons) of the complete Bicentennial Edition of *The Works of John Wesley*.

* * *

The underlying convictions of this ecumenical life began to take shape at an early age. On the one hand, growing up in a Methodist parsonage at a time when the "holiness controversy" was dividing Methodist congregations in the southern USA impressed the young seminarian with what he later knew to be the problem of Christian disunity. Throughout his life he thoroughly understood and affirmed the evangelical spirit and mind, and the Wesleyan "order of salvation" which explicated the healing "atmosphere" in which personal and ecclesial wholeness as well as human community were renewed.

On the other hand, that same parsonage family also venerated the classic Christian tradition, and already as a schoolboy Outler felt the beginnings of a lifelong hunger to understand and appropriate this patristic wisdom. A gift from a colleague of his father brought to the home library a set of the Ante-Nicene Fathers in English translation, and the young Albert was a fascinated explorer of its pages. One can only speculate at how early an age he sensed that the two streams — the patristic spirit and wisdom and Wesleyan sanctification — flowed into and reinforced each other. In any case, the realization that Wesley's "catholic Spirit" was the early Fathers' "Holy Spirit" marked Outler's characteristic theological existence from very early on.

His first student impulse was to face the question of what the Wesleyan "order of salvation" could mean in a post-Freudian age. He was one of the earliest seminarians in the 1920s to undergo the discipline of clinical pastoral education; he wrote his bachelor of divinity thesis on this topic, as well as his first book, *Psychotherapy and the Christian Message*, whose basic insight characterized all of his later theology as well: "Christianity must seek alliance with valid human wisdom, and it must at every point resist the rivalry of every merely human gospel."

This critically open attitude, rooted in the discipline of the gospel of salvation, nourished by the "catholic Spirit" of God and thus convinced of the wholeness of God's creation, opened up even wider horizons when Outler wrote the "Master Plan" for Southern Methodist University. "The aim of this university... is to educate its students as worthy human beings and as citizens, first, and as teachers, lawyers, ministers, research scientists, businessmen, engineers and so on, second..."

But it was when he turned to his own speciality of church history that Outler's conviction of the confluence of the two streams — the "catholic" amplitude of the Creator's Spirit and the clarity and power of that Spirit's apostolic revelation — acquired its most characteristic statement. The student of Outler can attest to the severity of his historiographical methods. But that severity expressed questions which never rest: Who really runs history? And is there such a thing as "our common history"? His often-quoted presidential address to the American Society of Church History put such questions unforgettably — "Theodosius' Horse: Reflections on the

Predicament of the Church Historian". How should Christian understanding evaluate the stumble in which an emperor died, clearing the way for the ultimate victory of Chalcedonian orthodoxy? Outler's answer was to insist upon God's "providence", understood as "God's total resourcefulness in dealing with his human children". And yet it was a concurrent providence which awakens and develops human freedom and participation in what happens. "God's providence does not amount to his predetermination of historical events. It is, rather, his real presence in every crisis of human decision — where history's meaning is born or aborted." And it is those ultimate "meanings" and "purposes" which create "our common history", a conviction which shaped Outler's view of history and illuminated his major work in systematic theology, the small but weighty book, *Who Trusts in God: Musings on the Meaning of Providence*.

Outler's basic approach to these early themes of human nature, the university and human history, with its insistence on both the prevenience of divine grace and the renewal of human ability, became a hallmark of his self-described "evangelical Catholicism". He found its deepest roots in the Wesleyan message of sanctification as the renewal of human nature and in the patristic tradition of the apostolic faith in God's grace. His work was a persistent quest for the reality which unites these two streams: human nature and human salvation, human history and the apostolic tradition, brought together in the providential presence of God.

Against that background, Outler's impressive ecumenical theology begins to take shape, a theology in which God's grace unites us, yet human ecumenical obedience "evidences" the presence of this grace. A divided people of God cannot bear credible witness to God's providential purpose to unite all things in Christ. Witness and unity go together. That is why he insisted that the ecumenical movement is "the growing edge" of the Christian church today and devoted a decade of his best theological work to the Consultation on Church Union, especially to its core problem of "the mingling of ministries". In living out that conviction, he dedicated another decade to the Second Vatican Council and its reception by non-Catholics as well as by Catholics. And, with genuinely creative ecumenical insight, the last twenty years of his career centred on showing his fellow Methodists that their own most distinctive convictions are best understood and most obediently lived out as a witness to the one ecumenical tradition of the gospel and its apostolic spirituality. Outler became for many in these final years the representative theological voice of US Methodism and, as such, a powerful advocate for many Methodists and non-Methodists alike of "the Christian tradition and the unity we seek".

It would require much more than a short essay to show how this work of Outler helped to open up for his denomination a quite new phase of reflection about authoritative church doctrine; or how his leadership in the Faith and Order movement helped many in recovering an understanding of the whole Christian tradition within which their own distinctive traditions acquired their real authority; or, quite specifically, how Outler's exacting historical-critical editing of Wesley's writings opened up fresh and often unexplored vistas of this "folk-theologian's" work and of the "traditionary process" in which the apostolic biblical message can become contemporary witness. Two aspects must suffice to sum up this perspective on his work.

First, for Albert Outler, it was not the sainted Wesley of denominational piety but the actual 18th-century "folk theologian" who could be most helpful to us today as we seek in our own language to be faithful witnesses to the apostolic faith. In consequence, he accepted the painstaking historical-critical labour required to recover this Wesley, undaunted by the mountains of historical material Wesley left behind. Among those materials was a list of all the books Wesley had read during his life. When Outler undertook to edit Oxford University Press's best-selling one-volume compendium of Wesley's works, he insisted on revisiting the British Museum often enough to get nearly every one of these centuries-old books in his hands and so to familiarize himself with the atmosphere in which Wesley had lived and breathed. This careful research led Outler to develop a quite new patristic perspective for understanding Wesleyan sanctification: Wesley as a student of the early Eastern fathers, especially of the Cappadocians. His conclusion is clear: this Wesley, the actual Wesley who lived and breathed the classic Christian tradition, is the figure who can help us to understand that the ecumenical vocation to an ecclesial as well as personal sanctification is essential to being a Methodist today.

Second, as the denominational Commission on Doctrine and Doctrinal Standards was deep in its work in 1970, it was Outler as chairperson who led the general conference to adopt "A Resolution of Intent" on how the United Methodist Church should understand and re-receive today the several anti-Catholic passages in its own constitution. These articles, originally an expression of the 16th-century Reformation and received by the US Methodists through Wesley's abridgment of the Anglican 39 Articles, are not to be abrogated in their historical intention, even as it remains an obligation for 20th-century Methodists to say how we understand these articles today in the light of our ecumenical understanding and commitments. This Declaration Outler then took to Rome, as he was authorized to do, and presented it to the Vatican as a gesture of ecumenical fellowship and hope, a gesture which was reciprocated in the Vatican's generous response and similar expression of our common ecumenical hope. This episode has not received the attention and analysis it deserves in either church. But as an enactment of how to understand tradition and the re-reception of our traditions in the context of the Spirit's traditionary process, it is an illuminating example of what Albert Outler had learned and sought to teach United Methodists about the ecumenical character of its understanding of the apostolic tradition.

Wesleyan holiness as ecumenically relevant "catholic Spirit": that is what animated this genuinely creative ecumenical bridge-builder in our own time.

BIBLIOGRAPHY

Works by Albert Outler:

Augustine, Confession and Enchiridion, tr. and ed. Albert C. Outler, Library of Christian Classics, vol. VII, Philadelphia, Westminster, 1955.

The Christian Tradition and the Unity We Seek, New York, Oxford, 1957.

"Doctrine and Dogma", *Encyclopaedia Britannica*, 15th ed., 1974, pp.927-29.

"Do Methodists have a Doctrine of the Church?", in *The Doctrine of the Church*, ed. Dow Kirkpatrick, New York, Abingdon, 1964, pp.11-28.

"History as Ecumenical Resource: the Protestant Discovery of Tradition", presidential address, American Catholic Historical Association, 28 December 1972, *Catholic Historical Review*, 59, 1, 1973, pp.1-15.

John Wesley, Library of Protestant Thought, ed. Albert C. Outler, New York, Oxford UP, 1964.

A Methodist Observer at Vatican II, Westminster, MD, Newman, 1967.

"The Mingling of Ministries", in *Digest of the Proceedings of the Eighth Meeting of the Consultation on Church Union*, Atlanta, GA, 17-20 March 1969, ed. Paul A. Crow, Jr, Princeton, 1969, 8, pp.106-18.

"Our Common History as Christians", in *The Nature of the Unity We Seek*, ed. Paul Minear, St Louis, Bethany, 1958, pp.79-89.

"The Person and Work of Christ in the Thought of Saint Augustine", in *A Companion to the Study of St Augustine*, ed. Roy W. Battenhouse, New York, Oxford, 1955, pp.343-70.

"The 'Platonism' of Clement of Alexandria", *Journal of Religion*, 20, 3, 1940, pp.217-40.

Psychotherapy and the Christian Message, New York, Harper, 1954.

"Theodosius' Horse: Reflections on the Predicament of the Church Historian", presidential address, American Society of Church History, 29 December 1964, *Church History*, 34, 3, 1965, pp.251-61.

Theology in the Wesleyan Spirit, Nashville, Tidings, 1971.

"Vatican II and Protestant Theology in America", in *Vatican II: An Interfaith Appraisal*, ed. John H. Miller, Notre Dame, IN, University of Notre Dame Press, 1966, pp.619-25.

"Visions and Dreams: The Unfinished Business of an Unfinished Church", sermon for the Uniting Conference of the United Methodist Church, 23 April 1968, *The Daily Christian Advocate*, 1, 3, 1968, pp.133-35.

"A Way Forward from Lund", *The Ecumenical Review*, 5, 1, 1952, pp.59-63.

Who Trusts in God: Musings on the Meaning of Providence, New York, Oxford, 1968.

The Works of John Wesley, vols I-IV, Sermons (The Bi-centennial Edition), ed.-in-chief Frank Baker, ed. Albert C. Outler, Nashville, Abingdon, 1984, 1985, 1986, 1987.

About Albert Outler:

John Deschner, "Albert Cook Outler: A Biographical Memoir", in *Our Common History as Christians*, Festschrift eds John Deschner, Leroy T. Howe, Klaus Penzel, New York, Oxford, 1975, pp.ix-xxi. Cf. also the bibliography compiled by Wanda W. Smith, with Carlotta S. Outler and Kate Warnick, pp.293-298.

Michael Ramsey
1904–1988

FRANCIS FROST

Arthur Michael Ramsey was born in Cambridge on 14 November 1904. His father was Congregationalist, his mother Anglican. During his secondary education at Repton, his elder brother Frank's avowed atheism challenged him to a more serious practice of his own faith. At 16 he obtained his father's permission to be confirmed in the Church of England.

He began undergraduate studies at Magdalene College, Cambridge, in October 1923. At the time, his mother, whose example had influenced his own interest in politics, was prominent in the Cambridge Labour party, but he himself opted for the Liberals, in spite of their heavy defeat in the 1924 general election. Political liberalism corresponded with his concept of the right balance between the freedom of individuals and intermediate bodies within the body politic on the one hand

and necessary state intervention on the other. He never departed from this position, which brought him close to William Temple's understanding of a Christian social order.

As he moved towards Anglo-Catholicism, religious preoccupations began to take priority over political. Anglo-Catholic worship at the parish church of St Giles had already awakened within him a sense of awe and adoration in relation to heavenly realities beyond the visible world and also to the centrality of the passion of Jesus. He became convinced "that the churches engaged at a more profound level with the predicament of humanity"[1] than did political parties.

Temple's influence on this change was considerable. A university sermon by Temple in February 1926 gave Ramsey the opportunity to compare the emotionalism of the Presbyterian evangelical from Belfast, W.P. Nicholson, with "Temple's quiet exploration of a Christian philosophy of life".[2] He felt that the latter approach was better able to commend the Christian faith to his contemporaries. To the end of his life he remained a deep admirer of Temple's mind and years later, at the end of his term as Archbishop of Canterbury, he asked to be buried near him.

In April 1926 Ramsey abandoned the study of law to devote himself to theology, with a view to preparing for ordination. This brought into his life the influence of Edwyn Hoskyns, another Anglo-Catholic, whose approach to New Testament criticism and the origin of the apostolic church offered a trenchant contrast to the shallow rationalism then in vogue in the Cambridge faculty. Hoskyns enabled Ramsey to grasp, within an English cultural setting, the importance of the neo-orthodox reaction of Karl Barth against continental European liberal Protestantism.

Through prayer, reflection and deep pastoral sensitivity, Ramsey moulded these various strands, including the contrast between a Non-conformist upbringing and a personal choice of Anglo-Catholicism, into a profoundly personal synthesis of Christian doctrine, ethics and spirituality, which made him a source of inspiration and spiritual strength to his contemporaries and prepared him for his future pastoral and ecumenical outreach.

Ramsey arrived at Cuddesden College at the end of July 1927 and was ordained to the diaconate on September 23 of the following year. During this period he went through great turmoil and distress. He discovered in himself a woundedness whose roots were probably in his early upbringing. It was brought to the surface by a tragic automobile accident in which his mother was killed and his father badly injured. The death of his brother Frank in January 1930 also affected him deeply. Later he said that these two deaths were the only two occasions on which he ever seriously doubted the truth of the Christian faith. He came to understand that all our wounds are to be taken directly to God and that the confessional is the place to do this. He also discovered that suffering can have a creative role in the spiritual growth of a Christian insofar as it is intimately connected with the mystery of the transfiguration of Christ's own suffering into risen glory. This truth took its place at the very core not only of his personal life of prayer and contemplation, but also of all his preaching and witness.

* * *

Ramsey's involvement in parish work did not last long. Six months after his ordination to the priesthood in September 1929, his superiors, knowing his aptitude for high-level academic work, sent him to Lincoln Theological College. He had ample time to complete his own theological education and clarify its doctrinal foundation, especially in the area of ecclesiology. In 1936 he published *The Gospel and the Catholic Church*, a seminal work which still retains ecumenical relevance as an attempt to fuse the Evangelical emphasis on the preaching of the Word with the Catholic emphasis on church order, an attempt inspired by the influence of these two strands on his own upbringing and subsequent development. Visits to the college of two able exponents of the Orthodox tradition — Nicolas Zernov and Georges Florovsky — deepened the love for Eastern theology and spirituality that had already been awakened in him at Cuddesden.

The year 1936 also marked the beginning of a strange interlude in Ramsey's life. The Bishop of Lincoln sent him back into a parish. Doubtless he saw the unique spiritual and pastoral qualities which destined Ramsey for service to the Anglican Communion as a whole, and knew that the somewhat hot-house atmosphere of a theological college was not adequate preparation. In 1939 Ramsey himself, in search of mixed work rather than a university lectureship, accepted the post of vicar at St Benet's, Cambridge, but found himself relegated to a backwater.

A month after the outbreak of the second world war, Ramsey was offered a professorship in the faculty of divinity at Durham and a canonry in the cathedral to go with it. He was instituted a canon of Durham Cathedral on 27 January 1940. He was only 35, but felt that he had found his right place in life. In April 1942, he married Joan Hamilton. She modified his tendencies towards austere eccentricity by making their house into a warm and welcoming home and introducing him to a much wider circle of friends and contacts. Ramsey expanded Durham's understaffed faculty by creating a second professorship of theology and a lectureship in New Testament studies, for which he chose a Methodist, Kingsley Barrett — an ecumenical initiative which did not go unnoticed.

A book on the resurrection (1945) was followed by what he considered to be the expression of his most treasured theological insights: *The Glory of God and the Transfiguration of Christ*. In this book he put all the resources of Western biblical exegesis at the service of what is central to Orthodox spirituality: the glory of the transfigured Christ as promise of our own future glory and of the transformation of the whole cosmos. As he wrote in the preface:

> The word "glory" is often on the lips of Christian people, but they have sometimes only a vague idea of its meaning... Within it are contained the greatest themes of Christian theology. The word expresses in a remarkable way the unity of the doctrines of creation, the incarnation, the cross, the Spirit, the church and the world to come.[3]

At the same time, Ramsey was becoming involved in international ecumenical relations, attending the first assembly of the World Council of Churches in Amsterdam (1948). With the support of his friend Georges Florovsky, he defended a Catholic understanding of church order and helped to prevent the WCC from becoming a federation of Protestant churches. At New Delhi (1961) he was elected one of the WCC presidents. His commitment to the World Council continued until the assembly at Uppsala in 1968.

From 1950 onwards Ramsey's career went through several rapid changes. As Regius Professor of Divinity in Cambridge University for only 20 months, he hardly had the time to overcome the suspicion of liberal theologians and make his mark before he was asked in May 1952 to be Bishop of Durham. He admitted that accepting this change was the hardest decision he had ever had to make, because he had thought that his appointment to Cambridge marked the definitive stage of the academic career for which he then felt himself cut out. Similarly, his three years in the see of Durham were just enough to enable him to find out what needed to be done without leaving him time to do it.

In April 1956 he was enthroned Archbishop of York. Assisted by three suffragans, he continued to combine pastoral activity and theological study. At the 1958 Lambeth Conference he was chosen to chair the main theological commission. His most scholarly work, *From Gore to Temple*, appeared in 1960. It traced the development of theological thought in England from the last decade of the 19th century to the middle of the 20th century.

At the same time, Ramsey began to travel more widely. In 1956, soon after his enthronement, he made his first contact with Eastern Orthodoxy outside Britain, as the guest of Patriarch Alexei of Moscow. It was the beginning of a friendship between the two. A long visit to East Africa in June 1960 embroiled him in the problems of decolonization with which he was often to be confronted as Archbishop of Canterbury.

In particular, he found himself in Nyasaland in the thick of the nationalist movement which changed this territory into Malawi.

* * *

It was through the decisive intervention of Prime Minister Harold Macmillan that Ramsey was chosen to succeed to Geoffrey Fisher as Archbishop of Canterbury. He was enthroned in June 1961; and into the thirteen years until his retirement on his 70th birthday on 11 November 1974, he packed a colossal amount of pastoral activity and decision-making. A few months before retirement, he commented wryly on the strain of such a weight of responsibility: "While I can do six things at once, I cannot now do twelve things at once, which my job requires."[4]

As head of the state church, Ramsey was deeply involved in the elaboration of post-war state legislation on moral and social issues and in major readjustments of church-state relationships which gave the church much greater autonomy in regulating its internal affairs. As primate of a worldwide communion, he responded generously to the challenge of young local churches growing rapidly in former British colonies. His tireless journeyings gave them the support and inspiration they needed for the growth of healthy community life and the establishment of sound pastoral oversight amidst agonizing social, cultural, political and racial upheavals. In his episcopal appointments he made many judicious decisions, such as the incorporation of Jerusalem, with the exception of St George's Cathedral, into an Arab diocese, with Robert Stopford as its archbishop.

Above all, there was the ecumenical challenge. The new possibilities for worldwide inter-church relationships afforded by improved means of travel were compounded by the entry of the Roman Catholic Church into the ecumenical movement. Ramsey's magnificent response to this challenge resulted in an unprecedented global ecumenical outreach. No Anglican leader before him would have been in a position to gain such stature.

Furthermore Ramsey's method of responding to the pastoral commitments imposed upon him by the religious and secular turmoil of the world in which he found himself immersed willy-nilly reveals a profound inner unity. This unity can best be characterized by its ecumenical thrust.

In committing himself to far-reaching changes in the relation between church and state, Ramsey had no political end in view. His one preoccupation was spiritual renewal. He wanted the church to have the freedom to achieve this renewal by being left free by the state to regulate its worship and prayer-life as it wished. Hence he did not favour total disestablishment. On the one hand, he saw that this would risk putting the appointment of bishops into the hands of a system that was much more bureaucratic than the existing one — even if giving the last word to civil authority was, strictly speaking, an ecclesiological anomaly. On the other hand, when the general synod came into existence in 1970, he saw it as a means not of wresting autonomy from parliament in every area of church government, but of achieving the clearly definable objective of freedom of worship.

An important corollary of the Worship and Doctrine Measure of 1974, which Ramsey fully supported, was that the clergy could now obtain relief of conscience in the vexed issue of subscription to language deemed obsolete in the Thirty-Nine Articles. According to the terms of the Measure, it was not possible simply to abolish this trust deed of Anglican identity, but the formula of subscription could be changed into an affirmation of belief in "the faith which is revealed in Holy Scripture and set forth in the Catholic Creeds and to which the historic formularies of the Church of England bear witness". Such a formula of subscription would have real ecumenical significance as the point of departure for convergence with confessions of belief of other Christian communions.

Above all, Ramsey had ushered in legislation permitting liturgical renewal, which eliminated once and for all the painful tension between rightness of conscience with English law and the imperative pastoral and spiritual need for such renewal. This was a major step forward in that total church renewal which genuine ecumenical commitment required of all the Christian communions.

More broadly, Ramsey established intimate contact with the highest leadership of two of the three major Christian traditions besides his own: Orthodoxy and Roman Catholicism. The very nature of his primatial responsibilities meant that his main preoccupation in relation to the Protestant world had to be the healing of the divide between the Church of England and British Methodism. Steeped as he was in English religious culture, he was able to make a less significant impact on representatives of Reformation churches of continental Europe. Yet he did reach out towards them, as is shown by his visits to West Germany and Sweden in 1964, and his visit ten years later to East Berlin.

In the realm of Orthodox-Anglican relations Ramsey was a pioneer, making full use of his deep empathy for Orthodox liturgical culture and spirituality and his charism for lasting personal spiritual friendship. His first visit as Archbishop of Canterbury, in 1962, was to Ecumenical Patriarch Athenagoras. On his way back he visited Metropolitan Chrysostom of Athens. Five years later Athenagoras was the first Ecumenical Patriarch ever to come to London. Ramsey also continued his relationship with Patriarch Alexei and became the first Archbishop of Canterbury to visit Moscow.

Mindful of the adverse political circumstances of the Orthodox churches in Eastern Europe, Ramsey reached out to them to draw them out of isolation. He made contact with Romanian Patriarch Justinian at Bucharest and with Serbian Orthodox Patriarch German in Belgrade, both of whom reciprocated by coming to Lambeth. These visits proved to Marxist government officials that church leaders, even when persecuted, were of international interest and concern. Because there were no Anglicans in the Balkans, Ramsey, even though representing a Catholic rather than a Protestant understanding of the church, could achieve certain results that would have been impossible for any representative of the Roman Catholic Church.

To be sure, Ramsey sometimes found himself in ambiguous situations where political power and even corruption were inextricably intertwined with church life. But he had the courage to confront all such ambiguity with personal moral rectitude. This gave to his pastoral action a transparency to truth which made it into authentic ecumenical witness. In short, he worked diligently at that exchange of charity with leaders of other Christian communions without which theological dialogue cannot be fruitful. His term of office at Canterbury did, in fact, mark the beginning of official dialogue between the Anglican Communion and Eastern Orthodoxy: a full joint commission representing the two communions met for the first time in July 1973.

The ecumenical initiative of Ramsey's which bore the most perceptible fruit was his visit to Rome in 1966. Nothing predisposed him to such a visit; on the contrary, his own Anglo-Catholic convictions risked raising the suspicion among Evangelicals that he would be willing to compromise Anglican-Protestant relations. However, his predecessor had already set a precedent by a visit to John XXIII; and the ecumenical openness of the Roman Catholic Church after the Second Vatican Council made a fresh initiative from the Anglican side not only possible but eminently desirable. Ramsey's first meeting with Pope Paul VI took place in the Sistine Chapel on 23 March 1966. The next day, the pope and the archbishop made a common declaration:

> They affirm their desire that all those Christians who belong to these two communions may be animated by these same sentiments of respect, esteem and fraternal love, and in order to help these develop to the full, they intend to inaugurate between the Roman Catholic Church and the Anglican Communion a serious dialogue which, founded on the gospels and on the ancient common institutions, may lead to that unity in truth for which Christ prayed.[5]

Yet there were areas in which Ramsey failed. He failed to carry his church with him in his ardent desire to see the cleavage between the Church of England and British Methodism overcome. The failure was such a humiliation to him that he no longer affirmed his Anglican belonging with the same enthusiasm: "What has vanished is the idea that being an Anglican is something to be commended to others as a specially excellent way."[6] His two visits to Northern Ireland achieved little if anything. After trying to heal conflicts between Catholics and Protestants all over the world, he now shared with his compatriots their failure to heal one of the worst conflicts of them all. Yet in his speech to the House of Lords he pointed out the duty to persevere, because (quoting Romans 14:7) "none of us lives to himself and none of us dies to himself".

* * *

Paradoxically, it was failure, and the humility it drew out of Ramsey, rather than his achievements, which gives us the greatest insight into that spiritual depth without which such ecumenical achievement would never have been possible.

In his preaching, lecturing and writing, Ramsey returned constantly to the truth of the absolute primacy of worship over service. We do not worship God in order better to serve our neighbour. Worship must be gratuitous. Since God created and redeemed us for his glory, we must give him this glory, by humble and loving praise and adoration. In other words, we must worship him. Service also has as its ultimate end the glory of God. Our service of our neighbours must include the material and spiritual needs in their this-worldly existence, but it is ultimately directed towards a fullness of union with God which glorifies God, because God is love and glorifies himself in his self-communication.

Above all, Ramsey saw a profound continuity in the depths of the soul between worship and service. His early Anglo-Catholic sympathies and his later more systematic study of Orthodox spirituality and theology made him acutely aware of how much the contemplation of the awesome, yet loving, majesty of God as revealed in the face of Jesus Christ leads away from all self-centredness. Self-forgetfulness then flows into all relationships with the neighbour. It frees our service of our neighbour from smugness, condescension and all other egocentric tendencies, giving it a breadth of generosity and even tender compassion which marks it out from the narrow moralism of a great deal of "doing good".

Ultimately, such sacrifice of all self-centredness is inseparable from sacrificial suffering. It is true that sharing in the paschal mystery of Jesus culminates in the resurrection which triumphs not only over sin but also over the suffering and death intimately connected with it. However, on this side of the grave, we have to have enough faith to see the suffering itself as glory, insofar as the suffering is the ultimate expression of a self-emptying love through which the full fruits of glorification are reached. Ramsey loved the gospel of St John, which he saw as the most perfect New Testament embodiment of this truth.

> In the New Testament it is St Mark who describes the total dereliction and death of Jesus. It was darkness, destruction and apparent defeat. But St John shows that because it was self-giving love it was also glory and victory. The self-giving love of Calvary discloses not the abolition of deity but the essence of deity in its eternity and perfection. God is Christlike, and in him is no un-Christlikeness at all, and the glory of God in all eternity is that ceaseless self-giving love of which Calvary is the measure. God's impassibility means that God is not thwarted or frustrated or ever to be an object of pity, for when he suffers with his suffering creation it is the suffering of a love which through suffering can conquer and reign. Love and omnipotence are one. [7]

The same seminal spiritual insight underpins all his attempts to reconcile the Evangelical emphasis on the preaching of the Word with Anglo-Catholic emphasis on church order. Perhaps more forcefully and realistically than any other Anglican theologian he understood that it is not possible to lay down one's life in imitation of Jesus in a private relationship to him through the Bible. One is called to do this laying down in the day-to-day acts of forgiveness, forbearance and patience which are asked of one in relation to the other members of Christ's visible body which is the church. Only thus does one triumph over one's own brokenness in union with the paschal mystery of Jesus. Ramsey gave this truth universal, ecumenical application when he said of Anglicanism as a whole: "It is sent not to commend itself as 'the best of Christianity' but by its very brokenness to point to the universal church wherein all have died."[8] He gave it application in the sphere of social ecumenism, when he persisted in disagreeing with the WCC over grants to armed liberation organizations. He applied it in his own life when he showed heroic forbearance to his enemies: in Northern Ireland he humbly accepted Ian Paisley's refusal to "shake the hand of a man who has just shaken hands with the pope"; in South Africa, he endured courteously the almost brutal rudeness of Prime Minister John Vorster during their conversation.

The activities of Ramsey's retirement were also an expression of the unity between the pastoral and the academic, the spiritual and the theological, which had underpinned his years of episcopal office. On retirement he wanted to do scholarly work and did, in fact, publish an academic book, *Come Holy Spirit* (1976), which complemented the more christological emphasis of his previous expositions of biblical theology. However, it was a book about prayer and the spiritual life, *Be Still and Know* (1982), which made the greatest impact on the reading public.

Ramsey died at the age of 83 still wearing the episcopal ring which Pope Paul VI had given him at St Paul's Outside-the-Walls. Was it not — for him and for us — one of the most precious symbols of an ecumenical achievement rooted in a presence to God which sometimes became almost tangible to those who had the privilege of a close contact with him?

NOTES

[1] Owen Chadwick, *Michael Ramsey*, London, Oxford UP, 1991, p.23.
[2] *Ibid.*, p.25.
[3] *The Glory of God and the Transfiguration of Jesus Christ*, London, Longmans, 1949, p.5.
[4] Chadwick, *op. cit.*, p.378.
[5] Cf. T.F. Stransky & J.B. Sherin, eds, *Ecumenical Documents: Doing the Truth in Charity*, New York, Paulist, 1982, vol. I, pp.285f.
[6] Remark of Ramsey to Fr Geoffrey Curtis, CR, quoted by Chadwick, *op. cit.*, p.346.
[7] *God, Christ and the World*, London, SCM, 1969, p.41.
[8] *The Gospel and the Catholic Church*, London, Longmans Green, 1936, p.220.

BIBLIOGRAPHY

An excellent biography of Ramsey, on which this sketch draws, is that by Owen Chadwick, published by Oxford University Press in 1991.

Works by Michael Ramsey:

Be Still and Know, London, SPCK, 1982.
Canterbury Essays and Addresses, London, SPCK, 1964.
Canterbury Pilgrim, London, SPCK, 1974.
The Christian Priest Today, London, SPCK, 1972, rev. ed. 1985.
The Church of England and the Eastern Orthodox Church: Why their Unity Is Important, London, SPCK, 1946.
Durham Essays and Addresses, 1956.
From Gore to Temple: The Development of Anglican Theology between Lux Mundi and the Second World War 1889-1939, London, Longmans, 1960.
The Future of the Christian Church (with Cardinal Suenens), London, SCM, 1971.
The Glory of God and the Transfiguration of Christ, New York, Longmans Green, 1949, rev. ed. 1967.
God, Christ and the World: A Study in Contemporary Theology, London, SCM, 1969.
The Gospel and the Catholic Church, London, Longmans Green, 1936, 2nd ed. 1956.
Holy Spirit, London, SPCK, 1977.
F.D. Maurice and the Conflicts of Modern Theology, Cambridge, Cambridge UP, 1951.
The Resurrection of Christ, Philadelphia, Westminster, 1945, rev. ed. 1961.

Oscar Romero
1917–1980

MARIA TERESA PORCILE SANTISO

When Archbishop Oscar Romero of El Salvador was shot to death as he was celebrating mass in the early evening of 24 March 1980, Latin America gave a new martyr to the universal church of Jesus Christ. At the same time Mgr Romero joined the long list of ecumenical pilgrims, men and women who were seekers after unity and now live within the communion of saints, persons who have gone beyond their cultural, social and even ecclesiastical frontiers to become the true promoters of unity among Christians through their experience of God and their fidelity to the gospel in our present day.

Oscar Romero was born in Ciudad Real, El Salvador, on 15 August 1917. After attending the Claretian Fathers' minor and major seminaries in San Miguel, he studied with the Jesuits at Central Seminary in San Salvador. From 1937 to 1943 he continued his studies at the Gregorian University in Rome, where he received his licenciate in theology.

Ordained priest on 4 April 1942 in Rome, he returned to El Salvador, where he worked in the San Miguel Diocese as parish priest in Anamoros, episcopal secretary and rector of the cathedral before being appointed rector of the interdiocesan seminary in San Salvador. He was the general secretary of the episcopal conference of El Salvador and in August 1967 became executive secretary of the episcopal council for Panama and Central America. In May 1970 he was appointed auxiliary to the archbishop of San Salvador. He was the president of the committee on communications media and national director of missionary foundations. In October 1974 he was appointed bishop of Santiago de Maria, and on 22 February 1977 he was invested as archbishop of San Salvador.

An exceptionally faithful priest and loving shepherd, Romero was a man of strict self-discipline. His poor rural origins and his traditional upbringing had made him humble and sensible. When he began his ministry as an auxiliary bishop, it was evident that his work was rooted more in the Second Vatican Council than in the more radical insights of the Latin American bishops' conference in Medellín. He was not one of those who used Marxist analysis for theological reflection; and his rectitude and his prudence made him advance step by step, never hastily or recklessly. It was only as a shepherd of his people that he slowly became the voice of the voiceless and his Sunday sermons turned into more and more vigorous accusations of social sins on the basis of the gospel. As he repeatedly called his congregation to conversion, he too began to walk along the path of conversion — radically, honestly and truly.

With a gift for dialogue and great human sensitivity, this shy and cautious man knew how to welcome people and discover their value. As human rights gradually became a central part of his pastoral work, this was internationally recognized, and numerous letters of solidarity came from people around the whole world. In 1979 the British Parliament nominated him for the Nobel Peace Prize (which went that year to Mother Teresa). Swedish Ecumenical Action granted him its Peace Award "in recognition of his work, based on the evangelical message, in favour of reconciliation among people, justice and human dignity, as well as his help for the oppressed". A few days after he received this prize in San Salvador he was murdered.

The turning point in his life as Christian believer, priest and bishop was the murder of a close friend, the Jesuit priest Rutilio Grande. Like Jesus' public ministry, the radical new phase that followed lasted three years — a period of conversion, prophecy, announcement of the new kingdom and denunciation of everything opposed to it.

Romero's own death came during the celebration of a funeral mass on the first anniversary of the death of Sara Meardi de Pinto, the mother of the director of the opposition newspaper *El Independiente*, a frequent target of violent attacks. When a nun who felt uneasy about the unusual presence of so many people at a virtually private mass tried to dissuade Romero from presiding over the ceremony himself, he urged her not to be so distrustful.

The day before Romero's homily had been very severe with the military forces, urging them in the name of God to stop repression:

> I would like to appeal in a special way to the army's enlisted men, and in particular to the ranks of the national guard and the police — those in the barracks. Brothers, you are part of our own people. You are killing your own *campesino* brothers and sisters. And over any order to kill that a man may give, God's law must prevail: "You shall not kill!" No soldier is obliged to obey an order against the law of God. No one has to fulfil an immoral law. It is time to listen to your conscience rather than to the orders of sin.
>
> The church, defender of the rights of God, of the law of God, of human dignity, of the person, cannot remain silent before such abomination. We want the government to understand seriously that reforms are worth nothing if they are stained with so much blood. In the name of God, and in the name of this suffering people, whose laments rise to heaven, each day more tumultuous, I beg you, I beseech you, I order you in the name of God: Stop the repression![1]

It is now believed that Romero's killing was not in fact directly connected to that memorable sermon but that the date had already been chosen earlier, when it was learned that he would celebrate a private funeral service at the small chapel of the Hospital de la Divina Providencia.

A faithful man, who led a life of prayer and fidelity to the church, Oscar Romero died celebrating the memorial of love, in continuation of the greatest act of the presence of God among his people, creating communion, trusting and placing his hope in the human being, building up the kingdom of God. He fell next to the altar with the word of God on his lips. While sowing the seed he became that same seed himself, reborn in the people who loved him, believed in him and trusted him. Reflecting a few days earlier on death threats against him, he remarked:

> I must tell you, as a Christian, I do not believe in death without resurrection. If I am killed, I shall arise in the Salvadorean people. I say so without boasting, with the greatest humility. [2]

He died hoping, celebrating eternal love, forgiving his enemies as the Lord did.

* * *

The situation that caused Archbishop Romero's death was social injustice: the accumulation of wealth in the hands of a few alongside the misery and poverty of the great majority of the population. This situation was not new; its origins were already evident in the 19th century, with El Salvador's successive economic booms based on export of indigo and, from 1875, of coffee.

At that time there were many small farms (about one hectare) and very few large estates. By 1971, the census reported that half of the more than 270,000 productive agricultural units in the country accounted for only 5 percent of its productive land. Only 500 owned 40 percent of the land (80 percent of the flat land). Sixty-three land-owners had more than one thousand hectares; and the production and commercialization of coffee, cotton, sugar and all the other important products of the country were in the hands of only six families.

In 1976 the congress passed a land reform law by which 150,000 acres belonging to 250 land-owning families were to be divided among 12,000 farming families. The estate owners then began a strong fight against the military government.

When Mgr Romero became archbishop, El Salvador was in the midst of an acute social and economic conflict. He himself did not naturally have the psychology of a hero or "superman". Those who knew him well describe him as fragile, even insecure.

Oscar Romero was rather a shepherd, listening to his people and engaging in a dialogue with history. A deeply human man, whenever he had to make a decision, he asked for advice, consulted and prayed. He felt weak, he reflected and posed questions and gradually, through an experience of conversion, he became a new man — just like every saint. Recalling his mysticism, puritanical attitude and attachment to the orthodoxy of the church, Carmelo Alvarez adds:

> One must, however, mark his process of conversion, based on the daily experiences of the people's faith and on a testimonial and pastoral situation: the murder of Fr Rutilio Grande, one of his priests. This experience — together with the murder of other priests — transformed and purified him little by little for the process that he himself had to go through. His biblical reading was accompanied by great humility and personal sacrifice. He fully identified himself with the suffering of the Salvadorean people, to the extent of completely apprehending the reality of martyrdom. The last months of his life clearly show the intensity of his pastoral task and the resolution to face his own martyrdom. [3]

Less than three weeks after Romero's appointment as archbishop, Fr Grande, a child and an old man were murdered. When Romero arrived at the Convento de Aguilares that night, he found many Jesuits, priests and nuns and hundreds of *campesinos* weeping. The reality of those deaths carried him to another reality. He began to ask for more help to see, think and reflect in order to lead his flock. For three days there were no classes at the Catholic schools, in order to provide time to read and meditate on the meaning of martyrdom, of giving one's life for others, of being real witnesses. Until the murders were investigated and justice was done, until all violence stopped, Romero declared, he would not take part in any official occasion. For three years he kept his word.

From that day onwards Mgr Romero became the symbol of hope in El Salvador. That hope came with a challenge, as he said in a homily in December 1978:

> How can we avoid asking Christians to incarnate Christian justice, living accordingly both at home and in their public lives, to be agents of change; to try to become new people...? If we change structures, if land reforms are implemented and other changes carried out with the same selfish minds, we will only end up with new situations of abuse and outrage. Changing the structures is not enough. This is what Christianity is all about and it is upon this that I insist. Please understand that the change preached by the church is based on the conversion of the human heart. New people who will know how to be the leaven for a new society.

The recorded memories of those who were close to Romero, the eight volumes of his diary, in which he wrote every day, his homilies and his four pastoral letters and the speeches he delivered when he received honorary doctorates from the Universities of Georgetown (USA) and Louvain (Belgium), help us to retrace his personal itinerary, showing how he reflected on what he was living as a process of personal discovery and transformation. Arnaldo Mora, who has edited an anthology of his writings, has discovered a real theology of dialogue in them. This theology is based on a clear consciousness of the fact that the church is the trustee of universal principles, but in order to apply those principles in a concrete way it is necessary to be open to reality.

Romero's apostolic mission was to announce the kingdom of God as a realm of justice and love for every human being, especially for the most oppressed. He expressed this in his second pastoral letter (6 August 1978), where he tried to place the role of the church in its historical context. To fulfil its mission of bringing down through history the kingdom announced by Jesus, the church must live constantly in a process of conversion:

> The church does not speak only about the conversion of others, but primarily of its own conversion. This consciousness of the need for its own conversion is something historically new, even though it has always been said that the church must always be reformed *(semper reformanda)*. And its urge for that conversion has been accepted not so much in looking at itself, even in its faults and sins, but in looking outside itself to the universal sin. The church has recovered the most original place for its conversion, to turn "our soul towards the most humble, poorest and weakest".

Romero's last pastoral letter showed his prophetic courage, not only in facing repeated death threats from enemies outside the church, but also by acknowledging the sins of the church, thus making enemies within the church as well:

> Today it is necessary to gather... the denunciations and criticisms that point to our own sins as human components of the church. For in a time of crisis, those who feel committed to denouncing the sins that lie at the root of the crisis in this country must be ready to be denounced as well in order to convert, in order to build up a church suitable for our people, a church that Vatican II defines as a "universal sacrament of salvation".

He then went on to enumerate the three principal faults which, according to the survey on which the letter was based, were pointed out by the basic ecclesial communities and the organizations of the popular church: disunity, lack of renovation and adaptation and the devaluation of the criteria of the gospel.

It is in his third pastoral letter that Romero's universal spirit appears as most revolutionary and evangelical. It is unique in the history of Latin American Christian theology as the first document by a bishop to recognize the ethical, political and Christian legitimacy of an insurrectionist movement. At the same time Romero rejected violence, classified different kinds of violence and defended non-violence.[4] The letter was signed not only by Romero but also by Mgr Arturo Rivera y Damas, bishop of Santiago de Maria, Romero's greatest and most faithful supporter, who later succeeded him as archbishop of San Salvador.

In an interview a few weeks before his martyrdom, Romero openly and unequivocally affirmed his attitude towards the revolutionary movements in El Salvador:

> In my third pastoral letter I defended the right to organization and, in the name of the gospel, I promised to support their claims of justice and to denounce any intention to suffocate them. Now, within the present situation of the country, I believe with more conviction than ever in the mass organizations. I believe in the need for the people of El Salvador to organize themselves, because I believe that these organizations are social forces able to attain an authentic society, with social justice and liberty. Organization is necessary in order to fight efficiently.

Romero's homily on the day before he was killed is his true spiritual testament. In it, his genuine evangelical spirit shines forth with splendour. A delegation from several US Protestant churches who had come to show their solidarity was present, and Romero referred to them:

> There is something that exists in every people: the group of those who follow Jesus Christ, the group of God's people that is not the whole people, but it certainly is the group of the faithful. And so the example this morning is most precious: followers of Christ there, in the United States, have come to share with the followers of Christ here, in El Salvador, our faith in justice. They are the voice of the gospel against the injustices in their society... They have come to offer us their solidarity so that we, the people of God here in El Salvador, may also learn how to bravely denounce the injustices in our own society.

* * *

When prophets die, they give birth to others. They die proclaiming life; they die and sing; they are never old when they die. A prophet dies as a new person, as the prophet of liberation, summoning everybody to conversion. Oscar Romero lived a life of conversion, begged for it, spoke about it persistently.

Mgr Romero had a premonition of his death. He announced it to a journalist from the Mexican newspaper *Excelsior*:

> As a shepherd I am obliged by divine mandate to give my life for those I love — for all Salvadoreans, even for those who may be going to kill me. If the threats are carried out, from this moment I offer my blood to God for the redemption and for the resurrection of El Salvador.
>
>   Martyrdom is a grace of God that I do not believe I deserve. But if God accepts the sacrifice of my life, let my blood be a seed of freedom and the sign that hope will soon be reality. Let my death, if it is accepted by God, be for my people's liberation and as a witness of hope in the future.

You may say, if they succeed in killing me, that I pardon and bless those who do it. Would, indeed, that they might be convinced that they are wasting their time. A bishop will die, but God's church, which is the people, will never perish.[5]

We may conclude by citing two testimonials to this ecumenical pilgrim. The first comes from an allocution of Pope John Paul II during the general audience on 29 March 1981 in Rome:

I particularly greet El Salvador, suffering serious tensions and violence that every day add new names to the already long list of innocent victims. A whole year has passed since the tragic death of the Archbishop, Mgr Romero, zealous shepherd murdered on 24 March 1980 when he was celebrating Mass. He thus crowned with his blood his particularly solicitous ministry among the poorest and the outcasts. His was a supreme testimony that has remained as the symbol of a people's torment, but as the cause for hope for a better future as well.

The second is by the Jesuit liberation theologian Jon Sobrino, when he received an honorary doctorate from the University of Louvain five years after Mgr Romero had been awarded his doctorate. Sobrino recalled the special way in which Romero continued to live in the hearts of the people of El Salvador:

In every home there is always his picture, a poster or, among the poorest, a faded photograph taken from a newspaper. Whenever Mgr Romero's name is mentioned during the Sunday sermons at the cathedral, there is always a moving clap of applause. All these external signs are the expression of something deeper. Mgr Romero lives in the hearts of the poor and crucified... He lives in the poor of this world who continue to proclaim the good news of their liberation, and they still cling to him who announced it in a credible way.

Mgr Romero lives... How does he live today? He lives in the same way as Jesus after his resurrection. This means that he continues to infuse his spirit in the people of El Salvador... Mgr Romero has been and continues to be the good news, God's gospel for today's world. Like the gospel, Mgr Romero is exacting and upsetting. We must give him an answer and through him an answer to the gospel of Jesus Christ. It is not enough to receive the good news and be thankful for it: we must make it yield a profit, even if this is very hard. And today the situation asks more than ever for its fruition.

The Body of the Lord is living, growing and developing in unity and holiness through the blood of his saints and martyrs as a leaven of new humanity, new heaven and new earth. It is the apocalypse: revelation of blood and glory. Nobody can remain indifferent to this.

NOTES

[1] Cited by J.R. Brockman, in *Romero: A Life*, Maryknoll, NY, Orbis, 1989, p.242.

[2] *Ibid.*, p.248.

[3] Alvarez' "Oscar Romero, Dietrich Bonhoeffer: Pastores, Profetas de Jesucristo", *Pasos*, no. 13, San José, Costa Rica, 1987, p.7. In 1975 Romero had written to Pope Paul VI asking that Mgr Escriva de Balaguer, the founder of Opus Dei, be canonized promptly. Romero said he owed a great deal of his own theological knowledge and formation to Opus Dei. The letter to Pope Paul was reprinted in the Madrid newspaper *ABC* in 1992; cf. Brockman, *op. cit.*, p.46.

[4] Cf. Brockman, *ibid.*, pp.142f.

[5] Quoted in *ibid.*, p.248.

BIBLIOGRAPHY

Works on Oscar Romero:

Carmelo Alvarez, "Oscar Romero, Dietrich Bonhoeffer: Pastores, Profetas de Jesucristo, en Pasos", San
   José, Costa Rica, *Revista del Departamento Ecuménico de Investigaciones*, no. 13.
James Brockman, *Romero: A Life*, Maryknoll, NY, Orbis, 1989.
Assassiné avec les pauvres: Oscar Romero, Archevêque de San Salvador, Paris, Cerf, 1981.
Arnaldo Mora, "Mons. Romero y la Teología Latino-americana, en Pasos", *Revista del Departamento
   Ecuménico de Investigaciones*, no. 48, 1993.
Por qué se lucha en El Salvador, Quito, Asociación Latinoamericana por los Derechos Humanos, 1983.
Jon Sobrino, *Oscar Romero, Profeta y Mártir de la Liberación*, Lima, Ed. CEP, 1982.

Ruth Rouse
1872–1956

See Franzen's biography of R.R.

RUTH FRANZÉN

editor,

One of those pioneers to whom the ecumenical movement today owes much, Ruth Rouse was a missionary, an evangelist, an apologist, a student leader, a friend and a person of prayer. She left a deep impression both on individuals and among an ever-growing Christian fellowship.

Ruth Rouse was born in 1872, the eldest daughter of an English cotton broker and his Scottish wife. Her father came from a devout evangelical family chiefly associated with the Plymouth Brethren; her mother was a Scottish Baptist. Although she was a Londoner and a globe-trotter for most of her life, her Scottish ancestry always meant a great deal to her. Spending many of her vacations in outdoor activities in Scotland, she gained new strength there. Into her old age she continued to hint with pride at her sturdy antecedents by recounting that she descended from "Scottish clansmen and cattle thieves".

WCC

Born in a day when most Victorian middle- and upper-class girls did not go to school but waited for appropriate suitors, Rouse had parents unprejudiced enough to send her to the best schools. Nor did they shrink from giving her the best possible university education, sending her to Girton College, Cambridge, although this place for pioneer women was an abomination to many conservative Evangelicals.

Growing up in a pious home during an era when religion was extremely important in everyday life, Rouse early felt challenged by foreign missions. At 16 she was drawn into the activities of the Children's Special Service Mission. On the sands of Bournemouth, where she was spending her holidays with her family, she was asked to supervise swimming classes for younger children. A wise lay leader and his colleagues saw the importance of encouraging this shy and sporting youngster. Later, Rouse dated her own conversion from those summer days.

In 1892 a significant new impetus entered the religious life of Cambridge through Robert P. Wilder and the Student Volunteer Movement for Foreign Missions (SVM). During his travels Wilder handed out SVM declaration cards which students could sign, thereby declaring their resolve to become a foreign missionary. The spiritual vitality of this new movement, born in the USA in 1886, was demonstrated by a swiftly growing number of young volunteers. On Wilder's visit to Cambridge, one of those declaration cards ended up in the right-hand top drawer of Rouse's desk at Girton, where it remained unsigned for two years.

One day in the middle of her final year at Girton, a verse from 2 Timothy 1 flashed through her mind as she stood looking out of the window in her two-room study apartment: "I know whom I have believed, and am persuaded that he is able to keep that which I have committed unto him against that day." Her insight was that a purpose or intention could be committed to Christ's keeping as well as anything else. This broke her indecision. Relieved from her fear of changing her mind, she signed the declaration card on the spot. Forty years later she told an interviewer that she had never again had the slightest uncertainty that God's purpose for her was worldwide and missionary, nor the faintest thought of changing her purpose from following that will for her life. Though still affected by indecision in other matters for a time, from that moment she began to "grow up".[1]

In 1895 she became editor of the SVM magazine *The Student Volunteer*, and the next year she was appointed travelling secretary of three British student organizations, all with a deep commitment to foreign missions and Christian student work. Gradually, her pioneering work among women students grew into a worldwide mission. Already in 1897, her field widened to include the Scandinavian countries, where she was instrumental in encouraging Christian groups to organize themselves in almost every university centre. Before leaving for her foreign assignment in India, she spent two years in North America. In fact, she was already in the midst of her life work, challenging women students with the Christian message and recruiting them into Christian service at home and abroad.

Involvement with the missionary cause was to be a life-long commitment, although she herself was on the foreign mission field, in India, for only two years (1899-1901). There she worked with the Missionary Settlement for University Women. Ill health compelled her to return to England, where she was drawn back into the field that was to be hers for decades, international student work.

From 1904 to 1924 she was travelling secretary for the World Student Christian Federation, appointed to take care of the work among women students in particular, though men liked to listen to her too, appreciating her logical reasoning. Attacks on the church and Christianity by philosophy and science had made it difficult for many students to believe. During her own first year at college, Rouse had been confronted with the conflict between science and faith, reason and religion. Unused to debate, she was hardly capable of defending her faith in discussion with her agnostic fellow students. But she knew how to pray, and she emerged from the clash with a stronger faith. Those early arguments forced her to study the evidence and to develop her apologetic skills. During her three decades of work among students, she developed a fondness for discussing intellectual questions, and she considered apologetics an indispensable part of evangelizing.

European women students especially were often "emancipated" and difficult to win for the Christian message. Rouse's outspoken aim was to gain a foothold among them in any university centre. Her reports show a deep sympathy and thorough understanding of those very radical women students. Although she profoundly disliked their manners, she understood the psychology of the circumstances that drove them into opposition, recognizing that the difficult struggle against men to win their right to study had also made many of them militantly opposed to a church dominated by men and against Christianity itself.

Working among women students in a period when women's consciousness was rising inevitably brought to the forefront many of the issues of the day. Although deliberately undemonstrative in argument, Rouse wielded a considerable influence by her own example and by offering a role model for men. Furthermore, her insistence on giving young women students their own arena afforded them a venue where they could develop their decision-making and organizational skills. Women students were thus drawn into full participation in the WSCF and its national movements in the early years of the 20th century, well before many societies even granted them citizenship.

Rouse was herself a real "gentlewoman", a person of comity. In opening the way for women to activities and decision-making on all levels, she made it a point never to give the impression of attacking men's privileges. The WSCF policy was always to add women's representatives, not to replace men by women. Another key principle was never to allow secondary issues to distract her from evangelization and Christian follow-up work. She warned the groups she started never to allow clashing opinions on issues at dispute — such as language, nationality, sex or race — to split up their Christian oneness.

An able speaker and writer, her outstanding gift was working with individuals, and even at her busiest she always looked for time to do this work. Nor did she shrink from the challenges thrown up by language barriers; with or without an interpreter, she handled innumerable personal talks on evidence for Christianity, the way of salvation, the missionary call, the deepening of the spiritual life.

She used her enormous gift for making friends to bring her many new friends into an international network of Christian friendship and cooperation. Remnants of her voluminous worldwide correspondence testify to her own capacity for continued personal concern. She took great pains in careful follow-up work through letters, conferences and regular visits. Constantly on the lookout for able and willing leaders, she succeeded in inspiring, often from among only a few interested students, many a germinating national effort, especially among women students.

During and immediately after the first world war, Rouse and her co-workers within the WSCF did much to re-establish mutual understanding between Christians from both sides of the frontlines. Her outstanding contribution was the launch of a cooperative undertaking by students known as European Student Relief. Visiting Vienna in 1920, she was confronted with incredible suffering and starvation among students. "After wakeful nights, wondering if an appeal for an immediate gift of £10,000 was too daring, the call of God to a venture of faith seemed clear." In her book *Rebuilding Europe: The Student Chapter in Post-War Reconstruction* (1925) she recounted the story of the campaign and its response. Within five years, over £500,000 (then equivalent to US$2.5 million) had been received from students in 42 countries and distributed to their fellow students in 19 countries. In 1926, the relief work of the WSCF was launched as an independent organization, the International Student Service, which was desperately needed again within less than 15 years.

In 1924 Rouse returned to England, where she served until 1939 as educational secretary of the Missionary Council of the National Assembly of the Church of

England, one of the most prestigious posts held by an Anglican woman in those years. The task was not easy. Most of her work was done in the shadow of bishops and other more visible male church leaders. Although she possessed a volatile temperament, her reputation as a reliable Evangelical seems to have been stable among friend and foe alike. A firm commitment to the missionary cause helped to reconcile even those of clashing opinions.

Another field in which Ruth Rouse made a contribution for almost half a century was in the international work of the World's Young Women's Christian Associations. She was a member of the world executive committee (1906-46) and was president during the difficult years of the second world war.

Her conference career began with the first Student Volunteer Movement Quadrennial in Liverpool in 1896, where she was one of six or seven young leaders instrumental in ensuring the success of that daring venture into the arena of international student conferences. Later she helped to arrange and personally participated in innumerable national and international missionary conferences.

Her last great international ecumenical conference was the first assembly of the World Council of Churches (Amsterdam 1948), where she was invited on a special visitor's pass. She was already deeply involved as an historian in what was to be her last great work. Together with Stephen Charles Neill, she shouldered the responsibility for planning and editing *A History of the Ecumenical Movement, 1517-1948* (1954), and she wrote two of the 16 chapters herself. That work and her other major work as a historian, *The World's Student Christian Federation: A History of the First Thirty Years* (1948) are still considered standard reference volumes.

Introducing the history of ecumenism to the readers of *The Ecumenical Review*, Rouse pleaded:

> The World Council of Churches should regard the issue of the *History* as but the modest beginning of an endeavour to rouse the whole church to a mighty effort to unite the churches. Such an endeavour should be rooted in prayer, and regarded as the supreme spiritual call to the church in the second half of the 20th century, intimately bound up with the revival for which we are praying and longing. Revivals in the past have centred upon a demand for faithfulness in carrying out some specific activity or duty incumbent on the Christian. May it not be that the revival we long to experience in the second half of the 20th century will centre on the question of church unity, and have as its outstanding spiritual demand the giving of all and everything to secure the coming together of the separated denominations into one universal church? Revival and worldwide missions! Revival and Bible study! And now revival and church unity![2]

Rouse learned early to find new strength, as is demonstrated by this passage, written in 1897 to Lydia Wahlström, a "great friend" in Sweden:

> I have been helped lately... by thinking of God as he is so often spoken of by the Psalmist as "my God". It is so wonderful to think what God is, really is for us, and that we are taught to claim for ourselves each one of the marvellous revelations that he has given of himself, of the exceeding greatness of his power, of his love that passeth knowledge. And the more we constantly look at what God is and not at what we are, the stronger we shall grow. We shall not then make ourselves miserable by constantly pulling ourselves up by the roots to see how we are getting on...

Her lifelong zeal for Christian unity flowed from the same deeply felt source. An obituary by her younger friend and fellow worker Suzanne Bidgrain offered this testimony:

To Ruth, a believer in the church universal, ecumenism meant the thrilling, and at the same time awe-inspiring, experience of fellowship in faith with all those who worship the Lord to whom her life was dedicated — she always shared the beautiful wish of the Church of England to act as "a house of reconciliation", and when, later on, she was given an almost unique opportunity of working all over the world for the fulfilment of Christ's prayer "that they may be one", she did so with all the enthusiasm and faithfulness in her, contributing, I believe, more than any other Federation leader to making the Federation, as she herself said, "an experimental laboratory of ecumenism".[3]

Ruth Rouse gained the strength for her long and demanding career from the reality of her faith in God, with whom she was eager to cooperate in a most natural way. She always underlined the significance of Bible study and prayer in the Christian's life and work. To her contemporaries Rouse's own life was the incarnation of her teaching.

NOTES

[1] Wilmina Rowland, "The Contribution of Ruth Rouse to the World's Student Christian Federation", unpublished master's thesis, Yale University, 1936, p.59.
[2] *The Ecumenical Review*, vol. 7, no. 3, 1954, pp.239f.
[3] *Student World*, no. 1, 1957, p.75.

BIBLIOGRAPHY

An unpublished M.A. thesis by Wilmina Rowland, "The Contribution of Ruth Rouse to the World's Student Christian Federation" (Yale 1936) was for many years the only piece of research about her. A bibliography of Ruth Rouse's major published writings has been prepared by Ruth Franzén and published, together with the article "The Legacy of Ruth Rouse", in the *International Bulletin of Missionary Research*, vol 17, 1993, no. 4. A book entitled *Ruth Rouse and Her Work in an International, Ecumenical and Ideological Perspective* by the same author is due to be published shortly.

Maria Gabriella Sagheddu
1914–1939

MARTHA DRISCOLL

Born in Dorgali, Sardinia, on 17 March 1914, Maria Sagheddu grew up in a typical shepherd's family. Life was not easy, and the death of her father when she was only four accustomed her to poverty and hard work from earliest childhood. She was a quick, intelligent student, always first in her class, but her formal education ended after the sixth grade when she began to work as a domestic servant to supplement the family's meagre income. A stubborn and wilful child, she had a passion to win both at school and at play, and a strong determination to overcome any challenge.

Although her environment was a very Catholic one, she was not particularly interested in church activities. Her deeply religious mother found her strength in daily mass, but Maria preferred to play games rather than accompany her mother to vespers. Sunday mass was enough for her.

Then at the age of 18 something happened. Maria Sagheddu changed. Evidently she had some kind of conversion experience, although she never spoke of it to anyone except her confessor. At the same time she voiced her desire to consecrate herself completely to God in the religious life. She began to direct all of her strong willpower into a very real effort to grapple with her impetuous temperament and follow the call of Christ. Her life was henceforth to be marked by a very deep sense of vocation. She began to frequent the sacraments — mass and communion every morning, vespers every evening — and to spend long hours in silent solitary prayer in church. She enrolled in Catholic Action and became very active in teaching catechism, serving the poor, the sick, the unwanted. The most profound change, however, was in herself. "She became sweet and calm," was her mother's brief comment about a daughter who no longer lost her temper or became annoyed by the contradictions of life.

After two-and-a-half years of determined day-to-day conversion, her parish priest chose for her the hard, simple life of the Trappists. At the age of 21, Sagheddu entered the small and poor Trappist monastery of Grottaferrata "on the continent", not far from Rome. She received the habit on 13 April 1936, made her first vows on the Feast of

Christ the King in October 1937, contracted tuberculosis in the spring of 1938, and died on 23 April 1939, at the age of 25.

What is the ecumenical significance of this very ordinary and very short life? Most likely Sr Maria Gabriella, as she was called in the monastery, had never even met a Protestant or an Orthodox before entering the cloistered community of Grottaferrata. There, however, she came in contact with the movement of prayer for the unity of Christians, the Octave of Prayer promoted by Abbé Paul Couturier. The prophetic vision of the community's Abbess, Mother Pia Gullini, perceived the importance of this ideal and began to direct the entire community to the special vocation of prayer.

The first of Couturier's leaflets to reach Grottaferrata was an invitation to participate in the Week of Prayer for Christian Unity in January 1937. It was possibly the first time that many of the nuns became aware of the scandal and the suffering caused by the divisions within Christianity and heard of the incipient movement towards unity in accordance with the prayer of Jesus on the night before he died: "that they may be one". Couturier's tract, calling for prayer, sacrifice, expiation and voluntary oblations, was read at the daily community meeting on 17 January 1937, and Mother Pia offered some brief explanatory comments. Almost immediately, an elderly sister approached the abbess, her face radiating joy. "What you just read to us is so beautiful. It is exactly for me. Today is the anniversary of my profession. It seems to me that you can offer your life for this cause. I have come to ask your permission to offer to the good Lord the little bit of time I have left. It is truly a worthy cause."

Mother Pia responded affirmatively. Exactly a month after the Novena for Unity, the 78-year-old Mother Immacolata died peacefully as a result of a stroke suffered the week before. The community was informed of her offering, and fervour for the cause of unity grew. When Couturier's request for prayer and sacrifice during the Week of Prayer for Christian Unity was read again the next year, it was the newly professed, 23-year-old Sr Maria Gabriella who felt called to offer her life. Surprised, Mother Pia deliberately responded coolly. Perhaps she viewed it as a burst of passing enthusiasm, not uncommon among young religious. She suggested that Sr Maria Gabriella think it over, perhaps assuming that the idea would be forgotten. But a few days later, Sr Maria Gabriella went back to her. "It seems to me that the Lord really wants it; I feel myself pushed to think about it even without wanting to." Once again, Mother Pia's answer was non-committal: "I won't say yes or no. Offer yourself to the will of God."

Shortly afterwards, Maria Gabriella developed a cough, signs of weakness and loss of energy. By Easter, the abbess sent her for an X-ray. She was to spend 40 days in a large public hospital in painful but futile attempts to cure the tuberculosis that had been diagnosed. The disease only developed more rapidly. When she returned to the monastery, she was taken to the infirmary, where she spent the remaining ten months of her life in peace, abandonment and growing joy as the definitive encounter with Christ drew near. The sisters were impressed by her serenity and by her deep and constant sense of gratitude. The longed-for day finally arrived, and after heroic patience throughout her illness and agony Sr Maria Gabriella happily went to meet her Lord on the evening of 23 April 1939. It was the Fourth Sunday after Easter, the Sunday of the Good Shepherd, and the gospel of the day proclaimed: "I have other sheep as well that are not of this fold. I must lead these also so that there will be but one Shepherd and one fold." This was seen as a confirmation that the offering of her life had truly been a response to a divine inspiration.

Normally, the story of Sr Maria Gabriella would have ended there within the walls of her beloved Grottaferrata. Many others had consumed their lives in love of Christ and prayer for his church in silence and obscurity. That was their vocation, but it was nothing unusual, and their deaths were as hidden as their lives had been. But Providence intervened, and the story of Sr Maria Gabriella was written and published thanks to the insight and courage of Mother Pia, who sensed a very special design of God in it. A popular biography appeared less than a year after Sr Maria Gabriella's death and was reprinted four times within twelve months. The cause of unity was made known throughout Italy, and Grottaferrata soon became an ecumenical centre of prayer and encounter. Many vocations streamed to the monastery, attracted by the ideal offered them by Sr Maria Gabriella. Visitors came from as far away as England and France to pray at her tomb, among them Frères Roger Schütz and Max Thurian of the newly formed community of Taizé. They brought word of her back to others.

In this way, Sr Maria Gabriella soon became a kind of popular "patron saint" of the ecumenical movement which was beginning to gain ground in the Roman Catholic Church. As the church renewed itself during and after the Second Vatican Council, her silent witness inspired others to imitate her prophetic example of the "spiritual ecumenism" mentioned in the Decree on Ecumenism. This popular recognition received official sanction quite rapidly. On 25 January 1983, less than 44 years after her death, Maria Gabrielle Sagheddu was proclaimed "Blessed" by Pope John Paul II during the annual ecumenical celebration in the basilica of Saint Paul's Outside-the-Walls at the end of the Week of Prayer for Christian Unity.

Sr Maria Gabriella never spoke of her offering for the unity of Christians to anyone except to respond monosyllabically to Mother Pia's repeated question as to whether she was renewing it faithfully every day. She rarely spoke of the cause of unity, and took little interest in the correspondence that the Anglican monks of Nashdom had begun with Mother Pia at the suggestion of Abbé Couturier. She did not seek psychological support or spiritual importance by accumulating information about the situation of the division among Christians nor about any new signs of openness that might be considered the fruit of her prayer and sacrifice.

In effect, Sr Maria Gabriella was completely unaware of having a message for anyone. She had no consciousness of doing anything extraordinary or having anything to teach to others. Perhaps her most specific characteristic was a deep sense of unworthiness, together with a profound gratitude for everything that had been given to her. It is up to us to seek and perceive the message of God for his church in Sr Maria Gabriella's simplicity. Perhaps it is that the path to unity coincides exactly with the normal path of Christian prayer and conversion in the joyful, loving gift of self in thanksgiving for all one is and all one has for the glory of God and the coming of his kingdom. Her offering was for unity, but her attention was on Christ, on his desire for unity. Her prayer for unity was not just one intention among many. It was simply her prayer to be personally ever more united to the heart of Christ and to repeat with him, "Thy kingdom come". For her, the unity of all people in Christ was the same as salvation for all. It was not a new intention; it was already the scope of her whole life consecrated to God.

Seeking unity means seeking Christ above all else. If we penetrate the heart of Christ, if his prayer lives in our heart through the Spirit, our entire life becomes a sign and sacrament of the unity that is already ours in him. Then we are capable of accepting any sacrifice in union with his sacrifice on the cross for the salvation of the world, which is the unity of all things in Christ.

Sr Maria Gabriella sought only to live her monastic life to the full, seeking and finding God in the ordinary activities of everyday life: listening to his Word and responding to it, forgetting self and placing all her trust in his mercy, loving the house of the Lord to which she was called, loving her community, loving each one of her sisters, struggling to overcome all the impatient instincts of her obstinate temperament. Some have suggested that she thus pointed to the "little way" of ecumenism by showing that the most important aspect of work for unity is personal conversion from the selfishness and pride which are the roots of division. The most effective way to promote the visible unity of all Christians is by promoting the real unity of your own ecclesial group, by learning to become *church* — one Body, one heart, one mind in Christ — by learning to live together in humility and forgiveness, in mutual service and readiness to sacrifice.

In a time of disappointments, delays and setbacks on the ecumenical journey, Sr Maria Gabriella's silent sacrifice is perhaps a call to patience, perseverance, conviction and hope in the humility of faith. She did not look for results. She had no human expectations as to when and how the desired unity was to be achieved. She did not wish to take any credit for that achievement. Thus she was free from discouragement, free from worries, free from the temptation of despair. She simply did what she felt that the Lord asked of her, thankful to have been given a small part in his suffering, an incomprehensible sign of his love. She found peace in trust and abandon to his mysterious design, certain that his victory was assured.

Sr Maria Gabriella left behind no books or articles or meditations on ecumenical matters; unwittingly, however, she left a clear sign as to what filled her mind and heart during the long months of illness. A section of her small gospel is stained yellow from the constant contact with her sweaty, feverish fingers, obviously the pages she read and reread: the last chapters of the gospel of John — the farewell discourse, Jesus' high priestly prayer, the passion. Her only extant writings consist of a small notebook with some very impersonal entries and about forty letters, most of them written to her mother. In them, she does not speak of unity, but rather gives us insight into her own experience of the salvific mystery of impotence, failure and death as the necessary path to resurrection and new life, the necessary path to unity.

From the hospital to Mother Pia:

I assure you that my sacrifice is totally complete because from dawn to dusk I do nothing else but sacrifice my own will in everything...

I would like to be strong, as strong as iron, and instead I feel as weak as a piece of straw... I have been convinced for quite some time that I am no more than a pygmy in the spiritual life, because I let myself be carried along by every wind that blows.

Before this there was no way of bending my will: now I understand that the glory of God does not consist in doing great things but in the total sacrifice of my "ego". Pray for me that I might understand more and more the great gift of the cross so that I might put it to good use from now on for myself and for everyone...

From letters to her mother:

Thank you, dear mother, for the way in which you have accepted my sacrifice. I am so happy not only to offer myself but to be offered again by my dear ones like a holocaust to be consumed, if God so pleases, for the salvation of souls... I know that our human nature needs to have its outlet and that you feel the need to cry, but after the first moment, just fling everything into the heart of Jesus that consumes everything like a fiery furnace... I understand your pain, dear mother, and my heart aches for you, but remember that the bigger the sacrifice, the bigger will be your reward in heaven... God will certainly recompense you for the love and resignation with which you have embraced the cross he has sent you...

I do not want you to get ideas and begin to pray for my recovery. Pray instead that the Lord will do with me whatever is to his greater glory... I am always content to do the will of God, whatever it might be, for that is my joy, my happiness, my peace... Remain firm in your dispositions of abandonment to the will of God and bless him always for whatever he chooses to do with me. Forget that I am sick and think only about the Lord: thank him and bless him for the graces and the gifts he has given me...

My happiness is great and no one can take it from me... There is no happiness greater than being able to suffer for Jesus and for the salvation of souls...

From conversations with Mother Pia:

I read this phrase of Ruysbroeck: "With a humble and generous heart, offer and present Christ as your own offering, as a treasure that liberates and rewards. He in turn will offer you to his heavenly Father as the precious fruit for whom he died, and the Father will embrace you with His love." I stopped there... it seemed that the Lord wanted me to understand, "This is for you".

Jesus has chosen me as a privileged object of his love, giving me his suffering to bear in order to make me more like him... I think that I will never fully understand the love that Jesus shows me in offering me this cross.

The aim of Sr Maria Gabriella was not so much to pray for unity as to seek the glory of God through personal participation in the paschal mystery of Christ. Hers is the gratuitous prayer of praise and thanksgiving. This is the exigency of the absolute. This is the intuition that if we seek only the glory of his name, all else will be given, including unity, *especially* unity. For the glory of God *is* the unity of all persons in Christ. The ecumenical journey is that journey of every Christian who lives and prays the Lord's Prayer, willing to follow Christ consistently right to the cross, open to the Spirit who conforms us to Christ crucified so that we may also be conformed to his glorified body in the full maturity of Christ. Ecumenism calls for that sanctity.

BIBLIOGRAPHY

Works on Maria Gabriella Sagheddu:

Maria Giovanna Dore, *Dalla Trappa per l'Unita della Chiesa: Suor Maria Gabriella*, Brescia, Morcelliana, 1940 (repr. 1983).

Maria Giovanna Dore, *Suor Maria Gabriella*, Rome, Edizioni Paolini, 1940.

Martha Driscoll, *A Silent Herald of Unity: The Life of Blessed Maria Gabriella Sagheddu*, Kalamazoo, MI, Cistercian Publications, 1990.

Marie de la Trinité Kervingant, *Le monachisme, lieu œcuménique: La bienheureuse Maria Gabriella*, Paris, Oeil, 1983.

Jean Leclerq, "Blessed Maria Gabriella Sagheddu: In Praise of Ordinariness", *Cistercian Studies*, 1983, no. 3.

Bernard Martelet, *La petite sœur de l'unite: Marie-Gabriella*, Paris, Mediaspaul, 1984.

Cristiana Piccardo, *Ritrovare una Sorella, Alla Scuola della Libertà*, Milan, Editrice Ancora, 1992.

Paolino Beltrami Quatrocchi, *Gabrielle dell'Unità*, Monastero Trappiste di Vitorchiano, 1980.

Monica della Volpe, *La Strada della Gratitudine*, Milan, Jaca, 1983.

Monica della Volpe, *Sr Maria Gabriella: Donner la vie pour l'unité des Chrétiens*, Collectanea Cisterciensia, 1983, no. 3.

Bishop Samuel
1920–1981

Stephen and I visited him in Cairo

MICHAEL GHATTAS

"Who can really fill the void left by Bishop Samuel? Who can fill the countless gaps he has left, not only as regards his work, but also his heart and sentiments?"[1] Those words from the funeral oration by Pope Shenouda III sum up simply what distinguished the personality and the contributions of a man who had been his own companion in spiritual endeavour and struggle for over 30 years.

Bishop Samuel was born Saad Aziz on 8 December 1920 in Cairo. After primary and secondary schooling in Cairo, he began law studies at Fouad I University (now Cairo University), from which he graduated in 1941. He then worked briefly with the Egyptian National Bank, but soon resigned his post to devote himself to Christian youth work and to service in the Sunday schools in Giza.

After completing his theological studies in Cairo in 1944, he obtained a scholarship to the American University in Cairo to study education and psychology, after which the Coptic Church sent him to Ethiopia to teach at the Theological Institute in Addis Ababa, which he did until 1946. He was decorated with the Star of Ethiopia.

Returning to Cairo, he was appointed general secretary of the Sunday school of the Coptic Orthodox Church. Already he was longing for a monastic life. He spent three years with his spiritual mentor, Archpriest Mina Al-Moutawahed (later Pope Cyril VI), who was then leading the life of a hermit, at the St Minas Church in Old Cairo. In 1948, he was robed as a monk, taking the name Makary Al Souriany,[2] and went to the Virgin Mary Monastery in Wadi El-Natrun. There he was consecrated as a priest in 1951. He was later consecrated as an archpriest.

In 1952 he was commissioned to become spiritual guide of theology students in Cairo. He earned a master's degree in education from Princeton University, writing a thesis on Christian education in the Coptic Church. Beginning in 1955 he taught pastoral care at the Theological College in Cairo. He served as secretary to Pope Cyril VI from 1959 to 1962, when he was consecrated Bishop for Public Relations and Social Services, receiving the name "Samuel". On 6 October 1981 during the assassination of Egyptian President Anwar Sadat, Bishop Samuel was tragically murdered and fell asleep in Christ.

Throughout his entire life as a layman, monk and bishop, he was self-disciplined and self-critical, firmly convinced that every virtue should impel one on towards another. He was very strict about his own spiritual life, holding himself accountable in all things large and small. He believed that sacrifices, suffering, trials and tribulations patiently borne by believers are not ends in themselves, for God's gifts and rewards are not granted in return for suffering and woes but are based on the humility called forth by suffering. He also practised Christian meditation, freeing his thoughts from vain wandering and cultivating purity of heart until the Lord Jesus Christ found place in it. [3]

* * *

As the person responsible for the external relations of the Coptic Orthodox Church, Bishop Samuel had frequent contacts abroad from 1954 until his death. He was active within the World Council of Churches; and the WCC's first general secretary, W.A. Visser 't Hooft, described him as "truly a civil engineer who built up ecumenical relations between the Coptic Church and the Council. Although the Coptic Church had been represented since the very first meeting of the WCC in 1948, it did not make use of its membership until Bishop Samuel became responsible for the external relations of the Coptic Church." [4]

As Makary Al Souriany, he was chosen by Pope Yusab II as part of the Coptic Orthodox delegation to the WCC's second assembly (Evanston 1954) — the church's first opening towards the outside world after centuries of isolation. Later he chaired several WCC commissions, including Church and Society, Diakonia and International Affairs. In 1961 he was elected to the WCC Central Committee.

Bishop Samuel's main concern in building bridges between other churches abroad and the Coptic Church was to see his church play a role in pursuing the unity of the church, so that the church with all its members could praise its Lord in the full flower of its strength. Pope Shenouda III spoke of the gifts which the bishop brought to this task: "He had a wealth of experience second to none; his actions were imbued with love towards everyone; he was always engaged in quiet but productive activity." [5]

While especially emphasizing the significance of the Coptic Church during the first centuries, Bishop Samuel also demonstrated its continuing impact on history and described its present work, its participation in theological debates and its cooperation with other churches. This earned the Coptic Church a respected place within the world church community today. Within the WCC he was also instrumental in bringing about many resolutions regarding inter-church relations, for example, concerning the cessation of missionary work aimed at luring members away from one church to another.

At the regional level, Bishop Samuel was active in both the Middle East Council of Churches and the All Africa Conference of Churches. He was one of the founders of the MECC in 1974, and served as a president of the Council from its establishment until his death as a martyr. For many years he was a vice-president of the AACC. In 1976 when it met in Cairo and Alexandria, he played a decisive part in drafting the report it drew up on the Church of Alexandria, setting out its significance since the beginnings of Christianity in Africa.

In addition, he represented the Coptic Church as an observer at the Second Vatican Council. He also worked assiduously to bring about harmonious relations between the

Coptic Orthodox Church and the other Oriental Orthodox Churches (Ethiopian, Armenian, Syrian and Indian). In January 1965 an agreement among the heads of these churches was signed in Addis Ababa, Ethiopia, in which Bishop Samuel had played a major role.

Within Egypt, one of Bishop Samuel's main concerns was forging harmony and fraternity between the Coptic Orthodox and other Christian churches. As President of the Council of Churches responsible for public and church matters, he pursued this goal until his death. He was often involved in discussions regarding interchurch aid among the Coptic, Catholic and Protestant Churches in Egypt.

Above all, the Coptic Orthodox Church owes Bishop Samuel a debt of gratitude for his efforts in fostering Christian-Muslim dialogue. He strove untiringly to achieve harmony and peace with the leaders of Islam. While convinced that agreement could not be expected on theological issues, he believed that Christianity and Islam should be at one concerning the worth of the human being and human dignity. Both religions should strive to counteract atheism, materialism and all other excesses threatening modern society, which jeopardize not only harmony among religions but also human dignity, justice and peace. Religions and their leaders should therefore be an example in the practice of human rights, and places of worship should be sources of peace and justice. Christianity and Islam should therefore not merely co-exist; Christian-Muslim dialogue should foster mutual assistance and a joint approach to social issues and problems. [6]

Bishop Samuel's commitment to the work of the ecumenical community reflected his own dependence on his Lord Jesus Christ. From the depths of his heart he always repeated: "No one has greater love than this, to lay down one's life for one's friends" (John 15:13). His life can therefore be seen as a sacrifice on the altar of humanity.

* * *

At the beginning of his life as a monk, Bishop Samuel wrote down the following prayer, which describes his complete surrender to God:

> My God and beloved Jesus, ten years ago you drew me unto yourself from the world and you have nurtured me in every way, with the fullness of your love, the generosity of your mercy, which by your power and guidance I came to feel in the midst of my weakness and shortcomings... Now you let me live in your dwelling and you prepare me to pray on the hill of your holy kingdom. Prepare me with your Holy Spirit and fill me with all his gifts, not for my sake, for I am not worthy, but on account of your great love which has wrought much good in me. It will continue to work much good in me so that no one may say, "it beckoned then abandoned him".
>
> Also not for my sake, but for that of your children whom you love. You have bought me with your love so that I may serve them. You have now filled me with your love so that I serve them, because of your love towards them.
>
> Also not for my sake, but for your church which you took unto you as your bride. It groans under the shackles of the world and the confusion of its departing from you. I therefore pray for mercy, for help and the outpouring of your love and your guidance. Increase, I pray you, that power from on high which accompanied me while I was in the world, even as I dwell day and night deep in your house.
>
> All time, all duration and every heartbeat are in your hands. I therefore prepare myself to use them, for you have nurtured me, you know my weaknesses, for I can in no wise rely upon my own strength. If you do not bless time and every minute, how can they bear fruit

and bring forth benefits? Your blessing can make much from little, can prepare the minutes to bring countless blessings...

My God and Saviour, take my heart and sanctify it. Bless all my time and accept it. Give me success with your blessing and your love at all times. Glory and honour be unto you for ever. [7]

Bishop Samuel believed that all those who engage in church service should prepare themselves spiritually for this. He could see that Christian virtue is the most important mark of a person of God. In one of his lectures on spiritual exercises he stated:

When a person discovers the treasure-store of grace within himself, he can receive from God the power of renewal which makes new life possible... A person who schools himself to learn from life cannot rest content with what has been achieved... For the Creator himself is constantly at work and cannot remain inactive within anyone.

Bishop Samuel then explained the bases of all spiritual exercises in three points: (1) the will to grow; (2) belief in our capacity for continuous learning; (3) discovering the possibility of positive action and renewal. [8]

Bishop Samuel delivered countless lectures at home and abroad. Deeply concerned with ministering to the Copts of the diaspora, he sent them many letters encouraging them to emulate the apostles of Jesus Christ in the countries where they found themselves, without abandoning their love of their fatherland.

Bishop Samuel's contribution to the ecumenical movement strengthens our own resolve to take up the torch he lit within the ecumenical community. As long as there are persons who strive like Bishop Samuel for the unity of the body of Christ, we may look forward in hope to the day when the unity of the church will be clearly visible to all humanity.

NOTES

[1] Quoted by Iris Almasry, *The Story of Bishop Samuel* (in Arabic), Cairo, 1986, p.129.

[2] In the Coptic Church, one's name is changed when he becomes a priest or a monk, suggesting that this signals the start of a new life (cf. Gen. 17:5; John 1:42).

[3] Cf. Almasry, *op. cit.*, p.21 n.1.

[4] Quoted in Friends of Bishop Samuel, *Enlightening Insights into the Life of Bishop Samuel*, Cairo, Al Giza, 1992, p.6.

[5] Almasry, *op. cit.*, p.129 n.1.

[6] Merit Boutros Ghali, in *Enlightening Insights, loc. cit.*

[7] *Ibid.*, pp.66f.

[8] Almasry, *op. cit.*, p.58

BIBLIOGRAPHY

The most important books by Bishop Samuel — all of which appeared posthumously — deal with the following themes: the mutual responsibility of church and parents; pastoral theology; the way of happiness; work and service of the individual; spiritual exercises; family counselling; Christian views on order in the family: contemporary issues; joy and peace; the basic truths of religious life.

In addition to the works cited in the notes above, a good deal of other material about Bishop Samuel has been published in Arabic, especially in the Coptic Church's *Sunday School Magazine*.

In English see:

Ans J. van der Bent, "Bishop Samuel", in *Dictionary of the Ecumenical Movement*, eds Nicholas Lossky et al., Geneva, WCC, 1991, pp.898-99.

"Bishop among Those Killed with Sadat", in *Ecumenical Press Service*, no. 28, 1981, p.1.

Marie Skobtsova
1891–1945

ELISABETH BEHR-SIGEL

An avant-garde poet in a highly intellectual circle in St Petersburg, a member of the Russian Socialist-Revolutionary Party, twice married and divorced, a mother of three, then a nun in the Russian Orthodox Church in exile, finally a resistance worker in occupied France, deported to the Ravensbrück concentration camp, where she died shortly before the liberation — this was in outline the life of Mother Marie Skobtsova.

She was born Elisabeth Pilenko on 8 December 1891 (old calendar) in Riga, Latvia. Her family belonged to the Ukrainian landed nobility, and one of her 18th-century ancestors had married the sister of the Empress Anne of Russia. Her father had created a model vineyard on the family estate near Anapa, on the shore of the Black Sea, and in this landscape of sun and sea Lise spent a happy childhood, but one which ended in drama with her father's premature death. The tormented adolescent was distraught.

She was 14 at the time. Shortly afterwards she and her mother went to live in St Petersburg. Although the family had relatives close to court circles, the young girl, whose poetic talent was already evident, was principally to be found among the avant-garde literary elite. Lise was close to the symbolist poet Alexander Block. At 18 she married Dimitri Kouzmin-Karavayev, a lawyer and member of the Social Democratic Party. The young couple went out a great deal, forming part of the refined group who congregated around the writer Vyacheslav Ivanov.

Eventually, however, the discussions in this milieu, which often went on into the early morning, bored the young woman. She condemned the progressive intelligentsia for talking and talking about revolution without being prepared to give their lives for it. She herself was drawn towards a mystic populism, a messianism of the Russian people and earth. At the same period she began to feel a desire to deepen her knowledge of the Orthodox Christian religion. St Petersburg was a centre of what has come to be known as the Russian religious renaissance of the early 20th century. She was one of the first women authorized to follow courses at the St Petersburg Theological Academy as a free student.

Meanwhile, her marriage had collapsed. When the Russian Revolution broke out, Lise joined the Socialist-Revolutionary Party, a group of idealists who believed, not without a certain confusion, in Russian populism with its aspirations to *pravda* (justice-truth) and the ideals of Western democracy. But the cynical realism of Lenin's Bolshevik Party triumphed in Russia, eliminating the Socialist-Revolutionary majority of the first democratically elected constituent assembly.

Fleeing from Bolshevism, Lise returned in January 1918 to the family estate in Anapa, where she was elected to the town council and eventually became mayor. In the difficult and dangerous civil war that followed the Soviet seizure of power, Anapa was occupied in August 1918 by a White Army group. An independent government was set up in Kouban. Accused of collaborating with the local soviet, the young woman was brought before a military tribunal, where she was given only a symbolic sentence; and one of her judges, the young officer Daniel Skobtsov, fell in love with her and they married.

Without renouncing her Socialist-Revolutionary ideals, or perhaps because of them, Elisabeth Skobtsova shared in her husband's struggle against Bolshevism. The events of the civil war separated the couple. After the defeat of the White Armies and the evacuation of Crimea, the only possibility was exile together with her mother and her daughter from her first marriage. The pregnant Lise embarked at Novorossisk on the last ship to leave for Georgia. The voyage was a nightmare, but her son Yuri was born safe and sound in Tiflis. Eventually Daniel Skobtsov managed to get to Constantinople, where their daughter Anastasia was born a year later. Following the stream of Russian emigrants, the whole family settled in 1922 in Paris, which had become the capital of "Russia outside the borders".

* * *

Here the life of Elisabeth Skobtsova was to take a new course. The bonds between her and her husband became looser. Though remaining friends, they parted in 1927. She became totally involved in the *Action chrétienne des étudiants russes* (ACER), an Orthodox youth movement which sprang up spontaneously among the Russian immigrants.

This movement benefited from the influence of the Russian religious revival which had re-opened a dialogue between the intelligentsia and the Orthodox Church. Prominent intellectuals like the Marxist economist Sergei Bulgakov and the libertarian philosopher Nicolas Berdyaev underwent a veritable conversion. These "great converts", whose faith had undergone the trial of doubt, inspired young people in exile who aspired (to use their own term) to "ecclesialize life", in other words, to allow the light of Christ to penetrate all of life in its social and personal dimensions, and to turn the actions of a culture into worship "in spirit and in truth".

Bulgakov, ordained a priest in 1918, taught dogmatics at the St Sergius Theological Institute, which was founded in Paris in 1925. He became Lise's confessor and "spiritual father". She also became involved with other leading representatives of this new Christian intelligentsia.

As itinerant secretary of ACER from 1928, Skobtsova visited Russian student groups being formed in university cities throughout France — Lyons, Marseilles,

Toulouse, Strasbourg. Soon she realized that she could not limit herself to the university world. More and more she went into industrial regions, in working class areas where Russian emigrés had found jobs in mines, steel mills and the budding chemical industry. During her travels she encountered Russians who were chronically ill: those with tuberculosis, alcoholics, persons committed to psychiatric hospitals who could not be cared for because they did not speak French and any communication with doctors and nurses was impossible.

During the summer of 1932, after her monastic profession in March of that year, Mother Marie, as she was now known, visited women's monastic communities in Latvia and Estonia, where a regular and traditional Orthodox monastic life continued. She returned convinced that these traditional forms were not appropriate for the Russian immigrants in Western Europe. Not only were they out of date, but they also struck her as contaminated by a "bourgeois" spirit diametrically opposed to the radicalism of the true monastic vocation. She believed that for many women monastic-ism represented an attempt to create a spiritual family that would provide them with security. The monastery was a refuge, the monastic community another family, where one could feel at ease, "protected by high walls from the ugliness and misery of the world".

Perhaps this concept was appropriate for another age, but not for the apocalyptic 1930s, with the victory of fascism. But it went further than that. Influenced by Fr Lev Gillet, Mother Marie rediscovered the eschatological dynamism of early Christianity. She dreamed of a monasticism creatively renewed to respond to the call of the "signs of the times": a monasticism lived out not in the desert or behind protective walls but "in the world".

Russian immigrants were often among the first victims of the severe economic crisis in France. Mother Marie decided to open a house where, as long as there was room, all who came would be welcomed as brothers and sisters. She had no money, but she believed that, like the Apostle Peter, fixing her eyes on Jesus, she must learn to walk on the water. Thanks to gifts — often from Anglican friends — she managed to acquire her first house, 9 Villa de Saxe in the 7th district. When this proved too small she bought a derelict building in the rue de Lourmel in the 15th.

The Russian nun, with her wide smile, her hair all over the place and her clothes stained with the traces of what she had most recently been doing in the kitchen or the paint workshop, became a popular figure. To the rue de Lourmel came two or three nuns, a priest, the house chaplain, but also a professor of theology from St Sergius, penniless unemployed people, Russian petty offenders who after serving their sentence had nowhere to go, people shut up as mentally ill but whom, since they were not considered dangerous, Mother Marie managed to have released from the psychiatric hospital. There, too, were young women whom she had brought out of prostitution, and, from time to time, artists and dancers from the Russian opera or the members of a Roman Catholic Gregorian choir.

It was with much love that Mother Marie decorated her chapel. But she had problems with the lengthy Byzantine services, which she openly admitted bored her and she only attended from time to time. She had so much to do! It was she who did the cooking and the shopping. Dawn found her at Les Halles where the shopkeepers who knew her sold her things at the lowest possible prices or gave her surplus perishable articles. Sometimes she would spend the night in the cafés and bistros around Les Halles, where vagabonds slept with their heads on the tables. She talked to them, and she invited them, in particular the Russians rejected by everyone, to come and see her and help look for solutions to their problems.

The academy of religious philosophy founded by Berdyaev met in her house, and she took part in its meetings. She herself, with some friends, set up *Action orthodoxe* in 1935: this was a body responsible for a variety of activities in society as well as a spiritual fraternity of Orthodox inspiration and a reflection group. As such it published a journal *Novii Grad* ("The New City") which dealt with religious issues and social and political problems in a spirit of ecumenical openness.

* * *

Mother Marie had long foreseen the coming of the second world war, which broke out in 1939. After the "disaster" of 1940 came the German occupation, the food shortages which hit the poor the hardest, then the hunt for the Jews, beginning with foreign Jews. Mother Marie, one of whose best friends was the Russian Jew Elie Foundaminsky, did not hesitate for a moment. Her house soon became a refuge for those who felt endangered before they could be smuggled into the free zone. False baptism certificates were provided to those who wanted them.

It was said that Mother Marie was betrayed by someone who had eaten at her table. One day while she was out, the Gestapo came and arrested her son Yuri, a student, Fr Dimitri Klépinine and Pianov, the administrator of *Action orthodoxe*. Mother Marie was informed that they would be liberated if she gave herself up to the German police. When she went to them, she was arrested, but neither her son nor her friends were freed. All four were deported: the men to Buchenwald, Mother Marie to Ravensbrück. Only Pianov returned.

About Mother Marie's behaviour during her captivity we have the testimonies of several co-detainees, including a niece of General de Gaulle, Madame Geneviève de Gaulle-Antonioz, who had a deep friendship and admiration for her.

Endowed with exceptional vitality, sustained by an unbreakable faith, Mother Marie was well armed to stand up to the terrible test of concentration camp life. "Everybody in the block knew her," recalled one of her companions. "She could get on with the young people in the camp and with their parents, with people of progressive ideas, with believers and with non-believers":

> In the evening, around her miserable pallet, we listened to her... She told us of her work in Paris, of her hope of one day seeing the union of the Roman Catholic Church and the Orthodox Church... Thanks to her we rediscovered courage when, shattered by the growing weight of terror, we were giving up.

Secretly bartering her bread ration to obtain thread, Mother Marie embroidered icons and even a symbolic fresco representing the disembarkation of the Normans in Great Britain. But the last months prior to the Liberation were terrible. Suffering from dysentry, Mother Marie saw her strength failing. On a scrap of paper she scribbled a final message to Metropolitan Eulogius and to her spiritual father: "These are my wishes: I fully accept suffering... And I wish to accept death, if it comes, as a grace from above."

Nothing certain is known of Mother Marie's end. According to Geneviève de Gaulle-Antonioz, she was separated from the other detainees, transferred to the Jungen-Lager, where the sick and the handicapped were left to die of hunger, and died in isolation and utter destitution. Others say her name appeared on a list of prisoners gassed on 31 March 1945. It has also been said that she took the place of a young Polish woman due to be gassed. A few days later, in early April, the camp was liquidated in the face of the advance of the Russian army.

Marie Skobtsova's life might appear as a total failure. Her two marriages were broken; her children died young. She may have felt responsible for the arrest of her son. She never saw the victory over the Nazis for which she had so much hoped. *Action orthodoxe* died shortly after her. She has no disciples within Orthodox monasticism.

Yet she is still alive. Her passionate appeals raise questions and arouse us. Her influence within Orthodoxy after her death could perhaps be compared to that of Dietrich Bonhoeffer in the Protestant world. Like Bonhoeffer she searched for a "secularized" Christianity. Over and above all the paralyzing structures, she continues to call us to go towards him who comes.

Nathan Söderblom
1866–1931

ERIC J. SHARPE

The generation of ecumenical leaders most active in the inter-war years possessed many qualities, among them deep Christian devotion and a no less deep commitment to the best scholarship of which they were capable. The first world war had torn apart the expansive cultural imperialism which had inspired the world missionary conference in Edinburgh in 1910. The work of reconstruction, which began before the war ended, was in large measure master-minded by one man, Archbishop (formerly Professor) Nathan Söderblom of Uppsala, Sweden. Never was a Nobel Peace Prize more richly deserved than that awarded in 1930 to the man who has often been called the father of the ecumenical movement.

Lars Olof Jonathan (Nathan) Söderblom was born on 15 January 1866 in the Swedish country parish of Trönö, where his father, Jonas Söderblom, was minister. His mother Sophie was Danish by birth. Jonas Söderblom was an intellectually gifted, but orthodox, ascetic and somewhat forbidding minister of the old school, deeply influenced by pietist revivalism while remaining fiercely loyal to the church. Despite his own intellectual liberalism, Nathan Söderblom's spirituality remained close to his father's, though it was modified by his education and international experience.

Entering the University of Uppsala in 1883, Söderblom immediately threw himself into student Christian activities, especially those of the YMCA and the newly-founded Student Missionary Association. But his reading soon gravitated towards the theological liberalism and historical scholarship associated with the names of Albrecht Ritschl and Adolf von Harnack. A decade or so later he was to move away from Ritschl, who he thought had left too little room for spontaneity in the life of faith, and towards Friedrich Schleiermacher. He never, on the other hand, ceased to be an admirer of Harnack.

Thanks to his YMCA connection, Söderblom went to the USA in 1890 to attend Dwight L. Moody's Northfield student conference, where he met John R. Mott for the first time. It was during this conference that the cause of Christian unity was forced upon him. He wrote in his diary: "Lord, give me humility and wisdom to serve the great cause of the free unity of thy church."

In 1894 Söderblom was appointed pastor of the Swedish legation in Paris, where he spent the next six years, adding French to his languages and a love of France to his sympathies. In 1901 he earned his doctorate from the Sorbonne with a massive dissertation on *La Vie future d'après le Mazdéisme*, which, though centred on ancient Iranian sources, was actually a comparative work in the field of eschatology. This made his name as a scholar, and in the same year he returned to Uppsala as a professor, teaching comparative religion and apologetics. He held this post until 1914, from 1912 to 1914 jointly with a similar post in Leipzig.

In 1914, to everyone's astonishment, he was appointed Archbishop of Uppsala. A known liberal, and therefore not trusted by conservatives, he barely reached third position in the official election. But he was favoured in high places, and in August 1914 he and his family (by now he and his wife Anna had twelve children) returned to Uppsala.

It was the war and its consequences which made Söderblom into an ecumenical leader. As an academic he already had contacts throughout Europe and North America. He spoke French, English and German fluently, and although his wartime sympathies were discreetly pro-German — as a Lutheran it could scarcely have been otherwise — he detested war totally. Up to this time, most ecumenical initiatives had come from the circle around Mott, but once the US entered the war in April 1917 this link was broken, as the Germans found further cooperation impossible.

Söderblom's point of entry into the ecumenical movement was the World Alliance for Promoting International Friendship through the Churches, founded on the eve of war in 1914. Late in 1914 Söderblom sent out an appeal for peace. It received a mixed response, but David S. Cairns in Aberdeen wrote to him, with great foresight, "You seem to me, if I may say so, predestined... to take a leading part in the great work of reconciliation."

The work of international Christian diplomacy which followed was delicate, intricate and often unrewarding. But Söderblom's breakthrough as an acknowledged ecumenical leader took place during these years, especially at the 1919 World Alliance Conference in Oud Wassenaar, the Netherlands. The same year he published in Sweden his manifesto *Evangelisk katolicitet*, which contained the core of his ecumenical theology and launched the idea of a World Council of Churches.

Söderblom's own Universal Conference on Life and Work was finally held in Stockholm in the summer of 1925. Unlike the World Alliance conference, it was a meeting of churches, not merely of interested individuals. It was by no means a guaranteed success, opposition from some quarters being bitter. That it took place and was held together can be attributed mainly to the force of Söderblom's own personality. Wartime tensions were still strong and the "kingdom of God" theme was particularly divisive. The unifying factor was worship, as delegates found at the altar a unity which had been elusive in the debating chamber.

As well as his own "Nicaea of Ethics", Söderblom was deeply involved in the Faith and Order Movement and took an active part in the Lausanne conference (1927). He had planned to participate in the Jerusalem conference of the International Missionary Council in 1928, but was prevented from attending. Energetic and extrovert as he was, he had battled with ill health for some years before the onset of a heart disease in 1922. In 1931 he was just well enough to visit Scotland and deliver the lectures published posthumously as *The Living God*. For a few short and delightful days he was again Professor Söderblom, living and working in a less troubled world. But the respite was brief. Shortly after his return to Sweden, he had to undergo emergency surgery for an intestinal obstruction. He survived the operation, but his heart was unable to stand the strain, and he died on 12 July 1931, at the relatively early age of 65. His grave in Uppsala Cathedral carries the text: "So likewise ye, when ye shall have done well those things which are commanded you, say, We are unprofitable servants: we have done [in Swedish "only done"] that which was our duty to do" (Luke 17:10, KJV).

* * *

The ecumenical message of Nathan Söderblom can be summed up in his own phrase, *evangelisk katolicitet*. Both words present problems in English translation, "evangelical catholicity" sounding almost a contradiction in terms. If we remember, however, that the primary meaning of *evangelisk* is "gospel-centred" and of *katolicitet* "universality", then his choice of words becomes more understandable.

No amount of manipulation will make Söderblom less of a Lutheran than he was. In a 1926 article on "Why I am a Lutheran", he stated that after Paul, "the history of religion has no genius... equal to that of Martin Luther". Söderblom's "evangelical succession" passed from Jesus, by way of Paul and Augustine and Francis of Assisi to Luther, and thence to such as Pascal, Schleiermacher and Kierkegaard. Each was a "genius" in the realm of religion. Translate "genius" into the language of religion, however, and one possible result is "saint" — one who exhibits to the world the reality of the living God. Saints are not of one tradition, one period, one church, one nation. The one thing needful is to have been seized by that mighty power: for it is a fearful thing to fall into the hands of the living God (Heb. 10:31).

There is nothing whatever to distinguish Söderblom's *ecumenical* theology and spirituality from other aspects of his Christian life and work. His personality was complex and his range of interests wide. Always, however, he returned to what was for him the self-evident centre: his first large theological work was on the kingdom of God, his last, on the sufferings of Christ.

Though born in an out-of-the-way corner of Sweden, circumstances made Söderblom an internationalist, adding the life and thought of the USA, France, Britain and of course Germany to the Swedishness which was always the core of his personality. He was in a sense a high-church pietist, at home with Moody and Sankey as with Bach (he was an excellent musician). Although he was something of a showman, loving pomp and processions and vestments and brave gestures, his spirituality was deep and reserved, having little in common with that of the more advanced Anglo-Catholics. His attitude to Rome was ambiguous. The modernists — Loisy and Tyrrell especially — he respected warmly; the Vatican machinery he quite obviously disliked. In the 1890s he had been interested in the Orthodox world almost as though it were a mission field, but having visited Constantinople for a World Student Christian Federation conference in 1911, he became determined to draw the Eastern churches into a living dialogue. The response he found gratifying. Of course there were political (or at least diplomatic) overtones even at Stockholm in 1925. The outcome, however, more than repaid the effort.

He was largely instrumental in bringing about theological rapprochement between the Church of Sweden and the Church of England, initiated in 1908 and brought to the point of intercommunion in 1922. In later years, though not in Söderblom's lifetime, a sector of Swedish Lutheranism was to turn more and more away from Wittenberg and towards Canterbury.

Söderblom's ecumenical theology was evangelical in its total gospel-centredness, catholic in its universality. For "the wider ecumenism" of interfaith fellowships he had very little feeling — though that is a quite separate subject which cannot be disposed of in a few words. Worship was the key to the mystery of unity, and the altar the only worthy meeting point of churches and nations, always under the canopy of the communion of saints.

* * *

We may conclude this portrait with three excerpts from Söderblom's writings. The first was addressed to students of theology in Uppsala in 1901:

Do not seek any power or party, but the salvation of souls. Do not, I pray you, shut yourself up within any circle of persons or ideas, but desire to understand people and try constantly to learn to write a few new letters in the copy-book of life... Remember this — that your true happiness and the happiness of your churches will depend on whether you take seriously Paul's rule: Not as lords over the faith of the church, but as helpers of the church's joy. Not lords but servants — not servants of a party or faction, but servants of the church, creating joy, pouring out joy, by your life in love and your proclamation of the pure gospel from the eternal source of joy for the refreshment of thirsting souls.[1]

His ecumenical insights are evident in these paragraphs from his manifesto *Evangelical Catholicity*:

I am convinced that forms of words which have created and still create separation will never again fill the role they once did. Not because Christianity has or should become something vague, whose characteristic features have been worn away, but because stark necessity, death and hunger and the threat of savagery have forced Christendom to abandon its speculations, which by comparison seem to be luxuries, games or anachronisms, and to concentrate on what is essential. What is at issue now is nothing less than the mystery of suffering, the tragedy of the world — but also the salvation of the world, atonement, forgiveness, the transformation and renewal of humanity and the presence of God.

It is here that religion is forced towards its centre. And what is the centre of Christianity, if not God? God is not a doctrine or an idea, but a living Spirit, closer to us than anything else. God is the terrible and merciful power with whom we must reckon at every moment...

Catholicity must not be imposed from above or from outside as though it were a mould; it must grow out of the Christian consciousness..., but how is the necessary organization to be created and set in motion without interfering with the individual's relationship with God, or subordinating personal devotion to organization? The answer is that catholicity emerges out of the individual's need for salvation. We are without excuse before God and our conscience if we neglect this Christian responsibility. Salvation comes first; the organization of churches at large in second place. But the second is not separate from the first; it is a necessary consequence of it. We must learn to think ecumenically...

Naturally, the ecumenical council of churches must not trespass upon or interfere with the internal affairs of any of its member churches. Least of all must there creep in any hidden wish to bring pressure to bear on any church in matters having to do with the free expression of its own life, religious experience, philanthropy, Christian thought, research and growth in the truth — all of which is an unconditional presupposition for the genuineness and the future of evangelical Christianity.[2]

The final excerpt is from a hymn that he wrote:

The vessel shatters, and the oil flows freely,
A perfume fills the sad and weary earth.
Your soul, entranced by soft celestial fragrance
Will rise, freed from its worldly dust and dearth.

Shatter the vessel! Let its perfume wander!
Cast away caution, give what your soul loves best.
What height of joyful waste! Love breaks asunder
Its precious gift for its most honoured guest. [3]

NOTES

[1] From *Svenska Kyrkans kropp och själ*, Stockholm, Norstedt, 1916, pp.61,63 (tr. EJS).
[2] From *Evangelisk katolicitet* (in Lehmann, Söderblom and Westman, *Enig Kristendom*, Stockholm, SKDB, 1919, pp.104-21, tr. EJS).
[3] *Den svenska psalmboken* (1986), no. 445 (tr. EJS).

BIBLIOGRAPHY

There is no complete biography of Nathan Söderblom in any language. The best and most up-to-date book on his ecumenical work is Bengt Sundkler's *Nathan Söderblom* (1968). Of Söderblom's own extensive writings in Swedish, the best insights into his ecumenical thinking are to be found in *Religionsproblemet inom katolicism och protestantism* ("The Problem of Religion in Catholicism and Protestantism", 1910); his essay *Evangelisk katolicitet* ("Evangelical Catholicity", 1919); and his almost 1000-page personal report on the 1925 Stockholm conference, *Kristenhetens möte i Stockholm augusti 1925* ("The Assembly of Christendom in Stockholm", August 1925), published in the following year.

Works by Nathan Söderblom:

Söderblom wrote relatively little in English. There is a full, though still incomplete, bibliography of his vast output in Nils Karlström, ed., *Nathan Söderblom in Memoriam*, Stockholm, SKDB, 1931, pp.391-451.
"The Church and International Goodwill", in *The Contemporary Review*, 116, 1919, pp.309-15.
"Communion with Deity", in J. Hastings, ed., *Encyclopaedia of Religion and Ethics*, vol. 3, Edinburgh, T. & T. Clark, 1910, pp.736-40.
"Evangelical Catholicity", in *The Lutheran Church Review*, 43, 1924, pp.1-10.
"Holiness", in *Encyclopaedia of Religion and Ethics*, vol. 6, 1913, pp.731-41.
"An International Church Conference", in *The Challenge*, 8, 1917, pp.55-56.
"The Unity of Christendom", in *The American-Scandinavian Review*, 8, 1920, pp.585-92.
Closing address at the Life and Work conference, in G.K.A. Bell, ed., *The Stockholm Conference 1925*, London, SCM, 1926, pp.725-30.

Works on Nathan Söderblom:

Charles J. Curtis, *Nathan Söderblom: Theologian of Revelation*, Chicago, Covenant Press, 1966.
Stephen Neill, *Men of Unity*, London, SCM, 1960, pp.26-38.
Eric J. Sharpe, "Christian Mysticism in Theory and Practice: Nathan Söderblom and Sadhu Sundar Singh", in *Religious Traditions*, 4/1, 1981, pp.19-37.
Eric J. Sharpe, "The Legacy of Nathan Söderblom", in *International Bulletin of Missionary Research*, April 1988, pp.65-70.
Eric J. Sharpe, *Nathan Söderblom and the Study of Religion*, Chapel Hill, NC, University of North Carolina Press, 1990.
Bengt Sundkler, *Nathan Söderblom: His Life and Work*, London, Lutterworth, 1968.

Dumitru Staniloae
1903–1993

ION BRIA

On 4 October 1993, just a few weeks before his 90th birthday, Professor Dumitru Staniloae, one of the greatest Orthodox theologians of our century, died in Bucharest. Born in Vladeni, Romania (16 November 1903), he studied history in Bucharest and theology in Cernauti, Bukovine, continuing his doctoral studies in Athens, Paris and Munich. In 1930 he became dean of the faculty of theology in Sibiu, then moved to Bucharest after the second world war. As a teacher of mystical theology and Orthodox spirituality, he became the leader of a new theological trend which combined doctrine and spirituality, faith and culture. Over fifty years his writings appeared regularly in Romanian theological reviews, exercising a great impact on several generations of theologians. Accused of "mysticism" by the Communist authorities, he was imprisoned from 1958 to 1963. After his release, he wrote a famous three-volume synthesis of dogmatic theology, which has been translated into several languages.

Staniloae wrote several studies on ecumenism and was a member of various inter-confessional commissions and centres. He was invited to join the reflection group on the theme of the World Council of Churches' sixth assembly (Vancouver 1983): "Jesus Christ — the life of the world". He prepared position papers for the Romanian Orthodox Church on many controversial subjects, including uniatism and fundamentalism. Before and after the December 1989 revolution in Romania, Fr Staniloae was a prophetic presence and critical voice denouncing the tyranny of the totalitarian system. [1]

Not only did Staniloae genuinely renew the traditional way of thinking based on patristic authority, but he also raised several fundamental issues for contemporary theological discourse. His approach differed from that of those who have presented Orthodoxy in the form of a theological introduction or synthesis for the purpose of communication with the Western churches (Sergei Bulgakov, Vladimir Lossky, Nicolas Zernov, John Meyendorff, Olivier Clément, Timothy Ware), in that Staniloae explored inductively and creatively all the basic issues of Orthodox doctrine.

Controversial subjects which have been a real stumbling block for many modern Orthodox theologians — society, state, nation, ethics, ecumenism — were familiar areas for his creative theological thinking.

Since it is impossible in a brief summary to do justice to Staniloae's vast and diversified field of research and reflection, we shall focus on a few areas of ecumenical interest. From the beginning, he was influenced by Byzantine theology on the one hand and modern dogmatics on the other. The crowning achievement of his early period was *Jesus Christ or the Restauration of Man* (Sibiu, 1945), which remains a landmark in contemporary Orthodox Christology. In this work he developed a profound theology of hypostasis and of man as eternal person.

Although a teacher of dogmatics, Staniloae saw the principal role of theology not so much in systematizing the faith into dogma, ecclesiastical traditions or private theological opinions as in helping students to penetrate the mystery of the faith and to disclose its meaning for the spiritual life. He wanted to liberate systematic theology from all the limits and obstacles which prevent Orthodoxy from becoming the true Catholic faith for everyone everywhere. As a result of this style of presentation, dogmatics became a favourite subject for students of theology in Romania for several decades.

One of the main thrusts of Staniloae's theology was to establish an organic link beween the articulation of the faith, spirituality and the knowledge of God. This meant that he was constantly challenging the language and images applied to God. Theology for him demanded freedom from both enslaving passions and intellectual idols. Theology is a gift of God which is offered within the context of a personal experience with God and his acts in history. It is doxological; its symbolic language evokes the language of prayer. Theology is an intellectual liturgy, centred on the revelation of the Holy Trinity and taking place in an act of personal invocation of and communion with God. Therefore prayer is the gateway to theology.

Staniloae sought a way to accept and speak of God that went beyond the typical Western rationalist separation between the transcendence and the presence of divine essence. He underlined the organic synthesis between God's transcendence and God's reality in creation, history and humanity, referring to the *uncreated divine energies*, as formulated by St Gregory Palamas, which flow from God's essence and presence. God's nature comprises both an incomprehensible essence and an accessible energy. The notion of *theosis*, which defines the heart of Orthodox soteriology, is based precisely on this discovery of the continuous flowing of the nature of God, which enables real human *participation* in the divine mystery. For Staniloae, the Holy Trinity is not only the mystery of a living and personal God, but also the mystery of God in communion and the origin and model of the unity of the church, of humankind and of the person. The living, personal and perichoretic Trinity is the revelation of the divine reality.

Living in a context where intercultural dialogue was an existential and intellectual necessity, Staniloae rediscovered the richness of the theology of *logos*. God's presence is transparent in the created world; the unity, order and holiness of creation are rooted in the living and "rational" *logos*. He formulated a Christian view of human responsibility in the world based on the idea that the cosmos is full of potentialities, for new forces and vitality are at work in it. The individual is not simply a part of the cosmic reality, but its paradigm, a new creation in creation. Through the baptismal mystery, he or she becomes a priest offering the holy creation to God. Here the inner link between creation, incarnation and redemption is seen, since the *logos* through whom all have been created is the incarnate Son, the Saviour, the suffering King.

Another key idea in Staniloae's theology concerned the relationship between holiness, theology and knowledge of God. Life in Christ, or spirituality, is a never-ending process of spiritual growth, overcoming selfishness and surrendering idols, the root of all sin. But spiritual growth is not mere moral perfectionism, for a new level of spiritual life means a new level of transcendence and of knowledge of God. Holiness and contemplation are inseparable. Staniloae liked to describe the human person as the temple of God. Open to God's presence, the person becomes the holy dwelling place for mystical devotion, the image of God in more than a nominal sense. The person is always subject to *metanoia*, which is not the destruction of human nature but the restoration of the *ikon* of God, a way to prepare for receiving the divine gift of God's grace through the Holy Spirit, who brings the divine energies into the life of each person.

Nevertheless, spirituality has an important ethical dimension. Staniloae opposed the excessive privatization of piety which he saw reflected in Christian existentialism in the West. He insisted on the ethical implications of Christian piety and on the quality of personal relationships as a mode of existence. *Theosis* meant for him the transfiguration of our style of life, implying concern for one another, mutual sharing, dialogue and openness. Responsibility, the sense of belonging, is at the heart of Orthodox ethics. The continuing invocation of the name of Jesus, the so-called "prayer of Jesus", is incompatible with closing the door on neighbours. Theology and spirituality cannot be separated from a clear and sharp witness to Christ in society and in the world.

In contrast to those who take the church for granted as the pillar and ground of truth, free from all historical involvements and cultural values, Staniloe highlighted the sacramental nature of the church, speaking of both "ecclesial transparency" and "ecclesiastical historicity". Since Pentecost, the Holy Spirit has been rebuilding the trinitarian fellowship in history in the form of the people of God, the body of Christ. The unity and catholicity of the church are not abstract notions, for they refer to a real historical people of God, the reality of the local church, an historical community rooted in the soil of a culture and nation.

In his ecclesiological studies Staniloae reacted, sometimes sharply, against Western theological methods and Western influences on Eastern theology. Having grown up in a Romanian community that suffered under the proselytism of the Greek Catholics (Uniates) in Orthodox Transylvania, he scrutinized critically the political implications of traditional Roman Catholic ecclesiology (*Catholicism after the War*, Sibiu, 1933). Yet his sense of the unity of all Christians was profound, and he never adopted an attitude of anti-ecumenism. On the contrary, one of his most important contributions to ecumenical research was what he called "open conciliarity" (*sobornicitak deschisa*), which for him was crucial to understanding the identity and the place of Christian confessions in the framework of the universal church. "Open conciliarity" is a sacramental space for *growing together*, each with its specific identity, within an embracing catholicity. Again, it was the convergence of theology and spirituality that held the key:

> It seems that here we can see not only something of the unifying power of the Orthodox tradition at its deepest and best, but also something of the way in which the ecumenical

dialogue between the churches must be carried on. The questions of dogmatic theology cannot and must not be avoided. But they need to be met at the place where theology and spirituality come together into one. When they are seen in relation to the living and praying experience of the Christian people, then we find unexpected possibilities of reconciliation between positions which appear at first sight to be absolutely opposed. [2]

While Orthodoxy is often regarded as having little concern for the human family living around it, as though salvation is beyond and above human nature and history, Staniloae insisted that the church must face the difficulties and the anguish of the world. "The world is not only a gift, but a task for many." It is indeed a place of suffering and death, but Christ is present in all those sufferings, struggles and anxieties. [3] One can see the value of the world only through the sign of the cross which Jesus Christ imprints on it.

Painful as it may be, the church is challenged to grow together with the world as part of its mission as a healing and servant community. There is an analogy between the incarnation of God in assuming human nature and the solidarity of the church with the world, in which it assumes and transfigures the world's difficulties and complexities. "Orthodoxy must go beyond its theoretical anthropology to become like a saint, involved in the specific human relationships found in the complicated circumstances of our daily lives."

Staniloae's theology related closely to the local church and to the culture, seeking an adequate expression of the Orthodox faith which is not alien to the authentic values of the people but nourishes their spiritual and social life and inspires their artistic imagination and poetry.

Finally, it must be said that the theology of Dumitru Staniloae was the best expression of his personality. One cannot detach his vision from the style of his life. He was a man of extreme tenderness, courtesy and sensitivity within the family, among colleagues on the faculty and in society. His soft and fatherly face emanated a fundamental simplicity and sympathy, a healing calm and serenity which overcame any hardness of heart. This charismatic mystery of his person, his *ikon*, led many students, scholars and friends to become his disciples.

Staniloae's influence led to the formation of a kind of "school", including intellectuals, writers, philosophers, scientists and theologians, not all of them academics, which has tried to discern his "creative vision", convinced that a renewal of theology is necessary. Despite the persistence of a certain type of fundamentalistic dogmatics in some Romanian theological institutions, where the need for a fresh theological method and language is not understood, these so-called "custodians of Orthodoxy" are more and more challenged by the young professors of the Staniloae school.

Three elements summarize Dumitru Staniloae's contributions as an ecumenical pilgrim. First of all, during the difficult period from 1948 to 1989 he was able, in spite of many ideological limitations, to keep alive interest in theology as an instrument of analysis of history and culture. He himself paid a high price for this tenacity; and if Romanian theology has crossed this difficult period, it is due to his constant plea to put the theme of holiness and truth at the heart of theology. Second, he introduced a new style of teaching, emphasizing contact with students rather than method. Professors have to *reveal* to students their own hearts. Theology means spiritual unction, a kind of tranfer of a "seal" to the disciples. Finally, Staniloae has shown that theological development in the understanding of the faith is possible. The future of Romanian theology depends on how this vision is implemented today. [4]

NOTES

[1] The following text is based on my article "Creative Vision of D. Staniloae", in *The Ecumenical Review*, vol. 33, no. 1, January 1981.
[2] *Ortodoxia*, vol. 23, no. 2, 1971, pp.165-80.
[3] D. Staniloae, "La dynamique du monde dans l'Eglise", in *Procès-verbaux du deuxième congrès de théologie orthodoxe*, Athens, 19-29 August 1976, ed. Savas Agourides, Athens, 1978, pp.346-60.
[4] See "Orthodox Theological Education: The Case of Romania", in *Ministerial Formation*, no. 61, April 1993, p.31.

BIBLIOGRAPHY

Works by Dumitru Staniloae:

Theology and the Church, tr. Robert Barringer, Crestwood, NY, St Vladimir's Seminary Press, 1980.
"Jesus Christ, Incarnate Logos of God, Source of Freedom and Unity", in *The Ecumenical Review*, vol. 26, 1974, pp.403-12.
"The Mystery of the Church", in G. Limouris ed., *Church — Kingdom — World*, Geneva, WCC, 1986, pp.50-57.
"The Orthodox Conception of Tradition and the Development of Doctrine", in *Sobornost*, series 5, no. 9, 1969, pp.652-62.
"Orthodoxy, Life in the Resurrection", in *Eastern Churches Review*, no. 2, 1968-69, pp.271-75.
"The Role of the Holy Spirit in the Theology and Life of the Orthodox Church", in *Diakonia*, vol. IX, no. 4, 1974, pp.343-66.
"Some Characteristics of Orthodoxy", in *Sobornost*, series 5, no. 9, 1969, pp.627-29.
"Unity and Diversity in Orthodox Tradition", in *The Greek Orthodox Theological Review*, no. 17, 1972, pp.19-40.
Some of Staniloae's studies appear in A.M. Allchin, ed., *The Tradition of Life: Romanian Essays on Spirituality and Theology*, London, Fellowship of St Alban and St Sergius, 1971.

Works on Dumitru Staniloae:

Ion Bria, "The Creative Vision of D. Staniloae: An Introduction to His Theological Thought", in *The Ecumenical Review*, vol. 33, no. 1, 1981, pp.53-59.
Ion Bria, "A Look at Contemporary Romanian Dogmatic Theology", in *Sobornost*, no. 5, 1972, pp.330-36.

Oliver Stratford Tomkins
1908–1993

PATRICK C. RODGER

When the time comes to quit an active international ecumenical ministry — to clear up and throw away a mass of paper — it is often the things which were never written down on paper which seem most precious and most permanent. For many who have been engaged in the ecumenical movement around the world, these lasting treasures have included the fact of having known Oliver Tomkins: his leadership, his friendship, his person.

Well into his 80s he still spoke for himself in that tone of gentle assurance, shot through with humour, familiar to all who knew him:

> Is not "retirement" precisely the relinquishing of one's charge? I do not think that it is only my over-conscientious temperament which makes me think not. A priest is ordained not primarily to a charge but for "office and work" in the church of God: so long as I have breath and a neighbour, there is no discharge. Yet the score is now marked *rallentando*, it is primarily a matter of pace — in prayer, in neighbourly caring, in reading and in sharing one's thought, the attitude remains that of the Godward side of men and the manward side of God, only with an even clearer awareness that we have this treasure in earthen vessels. [1]

Yet those who have loved and followed him in the ecumenical path may perhaps attempt some appraisal of his work and influence over the formative half-century of the ecumenical movement which we now almost take for granted.

Oliver Tomkins was born in Hankow, China, in 1908, the son of Congregational missionaries of the London Missionary Society. It was a prophetic beginning for one whose sympathies among the nations and the churches of the world were to be so large. To many who met him, perhaps, he represented the complete Englishman, in voice, manner, temperament, style — England at its best. It is not surprising that the notorious insularity of the English — a cultured disdain for other peoples, symbolized by an unwillingness to speak their languages and a mild surprise that they do not conform to the English way of doing things — has sometimes been found in Anglican churchmen. Oliver Tomkins must have done as much as anyone to belie that unfortunate national reputation. To his natural courtesy, which enabled him to "empathize" with Russian Orthodox, French Roman Catholics, US Protestants, Scottish Presbyterians and many others, was added a deep conviction about the wholeness of the church (to use the title of one of his books). Oliver Tomkins was emphatically not among those "ecumenists" whose real notion of unity is the gradual revelation to others that they have been right all along. His value to the ecumenical movement lay most of all in his ability to draw forth from other, and very different, Christians their own understanding and expressions of the common faith.

I recall attending the third assembly of the World Council of Churches (New Delhi 1961) as a brand new and very nervous member of the Faith and Order staff. Oliver Tomkins co-chaired the assembly section, which produced the eloquent and famous "New Delhi Statement" on unity. Its text had been largely worked out the previous year at St Andrews by the Faith and Order Commission; and it was characteristic of Oliver, as chairman of its working committee, not to approach an assembly without the most careful preparation of something likely to commend itself widely to the churches. But it was his guidance of that section in New Delhi which I remember with unfading admiration: the combination of the authority conferred by long experience and deep conviction with a patient listening to contributions and objections from many quarters of the globe. With such a skilful pilot we were steered into the haven, and people went away feeling that they had received every consideration, and yet that the churches had managed to take a step forward together and to achieve a consensus that might some day bear fruit in their respective countries.

* * *

Like many others, Oliver Tomkins began his commitment to the ecumenical cause in the Student Christian Movement (SCM), both in its British and international aspects. On completing his studies at Cambridge University, he combined a staff job with the SCM with the usual parochial curacy, and during this time he attended the 1937 Edinburgh conference on Faith and Order as a youth delegate. It was an anxious time for the whole of Europe, as the war clouds darkened. The Church of England, like the people of England, was still doubtful and hesitant over the seriousness of the threat Hitler represented to the peace of the world. Yet it was also a time when God had raised up some great leaders of large vision and tenacious courage, among them W.A. Visser 't Hooft, George Bell, William Temple, Leonard Hodgson and J.H. Oldham. If there was less nationalist hysteria in Britain during the second world war than in the first, a more sober judgment of universal human sinfulness and also of hope for the future, it was to such leaders that we owed the greatest debt. Oliver Tomkins entered into that heritage, which kept alive Christian friendships across the barriers of enmity and grim suffering and made possible the rapid relief work in Europe after the end of the war and the establishment of the WCC at Amsterdam in 1948.

Meanwhile, Oliver Tomkins had become a parish priest in Sheffield. Despite wartime shortages, he recalled this as one of the happiest periods for him, his wife Ursula and their young family. It is something of a tradition of ecumenists from the Church of England to return at intervals to the pastoral ministry in the setting of parish or diocese, rather than into the specialized areas of academic or administrative work. Thus Oliver Tomkins spent five years as vicar of an urban parish in the north of England, another five as head of a theological college (Lincoln), sixteen years as

Bishop of Bristol and, after retirement, served as part of the ministry of the Cathedral at Worcester. Thus he came to know the English scene intimately, as well as the international one, and had an influence on many fellow churchpeople of different generations, men and women, Anglican and otherwise, in their own places. He never became an "ecumenical tourist", insulated from the regular concerns of the people whom he might be taken to represent in the oikoumene.

Of course there is a price to be paid for this. Those whose early days were spent in the SCM enjoyed both the easy camaraderie of young people to whom denominational loyalty is not a prime consideration and the stimulus of keen discussion from different theological and social backgrounds. In particular, they accepted men and women as equal partners and colleagues in the Christian cause. The list of gifted and courageous women of Oliver Tomkins's generation who served the SCM and the ecumenical movement is as long as that of the men. Many subordinated their own considerable talents to those of their husbands as far as a "career" was concerned, yet provided the partnership, spiritual and intellectual as well as conjugal, without which that career could not have proceeded. Ursula Tomkins was a shining example: her combination of an independent and sometimes critical outlook with a fundamental unity of purpose made her the ideal partner for Oliver for more than fifty years.

To know what such Christian life can be like, both personally and ecumenically, and then to descend to the plain of everyday parish life can sometimes be dispiriting, and Oliver Tomkins' ministry also had its difficulties and disappointments. He himself spoke of the shock of passing from the fraternity of the WCC, where everybody used Christian names, to the paternalistic discipline of a seminary in the 1950s, where staff members were all addressed by their titles. Yet he also acknowledged the value of that discipline, especially in the structured prayer life of the college chapel. The blessings of another kind of discipline in church life — that of synods — is perhaps less obvious; indeed, the release which is usually welcomed the most by retired clergy is that from "the noise of solemn assemblies"! But again, my own recollection of Oliver Tomkins is of a conscientious and patient figure at synods and bishops' meetings, not speaking often but always worth listening to when he did, and occasionally producing a longer speech, carefully prepared and beautifully expressed. For most of the time he would sit, dispatch case open in front of him, and write and write. In another man one might have suspected that a good deal of correspondence was being worked off during the long debates; but with Oliver Tomkins it was much more likely to be a scrupulous note-taking for the benefit of his diocese later on.

* * *

And everybody praised the Duke
Who this great fight did win.
"But what good came of it at last?"
Quoth little Peterkin.
"Why, that I cannot tell," said he,
"But 'twas a famous victory."

—R. Southey, "After Blenheim"

Looking back on an ecumenical career, one may be inclined to recall this verse of Robert Southey, which British children once had to learn by heart. Did the ecumenists of the mid-20th century who strove so valiantly for their cause indeed win "a famous victory" — or should we be as sceptical of the outcome as Southey was about the aftermath of the Battle of Blenheim?

At first there seems little doubt of the answer. The whole scene of inter-church relations has been completely revolutionized since Oliver Tomkins was born, two years before the Edinburgh conference of 1910. Certainly it has become normal for separated Christians to accept one another as brothers and sisters, colleagues and fellow-workers; where exceptions still exist they stick out like a sore thumb. In England, for example, the political and social barriers which once marked off the established church so sharply from Roman Catholics and Free Churches alike have all but vanished; and the more recent divisions between "conservative" and "radical" have little or nothing to do with denomination. In the realm of theology, which was Oliver Tomkins' particular concern, the old disputes, hardened by proud denominational certainty and self-assertion, have given way to a new temperament. Who could have foretold that in 1986 the General Synod of the Church of England would give an overwhelming vote of confidence both to the Baptism, Eucharist and Ministry report of the WCC Faith and Order Commission and to the first report of the Anglican-Roman Catholic International Commission (ARCIC) as "consonant with the faith" as received by Anglicans? It can surely be said that the patient work of pioneers such as Oliver Tomkins and his predecessors has borne remarkable fruit in the life of the churches. Theologians, so often in the past blamed for the perpetuation of division among Christians, are now often in the vanguard of ecumenical advance.

The common understandings that theologians have achieved and the personal friendships they have formed no longer look remote or academic even to pragmatic Anglican souls, for their experience has reproduced itself at many other levels of church life. Ecumenism may remain an exotic word, but the reality is now present in many a local situation — from the common collections for Christian Aid to the remarkable exchange and friendship between the members of various religious communities. The number of local ecumenical projects now exceeds 800 in England and is growing all the time. Prayer in common is even more widespread. Even in the matter of the eucharist, which has so often proved the most intractable issue for those who seek visible unity, the Church of England has, since a Commission on Intercommunion over which Oliver Tomkins presided in the 1970s, quietly changed its mind vis-à-vis the other non-episcopal churches and by canon law admitted to holy communion the communicant members of other trinitarian churches.

All this gives grounds for deep thanksgiving to God. But there are other aspects of the situation today which may make us doubt if there was "a famous victory" after all. First there is the lack of progress towards union between the Church of England and the non-episcopal churches in England, mirrored elsewhere in the United Kingdom, in North America and in all the principal English-speaking countries of the world. Those of us who were members of the General Synod of the Church of England between 1970 and 1985 had to witness the failure first of the Anglican-Methodist Plan of Union and later of the wider Churches' Council for Covenanting. In both cases there had been an immense amount of preparatory work in theology and liturgy and a large degree of consensus and personal friendship had developed among the negotiating teams. It was all the more galling for the Anglicans that at the last stage it was their church which produced insufficient support and — in a church vigorously upholding the principle of episcopacy — the advice of the bishops, a large majority of whom wanted to carry these schemes forward, was not followed.

Of course it is possible to make the best of a bad job: the goodness and grace of God are not defeated by the failure of any number of ecclesiastical schemes. Nevertheless, in a largely secularized country, where all churches are easily pushed to the margins, it cannot be a strong Christian witness to see the church still fragmented and each denomination struggling desperately for survival in the face of rising financial costs and the competition of new sectarian movements. At the first British Faith and Order conference in Nottingham in 1964, over which Oliver Tomkins presided, a resolution was passed committing the delegates to the hope of union within the participating churches by Easter 1980 (a young African colleague of mine in Geneva exclaimed, "How could it possibly take as long as that!"). By now we have cause to know how tough and persistent church divisions really are — and largely for institutional and sociological reasons which have little to do with theology, much less with the gospel.

It must also be acknowledged that the spiritual climate in England, like the political one, has changed. Oliver Tomkins once read a paper at a bishops' meeting entitled "The Dilemma of the Middle-Aged Liberal". The middle-aged liberal flourished in the days of Clement Attlee and Harold Macmillan in politics and economics; or, in church terms, the period after the Faith and Order conference in Lund, when there seemed to be widespread interest in a common return to the Scripture and Tradition as the basis of a deeper unity of heart and mind among Christians. But that epoch, like every other, was destined not to last, and it has been replaced by a much sharper climate in England. The "liberal" type that instinctively sought consensus on "the middle ground" has fallen into disfavour, even a certain measure of contempt, as a person of insufficient conviction, the utopian product of a society that has now passed away, an armchair philosopher out of his depth in the harsh world of today. It may be forgotten that the temper of reconciliation which characterized Oliver Tomkins and his friends sprang out of and was tested in the terrible experience of two world wars.

It would be wrong to exaggerate the effect of this changed climate on Anglicans whose historic role is that of the *via media* in the universal church. If they have any wisdom, they will know that it is not their Christian calling to follow the spirit of the age but often to resist it, and to uphold moderation and gentleness in public life all the more when these are generally lacking. Nevertheless, the new asperity is not without its effects on the *oikoumene*.

The type of patient wisdom and courteous listening to others which Oliver Tomkins represented par excellence is certainly not in fashion. Too often it must yield to snap judgments and over-simplified utterances encouraged by television and press interviews, nearly always the enemies of truth in religion. And in spite of ARCIC and BEM, the centrifugal forces in Britain — the separation of white and black churches, the growth of sectarian movements, the indifference of individuals towards their own church traditions — are certainly powerful today.

It is not on any triumphalist note, therefore, that one can end an assessment of Oliver Tomkins' influence as an ecumenist in his own country. Yet Oliver Tomkins was much more than a middle-class liberal. He was a man of faith and hope who learned and taught others to wait upon God and his time. There have been some good foundations laid in the ecumenical movement of the mid- to late-20th century, and some shining examples given to posterity. Times change, new fashions arise, and in theology as in literature reputations rise and fall. The main thing is to be undismayed and to build patiently on the foundations which we owe to such persons as Oliver Tomkins.

NOTE

[1] Oliver Stratford Tomkins, "Essays Presented to Tom Baker", October 1986.

BIBLIOGRAPHY

Works by Oliver Tomkins:

The Church in the Purpose of God: An Introduction to the Work of the Commission on Faith and Order of the World Council of Churches, in preparation for the third world conference on Faith and Order, Lund, Sweden, 1952, London, SCM, 1950.
The Third World Conference on Faith and Order held at Lund, August 15th to 18th 1952, ed. Tomkins, London, SCM, 1953.
A Time for Unity, London, SCM, 1964.
The Wholeness of the Church, London, SCM, 1949.

Lakshman Wickremasinghe
1927–1983

S. WESLEY ARIARAJAH

His impact was total; and the quality of his personality cannot be accounted for by this or that particular trait. And that personality was enchanting, almost mesmeric in its influence. It was incapable of analysis; it was there; seeming almost ethereal. You could not go beyond it.

What is the secret of his greatness? It was greatness. What is the secret of his goodness? It was goodness. There our attempt at analysis must stop.

So wrote the late Bishop Sabapathy Kulendran of the Jaffna Diocese of the Church of South India in Sri Lanka after the death in October 1983 of the Anglican Bishop Lakshman Wickremasinghe.

Born on 25 March 1927, Lakshman Wickremasinghe had a distinguished academic record. After completing his University of Ceylon degree in economics and political science with first class honours, he studied political philosophy at Keble College, Oxford. Setting aside what could have been a remarkable political career, he decided to dedicate his life to the ministry of the church. Following a period of pastoral ministry and university chaplaincy, he was consecrated as bishop of Kurunegala, Sri Lanka, on 16 December 1962. At 35, he was the youngest bishop in the Anglican Communion.

Bishop D.J. Ambalavanar spoke of him as "a fine Christian gentleman, a great servant of God, a noble leader of the church and an ecclesiastical statesman of the highest quality". At his ordination Bishop Lakshman was presented as a "godly and well learned man". Many would recall his "eloquence, humour, charisma, magnetic personality, and the devout life rooted in prayer and fasting". Yet the title he himself most appreciated was that by which the people in the villages of Sri Lanka knew him: the "people's bishop".

Bishop Lakshman chose the people and the nation as the primary focal points of his ministry. By "people" he meant — in a nation where more than 65 percent of the population was Buddhist and another 25 percent Hindus and Muslims — *all* people.

And by nation — in a country torn apart by ethnic strife — he meant both Sinhalese and Tamils. Belonging himself to the majority Sinhalese community, he refused to accept the idea of a nation that was less than fully and justly inclusive.

He was a true ecumenist. He worked hard to bring about a planned union of churches in Sri Lanka, but when the Scheme of Union did not materialize, he decided to put ecumenism into practice in every way possible. His was a much-respected voice in Anglican meetings and Lambeth Conferences and in the Christian Conference of Asia. Few church leaders had the wide network of contacts that Bishop Lakshman had with clergy and laity from branches of the church other than their own.

His love for Sri Lanka and for his own Sinhala culture found concrete expression in worship, liturgy, preaching and in the observance of national festivals. He maintained close relationships with the Buddhist community. Many Buddhists, from the hierarchy who had considerable say in the affairs of the nation to the village priests in his rural diocese, looked upon him as a close friend. He was vigorous in his determination to change the "British image" of the Anglican Church in Sri Lanka. This he accomplished by giving importance to Sinhala language and culture in every aspect of church life.

While remaining a nationalist, he also showed an intense quest for justice in national life. He supported social movements which stood for justice in all aspects of society, and was the patron of the Christian Workers Fellowship, which struggled for the rights of labourers. He was chairman of the Civil Rights Movement of Sri Lanka, a position that brought him into prophetic confrontation with the political powers. Somasiri K. Perera, former president of the Methodist Church and a long-time partner with Bishop Lakshman in the struggle for justice, says that the bishop will be remembered "for his vigorous leadership [of the Human Rights Movement], his forthright utterances, his bold stand on public issues and his defence of the civil rights of the citizens of this country on issues like fair and free elections, the prevention of terrorism act, fair trials for political prisoners, rights of minorities and torture". On all these matters he spoke with courage and prophetic clarity.

But the greatest passion of Bishop Lakshman's life was reconciliation and peace among the two Sri Lankan ethnic communities. The communal strife took a toll on his spirit. No Sinhalese visited Jaffna, the heartland of Tamil aspirations, more often, especially after eruptions of communal conflict. The vicious outbreaks of strife between the two communities in July 1983, which brought immense suffering on the Tamil people, deeply grieved him, for he saw the unleashing of such brutality on innocent people as the sign of the spiritual decadence of the society as a whole. While the wounds were still fresh, he made a bold and courageous visit to Jaffna with no consideration for his personal security.

On his return, he made national reconciliation the theme of the pastoral address to the annual council of his diocese, which is made mostly of Sinhalese clergy and laity. In a bold, impassioned speech he challenged the council to share the shame and guilt of what had happened and insisted that they must apologize to the Tamil people as the first step towards national reconciliation. Tracing the history of the conflict and the immediate factors that led to communal riots, he contended that the suffering inflicted on innocent Tamils was morally indefensible:

> We must admit this and acknowledge our shame. And we must do so for the right reasons. It is not enough to be ashamed for the reason that inhuman passion enslaved a section of the Sinhalese for a short period. Nor must we be ashamed because our sense of moral outrage

will improve our image abroad. We must be ashamed because what took place was a moral crime. We are ashamed as Sinhalese for the moral crime other Sinhalese committed.

We must not only acknowledge our shame. We must also make our apology to those Tamils who were unjustified victims of the massive retaliation. An apology must be made for three reasons. First, as Sinhalese, we share in the total life of our people. We share in all that is good and great in our Sinhala heritage... In the same way, when a section of the Sinhalese do what is morally wrong or bad, we share in it. As members of the whole group, we claim that what one section did belongs to us all... Secondly, it is a mark of moral maturity to acknowledge a moral crime on behalf of those closely knit to us who do not realize that they have done so. An apology is made on their behalf... Thirdly, there is the example of Jesus in the midst of brutality and suffering. He shared in the guilt of all those who were involved in the moral crime of bringing about his unjust death. Because he shared in our humanity, he apologized for all those who did not know the moral evil they were doing. His compassion acknowledged both shame and guilt. He apologized so that he might begin the process of setting right what was wrong in a broken relationship. [1]

Only those who are aware of the socio-political climate of Sri Lanka in September 1983 would know the courage, spiritual stamina and pastoral passion that was needed to make this appeal to his Sinhalese compatriots. Those who were close to Bishop Lakshman during those months realized that in keeping with his own words, he carried in his heart and mind this tormenting sense of corporate responsibility and the burden of the need to reconcile the strife-torn nation. Only a few weeks later, on 23 October 1983, he succumbed to a massive heart attack.

"I do not know what Lakshman achieved," wrote Bishop Kulendran, "but that he lived among us for some years was a privilege granted to us. What a difference it made when he came into a room! One could feel that a benign presence had come among us. What a radiance he shed wherever he went! It was what the Bible calls 'the beauty of holiness'. I do not envy the generations that will not know him."[2]

NOTES

[1] Pastoral address at the 1983 annual council of the diocese of Kurunegala, *The Ceylon Churchman*, vol. 82, no. 1, 1984, pp.9-10.
[2] S. Kulendran, "A Benign Presence", in *ibid.*, p.23.

Olive Wyon
1881–1966

JANET CRAWFORD

Olive Wyon was born on 7 March 1881 in Hampstead, London. The eldest of five children, she grew up in a cultured Victorian family which was deeply committed to the English Free Church tradition. While studying in Germany she developed a deep and lasting interest in German life and German theology. This led her to study at King's College, London, then to take up missionary training in Edinburgh at what was later to become the St Colm's Missionary College of the Church of Scotland. Wyon became well known in the churches in Great Britain as the translator of a number of important works by European theologians, especially Emil Brunner.

R.R. Yerbury & Son, Edinburgh

Always keenly interested in the ecumenical movement, Wyon was one of a network of writers who contributed to the preparatory studies for the world conference on Church, Community and State (Oxford 1937), organized by the Universal Christian Council for Life and Work. Through this she became known to such ecumenical leaders as J.H. Oldham, W.A. Visser 't Hooft and H.P. Van Dusen.

After pastoral work among students in Cambridge from 1939 to 1946, she accepted an invitation from the Provisional Committee of the World Council of Churches to work in Geneva as Study Department secretary, which involved her in preparations for the WCC's first assembly in Amsterdam in 1948. One of her responsibilities was to work with Twila Cavert on the enquiry into "Life and Work of Women in the Church" and on preparations for the conference for women to be held in Baarn, the Netherlands, just prior to the assembly, though illness prevented her from going either to Baarn or Amsterdam. Shortly before the assembly the University of Aberdeen conferred on her the honorary degree of Doctor of Divinity — one of the first women to be awarded this honour.

In 1951 Wyon returned to St Colm's, where she herself had trained forty years earlier, as principal. This, her final appointment, lasted three years and was one for which her wide church and ecumenical experience had prepared her well.

After retirement, Wyon continued the work for which she was already well known by a large audience: writing books on prayer and spirituality. Written for the "ordinary" Christian rather than the specialist, these popular books, widely read both in Britain and in the United States, reflected her own deep interest in prayer and her growing appreciation of sacramental worship. Her book *The Altar Fire*, a series of meditations on the eucharist, was written, not for regular communicants but for persons unfamiliar with or puzzled by this "central act of Christian worship".

From the Protestant, missionary-oriented focus of her youth, with its emphasis on "the evangelization of this world in this generation", through her life of Christian service with its many ecumenical contacts, Wyon's theology and spirituality developed more ecumenically. For Wyon, there were three elements of religion: the historical and institutional, the intellectual and theological, and the spiritual and experiential. All three were essential, and if the third element, the spiritual, was overlooked, the whole life of the church was endangered. She saw the renewal of spirituality within both Protestant and Catholic traditions as a major force for Christian unity. She believed that all Christians are called to live "in unity, holiness, mission — and the three are one".

While in Geneva Wyon was deeply impressed by her contacts with the Protestant women's community of Grandchamp, Switzerland. Her book *Living Springs* described Grandchamp and other new religious communities in Europe — Taizé, Iona, the Ecumenical Sisterhood of Mary, the Michael-Bruderschaft, the Grail Society — as "part of the ecumenical spirit which is renewing Christianity in our time". Wyon saw these communities as "living springs", born of the Spirit of God and bearing within themselves the promise of renewal for the church and for the world. This renewal was, in her view, based on prayer:

> In every case, *this "new life" emerges from a praying group:* whether it is called a "community" or a "company" or a "team". In other words, the "living water" comes from Christ himself, where two or three meet in his name — and where, as in the first community of Jerusalem, they remain steadfastly together in *faith and fellowship*, in *sacramental life* and in *prayer*. For "renewal" always comes when we return to the source, to Jesus Christ himself. But all through the course of the history of the Christian church, this return to the source means going into *"the desert"*. It is there, in *solitude* and *silence*, that the voice of God is heard; it is there that the river of prayer is born, that prayer which is the life-blood of the church.

Wyon agreed with Abbé Couturier that "prayer is a cosmic force". The growing movement towards Christian unity she attributed to

> countless hidden currents of prayer... flowing through people in every part of the Christian church all over the world... As these people pray, they know that "the walls of separation do not reach to heaven". They feel the pain and sin of disunity, and they taste the joy of that 'given' unity which is a foretaste of heaven.

This emphasis on the essential role of prayer in the search for Christian unity was the theme of Wyon's earlier book, *Praying for Unity*. She acknowledges that reading, study, discussion and conference each has a part to play in this quest for unity.

> Yet these various ways do not create unity. They may remove prejudice and misunderstanding; they enlighten our ignorance; they may, and often do, create a new interest in, and concern for, Christian unity; and all this is valuable. But it is still true to say that God alone

can create unity; that is why prayer must be our principal activity. When we are faced by difficulties which seem quite insoluble, when we are brought to the end of our own thinking and planning, even with the utmost exercise of human intelligence and goodwill, then we realize that it is only as we acknowledge our ignorance, sinfulness and helplessness before God, and throw ourselves upon his grace, that anything at all will happen.

For Wyon the ecumenical movement was God's response to prayer which was itself inspired by God, the source of all renewal and unity. This movement towards unity was not so much an institutional or intellectual as a spiritual experience:

> Many of us know this reality at first hand. We have had experiences of common worship which have been like a foretaste of heaven. When we do "meet" one another in this way the reality of the experience is unmistakable. But it is almost impossible to put it into words. If we try to explain it, people only think we are saying something which is quite obvious. Yet all who have ever had this experience (either on a smaller or a larger scale) know that there is a freshness about it which means that something new has happened in our lives; it is the opening of a door into a larger world; it is the dawn of a new day; it brings enrichment and enhancement of life; indeed, it is a "new creation".

The experience of unity led Wyon to a greater awareness of the scandalous and sinful nature of Christian disunity, an awareness heightened by her understanding of the eucharist as the sacrament of Christian unity.

> It is after such experiences of the reality of our "given unity" that we become more fully aware of the sin of disunity. It is with deep distress, and even with horror, that we feel what it means to be separated from those with whom we know that we are closely bound; especially is this the case at the sacrament of the eucharist; where on the one hand, we are profoundly aware of the inner unity of the Body of Christ, yet with pain and sorrow and shame we also know that in the sacrament of Christian unity, the climax of Christian worship, we are divided. The more closely we have been drawn to one another, the more poignantly we feel that pain and shame of disunion.

In *On the Way*, Wyon based her reflections on the Christian life on the ancient symbol of the journey or the pilgrimage, linking this both with the way of holiness (Isa. 35:8) and the Christian way described in the New Testament. Those who have entered the Christian way are called to go on to "perfection", which means not an impossible purity or blamelessness but rather the idea of maturity or completion. For Wyon, "holiness" is akin to "wholeness" and thus to unity:

> To put it very simply: when we set out on the spiritual pilgrimage we are seeking unity: union with God in Christ; union with other people in life and work; a desire for unity which becomes so strong that it will drive us forward to serve in any way we can to right human wrongs, to seek social justice, to bring love and healing into every sphere of life. Above all, however simple and ordinary our outward life may be, in our hearts we desire to give ourselves to God for his purpose: for the unity of the church, for the peace of the world and for the salvation of all humankind.

Holiness is possible, because God both calls us to it and empowers us to answer that call. And according to Wyon, the lives of the saints give inspiration and hope to those who seek to follow the "way of holiness". The saints of the past and the present are living witnesses to God and to God's action in human life.

> Otherwise, how can we explain the quality of their lives? What else could have given them such a spirit of love and forgiveness in the midst of persecution and ill-treatment? What else

could have given them the power to endure suffering with joy? to pour themselves out in loving service for people who were wholly ungrateful? who saw human need at its darkest point and met it with the power of God's grace and wisdom? For all the names of such people which have been preserved there are countless more which are known to God alone. Yet they blessed the world in which they lived and their influence still goes on, in secret ways, from one generation to another, through their prayers, their sufferings, their love and their undaunted faith in God...

We may not be able to define "holiness", but when we meet the real thing we know it. There is an unmistakable quality about it; but we may miss or ignore it if we are looking for an impossible "perfection", or for some preconceived ideal, and not for the spirit of Christ working in infinite variety in *real* people. Fortunately, the true "saints" are found in every communion; they are all of one blood, because their lives are animated by the love and power of the one Lord Jesus Christ. They point forward to a unity which has still to be realized within the church on earth.

Wyon's spirituality was described both as "almost mystical" and as "earth-rooted and marked by happiness verging into fun". She delighted in common and community worship and, somewhat unusually, was a member of both the Church of Scotland and the Church of England, being drawn to the sacramental worship of the latter. Her writings on spirituality have been described as "scholarly and shrewd, profound and aware, with a deep biblical understanding", while she herself "mediated a joyful spirit of shared devotion and prayerfulness".

Wyon died suddenly in hospital in Edinburgh on 21 August 1966. She was 85 years old. Bishop Kenneth Carey wrote of her: "There can be few people who have ever been so ready for eternal life. She had lived in it and by it for so many years, and by her writings, her work and, most of all, by what she was, she had helped so many people to realize the glory of being a Christian." Another wrote, "Olive Wyon was an exceptional person and a remarkable character. Under a quiet manner there was an immense fund of intelligence and spirited ability... [She] will be long and gratefully remembered in all parts of the church for her quiet wisdom, charity and personal humility, as well as for her life of devotion."

Olive Wyon was indeed an ecumenical pilgrim and one who came very close to her own definition of a "saint" as one who outwardly seems very much like everyone else but who uses her God-given faculties to the utmost limit.

BIBLIOGRAPHY

Works by Olive Wyon:

The Altar Fire, Philadelphia, Westminster, 1954.
Desire for God, 1966.
Living Springs, London, SCM, 1963.
On the Way, 1958.
Prayer, London, Collins, 1962.
Prayer for Unity, 2 vols, 1955-56.
Praying for Unity, London, Edinburgh House, 1955.
The School of Prayer, London, SCM, 1943.

Stephan Zankov
1881–1965

TODOR SABEV

New theological insights and contacts with other churches in the 19th century opened hearts within Eastern Orthodoxy to the search for Christian unity. This process was enhanced as the church redefined its role within new social, economic, cultural and political realities in Russia and the Balkans. The encyclicals of the Ecumenical Patriarchate in 1902 and 1920 strengthened the concern for unity and set up a basic programme of ecumenism; and the integration of Orthodox youth into the World Student Christian Federation had a further impact on Orthodox ecumenical commitment.

The life and ministry of Stephan Zankov, who grew up in this historical context, are interwoven with the growth and maturity of the Orthodox involvement in the ecumenical movement. Born on 4 July 1881, Zankov studied in the Theological Seminary in Samokov, Bulgaria (1895-99), and graduated with a doctorate from the Czernowitz Theological Faculty in 1905. Soon after, he consecrated his life to a demanding ministry: as assistant secretary general of the Holy Synod (1905-08), co-adjutor to the Metropolitan of Varna (1908-11), director of the Holy Synod department on spiritual and educational work (1912-21) and secretary general of the Synod (1921-23).

Ordained in 1908, his administrative career in the church was interlinked with his priestly ministry, transforming authority and prestige into service to God and to the neighbour in need. Standing firmly in the line of the 19th-century Bulgarian national revival, Zankov was a fervent preacher of the gospel, "persistent whether the time is favourable or unfavourable", convincing and encouraging "with the utmost patience in teaching" (2 Tim. 4:2-3).

A major concern of Stephan Zankov was religious and theological education to strengthen the mission of the church and uplift the religious and moral state of the nation. After many centuries of foreign domination and hindrance of church life, priority had to be given to the formation of a well-educated clergy and laity, the

Zareh I of Cilicia
1915–1963

KAREKIN II SARKISSIAN

Though he died at an early age, Catholicos Zareh I of Cilicia was a true ecumenical pilgrim, a living witness to Christian unity. I first came to know him more than forty years ago in Aleppo, the second largest city of modern Syria and one of the ancient cradles of Christianity in that historic land.

I was a young priest, and he was a young bishop, the pastor of the largest community of the Armenian Apostolic Church in Syria. I had been sent to Aleppo to recruit students for the seminary of the catholicossate of Cilicia in Antelias, Lebanon, where I was serving as assistant to the dean. Staying with him at the archbishopric, sharing the modest living conditions, I spent hours of intimate conversation with him, particularly in the evenings, when the precincts of the diocesan centre were emptied of the administrative personnel. We took our evening meals in the solitude of his monastic dwelling, so rich with historical reminiscences. The meals were accompanied and followed by discussions, most of which he initiated. He knew how to ask questions and to draw me, a very shy young priest, into the conversation.

I felt that I was at a second school after the seminary, the normal school of theology. I discovered in him a teacher who used no textbook or notes, avoided lecturing, did not attempt any method of formal tutorial yet was a real tutor. Here was a true mentor, a guide in sound thinking. Sitting next to him, listening carefully and doing my utmost to express myself clearly, I felt that I was passing through a process of self-awareness, a kind of self-purification and inner assessment of my own ideas. There was no classroom, no desk, no other students, yet plenty of lessons, an abundance of learning.

But above all that I learned during these days, I discovered a person who was what he thought. A simplicity, a remarkable serenity and a profound spirituality permeated all that came out of his mind, whose second name was "heart". The openness I found in him was a window into the spiritual and intellectual dimensions of his person, in which a dominant place was occupied by sympathetic understanding of and genuine respect for churches other than his own, with all their diversities and differences in theology, liturgy, life and administrative and pastoral structures. That was a lesson in ecumenism without the name, an inner disposition of seeing Christ's presence, the gospel message as the bond of commonness and communality. Only years later, through my own readings and ecumenical engagement, did I first hear the term "spiritual ecumenism", so closely associated with Abbé Paul Couturier. But I had seen it first-hand in Aleppo.

* * *

In 1956, at 41, Zareh became catholicos of the Great House of Cilicia. He was chosen at a time of sharp confrontations among the various segments of the Armenian community under the jurisdiction of Cilicia, and his election was opposed by several groups on purely political grounds. In the midst of all that turmoil, however, he never lost the serenity of spirit that had struck me from the very first moments of my own personal encounter with him. He proved himself ecumenical in circumstances in which being ecumenical meant touching the realm of spiritual heroism whose name is holiness, sainthood. He was a saintly figure, a holy man, because he never lost sight of the gospel and always felt upheld by prayer. His sermons were imbued by love, pastoral concern and an appeal to reconciliation and unity within the Armenian community at large.

He was born in Marash (Cilicia) in 1915, the very first year of the genocide perpetrated against the Armenians by the Turks of the time. He lived all his childhood in Syria (Hama and Aleppo) under conditions of poverty. In 1930 he was one of the first students to enter the newly opened seminary in Antelias, and five years later he became its first graduate to enter the celibate priesthood by joining the religious order of the catholicossate. Then followed two years of university studies in Oriental Christian and Byzantine history in Brussels. Most of his clerical life he served the Armenian community of Syria as prelate of the diocese of Aleppo (1940-56), being consecrated bishop in 1947.

Throughout his life he was a personal witness to the suffering of his people and at the same time to the process of national recovery after the terrible blow of the genocide. He loved his people; and he believed in God's renewing power through the sacrificial ministry of his only-begotten Son, Jesus Christ. Whenever I think of him, I recall the words of St Paul: "We rejoice in our sufferings, knowing that suffering produces endurance, and endurance produces character, and character produces hope, and hope does not disappoint us, because God's love has been poured into our hearts through the Holy Spirit which has been given to us" (Rom. 5:3-5).

* * *

His ecumenism extended more broadly to all Christian churches on the world level. He followed the development of the ecumenical movement with joy, particularly the founding of the World Council of Churches in 1948.

I personally witnesssed his exuberant joy when the two catholicossates of the Armenian Church (Etchmiadzin, in Armenia, and Cilicia, in Antelias, Lebanon) were received into the membership of the WCC during the 1962 Central Committee meeting in Paris. He had sent me as observer at that meeting. When I returned to Antelias, now with the badge of a delegate, I gave him a brief report, and he embraced me affectionately and with fatherly love. His first words in response to my report were: "Thanks be to God; we have now joined the family of the Christian churches in their march towards unity."

Six months later, in early February 1963, W.A. Visser 't Hooft, the WCC general secretary, paid his first official visit to the catholicossate in Antelias. Catholicos Zareh invited representatives of all the WCC member churches in Lebanon, and at an agape meal shared his own joy with them, because he wanted it to become the joy of all.

Several years earlier, he had welcomed the Ecumenical Patriarch Athenagoras I — a great pioneer of the modern ecumenical movement — to Lebanon. He was spiritually uplifted during the three meetings — one of them a personal conversation — they had together. Such encounters were among the finest hours of his life. Christian brotherhood was a living word for him, as it had been since his early days of association with the heads of the local Christian communities in Aleppo. For Zareh, ecumenism started at the grassroots level.

Another great ecumenical experience came in May 1962, when Cardinal Johannes Willebrands (then a bishop), together with Cardinal Bea, visited Catholicos Zareh I on behalf of Pope John XXIII and informed him officially of the forthcoming Second Vatican Council. The catholicos spoke vividly about the unity of the church and strongly underlined the importance of such a Council. His words still ring in my ears:

> If we condense the whole content of the gospel into a hundred points, I am sure we will agree on ninety-nine. But we will forget the ninety-nine and will constantly speak about the one on which we disagree. All these past centuries we have spoken about what divides us; it is high time that we begin to talk about the ninety-nine in which we will find the firm ground on which we stand together. We just need *metanoia*.

Referring to how atheism, secularism and a materialistic understanding of life and values have become so dominant today and to the havoc created by indifference and apathy with regard to religion, he added: "For today it is not the form of the faith that is at stake; faith itself is a question."

Sadly, Catholicos Zareh did not live long enough to see the growth of the participation of the Armenian Church in the ecumenical movement. Shortly after the visit of Visser 't Hooft — on 18 February 1963 — Catholicos Zareh I succumbed to a massive heart attack.

He was a man of love, faith, vision and conviction. A learned person, a regular and ardent reader, a diligent student of history, he was also sensitive and receptive to the lessons of history. History had taught him that division leads to weakness and weakness cannot be part of Christ's legacy, for it was he who proclaimed in the full love and humility which characterized his life and work: "Be of good cheer, I have overcome the world" (John 16:33).

Catholicos Zareh left us early and abruptly. But we cannot leave him, because his love, faith, vision and conviction remain alive. Such a legacy transcends death; it speaks of eternal truth; it bears untarnishable witness to unity, the gift of God and the signpost to the kingdom for all God's children.

Contributors

Wesley Ariarajah, a Methodist pastor from Sri Lanka, is deputy general secretary of the World Council of Churches.

René Beaupère is a French Dominican priest and director of the ecumenical Centre Saint Irénée in Lyons.

Marios Begzos is professor of theology in Athens.

Elisabeth Behr-Sigel is a retired professor of philosophy and theology of the Institut supérieur d'études œcuméniques (ISEO), Paris.

Ans van der Bent was director of the Library of the Ecumenical Centre, Geneva, from 1963 to 1986 and ecumenical research officer of the World Council of Churches from 1986 until his retirement in 1989.

Alain Blancy is the former associate director of the WCC's Ecumenical Institute in Bossey, Switzerland, and the Protestant co-president of the Groupe des Dombes.

Gerhard Boss is ecumenical affairs officer of the Roman Catholic diocese of Bamberg, Germany.

Ion Bria, a Romanian Orthodox theologian, served on the staff of the World Council of Churches for many years, most recently as executive director of the programme unit on Unity and Renewal, until his retirement in 1994.

Olivier Clément is professor of theology at the Orthodox Theological Institute of St Sergius, Paris.

Martin Conway is a Church of England layman and president of the Selly Oak Colleges, Birmingham, England.

Janet Crawford teaches at St John's College, Auckland, Aotearoa New Zealand. She is a member of the WCC's Standing Commission on Faith and Order.

John Deschner (United Methodist Church) is professor emeritus of Perkins School of Theology, Dallas, Texas (USA), and a former moderator of the WCC Faith and Order Commission.

Martha Driscoll is a Trappist sister living in Indonesia.

Jim Forest is secretary of the Orthodox Peace Fellowship and director of Peace Media Service, Alkmaar, The Netherlands.

Ruth Franzén is professor in the faculty of theology of the University of Helsinki, Finland.

Francis Frost is Roman Catholic lecturer at the WCC's Ecumenical Institute, Bossey, Switzerland.

Adriaan Geense (d. 1994) was director of the WCC's Ecumenical Institute, Bossey, Switzerland, from 1983 to 1989, and professor in the theological faculty of the University of Geneva from 1989 to 1993.

Michael Ghattas (Coptic Orthodox Church) is a teaching assistant in the theological faculty of the University of Marburg, Germany.

Jan Grootaers is a professor in the theological faculty of the Catholic University of Louvain, Belgium.

Hans Hafenbrack is chief editor of the German protestant press service *epd*.

Susannah Harris-Wilson (Episcopal Church, USA) teaches English and drama at Community College, Philadelphia, USA.

Thomas Hopko is professor of theology and dean, St Vladimir's Orthodox Seminary, Crestwood, New York (USA).

Metropolitan Kirill of Smolensk and Kaliningrad is chairman of the Department for External Church Relations of the Moscow Patriarchate.

Emmanuel Lanne is a monk of the Benedictine monastery of Chevetogne in Belgium, and a former member of the WCC's Commission on Faith and Order.

William Lazareth is retired bishop of the Metropolitan New York Synod of the Evangelical Lutheran Church in America, and a former director of the WCC Faith and Order secretariat.

Gennadios Limouris, former executive secretary in the WCC Faith and Order secretariat, is coordinator of the Synodical Committee on Inter-Church Affairs in the Ecumenical Patriarchate of Constantinople.

Luis Odell is a lay leader in the Methodist Church in Argentina and Uruguay. He was the first lay president of the Methodist Church in Uruguay, and is a former executive secretary of Church and Society in Latin America.

Modupe Oduyoye is a consultant to the Project for Christian-Muslim Relations in Africa and the former managing editor of Daystar Press, Ibadan, Nigeria.

John Pobee (Anglican, Ghana) is programme coordinator for Ecumenical Theological Education in the World Council of Churches.

Elizabeth Pontoppidan is former prioress of the Protestant community of Pomeyrol, France.

Philip Potter (Methodist, Dominica) was general secretary of the WCC from 1972 until his retirement in 1984.

Maria Teresa Porcile Santiso is professor of biblical theology and ecumenism at the Theological Institute of Uruguay, Montevideo.

Patrick Rodger is a retired bishop of the Scottish Episcopal Church and a former executive secretary in the WCC Faith and Order secretariat.

Todor Sabev, Bulgarian Orthodox Church, is a former deputy general secretary of the World Council of Churches and former professor of church history at the Theological Academy of St Clement of Ochrid, Sofia.

Karekin II Sarkissian was elected catholicos of the Armenian Apostolic Church (Etchmiadzin) in 1995; prior to that he was Armenian catholicos of Cilicia. From 1975 to 1983 he was vice-moderator of the WCC central committee.

Stjepan Schmidt is a Jesuit priest and archivist and historian for the Pontifical Council for Promoting Christian Unity, Rome.

Eric J. Sharpe is professor of religious studies at the School of Studies in Religion of the University of Sydney, Australia.

Josef Smolik (Evangelical Church of Czech Brethren) is professor at the Protestant Theological Faculty of the University of Prague and a former member of the WCC Faith and Order Commission.

Thomas Stransky is a Paulist father from the US and director of the Tantur Ecumenical Institute, Jerusalem.

Emilianos Timiadis is former representative of the Ecumenical Patriarchate to the World Council of Churches.

Theo Tschuy is a Swiss Methodist pastor and a former staff member of the World Council of Churches and the Conference of European Churches.

Georges Tsetsis is representative of the Ecumenical Patriarchate to the WCC.

Hans-Ruedi Weber is former associate director of the Ecumenical Institute, Bossey, and former director of biblical studies in the WCC.

Index of Names